Johann Sebastian Bach.

From a recently discovered portrait in possession of
Doctor Fritz Volbach.

Courtesy of Doctor Volbach.)

JOHANN SEBASTIAN BACH

THE STORY OF THE DEVELOPMENT OF A GREAT PERSONALITY

BY

C. HUBERT H. PARRY

MUS. DOC., OXFORD, CAMBRIDGE, AND DUBLIN
DIRECTOR OF THE ROYAL COLLEGE OF MUSIC, AND FORMERLY PROFESSOR OF MUSIC OF THE UNIVERSITY OF OXFORD

ILLUSTRATED

REVISED EDITION

GREENWOOD PRESS, PUBLISHERS
WESTPORT, CONNECTICUT

Originally published in 1909
by G.P. Putnam's Sons, London and New York

First Greenwood Reprinting 1970

Library of Congress Catalogue Card Number 73-109818

SBN 8371-4309-8

Printed in the United States of America

TO THE MEMORY

OF

E. W. H.

PREFACE

THE exhaustive researches of Philip Spitta in every quarter which could afford even remote illustrations of the life and work of John Sebastian Bach, and the voluminous and comprehensive work which embodied their results, might seem to render any further efforts in the same direction superfluous. His devotion and ingenuity in unearthing such facts as were attainable after more than a century of public indifference, and his shrewdness in suggesting surmises when facts were not to be found, seem to leave little for those to do who come after, but to confess their obligations and to acquiesce in the arguments discussed and re-discussed without stint. But Spitta's position, as the first thoroughgoing explorer, was inevitably specialised, as he could not take anything for granted, and had to set down every insignificant detail of fact and inference which bore upon his argument. He felt himself bound to give in the utmost fulness the births, deaths, marriages, and careers of remote relations, to discuss the interesting and valuable evidence of the water-marks in the paper used by Bach at different times in his career, and the technicalities of ecclesiastical usage which throw light on the schemes of his Church Cantatas, and many other matters which are rather beyond the requirements of any but specialists. His work is inevitably rather confused through the vast array of evidence which has to be marshalled, and it is difficult to derive from it, without great effort, any clear idea of the personality of the composer, as a composer, or any clear impression of his work as a whole. Moreover, as the writer endeavours to supply technical analyses of most of the works he refers to, especially of works which are hardly ever, if ever, performed, and as musical analysis is, as a rule, quite unprofitable without the actual Music analysed, it is necessary, in order to get even a limited understanding of the book, to have all Bach's works in the huge forty and odd volumes of the German Bach Society, and possibly a few other editions; and it would also entail several years of ample leisure, and a devotion which is practically inexhaustible.

Under these circumstances a more condensed survey of Bach's life-work and his unique artistic character may seem excusable. Too copious a presentation of details is apt to obstruct that understanding of the works of any great composer or artist, and the manner in which human qualities are manifested in them, which is the object of all scrutiny of their lives. In Bach's case the mere events and facts of the life apart from Art are insignificant, and in consequence of the lack of public interest which he inspired in his own time even myths and legends are but scanty, so there is but little temptation to dwell upon matters of secondary importance. His life was unified by the persistence of strong and decisive qualities of character and temperament, which happened to be very characteristic of the race and period to which he belonged; and the unity is emphasised by the fact that he had very little help from outside in developing his powers, and that he went on educating himself and expanding his resources from beginning to end. For the purpose of understanding such things it is necessary to discuss technicalities to a certain extent; but, in view of the hopeful manner in which the actual knowledge of Music in its technicalities as well as its artistic aspects has progressed in recent years, there is little need to extenuate a consideration of the life of a great composer mainly from the point of view of artistic development and self-expression. But it is necessary in such a case to ensure the identification of the works referred to. In vocal works and those which have special names this presents no difficulty. But in connection with some Organ compositions, when, for instance, several works of the same kind are in the same key, it is necessary to supply other means of decisive identification; and in such cases, for the most part, references are made to the most easily accessible of catalogues, the Thematic Catalogue of Peters; the instrumental section of which is referred to, for brevity's sake, as P. T. V. I—(Peters' Thematisches Verzeichniss der Instrumentalwerke) with the numbers of the references. In a few special cases reference is made to the Catalogue of the Bach-Gesellschaft Edition, indicated by the letters B. G.

C. H. H. P.

LONDON, January, 1909.

FOREWORD TO REVISED EDITION

In preparing this revised edition for publication I have made no alterations in the text except for the purpose of correcting actual mistakes.

A number of corrections had been prepared by the author, and to these have been added others that seemed necessary or advisable.

I wish to express my grateful thanks to Dr. Sanford Terry for his valuable advice and help in the work.

EMILY DAYMOND.

February, 1934.

CONTENTS

ILLUSTRATIONS

JOHANN SEBASTIAN BACH

CHAPTER I

CONVERGENCES

ART seems to differ from other manifestations of human energy in welcoming so frankly the evidences of personality. Culture and progress alike deprecate aggressive individual prominence. The cherished ideal of the religious-minded is the effacement of self. The philosophical ideal is the entire and perfect accommodation of impulses and actions to the general well-being. But art not only welcomes the evidence of personal initiative; it demands as one of its first necessities copious and consistent proofs of individuality. Different kinds of art manifest the personal element in different degrees. It is no doubt less easily realised in music than in painting; for in that branch of art the mere attribution to a great master on the proofs arising from some trick of the brush, or some special subtlety in the drawing, is sufficient to make a canvas worth a hundred times its weight in gold. The conditions of musical valuation are quite different, and scarcely as favourable to the assessment of the money value of authorship.

Yet it is evident in this art too that not only is the personal element essential, but also that works which are devoid of it are of but mediocre value; and the greatest works of all are just those in which the personalities of the authors are most vividly and unmistakably expressed.

The reasons are surely not difficult to find. The man who merely repeats conventional types of thought with variations, who, without personal initiative, expresses the average commonplaces of his time in skilful and elegant diction can hardly boast of any justification for his achievements. He discovers nothing for himself, but merely says what he thinks other people will like him to say. He does not even deal with facts but merely with other people's opinions about facts and their semblances. He traverses no specious futility, and sets no hand to the seal to proclaim his "act and deed." The true conviction is the personal conviction, not the acceptance of the conventions of the complaisant majority; and those who have to find their way alone in tears and anguish, and hammer out their own salvation unaided, attain more frequently to the highest artistic achievement than those whose path is smoothed for them by favourable opportunities.

There are countless ways in which the personal element may be manifested. It may be in the preference for special types of subject; in peculiarities of design, colour, diction, or texture; in the choice of special types of artistic method; in characteristic crudities and odd habits and tricks of expression; in warmth, impetuosity, deliberation, tenderness, vehemence, fierceness, aspiration, or any other human quality; and even in the peculiarities which betray physical deficiencies and mental obliquities, as well as those which reveal the highest perfection of technical mastery and the most patient and courageous recognition of inevitable law.

There must also be infinite varieties of degree. The highly gifted nature, which proves at every moment the richness of its spiritual outfit as well as its technical resources, reveals its personality in a very different manner from the nature which is individual only in its littleness. A light nature easily led, or a temperament too easily affected by external influences, produces work which is inconsistent and lacking in unity, however much special traits of diction or method may identify the product with the producer. When the scope is great, the individuality is generally due to the unity and consistency of the man's character, and the persistence of firmness and conviction.

And herein lies the counterpoise to the excessive emphasis which seems to be laid on personality. The man, whatever his greatness or pre-eminence, is the product and representative of the conditions and influences of his time, and they are the fruit of the times that went before. However little the direct share which mankind at large have in the individuality of a great artist's achievements, it is clear that they could not have been accomplished unless his contemporaries were imbued with a spirit which ministered to and fed the exaltation of the individual; and they could not have been accomplished unless the workers who went before had prepared the way and provided the language or the artistic methods which were necessary. These facts are most easily verifiable in respect of the artistic methods. For it is manifest that their development is a thing of itself, and quite independent of the development of mankind in things outside the range of art. Great national movements have taken place, and periods of enlightenment have come about in which the standards of men's thoughts and habits have been elevated and disinterested, and have borne fruit in heroic and nobly purposed deeds, without any corresponding artistic utterance. Many instances occur in the story of art, of striking and vivid personalities missing the opportunity of expressing themselves adequately through the resources of art being insufficiently developed in their time. The vivid personality of Monteverde was defeated by the immaturity of methods in the special branch of art he cultivated, and Purcell, for all his initiative and mental vigour, most frequently suggests to the hearer how great his achievements would have been if his opportunities had been more favourable.

The great and lastingly convincing works of art can come into existence only when a strenuous temper of mankind and a high standard of sincerity and of mental and moral energy happen to coincide with great accumulation of artistic methods and adequate solutions of artistic problems. The great artist then becomes the exponent of the spirit of his contemporaries: his work is the sublimated essence of their finest aspirations. Men only express themselves heroically when noble disinterestedness is frankly appreciated; they only express the fervour and ardour of religion when religion is a deeply rooted reality, not of forms and ceremonies, but of the spirit.

It can hardly be denied that the seventeenth century was a time when men were fiercely in earnest, and ready to sacrifice their lives and their well-being for what they believed. But circumstances had combined to prevent their expressing themselves fully in music. For a time the call for deeds was more urgent than for words. And when the terrible wars, in which the old Church endeavoured to suppress the impulse to break away from her domination, wore themselves out and the turmoil died down, great manifestations of art followed, which presented themselves, not in the countries or among people who had submitted or had been coerced into acquiescing in the old order of things, but among those who had established their right to liberty of thought and to the exercise of those kinds of religion which were more consonant with the progress of enlightenment and complete spiritual sincerity. Other nations may have suffered more cruelly in religious wars, and may possibly have sacrificed more, but Germany not only suffered and spent her blood freely, she was also foremost in the expenditure of intellectual energy, and the most effectual of all nations in the argumentative war, in insistence on liberty of conviction, and in appeal to men's judgment and sense of right.

It was therefore appropriate that, when the Northern kingdoms and provinces established their independence from the ancient ecclesiastical domination, it should fall to their lot to find the highest expression of the purified religion in music. It was fortunate, indeed, that the Germans did not swing over into violent extremes as did some other nations; but adopted a form of religion and ecclesiastical arrangements which retained many of the best features of the old religion, and admitted art of various kinds as a help to devotion and as a vehicle of religious feeling. It was fortunate, also, that the artistic efforts of the previous century had evolved and accumulated methods, and roughly indicated certain types of form, which could serve for the purposes of religious music, though initiated under a secular impulse.

The artistic departure which made the great outburst of Teutonic art possible in the first half of the eighteenth century began in Italy at the beginning of the seventeenth; when composers and poets, moved to widen out the range of art beyond the somewhat narrow limits of the style which prevailed in the music of the old Church, endeavoured to find principles more suited for secular purposes. They attempted the setting of dramas to music, and having no knowledge of the problems of such secular art, they struck at first on very crude and unsophisticated interpretations of dramatic situations. The obvious inadequacy of such premature experiments soon made them adopt courses more within their scope. During the latter part of the 17th century, their efforts were mainly directed to developing simple forms of solo vocal music, and to laying the foundations of instrumental style as distinguished from choral style; and this they did by giving attention to the idiosyncrasies of instruments, such as the violin, domestic keyed instruments, a few wind instruments, such as trumpets and hautboys, and the organ.

The natural aptitude of Italians for music stood them in good stead, and, paying attention mainly to purely artistic effects of beauty of form and musical idea, they achieved, by the end of the century, the foundation of most of the modern forms of art, whether instrumental or vocal. They transformed the old style of choral counterpoint into more vivacious and rhythmical instrumental polyphony, instinct with figure and definitely secular feeling, and even began to find their way to new principles of design, the organisation of which implied the recognition of a system of harmony based on the relative degrees of importance of the constituent harmonic contents of keys. The Italians were in such respects leaders by right of pre-eminent musical gift, but races which were less musically endowed carried the work to a more triumphant issue in virtue of greater persistency of feeling, greater force and firmness of character, and more consistent seriousness of purpose The Germans took up the secular methods, but applied them mainly to religious purposes, and to an art intended to serve in one way or another for the functions of the Reformed Church.

Early in the 17th century Heinrich Schütz, with but slender artistic resources, and retaining in his work many traces of the pre-secular times, endeavoured to find utterance for the deep religious feelings which possessed him in settings of the Passion and of the story of the Resurrection, and various psalms and striking episodes from the Bible, endeavouring to convey the beauty of human sentiment rather than beauty of melody or form. His work remains unique for its innocent and unsophisticated sincerity of expression; but, though illustrating the German impulse toward music, it hardly served as the basis of any further artistic developments, or as the foundation of a school. The composers who succeeded him, such as Hammerschmidt, Tunder, Ahle, and Briegel, adopted something of his attitude, and in some respects imitated his ways in setting their words; but they soon came more decisively under the influence of Italian methods. They continued to aim at expression, but their phraseology and their treatment of solo voices were gradually assimilated to types discovered by Italians, and towards the end of the century they lost a good deal of the vital force and interest which attached to the old contrapuntal style in their attempts to produce effects which were conformable to the predominating tendency towards harmonic music. It was fortunately but a passing phase, and German sacred music was ultimately saved from being dominated by the somewhat stupefying influence of the Italian homophonic style by the persistence of the polyphonic style in their organ music. This branch of art exercised a very powerful influence on the style of all the branches of art they cultivated, especially their choral music; and it is necessary to take some cognisance of it.

When organ music began to grow into a distinct branch of art, the Italians cultivated it with as much success as the Northern composers. Andrea Gabrieli in the latter part of the sixteenth century, and his great nephew Giovanni Gabrieli, and Claudio Merulo somewhat later, and Frescobaldi in the early part of the seventeenth century, proved themselves to have fully as good an instinct for the essentials of organ style as Sweelinck and Scheidt and other Northern composers for the instrument. Indeed, they were the pioneers of genuine organ music, and led the way not only in laying the foundations of the fugue form, but also in more free and showy forms of art, such as Toccatas, in which Merulo showed his instinct for virtuosity. But the organists of the Roman Catholic Church soon lost hold of the types of style which were essential to permanently successful treatment of the music for this instrument, and lapsed into complacent vapidity; abandoning the richness of texture (which absence of expressive power in detail in the organ makes essential) for homophonic and simple harmonic types of procedure and conventional formulas of ornament and accompaniment, which were adopted from the secular branches of art, such as the opera.

A few of the Southern German Roman Catholic organists, such as Froberger and Georg Muffat, maintained a high standard of polyphonic style, but even in the latter's work the polyphonic texture shows some relaxation of the forcible and dignified kind of utterance which is appropriate to the giant instrument. It was among the representative Protestant organists that the right energetic spirit was maintained, and the more appropriate style step by step developed. While the organ music of the Roman Catholic Church became superficial and poor in quality, that of the Northern organists became more and more vivid with earnestness and intensity of artistic concentration. The branches of art which most decisively distinguished the Protestant from the Southern school were those in which their beloved chorales, the symbols and embodiment of their religious fervour, were worked up into movements of singularly subtle artistic interest. The method of procedure was such as tended to foster the polyphonic style of writing. For the chorale tunes were not simply harmonised as tunes, but were used in a manner analogous to that of *Canti fermi* in the old Church choral music, as a single part around which a complicated network of polyphony was woven. At first the secondary parts had been written in a simple diatonic style similar to real voice parts; but as composers' instinct for instrumental style developed, they introduced copious ornaments, and manipulated the simple basis of melodic contours with runs, arpeggios, and other figures, such as were appropriate to the nature of the keyed instrument endowed with such conspicuous persistence of tone, clearness of enunciation, and certainty of pitch.

By this means a new style of counterpoint was developed, far more elastic, free, and full of rapid figures than the old choral counterpoint, and the independence of organ style was thereby made more and more decisive. Skill in management of figures and in the maintenance of consistency of material was attained through the composers' delight in weaving the new style of counterpoint out of characteristic features of the chorales, and making the whole coherent in detail by part answering part, overlapping and interchanging with the same types of melodic figures. The fact that their hearts were engaged in compositions of this kind expedited the development of technique, which was available in other branches of art; and there are indeed some very close points of contact between the fugue form and that of the Choralvorspiel.

In all forms organ music arrived at an advanced standard of independent maturity before the end of the century, as is manifested especially in the works of Johann Pachelbel (1653–1706) and Dietrich Buxtehude (1637–1707). Of these two remarkable organists and composers the first occupied a peculiar position; since contact with Southern German organists in the earlier part of his life gave him a taste for simplicity and clearness of harmonisation. The Italian influence is most noticeable in his works for domestic keyed instruments, in which are found many of the simple formulas of accompaniment, such as afterwards became common property. In such cases the polyphonic style is often totally abandoned; and the aim seems to be to give a pleasant and orderly succession of harmonies, which produce an agreeable sense of well ordered design, without much interest in the details. In his organ works the polyphonic style is more predominant, and his fugues (such as those on the Plainsong of the Magnificat) are characterised by conspicuous fluency and ease, and his Toccatas by a considerable inventive gift in the direction of passages of display. He is at his best in his numerous chorale-fantasias and chorale-preludes or "Choralvorspiele," which have a more genuinely Teutonic ring, and are not only dexterously manipulated in detail, but display great variety of treatment and even touches of poetic insight which the somewhat complacent efficiency of his other works would not seem to foreshadow. In all such matters he was an important pioneer. The tendency towards harmonic music was inevitable, and Pachelbel's peculiar position, combining traits of both the Roman Catholic and the Protestant schools of organists, was a very strong, if not the most powerful influence, in directing composers' minds to the assimilation of the harmonic and polyphonic principles, and helping to the realisation of tonal schemes of design.

Buxtehude was a man of very different type. His work is rugged, brilliant, full of strong and interesting individuality and depth of feeling. He is one of those composers who give the impression of greatness and nobility of mind, and when compared with Pachelbel he makes that composer's work seem tame and superficial for all its dexterity. He had quite as much instinct for harmony as Pachelbel, but of a different order. With him the predominant feeling is that the function of harmony as the means of expression is higher than its function as the means of suggesting design. He delights in strange chords and powerful sequences; in successions of harmonies which produce the effect of the motion of overwhelming masses. With Pachelbel the contrapuntal texture often seems like the ornamentation of a succession of simple chords, with Buxtehude the harmonic substratum and the rich polyphonic texture are admirably balanced and welded together so as to produce an effect of splendidly rich sonority.

Buxtehude's instinct for instrumental style was phenomenal, and as an inventor of genuine organ effects he has had few rivals in the history of art. In his work it is rare to find the time-honoured imitation of choral music adapted for the organ. If anything, he at times overstepped the just limits of elaborate ornamentation and figure. He wrote with the true instinct of the virtuoso for brilliant and appropriate richness of detail, and his resourcefulness was so ample that he but rarely had to fall back on conventional formulas. The extent to which he outstripped all the organ composers who preceded him is a pre-eminent proof of his genius, and his influence upon art was so great that it may be felt through the great composers who succeeded him up to the present time. In his works based on chorales he broke new ground, giving his examples a far more genuinely instrumental character than his predecessors had done; while his fugues, and chaconnes, and the passacaglia, and works in more elastic forms, such as toccatas and preludes, present the features of true instrumental music not only in detail but in scheme and artistic method.

In his work the labours of the noble school of German organists of the seventeenth century found their culmination, and only one step was needed to reach the highest level of organ music of all time. It was indeed the one branch of art which was successfully cultivated in Germany up to this time; for in other branches, though good work was done, it was all more or less tentative and immature. In music for stringed instruments the Germans were comparatively backward, and only began to make progress when they adopted Italian manners. Music for domestic keyed instruments was almost entirely neglected by them until near the end of the century, and what was achieved was either strongly coloured by organ style, or thin and artificial, as is the case with Pachelbel's work. The most conspicuous pioneers were Froberger and Kuhnau. The former in his suites for clavier manifests a very high instinct for delicate treatment of the domestic keyed instrument, and had no little share in the development of that branch of art towards the noble culmination which was to come in the next generation.

Johann Kuhnau's contribution towards the differentiation of the style of this branch of art was even more decisive. He was a man of culture, intelligence, and enterprise, and having noticed the neglect into which the domestic branch of the art had fallen, deliberately set to work to remedy it by writing suites for the clavier modelled on the lines contrived by Italian composers for stringed instruments, and sonatas of a somewhat polyphonic character, and also some programme-sonatas called "Biblical histories," which are instinct with artistic ingenuities and expressive and realistic devices. His work in these directions was really of very great importance, as it served not only as an initiative but as an admirable model of texture and style; and prefigured the lines on which the finest examples of this branch of art were designed soon after his time.

But, while giving adequate appreciation to the work of the foremost representatives of German music, it is well to remember that a very large number of distinguished composers of lesser eminence ministered to the advancement of their art in their respective spheres. Though few of them attained to that decisive definition of their own personality which has been emphasised as of such urgency at the beginning of the chapter, the devotion of spirit which shines through crudities and insufficiencies in their work afforded the most favourable conditions for the ultimate achievement of great results. Great works of art are the fruit of earnestness and devotion, and the belief that art is worthy of our best attention. The composers of Germany gave ample evidence that this was their attitude, and among these composers one family stood out pre-eminent, for simple devotion to art, and for the number of distinguished composers and performers which it furnished to the world.

The family of the Bachs is traced back to the early years of the sixteenth century. They were peasants, farmers, or of such occupations as befitted that rank of life, and were scattered over various parts of northern Germany—at Gräfenrode and Rockhausen near Arnstadt, at Wechmar in Saxony. The first of the family of whom musical tastes are recorded was Veit Bach, who was a baker or miller in Wechmar, and delighted in playing on an instrument described as a "Cythringen." His son Hans combined the professions of carpet-weaver and musician, and studied his art under one Kaspar Bach of another branch of the family, who was one of the town musicians at Gotha in the latter part of the sixteenth century. Hans Bach played on a stringed instrument, probably the viol, and was well known in many towns of Thuringia, such as Gotha, Arnstadt, Eisenach, and Erfurt, as a merry fellow, and he seems to have been in request to play with the town musicians at those places. He died in 1626 and left a considerable family, some of whom were musicians. The eldest of his sons, Johann, born in 1604 in Wechmar, was driven by the scourge of war which devastated the neighbourhood, to seek opportunities elsewhere for the employment of his musical abilities, and settled in Erfurt, where he became head of the town musicians, and had many sons who in their turn became town musicians. Among them was Johann Christian, who settled in Eisenach. Another distinguished son of Johann, named Johann Ægidius, born in 1645, became organist of St. Michael's Church and director of the town musicians of Erfurt. One of his sons, Johann Bernhard, born in 1676, was one of the most illustrious members of the family, filling the post of organist of the "Kaufmann's Kirche" at Erfurt, and afterwards succeeding his cousin Johann Christoph as organist of Eisenach. He was not only a composer of organ music but essayed his powers as a writer of suites for stringed instruments. Many other eminent musicians there were belonging to various branches of the family descended from Veit, but the most noteworthy at the end of the seventeenth century were the brothers Johann Christoph (born in 1642) and Johann Michael (born in 1648), who were the sons of Heinrich Bach, the youngest son of the before-mentioned Hans. Johann Christoph's official career began early, as he was appointed organist of Eisenach Church in 1665, and in that town he spent the remainder of his life. Very little is known of him beyond his admirable compositions, but it is highly probable that he came into contact with Johann Pachelbel, whose eminent position in the story of art has been above described, and who was court organist at Eisenach for a short time. Johann Christoph's compositions are of considerable importance and represent the highest standard attained by the family up to that time. They comprise some admirable examples of organ music in the form of the "Choral-vorspiel," and some very remarkable Church music in the shape of choral motets, and also a very important and picturesque composition for voices and orchestra known by its first words as *Es erhob sich ein Streit* (*There was war in heaven*). The work is an attempt to interpret in musical terms the combat between the Archangel Michael and Satan in Heaven, which is related in the *Book of Revelation*, chapter xii. It is cast on broad and imposing lines for a double choir of ten voices with an accompanying orchestra for strings, trumpets, drums, organ, and bassoon. It is noticeable, in view of the admitted influence of the polyphonic organ style in German compositions for voices, that the treatment is hardly ever contrapuntal or polyphonic. The voices are mainly used to declaim the words in the simplest successions of chords, and the use of five-part writing is extremely limited. The violins, also, have very little independent work to do, and the only instruments which are conspicuously favoured are the trumpets, which have very elaborate and brilliant passages to play, with the view of suggesting the scenes of warfare. The effect of the work as a whole would be imposing and massive, but the style of the treatment indicates Italian influence in its harmonic simplicity, though not by any means in the matter of diction or figure, or by making concession to public levity by inopportune tunefulness. The better kind of Italian influence is perceptible again in Johann Christoph's motets, for they are not nearly so polyphonic as might be expected of a German organist of that date. There are passages in them quite like hymn tunes, and very few which are absolutely contrapuntal.[1] At the same time there are some very fine and impressive passages in which harmonic and polyphonic traits are combined, prefiguring the methods of the great generation which succeeded him.

Johann Christoph's younger brother, Johann Michael, who was organist of Gehren from 1673 till his death in 1694, wrote some choral motets, which show the Italian influence even more strongly than his elder brother's works, probably because he was a much weaker musical personality. The influence is, indeed, so pronounced that at times the simple rhythmic harmonisation looks more fit to be played on instruments than to be sung. This strange phase extended even to the romantic Buxtehude, who—so out-and-out German in his organ

[1] Exception must be made of the superb motet "Ich lasse dich nicht," which is generally attributed to him, though quite unlike his other works in style and texture.

music—betrayed Italian influence, by lowering the expressive interest of the inner details, directly he began to write for voices or other instruments than the organ. The point needs to be insisted on in order to give due weight and value to the complete endowment of choral music with genuine Teutonic style in the course of another forty years.

The various lines of descendants who spread out from Hans the carpet-weaver produced too many able and devoted musicians to be dealt with in detail. The line in which the faculties of the Bach family culminated descended through Christoph, the second son of Hans, who had held musical posts in Weimar, Erfurt, and Arnstadt. Among his sons was Johann Ambrosius, born with his twin brother Johann Christoph in Erfurt in 1645. He was taken by his father to Arnstadt in early years, but ultimately returned to his native place, Erfurt, in 1667 as a member of the Raths Musikanten, and here, in 1668, he married Elizabeth Lämmerhirt, the daughter of a furrier of that town, by whom he had eight children, few of whom survived. They did not remain long in Erfurt after their marriage but moved to Eisenach in 1671, where their youngest son, John Sebastian, was born in March, 1685. In him the gifts of this consistently and profusely gifted family, and the long traditions of earnestness and sincerity which had become characteristic of Teutonic musicians, bore at last the noblest and maturest fruit, and in his works are verified the words with which this chapter set forth.

Of all the composers whose personality gains in fascination and whose individuality becomes more and more eloquent with the passage of time, John Sebastian

Bach's Birthplace in Eisenach

From *Die Musik*.

(Courtesy of Messrs. Schuster & Loeffler, Berlin.)

Bach stands foremost. Many other great masters are identifiable through characteristic traits of diction, through peculiarities of method and brilliant strokes of art or effect which are their peculiar properties; or even by the width of their scope and their power of handling great and impressive subjects. But no other master shows in small things as in great the same degree of consistent humanity. Though up to his time art of the kinds which came into being in the seventeenth century had been almost universally immature, and though, of more than a century of manifold creative effort, hardly any work remains to the world which has not to be taken with some qualification and allowance for its immaturity, he gathered into his grasp so completely all the methods and experiments which had been devised in different quarters and in divers countries, and so welded them by the consistent power of his artistic personality, that the traces of their origin are forgotten; and the immense mass of great and noble works which he poured forth in a life of ceaseless activity seems to have but one nationality and one source in the steadfast and energetic working of a single mind.

CHAPTER II

PRELIMINARIES

It seems difficult to suppress the craving to become intimate with the circumstances of the life of any man who has achieved work that makes a powerful appeal to us and has exerted influence upon our lives. The great ones who have shared in the fashioning of our souls are in a sense our spiritual ancestors, and that in itself is sufficient to invite a personal interest. And, besides that, the mental picture of the incidents and ways of such men supplies a sort of background and an atmosphere which seems to enhance our interest in their work and to remind us agreeably that it is human. But the conditions of life are, in the highest sense, mainly worthy of attention in proportion as they throw light on the achievements and quality of the works which make the man memorable. Mere biographical details are superfluous unless their bearings are kept in sight, and the attention is easily distracted from essentials by laying too much stress on irrelevancies.

There are just a few cases in history when such distraction is impossible owing to the lack even of legends. This is especially the case where the type of work achieved is of the kind that appeals to the higher type of mind. If the records of those who have won great and popular successes are deficient, legends are always easily cultivated and greedily stored up. Their absence is a very high compliment. When a great man's life is deficient in such things, the austerity of the situation appeals to the imagination. The human mind seeks for the proofs of human origin in the works themselves and not in the accessories. The lesser minds are baulked, but those who are capable of communion with the highest manifestations of the human spirit are fortified.

It is, then, not so overwhelmingly regrettable that, as in the case of Shakespeare, the personal records of John Sebastian Bach are of the very scantiest, and suffice for little more than to locate the successive phases of artistic development, and to identify the influences which directed the attention of the expanding composer and performer to different branches of art at different times. The very bareness of the outlines makes the singular scheme of development clearer and more intelligible, and gives to the subject a greater and more impressive aspect than any that could be derived from the most picturesque anecdotes. The mind becomes the more free to follow without distraction the manifestation of that steadfast and strenuous concentration of purpose, in gathering together the necessary artistic methods from all quarters, and in making them amenable for the service of an individual artistic purpose.

For this, indeed, is the key to the story of the life-work of John Sebastian Bach. As has already been indicated, when he came upon the scene the conditions were favourable to the attainment of great results in certain large and general respects. From his lineage Bach inherited a tradition of musicianship and a whole-hearted belief in his art. By the temper of the German people, to whom he belonged and among whom he lived, he was inspired and fortified in simplicity of living, in sincerity of mind, and ardour of devotion. But on the other hand the resources of art and the technique of expression were quite inadequate; and even such as were available were scattered and dissevered.

Different men and different groups of men had been identified with different branches of art, and had in these several branches done a good deal towards the establishment of style and artistic methods. The earlier members of the great Italian school of violinists and composers of violin music had fairly established the style of their branch of secular art, by formulating the outlines of construction which were most apt for works written for it and the most practicable types of diction in respect to its physical peculiarities. And it is important to note that the most conspicuous members of their particular craft, such as Corelli, confined themselves entirely to making music for their own group of instruments, without attempting to expand their scheme by experimenting in other fields of art.

The composers of organ music had been even more successful and had brought the standard of their art within sight and touch of the highest point of artistic maturity. Composers dealing with forms of greater complexity and scope, such as operas, church music, serenatas and all those larger forms which necessitated the employment of various orders of resource, both vocal and instrumental, were still in comparative bewilderment. Their ideas of construction, of procedure, and of style were all in a nebulous condition, and everything they did manifested in every part the helplessness of explorers as yet uncertain even in what direction to turn. The true principles which should differentiate sacred from secular music were not ascertained or perceived. Inartistic makeshifts, such as the figured basses to solo music of all sorts, were not only admitted but even predominant. Orchestration had hardly begun to exist, choral music was either fluently academic, as in the perfunctory festal church music of the Roman Church, or so crude from the excess of deep feeling over the resources of expression as to become almost impracticable, as was the case with some of Schütz's works. There was no lack of workers, but there was lack of co-ordination.

It is inevitable in art, as elsewhere, that the lower order of human beings should provide the groundwork for the achievements of those of higher type. The mechanics and everyday workmen fashion the details and appliances, and the organisers use them for great and comprehensive works. At the end of the seventeenth century things were more or less in a state of preparation; the appliances were ready in plenty, but they needed the gathering together and systematisation—the comprehension which only a man gifted with the highest faculties and perception of the widest range can command.

At such a moment different types of men deal with the opportunities afforded in different ways. The two most notable men who availed themselves of the opportunities which had been built up by their forerunners were, obviously, Handel and Bach; and their methods were most instructively diverse. Handel, in a different field and under different influences, systematised the artistic methods which came in his way in a general and practical manner, which served the purposes of a man who was very much before a very large public. The purpose of Bach was much more subtle and concentrated, and very much more personal. His art, with certain inevitable and natural exceptions, is far more intimate than Handel's. It presents the difference of spirit and texture between the type of work which is made for a small circle of attentive and earnest people, who will dwell on details at close quarters, and the type which is made for a large public not much concerned with subtleties of detail, but mainly with large impressions.

The public circle of Bach was very limited throughout his lifetime, and the largeness of his conceptions came from innate promptings rather than from external influences; and hence the largeness of conception was not vitiated, as is so frequently the case with men who are in personal contact with large audiences, by the histrionic temptations; by the impulse to make a show on a large scale with any means that come to hand; by the endeavour to induce an audience to believe pasteboard to be mountains and mere exuberance of rhetoric the profound wisdom of the inspired prophet. Bach was under comparatively small temptation to gloss over imperfections of detail or false traits of style, and everything ministered to make his work the veritable mirror of his own nature and convictions.

There is no need to gloss over the drawbacks of such a position. By contrast of opportunities Handel seems fortunate. Almost from the first moment that his professional life began, he could easily come into contact with musicians of the first rank in every branch of the profession. He was in a position to master the secrets of his craft by observing those who understood them without having to go far afield. Everything was brought near to his hand and no great demands were made upon his personal individual effort. The confined area of Bach's life-work made it inevitable that he should make more use of his own inner consciousness. In a small corner of Germany he was not likely to come across brilliant virtuosos, or the most distinguished singers either of opera or of sacred music. Indeed, the area of music itself would at first sight seem to be rather limited, just as it would be in a fairly enlightened provincial district in any modern country. The highest standard of art would then, as till recently in provincial areas, be connected with church functions. The organist would almost inevitably be the ablest musician in the neighbourhood and his organ performances the most frequent manifestation of the talents of a solo performer to be heard by the generality. The predominant influence would be in the direction of serious art, even the art of religion, and a young musician developing in such surroundings would naturally be impressed and influenced by the atmosphere of the most serious and deeply felt types of music.

But in Germany, in those days, music was not confined entirely to ecclesiastical purposes. Every group of habitations which was large enough to be called a town had town musicians, who, in a sense, represented secular art. They had, it is true, to assist in church music both on State occasions and at Church festivals, but their viols, hautboys, bassoons, trombones, and cornets were not rooted in the sacred edifices, and could betake themselves without difficulty to places where dance music and secular music of a kind could appropriately be indulged in. Secular instrumental music at the beginning of the eighteenth century was not of a very high or exhilarating order in Germany, but, such as it was, it supplied a hopeful counterpoise to the risks of the predominating ecclesiastical type, and let into the scheme some of the fresh air of the active world.

By good fortune this useful influence of healthy secularity was conspicuously present in the earliest and most impressionable years of John Sebastian Bach. His grandfather, Christoph, the son of Hans, seems to have been essentially a town musician. He was one of the official musicians of the Rath of Erfurt in 1642, and became one of the court musicians of the Count of Schwarzburg and town musician of Arnstadt in 1653 or thereabouts, and in that town he is held to have died in 1661. Ambrosius and his twin brother, John Christoph, John Sebastian's father and uncle, were both town musicians; and the latter succeeded his father at Arnstadt, while Ambrosius returned to their birthplace. Erfurt, in 1667, and became a town musician there and afterwards at Eisenach, being himself a performer on the viola.

Thus the predominant direction of the artistic energies of this branch of the great Bach family was towards secular rather than towards church or organ music. These circumstances must be taken into account in considering the moulding of John Sebastian's musical disposition; for it was of no little importance that the young and expanding genius should be beckoned forward in his most impressionable years, by the qualities of secular instruments, in the direction of the human and energetic side of art. Moreover, it was not only in its natural expressive aspects that such secular influence was valuable, but also as embodying in a very pronounced degree the secular element of rhythm. In the earlier choral music rhythm had been practically non-existent, and in all church music it continued in very pronounced subordination, for reasons which have been explained elsewhere. The genuine church composer always has a sort of uneasy suspicion of rhythm, and does not dare to open his soul to it. It is like certain things which, though perfectly natural and innocent in themselves, are prohibited by the conventions of certain strata of society. The value of having such an obstruction to complete musical expansion broken down at the outset and sympathy with secular music aroused can hardly be over-assessed; and to these circumstances may be fairly attributed the strain of ingenuous peasanthood which is never quite lost sight of in the composer; and that vivacity, variety, elasticity, and frankness of rhythmic force which distinguish him above all the other composers of the century,—unless perchance, the peasant-born Haydn might be counted as his congenial compeer.

Apart from the actual health-giving effect of listening to such secular music, the secular influence was fortified by the young musician's addressing himself early to the mastering of a stringed instrument. Under such circumstances as have been referred to above, it would be natural for the boy's relations to take it somewhat as a matter of course that he should follow in the steps of his father and grandfather and become a "Raths Musikant"; and for that end it was natural and inevitable that he should be instructed from the earliest possible years in the manipulation of some instrument of the viol or violin type, and such instruction he did indeed receive from his father.

But it is evident that the clavier was not much behind in the matter of chronology. Bach was at all times singularly awake to other types of musical activity or expression besides the central ones with which his life seemed at special periods to be specially occupied; and the fact of a clavichord being accessible would make it inevitable that the young musician should explore its possibilities. But there is nothing to help the world to discover who guided the earliest steps which were due to lead him to the highest position among the performers of his time. Whether his ultimate pre-eminence was due to self-development or not, it is at all events clear that the prevailing influences of his childish years were on the side of secular instrumental music, and an impetus was thereby given which led to his supreme position among the secular instrumental composers of his time.

But domestic troubles soon brought the influence of the father and of his particular line of art to an end. In 1694, John Sebastian's mother died; and in a little over half a year Ambrosius married again; and then, in the short space of two months, he too died, leaving little John Sebastian an orphan at ten years of age. He was the youngest of a considerable family, of whom very little is known. One of the elder brothers, yet again named John Christoph (born in 1671), was a musician of some eminence. He had in his youth enjoyed the advantage of learning from the famous organist and composer John Pachelbel during the time when he was organist of the Prediger-Kirche in Erfurt, and in 1690 had been appointed organist of the principal church in Ohrdruff, a small town in the same Thuringian district as Eisenach and Erfurt, and here he had married one Dorothea von Hof and established himself. And when the home at Eisenach was broken up he took his youngest brother to live with him.

In such a home new influences inevitably began to operate. Without laying undue stress on the difference between the art of a town musician and that of a musician attached to a church establishment, it cannot be gainsaid that the regular, quiet, orderly, and sober existence of an organist of a church, the peculiar artistic atmosphere, and the kind of work which falls to his lot to do are liable to exert a great and lasting influence upon the unfolding mind of a young musician. The better part of such influence is sobering. It leads to the concentration of the faculties upon the actual facts of art and to finding pleasure and reward in them rather than in the applause which brilliant individual achievement, either as a performer or composer, may evoke. And under this influence it is easy to see that the character of the young musician soon received a permanent bent.

There is no period in his life in which it is more natural to wish for trustworthy details of daily life. But of the kind of familiar details which might throw light there is an absolute dearth. There is barely enough even to suggest inferences as to the elder brother's character. His having been a pupil of Pachelbel's is no doubt suggestive, and helps to explain the respect in which John Sebastian held that composer—a respect which is shown in his taking him at times for a model. For though Pachelbel often seems to lack depth and sincerity he was one of the most important pioneers of style in his time, and his instinct for effect was so great that it has sometimes been sufficient to deceive the very elect into thinking there really was something behind it. The earlier stages in the differentiation of style are generally developed on a flimsy basis, though the principles which they illustrate are substantially just; but what filtered through John Christoph to John Sebastian was useful, as it helped him to the recognition of the necessity of decorative treatment of detail, especially in secular instrumental music.

The only anecdote with any point in it which survives from these early times illustrates his eagerness to obtain the helpful guidance of the most famous masters of his craft. It is told that his brother John Christoph had a collection of the most valuable compositions by such men as Kerl, Froberger, and Pachelbel, which was kept locked up in a book-case with a latticed front; and that John Sebastian managed to extract the roll through the lattice-work and endeavoured to copy out its contents surreptitiously by moonlight; and that John Christoph found it out and took the collection away. The latter part of the story is superfluous, except as indicating a touch of human nature which might be interpreted in various ways; but the story itself is especially notable as the first recorded instance of the practice, which was characteristic of John Sebastian from first to last, of studying the works of men of undoubted ability in different branches of art, and gaining insight thereby into the methods and principles of art in order to apply them to the higher purposes which his finer insight and more richly endowed disposition suggested.

His general education appears to have been duly attended to. The local school or Lyceum of Ohrdruff was by his time a foundation of some antiquity, and the scheme of the pabulum for young minds was up to the average standard of the day, though it supplied more of concrete material in the shape of elementary Latin, arithmetic, and the inevitable theology than of subjects which expanded the mind. But, such as it was, the period of schooling must have had some little influence upon John Sebastian's character. His knowledge of Latin also was sufficient to stand him in good stead in after life when he was called upon to instruct the boys at St. Thomas's School in Leipzig in that language as well as in music. But a more important point was that the particular tradition of the school in respect of Protestantism was what was technically called "Orthodox" as distinguished from that which was defined as "Pietistic." For it was in the orthodox section that the church services included the softening and inspiring influences of art, which by the pietistic section were discouraged. It is also noteworthy that music was cordially recognised in the school. An appreciable portion of time was set aside for its cultivation, and there was a choir of boys who sang in church, and also (in accordance with the practice common in Thuringian towns of those days) in the streets, whereby they earned a little money. This was probably the beginning of John Sebastian's individual experience of the actual practice of choral music, and for several years he continued to sing in choirs, which is a most serviceable way of getting into touch with the mystery of writing choral music sympathetically.

Beyond this not much can be recorded of the five years during which he lived with his elder brother at Ohrdruff; and at the early age of fifteen he had to begin to provide for himself and find his own way in life. His independent musical career began in the choir of the convent school of St. Michael's at Lüneburg, in which he obtained an appointment with the small monthly salary of twelve groschen. Here he came into contact with a good deal of music, much of it of good quality; for a band of some sort was attached to St. Michael's and performed with the choir on festivals and grand occasions. It is also inferred, from the rich comprehensiveness of the library of the institute at Lüneburg, that John Sebastian had opportunities of taking part in the works of the most interesting composers of the seventeenth century, such as Heinrich Schütz, Hammerschmidt, Ahle, Scheidt, Briegel, Crüger, and Pachelbel, and some earlier members of his own family. The organist was Johann Jacob Löw, who came from Bach's own native town of Eisenach, but had travelled a good deal, even as far as Vienna and Italy, and had had the privilege of being acquainted with Heinrich Schütz himself.

But a more important influence was exercised by Georg Böhm, one of the most remarkable and interesting of all the performers and composers of the time, who was organist of St. John's Church in Lüneburg. The number of his compositions which is accessible in modern times is very small; but it is sufficient to indicate that he had a considerable instinct for instrumental style, and cultivated a more ornate manner than the earlier composers of organ music. It is highly probable, moreover, that it was from hearing Georg Böhm play that John Sebastian was inspired to set out on one of the pilgrimages to extend his understanding of his art, which occupy such a prominent space in his early history.

George Böhm had been a pupil of the famous musician John Adam Reinken, one of the aged heroes of the northern school of organists. Reinken had been born as long before as 1623, at Deventer in Holland, and had already been organist of the Church of St. Catherine at Hamburg for nearly half a century. His reputation was very great both as a performer and a composer, and, as Hamburg was at an accessible distance from Lüneburg, it was natural that John Sebastian should be possessed by the desire to become personally acquainted with his artistic powers. In the end he made several expeditions, mostly on foot, to that busy old commercial centre, which has always been so forward in its interest in music. It was in Hamburg that the enterprising German opera composer, Reinhard Keiser, had long been in full exercise of his remarkable versatility; and here also Handel had been exercising his powers as a violinist, cembalist, and composer in the opera house for some time, and was very likely so engaged at the time of Bach's coming to the town. Whether, indeed, Bach concerned himself with the opera we have no means of knowing, but the atmosphere of Hamburg was full of music, and the young composer had excellent opportunities there for extending his artistic horizon. As far as the veteran

Reinken is concerned, there is little to be said with certainty. That Bach went several times to hear him is proof that he was interested in his performances and his artistic personality; and his having based a work of his own on Reinken's *Hortus Musicus* in later years is proof that the early impression was not impaired by growth of maturer judgment.

In view of the ultimate quality of Bach's fame it was fortunate that his stay at Lüneburg was not a very prolonged one. For though he was in a position to absorb fruitful influences, to such a nature as his the example of Georg Böhm was not inexhaustible; and the learning which he could take to himself from listening to Reinken could only be obtained at a heavy expenditure of time and shoe-leather. In John Sebastian's time there was no good organ in Lüneburg. That in St. John's Church, played by Böhm, was the best. That in the church with which Bach was connected was very poor, and he could play on it only by permission. It is not possible to develop powers to any high degree of efficiency by merely listening to other people, so in a most vital respect his opportunities were inadequate. The situation came to an end in rather an insignificant manner; for all that is known is that in the year 1703 John Sebastian was no longer a member of the church choir at Lüneburg but in the service of Johann Ernst, younger brother of the Duke of Weimar. It is not implied that his appointment was essentially a musical one, but it is recorded that he took part in the performances of the court band as a violin player.

Weimar was always a great artistic centre, and the reigning family prided themselves on their encouragement of music, and their cosmopolitan taste. So the young musician had renewed opportunities of hearing plenty of secular music. But his stay at Weimar this time was very short. The episode makes but a narrow interim between the period of his youthful probation, and the acceptance of the appointment which marks the beginning of mature and independent activity. The short stay at Weimar was, however, the stepping-stone to this appointment. For it was the near proximity of Arnstadt which caused John Sebastian to go there from Weimar to see some relations, and this brought in its wake an opportunity to play on the new organ in the church there, when by good fortune, some of the people in authority heard and were impressed by his performance; and this led to his being offered the organistship.

Up to this time, when he was eighteen years old, there is little if anything which can be decisively identified as illustrating his powers as a composer. A few compositions are speculatively assigned to the Lüneburg time on the basis of intrinsic qualities, notably a primitive Chorale-Prelude (see p. 534) which shows the influence of Böhm; but they do not afford substantial matter to dwell upon. All that can be safely inferred is that he had obtained some efficiency as a player on domestic keyed instruments, whether harpsichord or clavichord, that he was an efficient performer on a stringed instrument, that he had, in spite of very limited opportunities, developed remarkable powers as an organist; and that he had taken every opportunity to develop his insight into the mysteries of his art, by keenly observing the performances of the most distinguished organists who were in accessible range and by taking part in choral and secular instrumental music, and thus preparing himself for the exercise of his own creative activities, which grew with steadfast continuity towards the supreme mastery in these branches of art.

The people of Arnstadt were very proud of the organ in the "New Church." It had only been completed in 1701, and though of moderate dimensions, as modern ideas go, it was fully adequate to such requirements as the organ music of those days imposed. It had a great organ, as it would now be called, of ten speaking stops, four of which supplied a good solid foundation of diapason tone; a choir organ of seven stops, in which it seems strange to find only one stop of eight-foot tone—the Lieblich Gedackt—with four stops of four-foot calibre and a quint, a sesquialtera and a mixture, which must have produced a strangely brilliant effect; and last, and by no means least, a substantial pedal organ of five stops, of which two were of sixteen feet, one of eight, and two represented the higher harmonics; which could, moreover, be coupled to the manuals.

It seems that the authorities were not well satisfied with their organist at the time when John Sebastian visited the town and gave proofs of his abilities; so the former was gently shelved and John Sebastian was appointed in his place in August, 1703, he being then eighteen years of age. Together with his duties of organist he combined those of training the choir of the church, and rehearsing a kind of musical society which provided another choir on a large scale. Here were plenty of opportunities for the exercise of his powers, and he was also fortunate in finding the people of Arnstadt well disposed towards music, a court theatre where musical performances were sometimes given, and also a few musicians of ability.

John Sebastian had, unquestionably, an ample supply of native independence of character, but he had also the common-sense to adopt courses which were most likely to lead him to the highest practical results in the long run. His career is a perfect study of natural and spontaneous direction of human energy in accordance with the opportunities he found for testing and establishing the results of his work. In every change in the conditions of his environment throughout his life he adapted himself to the line of work which fitted in with it. Here in Arnstadt his opportunities lay in the direction of works for choir and orchestra and works for the organ; and intrinsic qualities, as well as a network of interlacing circumstances given by Spitta in a note, make it fairly certain that the church cantata *Denn du wirst meine Seele nicht in der Hölle lassen* was composed at Arnstadt very soon after he was appointed there.

It must be admitted that the cantata is known only in a revised form dating several years later, and that it would therefore be unsafe to point to any of its excellencies as representing the standard of his art at this date or to draw inferences from them; but on the other hand there are features which evidently belong to the original form of the work, and are highly significant. The band for which it is written is of the constitution which was most familiar in those days in opera as well as in sacred music, in the works of Alessandro Scarlatti and Hasse as well as of Handel, comprising the usual group of strings, with trumpets and drums. A great many solo voices are employed for arias and recitatives, and the chorus is used but sparingly. In some respects, as for instance in the instrumental passage with which it opens (which is repeated with modifications in the latter part of the second half of the cantata), the style is bald and crude. Fanfares of trumpets which are built on the simplest harmonic successions make their appearance, and the treatment of the strings is dull and commonplace. The solo movements are very limited in scope and for the most part restricted to the simplest harmonies. In some of them there are attractive and characteristic passages of tune of a joyous and direct type, which bring some of Reinhard Keiser's tunes to mind; as in the duet *Weichet Furcht und Schrecken,* and the tenor solo *Entsetzet euch nicht,* and the soprano solo *Auf, freue dich, Seele.*

Most of these solos are cast in a very compact aria

form, and they are generally characterised by very long and elaborate runs, such as are met with in the works of German church composers of the latter half of the previous century, who borrowed the device from the Italians. In later days Bach used such decorative features with great aptness, usually for purposes of expression. But here the aptness appears only in a general sense, and the forms of the florid passages are conventional. There is only one chorus of any dimensions, *Mein Jesu, mein Helfer,* and this is as bald and as plain as the treatment of the instruments above referred to. The final chorale is so vastly superior in texture and interest to the other movements that it is natural to infer that it belongs to a later date than the rest of the work. The cantata is at a more consistently high level than the cantatas of Buxtehude, which seem likely to have been Bach's models, and there are plenty of characteristic traits of the composer in elementary disguises. But there is a lack of development, a lack of richness in polyphony, a lack of intrinsic distinction in the substance, a lack even of expression; though there are gleams in the recitatives where the true John Sebastian is momentarily revealed, as in the passage from the recitative for soprano.

SOPRANO.
Wie könnt es an - ders sein? Ein
CONTINUO.

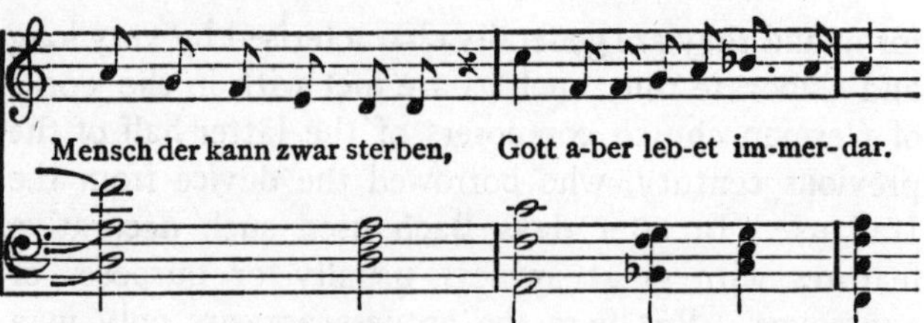
Mensch der kann zwar sterben, Gott a-ber leb-et im-mer-dar.

Circumstances which occurred later make it likely that John Sebastian did not compose any more cantatas while at Arnstadt; and though a good many organ compositions are referred to this period of his life for reasons which will be discussed later, the only work which known circumstances almost decisively prove to have been composed at Arnstadt is a work not for organ but for the domestic keyed instrument, the clavier. Interest in this work is enhanced by the fact that it stands by itself in a line upon which Bach never again adventured, rightly discerning that such a type of programme music was, for him, superfluous. The event which originated the composition is decisively identifiable. His brother John Jacob entered the service of Charles XII. of Sweden in 1704 as a hautboy player in the King's Guards, and his departure to take part in an enterprise of that impetuous monarch (whose service inevitably suggested copious risks) inspired John Sebastian to embody his feelings in a musical work in several movements, described in the title as "Capriccio sopra la lontananza del suo fratello dilettissimo."

Programme music of this kind was by no means a novelty in those days. Froberger, most interesting of South German organists, had astonished his admirers by his powers in this direction, and French composers for the clavier or harpsichord were beginning to cultivate it with evident preference and success. Moreover it had been but as recently as 1700, that the admirable Johann Kuhnau, organist of St. Thomas-Kirche and cantor of the Thomas-Schule in Leipzig, had published the notable group of biblical history sonatas before referred to, in which interest of workmanship and happy instinct for expression are combined with quaint fancy. It is very likely that Bach was influenced by these precedents, and there is a certain kinship between traits in his work and those in some of Kuhnau's which makes it likely that he was acquainted with them.

The importance of the work in the story of Bach's life is that it represents such a sudden attainment of a high and equal degree of mastery, and such a consistent revelation of the composer's personality. Were it not for the dates being identifiable almost beyond dispute it would be difficult to believe that it could have been produced so early. But the explanation is fairly evident. The programme happens to be an ideal one, and represents genuine and serious feeling; and this programme, by thoroughly enlisting his heart, caused his faculties to concentrate. One of the drawbacks of the youthful artist is that the eagerness to express himself is not always seconded by certainty as to what courses are most apt for the occasion. The meaning of methods by which purely artistic developments are achieved is only reached by experience. But the lack of such experience can sometimes be serviceably compensated by a clear and unmistakable emotional impulse which keeps the faculties from wandering. Bach was especially amenable to emotional impressions. Most of his greatest achievements are the fruit of subjects which moved him deeply—the episodes of the Passion, the words of the "Crucifixus," the "Sanctus," the "Incarnatus." The consciousness of having some definite feeling to express always helped him. He looked for it. In nearly all the great first choruses in the cantatas it is perfectly clear that the words generated an impulse in him to express in the many-sided fashion that belongs to music the actual phase of praise, prayer, contrition or exultation, which is embodied in the text.

So in connection with this programme the young Bach had something definite to which he could address himself, something which supplied a basis of consistency in many different aspects of the same root-idea. There are no less than six movements. In the first—a short arioso—the friends endeavour to dissuade John Jacob from his risky enterprise. The sympathetic listener seems to be able to see right into Bach's mind and to feel with him the reiteration of tender appeal.[1]

The second movement (a concentrated little fugue) represents the anticipation of dangers to which the

[1] Bach afterwards developed this idea in a marvellous fashion in the slow movement of the Toccata in D minor for Clavier, see p. 71.

traveller will be liable—a movement of foreboding and anxiety. The third movement has a remarkably subtle ground bass over which all kinds of plaintive melodic figures are presented; expressing very clearly the laments, the tears, the sorrowing gestures of the friends; such as the quite typical passage,

and the surprisingly frank chromatic wail,

In the fourth movement the friends see that protest is of no avail and endeavour to attain to dignified resignation. And then the whole aspect of things changes. In comes the postilion cracking his whip, to a bustling little burst of tune, which seems to tell the kind of adventitious gaiety which often accompanies the excitement of a departure on a long journey! And the last movement is a most entertaining fugue on a tune supposed to be played by the postilion on his horn, with the crack of the whip through it all! The mastery of thematic material—from the point of view of what each item means—is quite astonishing. It cannot be doubted that the actual scenes of the journey with the merry postilion and the galloping horses were actually in Bach's mind as he wrote; and it held him firmly to the matter in hand. The result is the most dexterous piece of work of the kind that had ever appeared in the world up to that time.

The whole work presents the individuality of the composer with perfect consistency; and the actual artistic execution and the modelling of the movements are at the highest pitch of finish. Such being the case it seems strange that Bach never again wrote a single movement of what may be described as programme music, and that a work so perfect should be so little known. The explanation of the first mystery would require a long dissertation on the whole question of programme music. All that can be said here is that Bach undoubtedly recognised that the actual naming of a programme for instrumental music has the effect of circumscribing and belittling the music. And that fact answers the second riddle. Beautiful as the music is, it is on a very small scale. Bach himself practically extinguished it by the weight and depth of expression of what he produced in later days. For a really great individuality the attitude of mind here manifested is not adequate to the highest purposes. Yet its being limited in this case suited the occasion, since Bach being as yet only nineteen and insufficiently sure of his methods, was likeliest to achieve a perfect work of art within a range which was necessarily restricted.

It was not long after this composition had been achieved that his ardour to extend the scope of his artistic mastery impelled him to make himself familiar with a master of higher gifts and stronger personality than he had ever hitherto met. Dietrich Buxtehude was at that time organist of St. Mary's Church at Lübeck, and his personal pre-eminence was enhanced by the musical traditions of the town. His predecessor, Franz Tunder, had been a composer of considerable mark, who had produced a great quantity of church music of fine and serious quality, worthy, indeed, of being linked by kinship of feeling with the works of John Sebastian. Buxtehude had married Tunder's daughter and succeeded him. His great position among the musicians of his time has already been indicated (page 12), but it must be further pointed out here that his line of work as well as his personal qualities would be most sympathetic and most opportune at the moment to John Sebastian. The breadth and power of his conceptions, the richness and novelty and elasticity of his treatment and his exceptional instinct for instrumental style were well calculated to attract the interest of a young composer of John Sebastian's disposition. Moreover it is easy to see from the texture of his organ works that Buxtehude must have been a brilliant performer; and not only that, but also endowed with a large human capacity to enjoy his art as well as to make it. His activities extended also in other directions which ran parallel to John Sebastian's work. For the institution of the "Abend-Musik" at Lübeck (an annual series of musical performances on a large scale which took place on several days in Advent) afforded him occasions, as it had done his father-in-law before him, to compose large works for voices and orchestra and put them to practical tests. The church cantatas he wrote for such occasions are historically important, as establishing the connecting link between him and Tunder; and they have moments of human feeling which speak the same sensitive language as John Sebastian in spite of their being on the whole rather tentative.

In this comprehensive kind of composition he was hindered by the backwardness of many branches of art which had to be brought into one sheaf. The backwardness of orchestration, and of the delicate arts of accompaniment, caused the demands on the inventive powers to be too heavy even for a man of his calibre. The language was inadequate to the utterance of his thoughts. In such things, he was toiling for others to achieve, but he had toiled far enough for it to be worth while for John Sebastian to take his work in this line into consideration, while in organ music there was absolutely no man living who could give him such an interesting and inspiring example.

Lübeck was about two hundred and fifty miles from Arnstadt, but to John Sebastian the distance was of no account, even if the journey had to be undertaken on foot, so urgent was his desire to observe the greatest achievements in his line of art. So in October,

1705, he applied for leave of absence from his duties and betook himself on another pilgrimage similar to that of earlier years to Hamburg. But there unhappily the curtain of oblivion descends again, for not a word of any kind of evidence is known as to what he did at Lübeck or how he spent the passing days. No one even knows what were his personal relations with Buxtehude himself—all that is known is that the attraction was so great that he could not tear himself away, and that he long outstayed his leave. By which means he had at least the opportunity of hearing the Abend-Musik, before mentioned, in the year 1705, for it was not till February, 1706, that he finally set out to resume his work at Arnstadt. It is not surprising that the consistory of the church where he had treated his duties with such scanty respect were not pleased, and he was summoned to give an account of his doings and to explain, if he could, his neglect of his duties. The record of the interview between John Sebastian and the consistory remains, and is one of the rare documents in which particulars of an episode in his life are accessible in complete and unmistakable fulness.

The consistory or its chairman asked him where he had been so long; to which he answered that he had been at Lübeck, where he had gone with the intention of learning some things connected with his art. He was then reminded that he had had leave for four weeks and had stayed four months; and he made the rather lame excuse that he hoped his deputy had replaced him satisfactorily. The consistory then took the opportunity to express their views on other matters which were not quite to their liking, and their complaints are enlightening. They said his variations on the chorales were "surprising," and that he bewildered the congregation by "many strange sounds" which he introduced into his accompaniments. That his preludes had been too long, and that when it had been pointed out to him he had made them too short. That he went to a wine shop during the sermon, and that he had not had any choir practices whatever. The indictment was grave, but apparently a peace was patched up and he resumed his duties. But the impulse generated by the influence of Buxtehude and the music he had heard at Lübeck impelled him towards absorption in composition; his relations with the authorities began to get strained again, and in November, 1706, he received another remonstrance from the consistory. The choir practices were again referred to as having been neglected, and the fact that a strange lady had been admitted by him into the choir and had been allowed to "make music" there was remarked upon. It becomes clear that John Sebastian was not altogether happy in the management of his work at Arnstadt, and it is not surprising that he took an early opportunity of accepting an appointment elsewhere. But meanwhile the reference by the consistory to the "strange lady" catches the attention. It is always construed as a reference to Maria Barbara, the youngest daughter of his cousin Michael Bach of Gehren, the younger brother of Johann Christoph who has before been mentioned as one of the most distinguished musicians of that generation. Their meeting is explained by her mother having been a native of Arnstadt, of which town her father had been town clerk; and it is supposed she may have gone there on a visit to her maternal relations. The ultimate outcome was her betrothal to John Sebastian.

But before the marriage could take place a new phase of Bach's career began at Mühlhausen, where he was appointed organist of the Church of St. Blasius, and installed on June 15, 1707. The musical traditions of Mühlhausen were of a high order. From 1654 till 1673 the organist of St. Blasius had been Johann Rudolf Ahle, a man of great mark, whose compositions rank very high among the best church works of the latter part of the previous century. And he had been succeeded by his son Georg Ahle, who was also a composer of considerable ability and of great repute in his time. He was John Sebastian's immediate predecessor, and his death in December, 1706, had left the place vacant. The appointment at Mühlhausen does not appear from a material point of view to have been any great improvement on that at Arnstadt. The salary of the organist was of about the same slender proportions, amounting to something under £10 of modern money: the principal enhancement of which consisted of a few measures of corn, two cords of firewood, some brushwood, and three pounds of fish per annum!

Even in matters more nearly connected with his art no striking improvement is noticeable. The organ in St. Blasius seems to have been in bad order, and one of the most interesting documents drawn up by John Sebastian himself which remains to the world, is his scheme of suggestions for making good its defects. The main trouble must be inferred from this document to have been that the bellows were insufficient for the work they had to perform, and John Sebastian made some simple and practical suggestions about them. Most of the other suggestions refer to new stops, and in these are some noteworthy features. It seems surprising to modern ears that he recommended the addition of no less than six new harmonic stops to the choir organ and only one soft stop of 8-foot tone. This, together with the strange constitution of the choir organ at Arnstadt suggests that musicians of the time had a liking for this quality of tone, comprising the least possible foundation and a crowd of harmonics, and that Bach, either from association or individual taste, endorsed it. Another feature, which chimes with what everybody must feel who knows his music, is the number of suggestions he makes with regard to the pedal organ, in which he wanted a better supply of wind, a 32-foot stop, and a complete set of new and larger pipes to the bass posaune, which would add weight and fulness. The most surprising of the suggestions, when coming from a composer of Bach's disposition, is that a set of twenty-six bells, which the parishioners had already procured and paid for, should be attached to the pedal organ. However, there seems no need to infer that Bach used the bells in the pedal parts of his fugues and toccatas. It was not at all an unusual thing in the Middle Ages to have peals of bells connected with mechanical appliances like organ keys or pedals, which were played upon by an individual performer; and elaborate music was written for such contrivances, and musical reputations, like that of Mathias van den Gheyn, were even founded on such compositions and performances. And, moreover, whatever artistic purists might say about it, the sound of carillons and bells mixed up with a hurly-burly of singing and organ and other instruments has a strangely exhilarating effect on brilliant festive occasions; and for such occasions these bells may well have been reserved.

The suggestions for these extensive alterations seem to have been taken in good part, and the work decided on. But so short was Bach's stay in Mühlhausen that the reconstruction was not completed before he had moved elsewhere. However, short as this stay was, it was signalised by important events. The first of these was his marriage with his cousin Maria Barbara Bach, to whom he had been but a short while before betrothed, as before mentioned, while he was still organist at Arnstadt. The marriage ceremony took place at the village church of Dornheim, near Arnstadt, on October 17, 1707, and the parish register recording it contains some quaint points about the late Ambrosius, "the famous town organist and musician of Eisenach," John Sebastian's father, and Johann Michael "the late very respectable and famous artist." And it was in Mühlhausen that John Sebastian began to experience the domesticities of married life, which always seem to have been so desirable to members of the Bach family.

But a yet more significant event than his marriage, as far as the world was concerned, was the production of his first really important work. It was customary in Mühlhausen for certain members of the town council to be changed once a year, and for the occasion to be celebrated by a church festival, including music, which the organist of St. Blasius was expected to compose. And for this occasion John Sebastian composed the "Rathswechsel Cantata," *Gott ist mein König*, which was performed on February 4, 1708.

Here indeed the composer already manifests an astonishing range of mastery. With the possible exception of an early Passion by Handel, there probably was no other sacred work of the kind in existence which could in any way compare with it. It has an air so commanding and forcible, and so wide a range of expression, that it is difficult to realise that it is one of Bach's very earliest works. The treatment of the chorus already shows his remarkable instinct for all manner of choral effects. With regard to the treatment of orchestral instruments, it is interesting to localise the historical position by calling to mind that Corelli's concertos did not make their appearance till several years later. The work is conspicuously noticeable for the number and variety of the instruments employed, which makes it even exceptional among his cantatas. It is scored for two flutes, two hautboys, a bassoon, three trumpets and drums, strings, solo violoncello, and organ; and in some ways the use of the instruments seems more nearly in touch with the methods of modern orchestration than in many of his later works, as the tone qualities are solidified by using the characteristic instruments in groups, instead of treating them purely contrapuntally.

The spacious scheme opens in a very bold and animated manner with full chorus shouting "Gott ist mein König!" to an accompaniment of three trumpets and drums and vivacious passages for strings, such as was eminently suitable for an important civic occasion. To such massive effects succeed some finely contrived polyphonic passages showing strength and freedom in the disposition of the several voices, and ending with repetition of the jubilant phrases of the opening passage. This is followed by a duet aria in which the tenor solo, *Ich bin nun achtzig Jahr,* is interspersed with the phrases of a chorale given to the soprano voice accompanied by the organ. Both the matter and the manner are very characteristic, and it is particularly interesting, in view of later phases of Bach's career, to note so early an appearance of a form in which phrases of the chorale are fragmentally introduced. Other choruses are alternated with the solos, and represent different moods. One, *Du wollest dem Feinde nicht geben,* is quite in a tender vein, and is accompanied throughout by a persistent figure for the violoncello which is elaborated with characteristic skill and certainty of handling, the effect being finely enhanced at the end by giving corresponding passages to the higher wood-wind instruments and strings. There are two fugal choruses of diverse character, which show already a considerable facility in the management of that form, though they are not developed so spaciously as many of his later fugal choruses. The solos are conspicuous for the energy and decisiveness of the musical ideas, but they too are short and broken up into contrasted passages following the meaning of the words. One of them, *Tag und Nacht,* is accompanied by wood-wind, and another for alto voice, of very forcible character, to the words *Durch mächtige Kraft,* is accompanied by three trumpets and drums. The cantata ends with a jubilant and energetic chorus similar in spirit to the first. The words are treated throughout with vivid sense of their meaning, often suggesting inferences which widen the horizon, and the whole scheme is carried out with surprising efficiency. The personality of the composer is already strongly in evidence, and if the short spell at Mühlhausen had nothing more to show, the production of this work, his first strong composition in cantata form, would signalise it.

There is amply adequate reason moreover for believing that another cantata, *Aus der Tiefe rufe ich, Herr, zu dir,* was also composed at Mühlhausen. It was probably a funeral cantata, and this gives it additional interest; as it was quite a characteristic quality of J. S. Bach to be deeply moved by the idea of death, and many of his most poetical cantatas are associated with that solemn theme—not taking it in a gloomy sense, but as a thought suffused with mystery and tenderness.

It may serviceably be compared on the one hand with the early cantata composed at Arnstadt, and on the other hand with later examples of funeral music. The standard of artistic execution is certainly higher than that in the Arnstadt cantata. The vocal subject allotted to the first words (and anticipated in the instrumental introduction)

is full of meaning, and even at this early stage illustrates Bach's liability to be influenced by the realistic suggestion of the words. The bass solo, *So du willst, Herr, Sünde zurechnen,* is exquisitely and characteristically expressive of the sentiment. The opening of the second chorus is finely conceived; and the tenor solo, *Meine Seele wartet auf den Herrn,* is a kind of preliminary study for the type of movement in slow $\frac{12}{8}$ time, which Bach ultimately developed into such lovely conditions. It is very significant that in both these solos (as in the tenor solo in *Gott ist mein König*) a chorale is introduced, the phrases of the tune *Herr Jesu Christ* being sung by a second voice at intervals throughout the arias. Thus both solos show close kinship with that beautiful Teutonic form, the chorale-fantasia, of which it will be seen in the sequel that Bach made frequent use in later times both in choruses and in the solo form here exhibited; in which the chorale seems to come in like an illuminative aside to the discourse of the aria or recitative. The frequent early appearances of such a device are very notable, as it is highly characteristic of his Teutonic attitude, which was most pronounced in the earliest and latest phases of his career, and only partially in abeyance in the central period in his life, when he was assimilating and co-ordinating in his own personality such cosmopolitan methods and forms as were needed for the full complement of his artistic armoury.

So much may be said for the intrinsic spiritual manifestation of the cantata; and yet the spiritual waits upon the development of the material. The cantata is even highly interesting on account of its immaturities. Metaphorically speaking, the limbs do not move freely. The introductory sinfonia, founded on the subject of the succeeding chorus, is rather heavy, styleless, limited in scope, and even—in its mechanical five-part harmony—academic. The chorus begins well, but it only goes on a little way and breaks off into different material. The bass solo is lacking in variety and force of progression. Similar defects, which arise from uncertainty in the composer's mind as to what to do at particular moments, are conspicuous in other movements, perhaps most noticeably in the last chorus, which, though in many respects very fine, is spoilt by the inability of the composer to get away from the key of G minor and a limited and rather conventional range of attendant harmonies. Exception may be made of the superb close of the chorus, which is suggestive of the third ecclesiastical mode, and keeps company with the many hundred instances in which Bach reserved one of his finest strokes for the conclusion.

One other characteristic feature cannot be passed over, which is a conspicuous early example of the device of realistic suggestion, such as he could hardly ever resist, and which was indeed in the main a symbol of the extreme vivacity of his mind. In the first chorus the composer several times conveys the suggestion of broken utterance to the word "flehen" by alternate rests and short groups of notes on the same syllable, as follows:

Before Bach had been quite a year at Mühlhausen he evidently received information that the court organistship at Weimar was vacant. He had already had some little connection with the Weimar court, and there could hardly be any question as to its being a better post than the organistship of Mühlhausen; he accordingly offered himself for it and received the appointment. The letter he addressed to the council at

Mühlhausen notifying them of the fact is fortunately still extant, and is one of the very rare relics which shed some dim light on his personality apart from his music. It is a lengthy document, a little involved, as was the way with such literary efforts in those days, especially when the writer had a good deal in his mind. The most interesting part of it is the passage relating to his reasons for leaving Mühlhausen, where he says:

> While I have always kept one end in view, namely, with all good-will to conduct well regulated church music to the honour of God and in agreement with your desires, et cet., et cet., still this has not been done without difficulty, and as at this time there is not the slightest appearance that things will be altered. . . . I have humbly to submit that, modest as is my way of life, with the payment of house rent and indispensable articles of consumption, I can only live with difficulty. Now God has so ordered it that a change has unexpectedly come into my hands, in which I foresee the attainment of a more sufficient substance, and the pursuit of my aims as regards the due ordering of church music without vexation from others, since His Royal and Serene Highness of Saxe-Weimar has graciously offered me the *entrée* to his Hof Capelle and Chamber Music.
>
> In view of this offer I hereby, with obedience and respect, report it to my most gracious patrons, and at the same time would ask them to take my small services to the church up to this time into favourable consideration, and to grant me the benefit of providing me with a good "dimission." If I can in any way further contribute to the service of your church, I will prove myself better in deed than in word so long as life shall endure.

The laconic consistency of barrenness of evidence leaves the world in ignorance of any further information with regard to his post at Mühlhausen, and the next act, and that a very important one, finds him installed at Weimar.

CHAPTER III

WEIMAR, 1708–1717

THE development of Bach's artistic personality was the result of many diverse influences, and among them may frankly be acknowledged to have been the personal tastes and dispositions of some of the lesser German potentates with whom he came into contact. Though in later times the hereditary principle has been a good deal criticised, it is futile to ignore that in the past it has produced rulers and leaders of men who have exercised far-reaching influence for good. In the history of German music, the German aristocracy and men of royal blood have played honourable and distinguished parts; and it is no exaggeration to say that without the material help and enlightened sympathy which some of the greatest composers, such as Haydn, Beethoven, and Wagner, received from them, it is unlikely that many of their greatest compositions would ever have been written.

In Bach's case the influence was mainly indirect. He was influenced by the circumstances in which he found himself because he always adopted the sensible course of making the best available use of his opportunities. On several occasions the circumstances were the fruit of the tastes and temperaments of hereditary magnates. Among these Duke William of Saxe-Weimar, whose service he entered when he left Mühlhausen, deserves honourable recognition. Duke William was a man of earnest and clearly defined character. He had little care for the frivolities of courtly life, but preferred a well-regulated, orderly existence devoted to the well-being, moral and physical, of his subjects. Though his tastes lay strongly in an ecclesiastical direction, leading him to take pleasure in the company of clergy and in having them much about his court, his devotion seems to have been genuine and deep-seated.

As far as German Protestantism was concerned, he belonged to the group which was distinguished technically as being Orthodox, among whose objects it was to maintain the ancient musical traditions of the Church, as distinguished from the Pietists, to whom anything in the shape of artistic accessories and appeals to the poetic imagination was abhorrent. So in this respect John Sebastian was sure of a field for the exercise of his powers.

There were also other men of culture and ability in Weimar with whom Bach could maintain friendly relations, such as Walther, the organist of the town church (who is known to posterity for his *Musik Lexicon* and some admirable compositions, especially Chorale-Preludes); Drese, the Capellmeister, and Kiesewetter, the head of the gymnasium. It was also an advantage to him that there was a court band, which performed the best secular music of the time, and in which he could exercise his powers both as a violinist and a clavier player. But it must be said that this branch of music took a second place in the court of Duke William, since his mind was so much engrossed by the interests of religion. Hence the greater part of Bach's compositions during his time at Weimar consisted of organ music and church cantatas.

The organ in the chapel of the Schloss appears to have been of nearly the same size as the organ he had at his disposal at Arnstadt. It had two manuals, with eight speaking stops apiece, a carillon, and a very substantial pedal organ of seven stops, one being of thirty-two-foot calibre, three of sixteen, and two of eight; which must have supplied a grandly substantial bass such as his heart delighted in. For this organ he soon began to write works which have been the joy and the wonder of discerning musicians till the present day.

It must be said, however, that the establishment of chronology is more difficult in connection with his organ works than with any others. It is quite impossible to decide the dates of some of his finest and best known compositions; and the evidence for allotting certain others to certain periods is more subtle than conclusive. But nevertheless the intrinsic evidence of the quality of the compositions themselves is of some little service; and judging from that evidence and what little there is of more tangible kinds it seems as though Bach passed through three phases in the complete establishment of his personality. The first phase presents the condition of the performer, and is illustrated by works which were, likely enough, written at Arnstadt, to serve as pieces for himself to play. They contain the germs of many devices which he afterwards developed to stupendous proportions. One of his favourite effects of form is the contrast of brilliant bravura passages and passages of great weight and solidity—a scheme which is profusely illustrated in music before Bach's time, as in the Toccatas of Merulo and Pachelbel. Of this type there is a charmingly naïf example in a Fantasia in G[1] in three well-marked divisions, which was most likely written at Arnstadt.

The actual material of the bravura passages is not very characteristic (so far as it is Bach), but the lineaments are recognisable. The slow portion in the middle is very severe and simple in style, but the five-part writing has a very rich and noble effect, and the splendid sound of the big suspensions suggests to the mind that Bach was becoming aware of the aptness of the organ for such purposes and was trying his youthful hand at an artistic way of introducing them. The final portion is a kind of cadenza, in which a rather obvious series of chords is presented in a brilliant figure of demisemiquavers.

Another work which is obviously of a very early date is a singular group of four movements in C major,[2] beginning with a Prelude

presenting the same device as the before-mentioned fantasia, bravura passages alternating with fine successions of harmonies followed by a Fugue with a very long and rather monotonous subject in $\frac{3}{4}$ time with close in C—a bravura passage, which as a matter of

[1] Peters T. V. I. 855. [2] Peters T. V. I. 826.

fact is a kind of cadenza, and a second Fugue, in $\frac{3}{4}$ time. The figures of the bravura passages are all rather mild and commonplace, especially in the cadenza, and both fugues, but especially the second, are wanting in decisiveness of personality. An attractive isolated Prelude in A minor[1] may also be referred to the Arnstadt time.

These works have all the tokens of being the productions of a performer who wanted to supply himself with something to perform, and the element of virtuosity is very prominent. This quality arrives at a very high pitch of perfection in some of the works which may be safely referred to the early part of the Weimar period. The earliest Weimar works were probably a Prelude and Fugue in C[2] and a similar group in G major.[3] The former is of quite a showy character. The Prelude sets off with a pedal passage which suggests drums—and the style in general is rather Italian, in the simplicity of its harmonies. There are several experiments in bravura effect which are the germs of later and more perfect devices. The Fugue, on a persistent semiquaver subject,

is also extremely lively, full of interesting premonitions of what is to come after. The Prelude and Fugue in G major is also very animated, but weightier than any of the preceding pieces. The Fugue affords an illustration of Bach's faculty for making his concluding pas-

[1] Peters T. V. I. 859. [3] Peters T. V. I. 840.
[2] Peters T. V. I. 838.

sages impressive, for the abounding energy of the last few bars bears the seal of the most absolute mastery of organ effect. But still the presentment of his personality is not entirely convincing. The next work, however, which probably was the familiar Prelude and Fugue in D major,[1] shows the composer at a very high pitch of mastery. The Prelude has much more solidity than any of the previous works of the kind, and more variety, and the Fugue

is the delight of all organists who lay claim to virtuosity; since it is not only superb music, but one of the most dazzling movements of its kind in existence; and affords the performer special opportunity to delight his auditors by the long cadenza for the pedals at the end, which rises by an apt expansion of the semiquaver subject through the whole compass of the pedal scale, rushing into the incisive closing chords with jubilant and exhilarating confidence. The Fugue, moreover, is interesting historically, in consequence of the resemblance of the subject to one by Buxtehude in F, and in many points of artistic treatment as well. It is hardly necessary to add that though Buxtehude's conception is a stroke of genius, John Sebastian's work is so much wider in its scope and so infinitely richer in resource and interest that the suggestion of plagiarism falls disarmed. It can hardly be said whether John Sebastian had Buxtehude's Fugue in his mind, or whether it was the development of the unconscious rèvival of an old impression. If it was

[1] Peters T. V. I. 842.

deliberate, it was quite in conformity with his practice, which was to copy, rearrange, and amplify works by men who excelled in special departments of art, not with the view of passing off other men's work as his own, but to get as closely as possible into touch with their special artistic aptitudes, and to find a way to fill up their inaptitudes and improve upon their most skilful strokes of art. It was, indeed, only putting in practice personally the principles on which all art progresses. Plagiarism is mainly vicious when a man tries to pass off as his own something by someone else which is better than anything he could do himself. In Bach's case the object was not to foist other men's better work upon the public as his own, but to find out how to do better than the most skilful composers in the lines in which they specially excelled.

There is another work which also shows the influence of Buxtehude and an immense advance in intrinsic interest of detail, and even of actual effect, which was probably produced in the early Weimar period. The well known Toccata and Fugue in D minor[1] is indeed one of the most effective of his works in every way and indicates considerable rapidity in the composer's development. The Toccata is brilliantly rhapsodical, even dramatic in the intensity of its weird contrasts of rushing semiquaver passages and overwhelming masses of powerful harmony. There is a great deal more invention in the actual manner in which the passages are presented and more intrinsic interest in the material. The Fugue

[1] Peters T. V. I. 845.

is based on a rolling subject, most apt for the pedals, and is developed with a fine sense of consistency and power, ending with a coda in which the resources of the organ for presenting magnificent successions of chords and pouring out a majestic volume of sustained tone are put to the highest uses. As a matter of fact it would be hard to find a concluding passage more imposing or more absolutely adapted to the requirements of the instrument than this coda. The work might be taken as the culmination of Bach's first phase. Between this and the second phase a little work of very serious character, and almost unique among Bach's organ works, presents itself. This is a short Prelude and Fugue in E minor,[1] which is exceptionally distinguished by an atmosphere of sadness. The Prelude is not brilliant, though it has passages of the bravura type. It is solemn and dignified and weighty. The Fugue, of quite simple character, maintains the mood and, in spite of its limited proportions is at once interesting and impressive.

It is possible that a change which came about in the course of Bach's stay at Weimar was owing partly to his studies of other great organists' works. As at all times, he subjected the works of other composers to the most careful scrutiny, copying them out and even re-writing them. It must often have struck him that other composers had not got nearly so much out of their subjects and cues of development as he could, and then he set to work to remedy the defects. Acting on such a principle he wrote fugues on subjects by both Legrenzi[2] and Corelli,

[1] Peters T. V. I. 836. [2] Peters T. V. I. 849.

and reconstructed and amplified at least two fugues by Albinoni. At other times he deliberately set to work to write works in the same style as great masters of earlier date. He was evidently an admirer of the Roman organist Frescobaldi, and possessed a copy of his *Fiore Musicali*, which had been printed as long before his day as 1635, in which he inscribed his name and the date of its coming into his possession — "J. S. Bach, 1714." Frescobaldi was greatest of all the Italian organists, and John Sebastian, to widen his mastery of resource, wrote several works in imitation of his style, without entirely succeeding in keeping out his own. As an example may be quoted a Canzona in D minor[1] in Frescobaldi's style, very severe and simple, and dispensing with all the adjuncts of brilliant effect which are so prominent in works of his first phase. This may have been one of the sources of the changed aspect of the works which represent the second phase of Bach's development in organ music. They are all distinguished by great solidity and dignity. Even the energetic portions of the preludes, which have the same function as the bravura passages in the earlier works, are much more substantial and represent more definite musical ideas, while the fugues are almost invariably written on subjects in slow notes, and are developed with more concentration of material. Of this kind is the Prelude and Fugue in F minor,[2] of which the Prelude presents a new and weighty type of which he afterwards availed himself frequently, and the Fugue is slow-moving and dignified. There is also a Prelude and Fugue in C

[1] Peters T. V. I. 853.

[2] Peters T. V. I. 801.

minor,[1] of which the Prelude is massive and very decisive in form, suggesting the influence of the Italian Concerto. It is much more mature than the Fugue, which, in spite of a fine subject, is weak and monotonous in parts. This also betrays Italian influence, but was probably written before the Prelude. A Prelude and Fugue in C major[2] also belong to this group. A Toccata and Fugue in D minor[3] present some suggestive features. The Toccata is not so interesting as the earlier one in the same key. A form which depends so much upon a rhapsodical quality, like a brilliant improvisation, does not gain by too thoughtful and premeditated an air. The Fugue (known as that "in modo Dorico") is a very noble piece of work in a distinctly melancholy vein, which is notable as presenting a trait in common with the last fugue of the first series of the "Wohltemperirtes Clavier," as the greater part of the interest of the movement is based on an afterthought.

Developing into the following at the end.
Etc.

[1] Peters T. V. I. 802.
[2] Peters T. V. I. 792.
[3] Peters T. V. I. 818.

One more fugue evidently belongs to this category, and that is the slow-moving Fugue[1] which is so strangely mated with the colossal Toccata in F. The Fugue is reserved and quiet and in the same style as the works above described as representing his second phase. The Toccata with its immense development, its spacious cadenzas, and its dignity of manner must have been written later. It was, indeed, by compounding the essential qualities which are manifested in the two earlier phases that Bach arrived at his third phase in organ music, in which such triumphs as the Fantasia and Fugue in G minor, the Prelude and Fugue in A minor and this Toccata in F fully represent his personality. In these he revived all the elements of brilliant effect which were manifested in the earliest phase, but infused the works throughout with the elements of dignity and solidity which he had presented in the works of his second phase. There is one little bit of evidence referring to the great Fugue in G minor,[2] which is that Mattheson (Handel's friend and a very valuable writer on musical questions of his time) quoted in his *Generalbass-Schule* a slightly altered version of the subject of that fugue, and also the countersubject, as having been given to candidates at an organ test to work out extemporaneously, not mentioning Bach's name but indicating that the subjects were well known. From which it is inferred that the Fugue in question must have been written before 1720; which, at all events, was before the Leipzig time. If this is so, it seems to follow almost as a matter of necessity that the brilliant Fugue in A minor[3] was also written before the Leipzig time,

[1] Peters T. V. I. 817.
[2] Peters T. V. I. 799.
[3] Peters T. V. I. 807.

since they belong essentially to the same phase of his development—the phase in which solidity and brilliancy are completely co-ordinated, and the enthusiasm of youth is still manifested in the very exuberance of delight in the fullest consciousness of vitality. The two fugues stand out pre-eminently from all works of the kind through the vivacity of their rhythmic qualities, the definiteness of their subjects, and the spaciousness of their development, which make them the most permanently enjoyable organ fugues in existence.

There is no external evidence to define the periods when the Fantasia in G minor and the Prelude in A minor and the great Toccata in F were written. It is possible that the Prelude in A minor was written earliest. It bears tokens of the type which, as has been said, was influenced by the instinct of the performer. But on the other hand it is carried out with such extraordinary knowledge of what to do, and there is such a decided atmosphere about it—created by the chromatic successions and the strange gloom of the early part, which is confined to a low part of the scale—that it must represent a mature condition of faculties. It may not be so full of matter as the G minor Fantasia, but what has to be done is done in masterly fashion. A passage 3 and 4 bars from the end suggests connection with the great Passacaglia. The Toccata in F[1] seems necessarily to have been a work of this period on the grounds of the amplitude, consistency, and solidity of its development, the splendour of its final climax and a certain exuberance in the bravura passages. The Fantasia in G minor is one of the very greatest and

[1] Peters T. V. I. 816.

richest manifestations of his genius. Its richness, indeed, and the extreme daring of the progressions point to its belonging to the middle period of Bach's life—either quite at the end of his Weimar period or while he was at Cöthen. Here indeed are all the elements of bravura, the weightiest and most surprising progressions of harmony, of variety, of volume of tone, of every phase of contrast of feeling and character, all infused with the fullest interest of detail. It is at once majestic and full of feeling, and at the same time manifests that sense of spontaneity which makes it almost like an improvisation. It would almost seem as if the last word in organ music had been said. But Bach had yet in his later days to resume such compositions, and consideration of the works of that period must be deferred till the intervening phases of his development have been discussed.

Passing to other branches of art similar lines of development are revealed. His clavier music underwent much the same kind of transformation as his organ music—with the difference that, under circumstances which have been described, his first clavier work of any dimensions was so exceptionally interesting. In turning to a fresh branch of art, the general principle may be serviceably indicated, that differentiation of style proceeds in proportion to the development of individuality. In works which are comparatively colourless the style of clavier music does not differ much from organ music. It follows that when clavier works present an identity of form with organ works, and lack conspicuous differentiation of style, the inference is that they are early works. For such reasons it is safe to infer that a small group of toccatas were among Bach's earliest ventures in clavier music. On the basis of style, the Toccata in D minor would come first. It is an agreeable work, but—with the exception of a wonderful slow passage in the middle—quite commonplace in detail, and even mildly Italian in style. It is this which gives it the feeling of being like Handel. It is, in fact, like many other composers and therefore essentially unlike the true J. S. Bach; and the remarkable passage in the middle, where all of a sudden he was momentarily inspired to reveal his real self puts all the rest of the work out of countenance.[1] Bach was here trying to transfer an organ form to the clavier in terms of the Italian style; and from intrinsic qualities it is evident that after his fashion he pursued a course which ministered at once to self-development and artistic achievement. The Toccatas in E minor and G minor were probably written in the Weimar time and in connection with that in D minor. The steps of progress are quite clear. In both these later toccatas the complacent Italian style falls into the background and fades away. The details become more individual by degrees—a little more so in that in E minor, and a good deal in that in G minor. A growth of strength and decisiveness is perceptible, the scope of development in the G minor being much greater than in the earlier work; and so step by step the process of development can be watched. The fact that all the toccatas are on the same scheme of design makes this group of works specially illuminative, as they throw much light on Bach's unconscious methods of self-development, which in this case

[1] This passage is a development of the idea of pleading in the Capriccio to his brother, John Jacob (p. 42).

ultimately led to such splendid achievements as the Toccatas in F# minor and C minor (see p. 508).

A work which belongs to this period and illustrates the same phase of development is a very simple series of variations in A minor in the Italian style. The theme is singularly plaintive in expression and exquisitely finished in detail and form—quite a singular piece of spontaneous beauty, the evident product of poetic youth. The variations are commonplace, even dull. The work was an experiment, and Bach did not find the result worth following up or attempting to mend. He was indeed trying experiments and eagerly examining all manner of artistic regions, to enhance his powers of expressing himself. He took several movements from two of the sonatas for two violins, viola, and bass in Reinken's *Hortus Musicus* then recently published in Hamburg, and rewrote and reconstructed them for the clavier—filling the bald places with life, and beautifying them with subtleties of texture, mending the weak progressions, adding parts to the fugues, and amplifying them into movements of imposing proportions. The results, as shown in the two Sonatas in A minor and C major (Peters T. V. I. 97 to 107), are worth very careful comparison with the originals.

Yet again it must have been about this time that he took in hand Vivaldi's concertos, and arranged a large number of them for the clavier. Vivaldi was a contemporary of Corelli, but differed from him in that his brilliancy was in excess of his solidity and musical inventiveness. Corelli represented a dignified tradition still bearing the traces of the old solid choral style; Vivaldi represented the tendency of

Italian art towards harmonic forms, such as were met with in Italian opera, in which, so far, simple clearness of design and superficial effectiveness were the principal virtues. He was essentially a violinist, and at times, especially in slow movements when the aptness of the violin for expressive melody invited him, he wrote really beautiful music. In quick movements he showed facility, glibness, and a certain mastery of technique, but his ideas in such movements were little more than poses. But he had a great reputation as a representative of Italian instrumental art, and it was possibly on that ground that Bach subjected his works to the close study which arranging them for the clavier implied. Many of the original scores have been lost sight of, so it is not possible in such cases to say how much Bach added. Even in his versions they are for the most part dull and bald, which is sufficient to show that not much alteration had been made. But in some cases he evidently satisfied himself by making details more interesting, by filling in emptinesses with additional parts, and by adding touches here and there which gave life and vigour to the somewhat inert complacency of the original.

Bach made a good many experiments in the Italian style at one time or another, and though he enriched it out of the wealth of his own personality the works in which that style prevails are, with some few exceptions, of less intimate interest than his other works. The advantage he gained by such practice was that he assimilated with his own resources such points of Italian procedure as were capable of making his range of art more complete and comprehensive. And, as will be seen later, he adopted much the same course with French music, and often made use of the form known as the French overture—a type which had been employed by Cambert and Lulli, and was very generally adopted later by Handel in his operas and oratorios, and by countless other composers up to Spohr and Mendelssohn.

His opportunities at Weimar led to his resuming the composition of church cantatas, and some of the noblest and most poetic of his works of the kind belong to this period. Among the earliest must certainly be placed the cantata, *Nach dir, Herr, verlanget mich*, which is interesting for at least three conspicuous reasons. It forms more or less of a link between his early works of the type of Tunder and Buxtehude and his maturer cantatas, leaning, if anything, rather in their direction. It is also interesting because it contains some inchoate types of thoroughly Bachish strokes of art, which in their completer manifestations were almost exclusively his property. And thirdly it is interesting for the deficiencies which (as in the Mühlhausen cantatas) remind the observer of the gradual growth of his musical personality. It was not only that he by slow degrees attained the full power of development which is shown in such amazing proportions in many of the first choruses of his latest cantatas, but that, like Beethoven, he only found the full expression of himself in his finest thematic material comparatively late. Occasionally, when he was deeply moved, a wonderful musical thought makes its appearance; but for the most part the earlier works manifest the gradual transition from the semi-conventional to the absolutely characteristic.

As this is contrary to the commonly accepted view of composers' inspirations, it may be well to point out that there are two types. The kind of composer whose impulse comes from purely musical gift is likely to produce all his most attractive subjects and tunes when he is young; but the composer who combines musical gift with a great temperament and a great personality keenly alive to things external to music itself, only by degrees hammers out of himself the fullest and most unalloyed expression of his personality in his musical ideas—and of this order Beethoven, Bach, and Wagner are the most conspicuous examples.

The cantata under consideration has some superb strokes in it which show the composer's growth of grasp, such as the opening passage of the first chorus, but his personality does not shine out with uniform consistency. The one aria for soprano is very short and the level of its intrinsic interest is comparatively low. Two of the choruses are broken up into short, distinct episodes with but little inherent musical continuity. On the other hand, the composer's enterprise is shown in the adoption and management of the chaconne-form in the final chorus, and in the superb passage which concludes the last chorus but one, *Meine Augen sehen stets, zu dem Herrn.* And incidentally it may be mentioned as a curiosity that the cantata comprises a very notable solo part for the bassoon, and (as a subtle indication of its exact date) a very peculiar device of interlacing parts which lie so close in the scale as practically to overlap, which also occurs in the introductory Sonatina in the work next to be mentioned.

It may seem strange that very near the time when

the above cantata was written, was also produced the wonderful cantata *Gottes Zeit ist die allerbeste Zeit,* one of the earliest of Bach's works of this kind which has taken a very deep hold on the affections of musicians. This cantata is in many ways so unlike his later cantatas, and so much hinges upon the change of attitude which is manifested in them, that it renders exceptional consideration inevitable. The period when it was written is almost guaranteed by the fact that it is essentially Teutonic in treatment and style. In the earlier cantatas he was naïvely following native types in which an ardent spirit expressed itself in rather indefinite forms. To the mind that likes orderliness and clearness of exposition this kind of artwork is always rather uncongenial; but to the nature that is more concerned with what is said than with the manner in which it is said, works of this type are often more enthralling than the most perfect examples of the purely classical and formal art. *Gottes Zeit* represents the genuine unalloyed Teutonic John Sebastian, before he was impelled by the universal trend of art to accept the formal regulations of the Italian composers. The mind and poetic intention manifest themselves more plainly through not being trammelled by the restrictions of exposition and recapitulation, which are entirely impersonal, and the subject, death, is just the one that a man with such infinitely copious humanity would deal with most effectually when free from conventions.

The subject is, first of all, treated in a very singular colour. No other score for such a group of instruments exists. There are two flutes, which might supply an element of brightness if the composer ever used them in the bright part of their scale, which he does not. He never allows them to pass out of the low region which gives the strangest tone in the orchestra—a tone which is a mere shadow, inanimate, almost incapable of expressive increase or decrease; which would be repellent for its very intractableness if it had not (especially in the few lowest notes) an uncanny suggestion of sombreness. Flutes have been associated with death from time immemorial, and, as a rule, the association seems perverse and exasperating. But used in the way Bach uses them, no instruments could be more suggestive. The only other instruments which supply character and colour are two viole da gamba, instruments which have passed out of use since Bach's time, and can only now be occasionally heard at archæological functions. The instrument may fairly be described as an inadequate violoncello. It was of the same shape, though smaller, and having a flat back it lacked all the sonority of the more modern instrument in every part of the scale. It had neither the warmth and fulness of the lower string, nor the vibrating, soul-melting intensity of the upper part of the scale, which makes the 'cello the instrumental counterpart of the impassioned tenor among vocalists. The quality of tone was sometimes made more interesting by having sympathetic strings under the essential strings, as in a viola d'amore; but it seems hardly likely that this was the instrument Bach meant to be used. Rather must it be assumed that it was an ordinary "gamba" with a tone more akin to the viola, though not so cadaverous—a tone which is capable of a great deal of gradation and of expression, which in this case was exactly what the composer wanted, but neither too familiar (for men seem to lose their respect even for death, when it becomes too familiar), nor too warm and bright as violins would have been. To these flutes, representing cold inflexibility, and the gambas, representing the pathos and the shadowiness of death, nothing is added but the colourless "continuo"—meaning basses and organ bass, with figures to indicate what chords would be wanted to fill in the harmonies.

The scheme is Teutonic in its drawbacks as well as in its advantages. Its limitations made it liable to monotony, and it must be admitted that the risk is not relieved by the Teutonic habit of dwelling persistently upon any idea which takes possession of the soul. This persistence is illustrated frequently by the constancy with which Bach uses the characteristic figure of an accompaniment, without break or change from beginning to end of a movement. Such a proceeding is quite consonant with the Teutonic disposition, which enjoys absorption in a symbol, a figure, a thought, even a detail of mental construction, and does not ask for the nervous centre to be relieved so soon as beings of Southern races. Slow and weighty in movement, the actions of Teutons persist longer, while representatives of other races, effecting what they aim at by violent explosions of temperamental force, absolutely require relief by contrast of some sort after the concentrated expenditure of energy.

To those who cannot get into touch with an attitude so patiently reflective, the singular colour of this work, through being unrelieved, becomes monotonous. Wonderful as the conception is, it lacks, as far as the average mind is concerned, the very essentials which make the intention fully effective, because there is no contrasting alternative whereby the effect may be gauged. The earnestness of the intention is emphasised by the absence of the relief of any high strings or higher instruments—for the flutes are here used as low instruments—but the purely artistic effect is hindered.

On passing from colour to form the same Teutonic spirit is visible. The aria types of solo had not yet fully taken possession, and the scheme still bears the traces of the earlier Teutonic efforts, which were dictated rather by depth of earnest intention than by perception of beauty of effect or design. The solos bear the traces of the traditions of Schütz, Hammerschmidt, Tunder, and Buxtehude, enormously widened, deepened, expanded, but still showing the kinship, and a certain artistic crudity, which, to a mind fully in sympathy with the poetic intention, is even attractive. The crudities, such as they are, are saved from becoming painful by the attitude of mind. It is not the terrors of death which are dealt with, but the mystery of it; not the tragic side or the despair, but the consolation which the devout Christian of that time found in a personal love of Christ and a confident belief that His promises of comfort were sure of fulfilment.

Thus the opening Sonatina for the flutes, gamba, and bass is pathetic and tender. It suggests no terrors, but breathes only of loving regret. The first chorus is broken up into short distinct sections, beginning with the simple enunciation of the words "God's time is the best time," and treating each thought and sentiment that succeeds with subtle appropriateness of musical expression; and so also with solo passages which succeed it. The sentiment, "It is the ancient law, man, thou must die!" is given to the three lower voices of the chorus in a fugal manner expressing something of the sternness of fatality, but it is answered by the sopranos offering the suggestion of consolation in the words, "Yea, come, Lord Jesu." The close of the chorus is one of the most wonderful examples of the vividness of Bach's musical perception of things external to music. The lower voices continue to reiterate the gloomy words, "Man, thou must die!" while the trebles refer to the other aspect of death, as the door through which the personal communing with the Saviour, the Beloved of the Soul, is to be attained. The pathetic utterance of the word "sterben" by the lower voices breaks off abruptly, while trebles, as it were floating in a higher region, keep the mind occupied with the idea of the coming of "the Lord Jesus" by the use of a strangely beautiful melismatic passage, which seems hardly to end at all but merely to dissolve into space. There can hardly be any more suggestive use of the melismatic device in all music! (See page 81.)

The duet for alto and bass which follows is also one of the marvels of Bach's devotional genius. The alto has an exquisite series of phrases, to the words *In deine Hände befehl' ich meinen Geist,* and after considerable development of the musical presentation of the sentiment, the bass voice gives the answer which the devout Christian cherishes as his hope, *Heute wirst du mit mir im Paradies*—to which the alto responds with the long-drawn melody of the chorale, *Mit Fried' und Freud' ich fahr' dahin.* The combination of the slow notes in their steadfast firmness of gait with the flowing figures of the accompanying gambas and the free melodic passages of the bass voice makes a subjective suggestion of the firm confidence of the soul in the promise of Christ; and the movement closes fitly with the touching and trustful words, *Der Tod ist mein Schlaf worden.*

In the spiritual sense the connection of the scheme with such earlier German works as Hammerschmidt's *Dialogues between God and the Soul* is evident, as is also the technical connection with the beautiful art-form of the choral-fantasie, by which the effect of the firm slow church tune with diversely moving passages in other parts was most probably suggested. The last movement begins with a chorale, but not after the manner of the later cantatas, in which the chorale is presented in a simple concrete form, but with elaboration of figurate accompaniment such as enhances the artistic and expressive interest; and it passes after a manner practised by earlier German composers, into a fugal movement, giving the last words of the hymn *Durch Jesum Christum* with the "Amen" in rich and elaborate polyphony; rounding off and expressing finally the affirmation that is embodied in the opening words, *Gottes Zeit ist die allerbeste Zeit.*

Bach's attitude towards the church cantata was destined to undergo considerable changes, under the influence of men of poetic gift and temperament who were much interested in the literary side of the art-form, and also of his own careful study and observation of Italian art. The change indeed is so significant and suggestive that it needs to be considered a little in detail.

He certainly knew a great deal about Italian art even before he settled in Weimar. It would have been impossible for him to avoid it; for however much German music had been spiritually distinguished from Italian music and identified by its racial characteristics, the greater natural musical aptitude of Italians made it inevitable that in things which were specially art-regardant the Germans had to look to the Italians for guidance and for types of procedure. Thus Heinrich Schütz had brought back to Germany the semi-Netherlandish Venetian tradition which he gathered under the inspiring guidance of Giovanni Gabrieli. So, later in the century Hammerschmidt, Ahle and Tunder, had imitated the

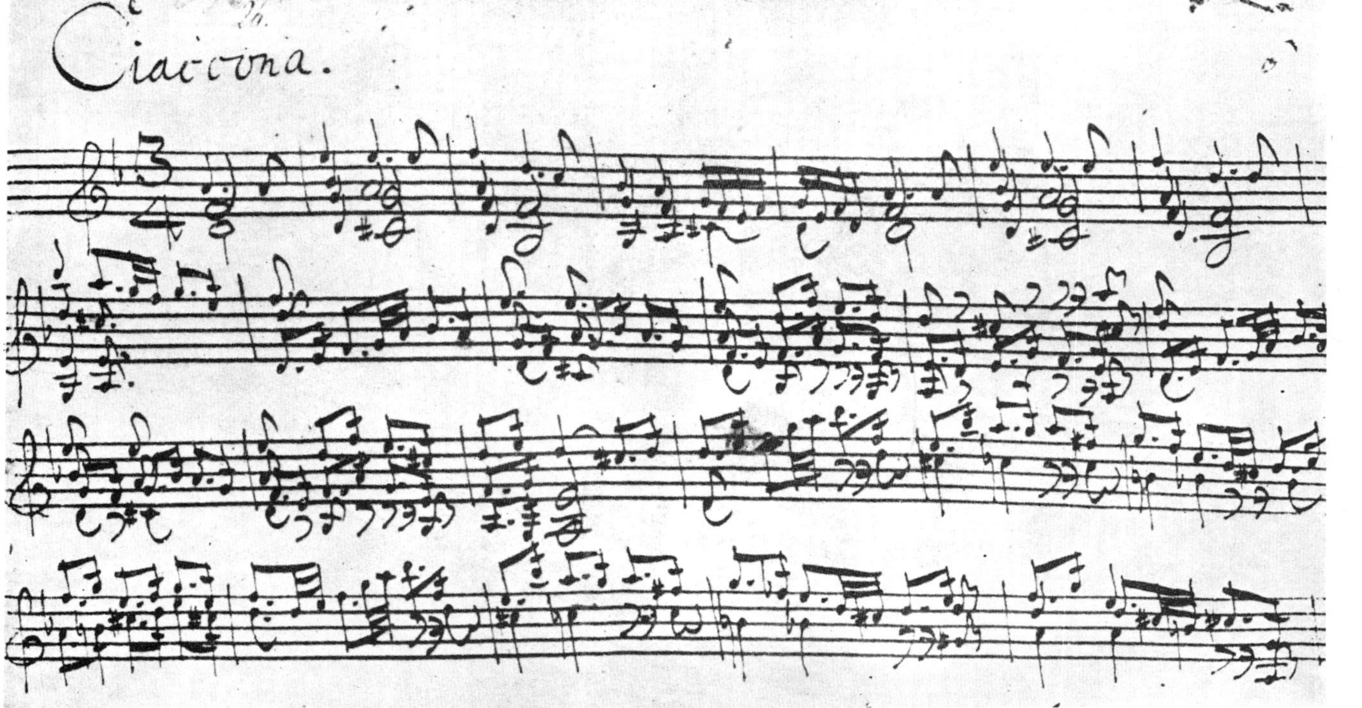

Bach's Musical Autograph

Reproduced by the courtesy of Messrs. Brietkopf & Härtel, from the Leipzig Edition of *The Works of Bach.*

treatment of soli, and borrowed types of artistic procedure from the Italian art of their time, which was not so noble as the earlier art of the Venetians; and again, later, even John Michael and John Christoph Bach and Buxtehude had been most deeply influenced by the Italian art of their time. Italian art was progressing step by step, and German art in its own line was keeping pace with it. But so far the models to which the German composers had confined themselves had been mainly in the department of sacred or ecclesiastical music to which they gave the best of their own attention. But the peculiarity of the situation was that this was not the department in which Italians of the century excelled. Indeed the kind of church music to which Italians were now more and more devoting their really productive energies was an imitation of the new kind of secular music. So the Germans who were following the lines of Italian composers of sacred music were by degrees drifting into the position of being imitators of imitations.

It was principally in opera and secular instrumental music that the Italians were making artistic strides. Their instinct for beauty of form had driven them to abandon the path which Monteverde had indicated, and to solve the problem of organisation before they faced the problems of expression. This, quite as much as the levity of taste of the operatic audiences, had brought about their over-profuse cultivation of the aria form. When the type had been established, composers were too easily content with merely producing variations upon it. But the assiduity with which they cultivated it tended to explore its possibilities to the utmost, and to show in what a variety of guises it could be presented. And this aria type, though devised for secular purposes, was applicable to sacred music. That is, it was serviceable as a principle with certain important changes of attitude. The attitude of the old sacred choral music of the Roman Church had been impersonal. The individual was merged in the devotional exercise of the many. The music was performed by many voices in combination. Individuality did not enter into it. But with Protestantism a much more personal note was struck. The individual man realised with fervour his personal relation with God or with Christ, and this soon became a characteristic feature of German sacred music. The love of dialogues between God and the soul, so frequently referred to, illustrates this point, and it is felt all the more when the spirit in which they were carried out is examined. The intimacy of communion between the individual man and a Divine being was a new and most attractive phase of religion to the devoutly minded; and nowhere is it more conspicuously illustrated than in the work of John Sebastian; and it was by adopting in sacred music principles which the Italian composers had evolved for solo music, both in the form of the aria and the recitative, that he found a more convincingly artistic solution of the requirements of this branch of art.

But for the achievement of this end it was necessary that the poet should lead the way. For, without poetry written in the form which admitted of treatment in the Italian types of solo music, the composer was helpless. It so happened that the subject of the form of poems for church music occupied a good deal of the attention of religious-minded men, and just opportunely there came to Bach's hands sundry poems for church cantatas by Erdmann Neumeister, a native of Vechtritz near Weissenfels, which had been written for church use early in the century. And the fortuitous concurrence of circumstances thus caused him, about the year 1714, to take a new line in the scheme of his church cantatas, in which the solo element from this time forward becomes so much more definite in form. This is illustrated very strongly by the cantata *Ich weiss, dass mein Erlöser lebt,* which is confidently attributed to this time; for the cantata is written entirely for a tenor voice, and consists of three arias, two of which are in the regular *da capo* form, with two interstitial recitatives. The form of the work is precisely the same as the familiar "cantata a voce sola" of which the Italian composers of the latter part of the previous century and the early years of the eighteenth had given countless illustrations. But Bach rightly adopted the principle only, and escaped the common mistake of imitating the manner as well as the method. The music is as much his own in its dignity and exact observance of verbal meaning as his earlier and more purely Teutonic work. Apart from the emphatic way in which it illustrates the adoption of the Italian type both of the aria and of the form of the whole work, the cantata is not musically very interesting.

Another setting of words by Neumeister of this time is *Uns ist ein Kind geboren,* which is more interesting for what it suggests than for what it accomplishes. It was written for Christmas Day, and Bach evidently meant it to have a very direct and festal character. As a matter of fact it is strangely commonplace and bald, and the traces of conventional types of figuration and scheme are everywhere manifest. It begins with a concerto of matter-of-fact and burly character. The first chorus is fugal but has little distinction or point, and another chorus farther on is even more elementary and bald. There are a few undeveloped airs with tuneful passages, and the final chorale is accompanied throughout by a violin solo, which keeps up an almost ceaseless motion of semiquavers in purely conventional and commonplace figures. The whole work serves as an excellent example of the elementary standard from which Bach developed such wonderful results; and it presents in crude forms many of the actual conceptions which he expanded into more artistic conditions later.

Another cantata of the period, which was set to Neumeister's words and which has many very attractive features, is *Gleich wie der Regen.* It begins with a delightful and characteristic Sinfonia in which much happy use is made of the effect of massed strings; there is a remarkable movement in which long passages of recitative are alternated with short bursts of chorus with an accompaniment to which four violas and two flutes afford special colour; and the soprano solo *Mein Seelenschatz* has a very characteristic accompaniment of violas and flutes playing graceful figures in octaves.

Of yet greater importance is the remarkable cantata written to Neumeister's words, *Nun komm', der Heiden Heiland,* about the date of which there can be no possibility of mistake, for the manuscript (which is in the Royal Library of Berlin) does for once in a way bear the date of its composition, 1714, written on it in Bach's own hand; and as it was written for the first Sunday in Advent, the exact day of its first performance is ascertainable as December 2 of that year. In this case we have the proof of Bach's cosmopolitanism in the adoption of artistic methods from all sources; for not only does it contain examples of the Italian type of *da capo* aria, but the first chorus is a very interesting and effective adaptation to new conditions of the form known as the French overture, from its use by Cambert and Lulli and the imitators of the latter composer. Bach's manner of adapting the form is illustrative of the happy possibilities of such transplantations. The first part, as in a regular French overture, consists of a weighty, broad, and energetic slow movement; and Bach even adopted the characteristic trochaic rhythm, which is so familiar in the overture to The *Messiah* and many of the other overtures of Handel which are in the French form. Bach's presentation of the type is naturally much more highly organised, and richer in harmony and detail than the works which he was, in principle, imitating. The peculiarity which gives this movement special significance is that the voices of the chorus come in one by one with the slow-moving strains of the chorale, *Nun komm', der Heiden Heiland,* which stand out in grand independence from the busy and complicated network of the instrumental music. The end of the portion representing the slow movement of the French overture is made imposing and massive by combining all the voices together in the last line of the chorale, while the instruments minister to the general vitality by continuing their own independent forms of motion. Then, as in the French overture, follows the fugue, in which the voices naturally and rightly take the lead. It is worthy of note that Bach is so faithful to his models that he makes the subject exceptionally short, as the subjects had always been in Lulli's works, and his treatment of the fugue form, as his had been, is exceptionally free and unacademic.

The solo music is worth dwelling on as illustrating the personal character of the new kind of sacred music. The first aria, which is developed at great length in complete *da capo* form, is to the words *Komm', Jesu, komm'* and breathes that atmosphere of personal love for Christ, which is one of the most consistent features of Bach's solo music. This is followed by a very remarkable recitative accompanied by strings pizzicato ("senza l'arco," as Bach has it), which from the very first chord (which is a shrewd discord) shows both the composer's boldness and his wonderful power of conveying the most intimate meaning of the words, and of fitting the music with ideal exactness to the phraseology.

It will be observed that the form of the accompaniment symbolises the persistent knocking at the door, and that the voice also, at the word "Klopfe," is made to execute a group of notes which is realistically suggestive. Even as early as this the composer shows his complete mastery of the possibilities of elastic recitative, in which melodic passages are intermingled freely with the purely elocutionary passages, graduated with perfect instinct for the particular type of procedure which is best calculated to convey and intensify the meaning of the words. The remaining aria is, again, in the *da capo* form, though short, and again it breathes the intimate personal note, in the words "Oeffne dich mein ganzes Herze," beginning, indeed, with the same phrase which Brahms used in a well-known song, to the words, "Oeffne mir." A point which is noticeable in the final chorus is that the final chorale is not given in its concrete simplicity as in most of the later cantatas, but is introduced in detail in single parts and worked up into an elaborate fugal movement.

A short cantata, *Wer mich liebet,* which Bach wrote in 1716 is also a setting of verses from a hymn by Neumeister. It is rather unusual in form, as it begins with a duet for soprano and bass, and has a chorale in the middle, and in the earliest manuscript extant ends with a bass aria—though one of the manuscript parts indicates that a chorale was to follow. The cantata is mainly interesting for the use to which Bach put it nineteen years later; when having to write a cantata for Whitsuntide, possibly in a hurry, he turned the opening duet into a chorus, making the slightest possible alterations, transposed the bass solo, and transferred it to a soprano, and adapted it to different words, and added some masterly arias, one for alto being among the boldest and most brilliant he ever wrote for that voice, with some remarkable effects in the accompaniment.

A more remarkable example than any of these, which belongs to this time, is the cantata *Ich hatte viel Bekümmerniss,* which is probably the best known of all Bach's church cantatas. In this he had the advantage of the words of another poet, Salomo Franck, a native of Weimar, which were eminently calculated to wake a sympathetic response in the mind of the composer. The cantata is on an exceptionally large scale with an introductory sinfonia and many choruses, arias, and recitatives. It is not necessary to discuss the choruses in detail. The first illustrates Bach's rugged daring in the use of clashing progressions, and the last, in which three trumpets are introduced in the accompaniment to the words "Lob und Ehre," is in his most brilliant and ornate manner, presenting examples of the phraseology of the organ, including types of passages which are evidently induced by the habit of mind of watching for formulas which were apt for the pedals, and which, fortunately, were effectively presentable by voices.

The solo music emphasises as prominently as ever the gradual acceptance of Italian methods and the intimate personal attitude of the worshipper; presenting a more complete adaptation of the former to German mood, and the latter in even richer and more deeply expressive passages. The solo, *Seufzer, Thränen,* is notable for the characteristic use of short, broken phrases; a favourite device with John Sebastian, and a most effectual manner of representing strong feeling of any sort, whether of joy or acute sorrow. The aria is not in complete *da capo* form, but in the familiar modified form in which a return is made to the opening ritornello to make the close, without repeating all the first part of the vocal solo. The aria for tenor, *Bäche von gesalz'nen Zähren,* is notable also for its deeply expressive character, for the richness of its instrumental accompaniment, for the extent of its development, for its thoroughly German character in matter and texture, and for the completeness of the adaptation of the Italian principle of the *da capo.* The type is thus seen to be completely assimilated by the composer without making any concession in the direction of Italian manner, or losing a tittle of the deep sentiment and earnest feeling which were building up the great edifice of German musical art. The two duets in the second half of the work are also notable as examples of that favourite form with German composers and poets, the dialogue. They are both for soprano and bass—the first is nominally in recitative, though abounding in melodious phrases and the kind of ornate passages to which the composer contrived to give so much meaning; and the second is a melodious duet for the same voices in which the Soul begins, "Komm, mein Jesu," and the bass, representing Christ, "Ja, ich komme," the dialogue being carried on with very rapid interchange of phrases, exactly as an analogous dialogue might have been presented on the Italian operatic stage, but with very different sentiment. Thus the transference of an Italian artistic device is seen to minister to the carrying out of an essentially Teutonic, or at least Northern conception; for the dialogue form had been just as popular with English composers of the latter part of the seventeenth century as with the Germans. The remaining aria for tenor, to the words "Erfreue dich, Seele," is again in *da capo* form, and is a happy and brilliant example of the adaptation for a solo voice of the ornate musical phraseology originally devised for the organ.

This may seem an odd quarter to draw upon for vocal ornamentation. But indeed it is difficult to see where else Bach could have gone for his models. The Italian types of floridity had all been developed in secular branches, and were indeed purely frivolous; for they meant nothing beyond the supply of an opportunity for display. The associations with such types were frankly impossible in sacred music. But the types of ornament used in organ music had always been associated with serious art, and though not developed with any respect to vocal aptitudes were still ultimately derived from church music, and as yet not very strongly differentiated from that ancient stock. To Bach ornamentation of detail had become almost a matter of course. Every musician was brought up in an atmosphere of turns and trills in those days. But the difference between Bach and the average commonplace musician was that he turned everything he could lay his hands on to some purpose; and he gradually assumed the practice of making all ornamentation serve the purpose of personal characterisation and expression. And it may be admitted in passing that his bent for putting the ideal before the practical frequently resulted in making some of the ornamental work provided for soloists extremely uncomfortable to sing. But taking the whole subject into consideration it must be said that enrichment of the fundamental outlines of melody by accessory notes, whether in instrumental music, vocal solo music, or choral music, is a most familiar and most characteristic feature of his work, and may be differentiated into two definite classes.

There are innumerable cases when the use of rapid passages is made to minister to a sense of exaltation, fervour of joy, or heightened animation, when the passages of themselves are not decisively characteristic; and to this order belong the ornamental passages in the final aria of the cantata above referred to. This type of rapid passage was, in the majority of cases, borrowed from the phraseology of organ music. But another kind, of which he made more use than any other composer, was what may be called an expressive melisma. It occupies relatively the same position as a vocal ornament in Italian music, and the device was possibly adopted by the composer as an adaptation of their practice. But whereas, with them, such a passage was merely introduced as a decorative element, or an opportunity for display on the part of the singer, with him it is used as a means of even exceptional expression. It seems, indeed, at times as the efflorescence of the ultimate fervour of the mood, the means whereby the culmination of human feeling may be presented. Of this illustrations occur most frequently in his later and most highly organised compositions; but already by this time many examples may be found. A very characteristic instance before referred to occurs in the cantata, *Gottes Zeit*, at the end of the movement, "It is the ancient law, man, thou must die" (p. 81). Of this kind there are many examples in the cantata at present under consideration. This type of quasi-ornament is not drawn from organ music, but most probably from early German vocal music, or even from folk music, and finds its counterpart in the most primitive music of savage races, so deeply is it rooted in the human mind. But in the more highly developed stages of art it implies the dwelling upon a significant or climacteric word—the prolonging, by an acutely felt melodic passage, of the essential points of a sentence. Bach was especially fond of introducing such passages in recitative, and it may even be said that in making use of the device he sometimes approached to formality; for when he discovered the most suitable place to introduce it as part of the artistic organisation, he presented it very frequently in the same portion of the movement. But at the same time his treatment of the matter illustrates in a subtle manner his constant endeavour to make everything minister to the expression, wherever language was combined with music, and wherever the essential function of the music is to convey and intensify the meaning of that language.

One of the most remarkable of the cantatas written at Weimar, and of very different character from the preceding, is *Wachet, betet,* a work of very large dimensions, in two parts. Unfortunately it is only known in the revised form which Bach gave it later, which may account for the Italian influences being a good deal in evidence.

In considering the words, Bach was evidently more impressed by the word "wachet" than by the word "betet," as the first chorus is in a very vivacious and strenuous mood, ushered in by a trumpet call, which is significantly reiterated at intervals throughout the movement.

It is indeed evident that he had the Last Judgment in his mind, for the upward rush of the vocal passages when the voices join in is symbolical of the rising of the dead. He does indeed make contrasts between the two words, but there is very little of the prayerful mood! The form of the chorus is suggestive: as if devised for the aria form, but giving only a hint of the reiteration of the opening phrases when the principal key comes back, and grafting on a grand series of characteristic progressions to make an impressive conclusion. The most remarkable solos in the work are both for bass voice, consisting of an accompanied recitative, *Erschrecket, ihr verstockten Sünder,* in the first part, and a very remarkable group of four movements, combined for purposes of expression and contrast, in the second part. The first of these combined movements refers to the great day of the end of the world, the sound of the trumpet, the voice of the Judge, the terrors and shuddering of the sinful, in terms which are harsh, crude, and vehement. But when this restless movement comes to an end, a short, slow, peaceful aria makes the most profound central contrast, referring to the *Seligster Erquickungstag* in broad and gracious phrases. But this again gives way to a more agitated movement, expressing the wild confusion of the Earth and Heaven being shattered. And yet again a passage of melodious adagio, in precisely the same mood as the aria—almost giving the sense of being a continuation—to the comforting words, *Jesus führet mich zur Stille,* whereby the soul is restored to peace; and the final chorale, *Meinen Jesum lass' ich nicht,* follows with the most complete aptitude. The contrasts between the four sections are evidently intentional. Among interesting traits it is to be noted that when the last trumpet is mentioned, the trumpets in the accompaniment begin playing the chorale well-known in England as the Advent Hymn, "My God, what do I see and hear?" which is played right through in the course of the recitative. There are recitatives and melodious arias also for other solo voices, but they do not call for special comment.

Bach was constantly experimenting at this time, and the impression that he is trying and testing procedure and processes is frequently conveyed to the mind. The cantata *Himmelskönig sei willkommen* is most suggestive in this sense. It begins with a "Sonata" for instruments in one movement, in which the trochaic motion of the melody and slow beats of the accompanying chords finely suggest the dignified approach of the "Himmelskönig." This is followed by a fugal chorus and a series of recitatives and airs. The usual four-part chorale is not introduced at the end, but in place of it there is a fine chorus, which is in the "Pachelbel-Choralvorspiel" form, on the chorale "Jesu, deine Passion," and even after that there is a "Schluss Chor" of lively character in aria form, and in the $\frac{3}{8}$ time which was so often used in the last movements of Italian concertos.

Here, indeed, is ample compounding of Italian and German forms.

Der Himmel lacht presents a good deal of diversity, and is a most imposing work. But unluckily it cannot be decisively said how much is genuinely Weimar work, as Bach is known to have revised it considerably later. It opens with a vigorous and fully developed "Sonata" for a very full band, then follows a brilliant chorus mingling fugal methods with rhythmic harmonies, some beautiful arias and arioso passages (which are mainly infused with Bach's earlier and warmly romantic manner), and a chorale at the end which is fully accompanied, but without any adornment of instrumental effect.

Bereitet die Wege is a short cantata for solo voices which gains an adventitious interest from the fact that Bach inserted the date of its composition (1715) on the title-page. It is also notable that he there calls the work a Concerto, and that having spent an unusual amount of trouble on the title-page, he was for some reason or other prevented from devoting the necessary time to the filling in of all sorts of details in the score. The names of the instruments are omitted, lines in the score are not filled in, and the final chorale is wanting!

Tritt auf die Glaubensbahn (a solo cantata) also belongs to the year 1715, and is set to words by Salomo Franck. It begins with two introductory movements which are scored for a singular group of instruments,—flute, oboe, viola d'amore, viola da gamba, and continuo. The viola d'amore also has a very important solo part in the soprano solo, *Stein, der über alle Schätze, hilf.* There is a quaint suggestion of realism in the first phrase of the first aria.

Der Friede sei mit dir is very characteristic of the Weimar period. It begins with an expressive recitative for bass. In the central aria-duet the melodious phrases of the bass are answered at intervals by the soprano in phrases of a chorale; and later the bass sings an arioso.

Barmherziges Herze, is also a cantata for solo voices. The first movement is a duet for soprano and tenor in the accompaniment of which the chorale *Ich ruf zu dir* is played by oboe or trumpet. There is an important accompanied recitative for alto and an interesting aria for the same voice, and a solo for bass; and it ends with the same chorale which was played in the accompaniment of the first duet harmonised with a simple free part for violin.

Komm, du süsse Todesstunde is a very interesting cantata with many beautiful features. It is rather unusual in form, as it begins with a tender aria, with a Chorale in the accompaniment, for alto solo. This is followed by a recitative and a serious aria for tenor. Then follows an interesting accompanied recitative for alto, in which Bach anticipates an effect he used again more than once, of suggesting, in connection with the words "Schlage doch, du letzter Stundenschlag" the effect of bells—which in this case is effected by reiterated notes in the flutes and pizzicati strings. Then there comes, at last, a chorus in flowing style and $\frac{3}{8}$ time, the vocal portions alternating with orchestral episodes. The final chorale is also very happily accompanied by the two flutes in unison.

Ach, ich sehe is also a solo cantata. The most interesting feature is the aria for bass at the beginning, in which the basses of the accompaniment keep up ceaseless quaver motion almost amounting to a ground bass.

The texture of the accompaniment is altogether very richly and highly organised—indeed, most masterly in detail. The other solos—a soprano aria, and a duet for alto and tenor—are not so interesting.

Nur Jedem das Seine is also a solo cantata to words of Franck's, of which the first aria for tenor is again the most important. The duet for soprano and alto, *Nimm mich mir,* has the character of a dialogue. The final chorus is not filled in, but only a figured bass is given with the words "Choral in simplici stylo" written over it.

Mein Gott, wie lang'—another solo cantata—is headed "Concerto." It begins with a very expressive and singularly metrical recitative for soprano with a beautiful melismatic close. This is followed by a duet for alto and tenor with elaborate obbligato part for bassoon. A recitative for bass and a strenuous aria for soprano, and the final four-part chorale complete the scheme.

Herz und Mund is on a grander scale than these solo cantatas, being divided into two portions. The most important feature is the opening chorus, which is in very florid style with fugal treatment and elaborate runs and a brilliant accompaniment for trumpet. There are several interesting solos with intricate accompaniments, and both halves conclude with the same chorale with florid accompaniment of strings.

The solo movements of another cantata of this period, written to Franck's words, *Alles was von Gott,* were revived, probably with revisions, in the great cantata, *Ein' feste Burg,* in Bach's latest years (p. 391).

Of the more intimate details of Bach's life at Weimar nothing is ascertainable, and of his public life little is known, and that mainly by inference. A fairly full record can be pieced together with the help of existing documents of some negotiations with the authorities of the Liebfrauen Kirche at Halle, Handel's Halle, for the post of organist there, which was vacant. An exceptionally large organ of 63 stops was being built, and Bach appears to have gone there to play on it in 1713. He offered himself for the appointment, and even went to the length of acceding to the invitation to write a church cantata, and conducting it, to prove his powers in that direction as well as in that of a performer, but he could not stay till the matter was decided, as his duties at Weimar demanded his return. But he then wrote to one of the principal men at Halle on January 14, 1714, explaining some little point with regard to his salary and his work which he desired to have considered, and, unfortunately, his application was not favourably received and the matter fell through—leaving some little ill-feeling behind. The people of Halle took it into their heads that he had not acted quite fairly by them, which caused him to write another letter on March 19th, protesting against the interpretation which had been placed upon his conduct, and throwing some little light on what had taken place. This appears to have appeased the authorities, for in 1716, when the great organ was finished, he was invited to come over and play upon it, and, in company with Johann Kuhnau of Leipzig and Rolle of Quedlinburg, to report upon it. This was accordingly done; and the report, a favourable one to the organ builder, Cuncius, was duly furnished. But of Bach's performances or any circumstances of his visit no record remains and no particulars are ascertainable.

He is known to have gone to Cassel by invitation of

the Crown Prince, from a Latin pamphlet published in 1743 by one Constantine Bellerman, Rector of Minden, and it is deduced from certain historic circumstances which seem to prove that the Crown Prince Frederick mentioned in the pamphlet was absent from Cassel from the latter part of 1714 till 1731, that the visit must have taken place late in 1714. The visit was signalised, according to the writer, by Bach's having played to the Crown Prince, and so stupefied him with astonishment at his facility in pedal playing that the Prince took a jewelled ring from his own finger and gave it to Bach.

Of another journey proof is supplied by some notes he had made on his copy of the cantata *Nun komm', der Heiden Heiland,* before referred to. They are merely particulars of the musical portion of a service at one of the churches in Leipzig where the cantata was performed, and as he was responsible for the conduct of the rest of the music on the occasion, which was rather elaborate, he made notes of what he had to do to help his memory and make sure of everything being ready and in order. His share, as so recorded in anticipation, consisted of a prelude before the service, the conducting of a motet, several interludes, a Choralvorspiel or two, and a final performance such as would be called in England a concluding voluntary. Of any particulars beyond those suggested by this list, we remain in ignorance. It is only to be inferred that these events prove the growth of his reputation as an organist and a composer.

One of the most familiar episodes in his life, which is vouched for with sufficient consistency by several chroniclers, occurred about this time, and points to his great reputation as a clavier player. It seems that he journeyed to Dresden in the latter part of 1717, and that J. L. Marchand, the French composer and clavier player, was there at the time. Marchand's reputation in Paris was very great, and it is evident that the amateurs at the Dresden Court also had a very high opinion of him; but John Sebastian's powers were more or less known by this time, and it somehow was brought about that there should be some sort of an artistic contest between them. The embellishments of the story in point of detail, which are given by various narrators, are naturally rather the outcome of a desire to make it effective than to be exact; but on one point at least they most of them concur, which was that time and place were agreed upon, and John Sebastian was ready, but not Marchand, who had taken an early departure from Dresden that very day. It was of course assumed that he had gauged the powers of his antagonist, and had foreseen defeat, and fled; and that view has met with general endorsement. The only points really worth notice are that Bach had by this time attained supreme pre-eminence as a clavier player as well as an organist, and that the zest with which the chroniclers report the story implies cordial admiration.

It must have been about this time, towards the end of 1717, that Bach resigned his position at Weimar. But little is known of the circumstances, and even the exact dates are uncertain. It is only certain that at the end of the year he was no longer in the service of the Duke of Saxe-Weimar but in that of Prince Leopold of Anhalt-Cöthen. The circumstances were destined to lead him to explore new artistic fields. While at Weimar, the duties of his office and the opportunities it afforded him had caused him to address himself especially to the composition of organ music and church cantatas; and the results are supremely interesting. The Weimar cantatas have indeed a special quality about them—a romantic fervour and sensitiveness of poetic feeling which are most characteristic of his personality. But organ music was the only department in which he had as yet attained to the fulness of his powers. He was one of the composers who grew in scope and resourcefulness all his life long, and wonderful and delightful as the best of the other works are, they are surpassed in grandeur and scope by works of the same order which he produced later in life.

By the time Bach left Weimar he already had several children. The eldest child was a daughter named Katharine Dorothea, born in 1708, probably at Mühlhausen, and the eldest son, Wilhelm Friedemann, was born during the Weimar time, in 1710. At Weimar, the best known of his sons, Carl Philip Emmanuel, was born in 1714, and also Johann Gottfried Bernhard in 1715. No traces remain of the story of the domestic life of this time, and speculation and surmises are fruitless. With John Sebastian the artistic life is all in all, and of that a new phase was opened when he transferred his allegiance to a new master.

CHAPTER IV

CÖTHEN, 1717–1723

THE reasons which caused Bach to give up a post where he had a good organ at his disposal and ample resources for performance of choral and instrumental works on a large scale, for the post of Kapellmeister in a small court, where there was no adequate organ, no adequate choir, and not even a theatre to draw upon for instrumentalists and singers, must have appeared to him very weighty, but there is very little to show what they were. The immediate impetus to leave Weimar may have been given when Duke Wilhelm August, his master, conferred the Kapellmeistership on Johann Wilhelm Drese when his father died, late in 1716. But there is no reason to think that the appointment was any reflection on Bach. The family of Drese had occupied the foremost position in the musical establishment at Weimar for more than half a century; and as the Duke is reported to have been very loyal to his dependants, it is very likely that he made the appointment in consideration of the long service of the Dreses, rather than from any lack of appreciation of Bach. At the moment, possibly, there may not have been any other post available, and Bach's disposition being impetuous and impatient, he would no doubt see any change that offered in a favourable light. He was attracted by what he knew of the young Prince Leopold of Anhalt-Cöthen, and he may have welcomed the idea of being a Kapellmeister, and he may have felt attracted by the idea of occupying himself with a different kind of music from that which he had hitherto cultivated. The world has so identified him with organ music that it seems almost incredible that he should have accepted a position in which he was almost cut off from it, and where his duties would mainly lie in a department of music which at that time was more backward than any other. For indeed secular instrumental music was but just beginning to emerge into any kind of definite independent existence. The Italian school of violinists had done something towards establishing the style of violin music, but even Corelli's concerti grossi had only made their appearance about five years before. Clavier music had been slumbering till but a few years before. Kuhnau had broken new ground with his suites and sonatas. Froberger's interesting suites, Couperin's elegant "Ordres" in the same branch of art, Muffat's "Florilegium," Purcell's sonatas for strings, Vivaldi's concertos, and Biber's violin sonatas indicated the direction of composers' aspirations, but extremely little had been done in which inadequacy of some sort or another, as pure instrumental music, is not apparent. It is conceivable that this may have been an inducement, and that Bach felt that an opportunity worthy of him was to be found in this hitherto slenderly cultivated branch of art. But at the same time it must be admitted that Bach's cultivation of secular instrumental music may have been caused by his being forced to realise the inadequacy of all existing music of the kind through hearing it so often at Cöthen. Which was antecedent and which consequent in this case is too subtle a question to be discussed here; and, indeed, it is of no very great consequence. The essential fact is that he applied himself with marvellous energy to make the best use of the special opportunities which Cöthen afforded him.

It needs to be kept in mind that, though hereditary, local and national influences all converged to impel him to concentrate his energies on sacred music and music connected with the church, he was inevitably influenced by the fact that the greater part of artistic method since the beginning of the seventeenth century had been developed in secular branches of art. Bach himself had already adapted secular methods and forms to sacred uses. And great as his natural musical aptitudes were, there can hardly be any doubt that a frank and uncompromising cultivation of secular music for itself was a necessary preliminary to the full expansion and attainment of his artistic personality. When men cultivate any branch of intellectual activity merely as a secondary accessory, while the main energies of their minds are occupied with other lines of thought, they never get thoroughly hold of the essentials. If Bach had continued through life to concentrate his attention on church music, and had given no more consideration to secular music than his quick perception needed to divine the methods which were equally applicable to serious art, the world would not only have been the poorer for the lack of a large number of secular works which are among the most permanent delights of artistically minded people, but the sacred works which he produced in later years, which are the crown of a life unconsciously devoted to self-development, would have been shorn of a great part of their completeness.

Thus, whichever way it is considered, the Cöthen period is one of pre-eminent importance; and the world owes some recognition to the young prince whose peculiar and well-defined tastes exercised so much influence in the development of the composite sum-total of the artistic personality of John Sebastian.

It would have been gratifying to human curiosity, and also in some ways historically useful, if it had been possible to fix the exact dates of production of the most important of Bach's secular compositions. For the greater part of them the world has to be satisfied with the result of a process of elimination. It can be inferred with a certain amount of safety that special works could not have been produced either in his least mature or most mature periods; that they have traits inconsistent with influences which are known to have been paramount at particular periods, and the inference so attained may be strengthened by the knowledge of those influences. In this manner most of the great secular instrumental works can be narrowed down to the Cöthen period. But it was not till some time after he had been settled in Cöthen that his productivity in this new line of art can be safely referred to. In the earlier years he was probably assimilating and learning from practical experience of the works of experts in several different forms of secular instrumental art how to improve upon their efforts and show the utmost that could be done in the various lines which were cultivated in the old style of instrumental counterpoint. And in these earlier years there are a few incidents which require to be enumerated.

The young prince seems to have been attached to his musicians, and when he went away from home he generally took a few of them with him, and his Kapellmeister was of course included. On one of these occasions they went to Carlsbad in May, 1720; and when Bach returned he found his domestic circle broken up by the death of his beloved wife, Maria Barbara. As has been before observed, nothing is known of their private life and nothing can be said on the subject. The Bachs were a domestic race, and John Sebastian's noble disposition justifies the surmise that he suffered from what must be the severest blow in any well constituted man's experience. But it is also clear that he was not overwhelmed, and found solace in his work. A church cantata, *Wer sich selbst erhöhet* is attributed to this time. It begins with a fine fugal chorus in a rather conventional contrapuntal style—not presenting Bach's personality very forcibly except in its skilful development. A soprano air has an elaborate organ part, obbligato. A fine accompanied recitative for bass is highly characteristic of his interpretation of such grim words as "Der Mensch ist Koth, Staub, Asch' und Erde." It may be mentioned here that one other church cantata, *Das ist je gewisslich wahr,* is attributed to the Cöthen time. It must be admitted to be rather commonplace.

In the latter part of this year 1720, also, another journey to Hamburg is recorded; when Bach came into contact with Johannes Reinken, the ancient organist of St. Katherine's Church, for the last time. His previous journeys there had been the pilgrimages of an ardent student, bent on penetrating the artistic secrets of the famous master; he now went as the full-fledged master himself and, without doubt, far greater and more efficient than the man whom in former days he had reverently subjected to close observation. There are sufficient proofs that he still respected the powers of his former exemplar; and if the old man knew little of the power of the younger, it is satisfactory to find it credibly recorded that he availed himself honourably of the opportunity to inform himself. According to Mizler—one of the chroniclers—some of the notabilities of the ancient town assembled to hear a performance by Bach, and Reinken himself came also. As he played for over two hours he must have given his auditors a variety of works, but what seemed to have impressed Reinken most of all was his performance on the subject of the chorale, *An Wasserflüssen Babylon*, which must undoubtedly have been in the form and style of the "Choral-Fantasie," a form which was not only most apt for extempore treatment, but very likely originated in the extemporaneous preludising of organists in the church services. The remark which Reinken is said to have made to him, "I thought that this art was dead, but I see that in you it still lives," has rather more than average verisimilitude, and it suggests a fact that is often overlooked.

As a rule, the world is right in assuming that where novelty is attempted, the likelihood of vital progress and achievement is greatest; and that a great line of art does not come to its culmination after a new line has become firmly rooted and arrived at vigorous growth. The fundamental idea is that two systems of art cannot flourish simultaneously, and that new developments do not come before the older developments have exhausted all their utility. But the idea is proved by facts to be erroneous. The world which often mistakes impatience for genius, and novelty for inspiration, sometimes concludes that the old paths are worn out long before men have followed them to their destinations. The men who had been laid hold of by the dramatic power of Monteverde's experiments thought that the old style of polyphonic choral music was utterly dead and done with; yet many of its most interesting products came into being after the appearance of "Arianna" and "Orfeo." Bach's case is particularly enlightening; for whereas the harmonic style of opera and instrumental music had become well established and had taken firm hold of the public mind before he was born, and art in general was gravitating in the direction of Italian style and Italian methods, he devoted himself to bringing various branches of art to perfection in the polyphonic style, and, while assimilating all that was to be learnt from the Italians, applied it for the first great manifestation of purely Teutonic art, and for the absolute vindication of principles of development and texture which were entirely alien and uncongenial to the Italian temperament.

From such considerations it is evident that John Sebastian is the pre-eminent example of the type of artist who follows deeply rooted principles, without regard for the popular trend of taste and style. His artistic instinct could not rest content with anything less than the richest and most copious resources of art, and it was only in the polyphonic methods of the North German organists that he found adequate scope for the employment of the characteristic and vivid details which were necessary for the full execution of his purposes. The impulse of the composers who had adopted, without compromise, the new Italian secular methods, was to seek mainly for effects of melody supported by conventional and purely secondary accompaniment, and to strive after simple elegance of form. And to such composers a scheme like that of the "Choralvorspiel," which is full of intimate subtleties of detail and expression, had become almost impossible. So Reinken's remark seems to be singularly to the point; and though to some it might suggest the pedantic overvaluation of times past, it was just in its estimate of the special nature of Bach's artistic position.

Reinken was at that time no less than ninety-seven years old, so his experience of art was exceptionally extensive; for he was born before Monteverde's later operas saw the light, and more than a decade before Cavalli began his work, and lived through part of Handel's brilliant career as an opera composer, and till within ten years of Haydn's birth. Few men could have seen more comprehensive changes in art; and if it be admitted that in the main body of art immense advances had been made, as illustrated by the operatic work of Alessandro Scarlatti and Handel when compared with the somewhat infantile and speculative experiments of the early cultivators of the "Nuove Musiche," it must be observed that the branch of the art which Reinken followed was just the one which had begun to fall backwards. The influence of the new harmonic style was beginning to make itself felt in organ music, and wherever this was the case, deterioration set in. So, though Reinken had the reputation of having even more than an adequately good opinion of himself, he would indeed have been more than human if he had not been gladdened to find a man of such supreme powers on his own side, just at the time when all the world seemed disposed to give him the cold shoulder. His sympathetic utterance in this case was probably his last communication of any importance to the world, as he died two years later at the remarkable age of ninety-nine.

John Sebastian had occasion to prolong his visit at Hamburg, as he heard that the organist of St. James's Church had recently died, and as the organ there was an exceptionally fine one of sixty stops, and the appointment in such an important town as Hamburg offered many favourable opportunities, he presented himself for the post. There were several other candidates, and it was decided that they should all perform on the organ before a kind of committee of local organists, one of whom was to be Reinken, on November 28th, and that the selection should be made afterwards, presumably on their recommendation. However, the Prince, his employer, required him at Cöthen five days earlier, so Bach never took part in the competition, and was not elected. The history of the art of music would have read differently but for this trifling accident; for if Bach had so soon severed his connection with Cöthen and resumed the work of an organist, it is unlikely that the greater part of his secular instrumental music would have been written.

The year 1720, in which his first wife died, is noteworthy as the beginning of the period when Bach's mind was specially projected towards secular instrumental music; and it seems as if domestic circumstances were again exercising influence on the course of his activities. It is worth recalling that the first of his secular instrumental works for the domestic keyed instrument which can be definitely dated was the outcome of family circumstances, as it was the parting with his brother John Jacob in 1704 that caused him to write the Capriccio for clavier which has already been referred to (p. 40). Now, again, it was the wish to develop the expanding musical gifts of his eldest son Wilhelm Friedemann, who was nine years old, which supplied the impulse to devise the *Little Clavier Book* or *Clavier-Büchlein.*

The work is surprisingly full of interest; but nothing in it is more significant than some short passages to which Bach has added numerals to indicate to little Friedemann how to use his fingers. These, in view of the complete and radical reorganisation of the old system of fingering which Bach effected, become historic landmarks.

Previous to the seventeenth century, players of the domestic keyed instruments had for the most part been content to use only the four fingers of either hand, and the thumb was hardly used at all. Nothing was gained in respect of power of tone by increased force of the blow of the finger on a key in either spinet or harpsichord, so the hand and fingers were kept almost flat; and in that position the thumb was too short to reach the keys without awkward movements of the wrist and arm. This entailed the passing of longer fingers over short ones, and of short ones occasionally under long ones. The middle finger was the principal resource for such processes, and crossed over the back of either the pointer finger or the clumsy finger as required, and the little finger had to be occasionally slipped under the clumsy finger.

With such limitations, a good deal of such music as John Bull's virginal music seems almost impossible, and it is quite clear that a great many passages in the old music in which several parts are moving simultaneously could not have been played without a wider reach than the fingers alone were capable of attaining. But the thumb was, nevertheless, in theory more or less tabooed, and there was no system. Some players who attained great reputation with the musical public probably had their own little secrets and their own ways of coping with difficulties; and different authorities had different views even on such a simple matter as fingering the scale. The impulse of John Sebastian to achieve the utmost possible in execution soon caused him to bring the thumb into activity; but he cannot have all the credit, for there is no doubt that the moment had arrived in the history of the art when all means of execution must be brought into requisition, and the discovery of the function of the thumb was being made simultaneously in various parts of the civilised world. Thus, Couperin, the famous French clavecinist, in *L'Art de toucher le Clavecin* (which came out in the very year that John Sebastian went to Cöthen), gives copious examples of fingering in which the thumb is liberally used. But it illustrates the helplessness of the human mind to speculate far ahead of the limits of experience, that he evidently did not realise the special advantage of the thumb passing under the hand, but made it frequently pass over the middle finger when a white key played by the middle finger had to be succeeded by a black key on the far side of it from the thumb. Such a procedure is so contrary to modern practice that it is almost unthinkable, and emphasises to a very striking degree the limited extent to which players had been accustomed to use the thumb, and their consequent lack of understanding of the ways in which it might become most serviceable.

John Sebastian, at all events, divined the usefulness of crossing the thumb under the hand, and thus became in a sense the precursor of the modern system of fingering; but he also maintained many of the ancient habits of fingering, and continued frequently to cross long fingers over short ones. This was partly a result of the character of the instruments he played upon, with which specially artistic effects were obtained by gliding from note to note; and the modern system, in which the passing of the thumb under the hand plays so conspicuous a part, did not attain to complete recognition till the harpsichord and the clavichord were superseded by the pianoforte, which required a totally different position of the hand to give full effect to its capacity for varying the tone in connection with the force of the blow on the key. Bach's fingering was, in fact, a transition stage, retaining some of the old traditional usages of harpsichord players and clavichord players but anticipating some of the devices of piano players.

But it is evident that it was not completely systematised. For it is noteworthy that though his son Philip Emmanuel (who was the greatest authority on clavier playing in the next generation) referred to his father's practice as the foundation of his own, there are many discrepancies of detail in their usage. Indeed, at that time there was no recognised system, and the great players had their own individual ways, and used such devices of crossing fingers over one another as suited their particular hands or their particular fancies in the way of phrasing. Of the habits of such players as Handel and Domenico Scarlatti nothing definite is known. From some observations of Mattheson's it has been inferred that Handel did not pass his thumbs under his hands, but passed the fingers over one another in the traditional manner. It is the good fortune of having a little piece in the *Clavier-Büchlein* fingered for Friedemann that affords proof of Bach's being in the forefront of those players who immensely extended the range of technique by adding another serviceable member to the group of fingers of each hand. Some of the fingered passages are as follows:

Beyond this, as has been said, the book is interesting as representing Bach's ideas of the order in which technical and artistic difficulties should be taken. The explanation of clefs and scales is necessarily in the forefront, and thereupon follows the consideration of the signs used for embellishments. The prominence thus given to these departments of art recalls to mind how great the sphere of ornament was in those days, and how essential it was to the clavier player to make the ready interpretation of the most familiar turns, mordents, and shakes a second nature. But after providing for knowledge of that department of art, Bach passes on to the mastery of such matters as simple scale passages and arpeggio formulas, which are presented in a piece called "Applicatio" (one of the pieces in the collection which is fully fingered) and some little preludes. Then he passes on to part playing, which is provided for in two arrangements of chorales, adorned with the usual ornaments of the day. Then come two short and simple allemandes; and so by degrees more complicated difficulties are presented, both in passage playing and part playing. The book increases in interest when several of the preludes which have become familiar to all the musical world in the *Wohltemperirtes Clavier* make their appearance; some, as for instance the tranquil meditative first prelude in C major, in a simpler and shorter form than the version generally known; some, like the second in C minor, with the bustling energetic figures in both hands almost complete, but an abbreviated coda; some, again, like that in E minor in the first book, not only in a shorter form but with a totally different treatment of the work for the right hand. Later on several of the preludes in more difficult keys make their appearance, such as the prelude in E major of the first book, the serene and expressive prelude in C sharp minor, and the wonderful song-prelude in E flat minor, which was probably introduced to develop the powers of the young player in cantabile expression and phrasing. Many other familiar pieces make their appearance; such as some of the two-part and three-part "Inventions," including such an exquisite work of art as the three-part invention in G minor, which is here called "Fantasia." Besides these, in the latter part of the collection, with less apparent order in relation to difficulty, are minuets and other dance movements, and a little fugue.

The whole scheme is enlightening in respect of J. S. Bach's views and feelings about education, showing how he instinctively felt the advantage of developing the musical intelligence simultaneously with the technique, instead of stupefying the learner with meaningless mechanical exercises. His views in this connection were again indicated when, two years later, he made two collections of pieces of the type of the movements referred to above as two-part and three-part inventions, calling the three-part movements "Sinfonia," and he then added a preface in which he explains his object to be to "show a plain way to lovers of the clavier to play clearly and well in two and three parts, and to attain above all to a cantabile manner of playing." They are all in the polyphonic style of instrumental counterpoint, with definite ideas beautifully woven into complete and finished works of art.

But before this collection was completed other important events had occurred. As far as can be ascertained, the next work which was completed after Friedemann's little Clavier Book was of very different calibre, and represents Bach's first departure on a large scale into the region of secular music for large groups of instruments. It appears that some years before, he had come into contact with a Markgraf of Brandenburg, who was some eight years older than himself and was an enthusiast for music, and made a collection of concertos by famous living composers; and that the said Markgraf, being struck by Bach's musical powers, had invited him to compose something for his private band to play; and it was in March, 1721, that the composer completed the set of six remarkable works which are known as the Brandenburg Concertos, and sent them to the Markgraf, who was then in Berlin.

Though he had written many instrumental pieces of considerable dimensions in his cantatas, these were probably Bach's first ventures into the realms of absolute instrumental music on a symphonic scale, his age at the time being thirty-six. Such being the case, a little attention may fitly be bestowed on the form of art which he used and his attitude towards it.

The scheme of the early type of concerto (which was the first form of orchestral music cultivated by the secularist composers of the seventeenth century), suggests that it was the outcome of private musical establishments in which there was a select few of efficient performers and a number of hacks who combined the capacity to play easy parts, in company, with the execution of menial duties. In the earlier days most of the works of the kind were written for stringed instruments only. For instance, Corelli's twelve concertos, which are the most familiar of the works of the type which have survived, were written for a "concertino" of three soloists, and a "concerto grosso" of assistants; the former consisting of two violins and a violoncello, and the latter of two violins, viola, and bass with figures, for the harpsichord. It is important to realise that the conception of such a concerto was quite different from the modern idea. The prominence of the individual solo performer and his "virtuosity" did not enter into it in anything like the degree which it does in later times. The object of the group of soloists was to deal with the music which required finished execution; and the "tutti" came in to supply contrast and give the attention of the audience a rest, like the instrumental "ritornelli" in the early Italian operas. The alternation of the "soli" portions and the "tutti" portions became the most conspicuous feature of the form; and the certainty with which the bustling entry of the "tutti" at the end of each section of the "concertino" responds to the hearers' anticipation is almost laughable. Amateurs who are not familiar with the actual concertos of the period will be able to realise the feeling for themselves at the conventional entry of the full orchestra after a solo passage in the early pre-Beethoven concerto of the Classical period, which is a rudimentary survival from the earlier stratum of evolution.

Bach interpreted his opportunity liberally as an invitation to show something quite out of the common in every way. Though he had never essayed anything of the kind before, still he may have felt sure that in the actual musical material and its development he could surpass anything which had been produced by man so far. But that would not satisfy the spirit of enterprise within him. He must needs show that he can make concertos for all the different kinds of solo instruments available in those days, and not restrict himself solely, as usual, to string soloists. The intention is manifestly admirable from the practical point of view. Whether the Markgraf had so many soloists in his band is not necessarily in question. If he had, the writing of concertos for each of the more distinguished players was a timely compliment to the musicians themselves. If he had not, Bach at least offered him the opportunity of presenting to his fellow amateurs a vast enhancement of the usual monotonous limitations.

The feast of variety which Bach thus offered was provided for by writing each concerto for a different group of instruments. The first, in F major, is for strings (including a violino-piccolo), three hautboys, two horns, and a bassoon, with harpsichord, as usual, to fill in the harmonies when needed. The second, also in F major, is for strings, together with solo violin, flute, hautboy, and trumpet. The third, in G major, which consists of two remarkably brilliant and energetic movements, is for three violins, three violas, three violoncellos, and bass. The fourth, also in G major, is for solo violin, two flutes, and the usual strings; the fifth. in D major, for harpsichord, violin, and flute solos, with strings; and the sixth, in B flat, for two violas, two "viole da gamba," violoncello, and harpsichord.

This method of diverse grouping of instruments shows how different the conception of orchestration was in those days from what it is now. The principles of modern orchestration, in which the special aptitudes of all the different instruments are made to minister in the highest degree to the richness and variety of effect and meaning, and to offer constant changes of tone-colour, had scarcely begun to dawn upon men's minds. The instruments, as far as they were able, played the same types of passages as parts in a polyphonic whole (analogous to voices), and they were not identifiable in the general complexity through the individuality of their diction, but merely through the difference of colour which each particular line represented. The stage of evolution is the definite but transitional one of lines of different colour, following upon the earlier system of lines of the same colour (such as voices), and preceding the system of masses of colour produced by grouped instruments, which in its turn preceded the system in which subtleties of colour are produced by combinations of melodic lines and musical figures. In the stage in which Bach worked (and he had to work under the inevitable limitations of evolutionary progress), the lines of colour or tone-quality which the individual instrument represented were spread over much wider areas. For inasmuch as all the instruments were treated melodically and without much difference of type, they had to be used for a longer time at a stretch, in order to provide the basis of contrast, than is the case in later orchestral music, in which masses of varying tone quality or colour are incessantly playing on the senses.

These concertos illustrate the same attitude of mind as the many movements in Bach's Cantatas and Passions and other works on a grand scale in which a single characteristic instrument or a group of characteristic instruments is employed throughout to give a unity of tone-colour to the whole. Indeed, they are even more conspicuous examples of the attitude of mind, as each work as a whole has its individual characteristic grouping of tone qualities, and it is not even so much the individual movements which are contrasted with one another as one complete work with another.

The scheme of the early concertos is indeed a further illustration of a primitive conception. Composers were slowly feeling their way towards the complications of modern orchestration by various experiments, and they frequently essayed to obtain variety of effect by contrasts between instruments of the same type, instead of between instruments of different types. They did not, even instinctively, realise the connection between style and physical characteristics; and as their work had a contrapuntal basis (in which the linear function of violins and oboes and flutes was almost identical), it seemed as natural to them to obtain a modified effect of contrast between groups of solo stringed-instruments and groups of massed stringed-instruments as between stringed instruments and wind instruments. Their minds were undoubtedly beguiled by the traditions of their peculiar musicianship, which still, notwithstanding many temptations, regarded good free contrapuntal writing as the most essential object of the true artist's efforts.

The foundations of the harmonic usage, which was the necessary preliminary to the development of modern orchestration, had been laid long before Bach's time, and it was mainly the helpless followers of tradition and convention who at that time were on the side of counterpoint. Yet Bach himself remained in the camp of the unconverted, and took little advantage of the glimmering lights which already showed the way in the direction of modern instrumental art. To understand his position in relation to secular instrumental music it is necessary to give some attention to the state of that branch of art in its larger manifestations.

One of the essential differences between the old style of contrapuntal music and the new style, which grew out of the experiments in "Nuove Musiche" made at the beginning of the seventeenth century, was that in the earlier style the parts which served as the strands of the contrapuntal texture moved, for the most part, step by step, in the manner which was best adapted for voices; and the new style recognised the capacities of instruments for taking any interval required of them. The composers who maintained even in their instrumental music the methods of contrapuntal art, with its richness of texture, still founded their parts, however florid, upon an underlying basis of conjunct motion, or, in simpler words, on scale passages, whereas the representatives of the new style soon fell into the habit of basing their passages on the component notes of chords, in other words, on figures based on arpeggios. It is not to be inferred that either party restricted themselves entirely to one or the other procedure. Vivaldi, for instance, wrote plenty of scale passages, and J. S. Bach wrote plenty of arpeggios, but their attitude of mind was diverse. The representatives of the old order of art, who were mainly writers of organ music and founded their style upon the style of organ music, thought of their music mainly in combined lines; while the representatives of the new kind of art, which was destined to blossom into modern music, thought of their art in successions of chords. The former kind of music was better supplied with type of musical idea and artistic method, for it had a longer tradition and had been cultivated by a higher order of composer. But it did not lend itself to orchestration.

As before pointed out, the tendency was for all the instruments to be treated on the same terms and to take parts like voice parts, and there was little recognition of their natural aptitudes. The fact that some were better fitted for long notes or slow passages, and others for rapid passages, was not conspicuously recognised, and this partly because scale passages and contrapuntal treatment did not lend themselves to such purposes. But music mainly founded on chords, and containing passages founded on arpeggios, lent itself much more readily to the combination of instruments according to their aptitudes. For while agile instruments played arpeggios or passages founded on chords, the less agile instruments could hold on the chords themselves, and supply a good background of tone and colour. And in order to arrive at modern orchestration it was necessary for music to pass through a phase in which wind instruments were to a great extent used to play holding notes without any other definite musical purpose, as is so frequently seen in Haydn's and Mozart's symphonies. It was in this way that the cembalo with figured bass was ultimately rendered unnecessary. And it was by this elementary recognition of difference of function between one class of instrument and another that the modern composite orchestral style was approached. In course of time the mere blank holding notes were transformed into more definite types of figure and melodic and rhythmic passages which were each apt for the instrument which had to play them; and the highest ideal of modern orchestral style is that in which all the different instruments supply such elements of effect as they are best fitted to supply, in the terms that are best adapted to their capabilities of diction. This entails polyphonic treatment, and thus practically returns to the principles of J. S. Bach, but with this difference—that the things which the different instruments now have to do are specially consonant with their aptitudes, and not, as in J. S. Bach's works, mere general types of figure or passage which were made to serve for all instruments alike.

It must appear from this that Bach's manner of writing for a large group of instruments of different calibres belonged to an order of art which was more primitive and less in touch with the inevitable progress of art than the works of Italian composers of his time and those who followed them. This, indeed, is consistent with what has before been said of the general character of his artistic work, and the reasons are the same. It always happens that when men attempt a new departure in art they have to go back to a much lower level both of intrinsic and of artistic interest, until they have developed a mass of new methods and resources. The new kind of art was making progress and Handel may be said to have occasionally employed it to good purpose, as, for instance, in such an unlikely line as his organ concertos; and Alessandro Scarlatti had also shown many premonitions of its possibilities, if indeed he might not be described as the first notable composer to divine the essentials of orchestral music.

As a matter of fact, the composers of the new kind

of music were always at their worst when they were exploring the new paths, and whether it was Handel or Alessandro or Domenico Scarlatti or Vivaldi or Pachelbel, whenever they are found writing anything genuinely interesting and full of life, they are found to have reverted to the old polyphonic methods.

The new style was not adequate either for the expression of ideas such as John Sebastian's, or for interest of artistic treatment such as a man with such a supreme artistic instinct would find indispensable. In this respect the individuality of the man counts for much. It was possible for a man of talent to be satisfied with a trend of art which did not give him much artistic scope, as long as his own instinct did not demand much of him, or when his test was whether he, as a public man, satisfied his patrons—which was certainly the main consideration with Italian opera composers of the time. But J. S. Bach was not, in this sense, a public man, and what he gave to the world had first to satisfy him as adequate. And this could not be done in the new style for the simple reason that it was impossible. He therefore took the only course which afforded him adequate scope for his individual artistic aspirations with any chance of satisfying his high sense of responsibility.

This applied to such a detail as orchestral method as well as to the general question of polyphonic or harmonic method. He occasionally made experiments in the harmonic method, and infused something of his personality into the products, but they are not the most convincing examples of his work. In the Brandenburg concertos there are hardly any anticipations of modern orchestration. Such a simple thing as the wind instruments being employed to sustain tone and to solidify the whole is hardly found in them anywhere. Indeed, almost the only place in which the effect is employed is in the first movement of the second concerto, and then it is not the wind instruments that have holding notes but the strings, and the wind have to bustle about in the same semiquaver passages which are elsewhere given to the strings, making a kind of cackle which may fairly be described as primitive!

But though Bach in these remarkable works steadfastly clings to the old polyphonic methods, it cannot be said he is not enterprising and speculative. Every concerto shows a great variety of novel and striking inventiveness, both in scheme and effect. The principle on which early concertos were devised, of contrasting a group of solo instruments with the "tutti," a mass of accompanying instruments, appears in a new guise, mainly the result of the original selection of the instruments better adapted to be used as solo instruments, or in pairs, than in masses.

In the first movement of the first concerto there is plenty of merry banter between the solo instruments and the tutti in short passages, but the effect in general is rich and full and is gained by almost persistent employment of the tutti. The second movement is a development and expansion of a type which is met with in Vivaldi's concertos, being a kind of ornate expressive song simply accompanied by the tutti. But its interest is enhanced by its being made a duet between the hautboy and the solo violino-piccolo—and it may be mentioned in connection with what has been said above of the lack of differentiation between the music allotted to instruments of different types, that both instruments have to deal with identical passages and passages of absolutely the same type, without any attempt to give them passages which are specially illustrative of their idiosyncrasies. The work ends with a group of dance tunes of delightful quality, in which most entertaining effects are obtained by special grouping of instruments. The trio to the minuet is scored for two hautboys and a bassoon; a delightful polacca is scored for strings alone, and has a trio for two horns with hautboys for the bass—all gay and playful.

The limitations of the trumpet cause the subject of the first movement of the second concerto to have rather an Italian air, as it was inevitable to base the passages allotted to it mainly on the component notes of a chord; otherwise that instrument does its best to play the same type of passages as the violins. The middle movement is a kind of quartet between the flute, hautboy, violin, and 'cello; and the last a showy movement in which the trumpet figures very gaily, and has a part which is almost unplayable in modern times owing to the extreme altitude to which it is called upon to rise.

The third concerto is much the most remarkable of the group, as it really departs from the old conception of concertos and depends upon the remarkably rich effects which can be obtained by having three groups of three instruments—that is three violins, three violas, and three 'cellos—with double bass and continuo to add to the sonority. The grouping of three instruments is maintained almost invariably throughout with astonishing effect, so that the chord-passages of one group are constantly pitted against the chord-passages of another group, except where for variety and sonorous enforcement of some characteristic idea the three like instruments are massed in unison. The artistic conception is superb and superbly carried out, especially in the first movement. There is no slow movement, but only two long sustained chords between the first and the brilliant last movement. This latter is in $\frac{12}{8}$ time and most vivacious, but not so interesting as the first, as it has less variety and less genuine force in the subject matter.

The main feature of the fourth concerto is the extremely brilliant part for the solo violin, which is attended by two "echo flutes" or "flûtes à bec." The work of the "tutti" instruments, especially in the first movement, is unusually subordinate. The fifth concerto is notable again for a remarkably brilliant solo part for the clavier, which in its turn has a flauto traverso and a solo violin as attendants. There is indeed an enormously long passage of the most brilliant description for the keyed instrument, unaccompanied, with every device of execution embodied in it, illustrating Bach's extraordinary inventiveness in the line of virtuosity, not for itself but as a means of expressing musical ideas, and of course, in this instance, departing from the rule of making all the instruments play similar passages; for a great cembalo player like Bach could hardly be contented with setting down anything for it which any other instrument could play. The slow movement is a very expressive trio between the cembalo, the flute and the solo violin, marked auspiciously and suggestively "affettuoso," and full of elaboration of beautifully conceived figures beautifully interwoven. Bach was evidently in the humour for expression at the time he wrote this concerto, as the last movement, in $\frac{6}{8}$ time, has many directions for interpretation, among which the word "cantabile" frequently occurs.

The sixth and last concerto is a kind of mysterious counterpart to the third concerto; as the singular grouping of two violas, two viole da gamba and a 'cello and bass, prefigures. The colour is weird and picturesque throughout, and the subject matter such as befits the unusual group of instruments employed. The two groups of instruments maintain their apposition to a great extent in the first movement. In the second the gambas remain silent, and they have not much to do in the last, which must be admitted to be more perfunctory than the first; as though it had dawned upon the composer's mind that the strange colour of the instrument tended to become monotonous; and this impelled him to rely rather upon general animation and the body of tone supplied by the copious use of the 'cello.

This group of works illustrates, like many another, the singular extent to which Bach allowed himself to be guided by his opportunities. The invitation of the Markgraf afforded him one, and he made ample use of it; and though it can be read in the works themselves that he enjoyed the composition of them, and though the works were by far the finest of their kind produced in that generation, yet, inasmuch as no fresh opportunity offered, he never again wrote works of the same kind. Sometimes his impulse seemed to lead him to follow up a newly attempted form of art by many works of a like kind, and to go on exploring the new paths. Sometimes he contented himself with producing the finest examples in some form of art that he had not before attempted and then passed on to something else. The paradoxes force themselves on the attention. It is possible that the Brandenburg concertos were never played in his lifetime, except in such fragments as he transferred to other works. They just went into the Markgraf's celebrated collection and there was an end of it. At any rate, they were quite unknown. When the collection was sold at the Markgraf's death, the catalogue took special notice of concertos by all sorts of popular composers of the day whose names are now naturally forgotten; and Bach's were not even mentioned by name, but were sold with all the stuff considered of no value in what are called the "job lots."

Though Bach did not again experiment with orchestral concertos of this kind, he wrote a very large number of concertos for solo instruments and groups of solo instruments, which may be serviceably referred to in this place, though they may have been composed at all periods in his life. Most of these accord more nearly with the modern idea of concertos, and it is worth while to consider how much share Bach had in turning the course of events in that direction.

As has been said, the original idea of the concerto did not include the extreme prominence of the solo instrument; but the ultimate consummation of the modern type was inevitable. The tendency is prefigured even in the fifth Brandenburg concerto, in which the clavier is allowed to have the field to itself for considerable spaces of time. And when later Bach wrote concertos for clavier and for two and more claviers with orchestral accompaniment, it was inevitable that the individuality of the solo instruments should be more and more emphasised, because Bach's impulse, begotten of ample experience, necessarily impelled him to get the utmost effect out of the passages which the performers had to play alone, and this could not be effected without giving them a conspicuous share in the proceedings. The tendency in the modern direction was more noticeable in concertos for claviers than in concertos for violins or wind instruments, because the clavier was so much better adapted to play solo passages without the orchestra.

It seems probable that the violin concertos were written in the Cöthen period, and they are more akin to the Vivaldi type. The claims on the soloist are not very exacting, though the violin has interesting work to cope with, and the functions of the orchestra are not so subordinate as in the clavier concertos. Both the concertos for violin solo, in A minor and E major are, as a matter of fact, works of the most delightful quality. They are cast on the Italian lines, with quick movements first and last and a slow movement in the middle, and the style is simple, direct, and melodious. The quick movements are essentially practical in their relation to an average audience, and the slow movements are of supreme beauty and interest. In the latter Bach adopts his favourite device of using characteristic figures in the accompaniment, which in these cases are given mainly to the basses. It is worth while to note their kinship in this particular with the wonderful slow movement of the Italian concerto. But in both the present instances Bach's cue is definite and special, and gives the scheme a distinct character of its own. What was most probably in his mind was to make the subject which is given to the basses a kind of text or psychological entity which recurred persistently in the manner of what the French call happily an "obsession" to which the violin solo constantly discourses in answer, as though arguing the contention of the basses from different points of view. The slow movement of the E major concerto might even be compared with the "dialogues" in the cantatas, or perhaps even more aptly with the slow movement of Beethoven's concerto in G. The great fascination which such movements exercise over people who are not essentially musical (as well as over those who are musical as well as poetical) lies in the fact that the form is psychological rather than essentially musical. The form is of the spirit rather than the letter. Bach spent a great part of his life feeling his way in this direction, and never till his last days quite made up his mind whether the usual mechanical view of form (the view based on distribution of keys and themes), or the view which puts the psychological scheme in the forefront, was the right one. But it is in his wonderful slow movements that he reveals the actual intention to use music as the vehicle of psychological concepts, and touches the fringe of the question, which was due to excite so much attention a century and a half later, of programme music. The adagio movement in the violin concerto in E is particularly illuminative in this sense, and has even a dramatic character, owing to the very definite manner in which the dialogue is carried on. In the well-known concerto in D minor for two violins and orchestra the slow movement is again, by a very long way, the most attractive feature of the work. It is quite possible that it stands absolutely in the front rank of all Bach's movements whose reason of existence is pure beautiful melody. But in this case the psychological element is not so much in evidence. Bach's mind was not in this case moved by the possibilities of such a contrast as that between the basses and the solo violin in the other concertos, but by the æsthetical possibilities of alternation between two solo violins, in which the cue would not be so much in apposition or contrast, but in sisterly discourse. Here is a case in which Bach, probably unconsciously, was carried by the force of circumstances in the direction of the modern conception of the concerto, for in making use of the qualities of the two solo violins ample material was supplied for the development of the whole movement, and consequently the orchestra comes to occupy a very subordinate and insignificant position, mainly contenting itself with supplying the harmonies and indicating the rhythmic pulse. In the quick movements the soli and the tutti resume more or less the normal relations of the concerto of that time. Both movements are animated and direct and serve sufficiently well as preface and after-word to the slow movement, with just the same functions as the first and last movements in the Italian Concerto for clavier, to be discussed later.

The aptitude of the violin for expressive melody induced the composition of many movements of extraordinary beauty like those in the concertos. The qualities of the clavier moved Bach in a different manner. He was very urgent about executing melodious phrases in a cantabile manner on that instrument, and not infrequently essayed movements of a song-like character for it; but for the most part the influence of the keyed instrument was more in an abstract direction, suggesting purely artistic developments. It would be hard to find more suggestive contrasts than such as are presented between the slow movements of the violin concertos and those in the fine concertos for two claviers in C and C minor. The latter were probably written later in life and present the tokens of much more spacious development and more maturity of style, especially in the quick movements; and in these cases the order of merit is reversed, for the slow movements are of less appealing quality than the quick movements. Bach in these cases laid hold of the rhythmic capacity of the keyed instrument and the opportunity which the activity of so large a number of human fingers afforded for producing rich effects and giving the impression of great fulness of tone. The differences may be summarised in the sense that the violin is superbly suggestive for melody and the clavier specially adapted for part-writing; so when Bach writes slow movements for the clavier he makes them serve as phases of contrast to the quick movements, in which some rather abstract melody is discussed with a certain aloofness of manner, or treated with elaborate ornamentation, such as was more suited to the instrument than passages of sustained melody pure and simple. The alternative presented in the admirable concerto for the clavier in D minor is to give a Siciliano in place of the central slow movement, a course which provides a type of melody well adapted to the limited sustaining power of the harpsichord.

Bach does not seem to have been so much attracted to the composition of concertos for a single clavier with orchestra, and he did not write many original works in that form. The finest of them is that in D minor above mentioned, which from its style would appear to have been written at Cöthen. In all the concertos for clavier, whether for one instrument or many, there are passages for the solo instrument unaccompanied which anticipate the procedure of modern concertos, with considerable use of arpeggios, and even occasional cadenza passages. Bach follows the Italian types in the general scheme and easy style of the quick movements, and they are rather homophonic in feeling, with the exception of the last movement of the double concerto in C major, which is a fugue of a most vivacious description. It certainly gains by being cast in a form which was so congenial, as it is quite one of the most effective and delightful of all the quick movements, and has a cadence-passage developed on the basis of the final clause of the fugue subject which is positively exhilarating, and most characteristic of the composer, in which a small nucleus is expanded into a passage of considerable proportions. Bach clearly enjoyed writing in the concerto form and found it congenial. It would be even natural to infer that he found opportunities for performing the works, as in many cases the same concertos appear in versions both for violin and clavier. Both the concertos for violin and that for two violins exist for claviers, and transposed—the concerto in A minor into G minor, the concerto in E into D, and the double concerto in D minor for two claviers in C minor. He also made a clavier concerto in F out of the fourth Brandenburg concerto, which is in G.

In the same year in which John Sebastian completed the six concertos through which the name of Christian

Ludwig, Markgraf of Brandenburg, is still known to the musical world, he took the very important step of marrying a second time. His first wife had been dead little over a year, but the sane, wholesome humanity of the Bach family predisposed them to domestic life, and the tenderness and warm-heartedness which can be so amply read in the composer's works made him need one fully sympathetic being in his home life, upon whom he could bestow the full measure of his affection. The matter brings into relief the individual character of the man which has been before insisted upon. If he had been a public man like Handel, married life would have been more or less a superfluity. But John Sebastian was never at any period of his life much of a public man. The centre of his life was not the concert room or the theatre, but the home, where he must have been constantly at work writing the truly enormous mass of compositions upon which he concentrated his attention, and which he often rewrote again and again to bring them up to his highest conception of perfection. And for the completion of the home circle to a man of his temperament a wife was a very important adjunct.

His second wife, Anna Magdalena, came from Weissenfels, where her father, Johann Caspar Wülcken, was court trumpeter. She was only twenty-one years old, and therefore fifteen years younger than John Sebastian. But little more in detail is known of their domestic circumstances than there is in his first wife's time, but a number of side lights illuminate their relations most happily. There is no doubt that she was extremely musical. She not only played on the clavier, but she sang and had been a court singer at Cöthen before her marriage. She also wrote a very good musical hand, and did a good deal of copying for her husband, both of his own works and those of other composers—such as Handel, a great part of whose Passion to the text of Brockes was written out by her.

He, in his turn, delighted in developing her musical aptitudes, and one of the first works to which he gave his mind after their marriage was a collection of pieces for her to play, which is known by the name of "Clavier-Büchlein vor Anna Magdalena Bachin," the date of 1722 also being on the MS. Bach himself playfully described the contents as "*anti Calvinismus, und Christen Schule, item anti Melancholicus,*" which is interpreted as a little hit at the unsympathetic attitude of the Pietists towards music.

There is something specially attractive about the idea of Bach's making this collection of pieces for his young wife to play, and the spirit of the works themselves seems to suggest the tenderest and most loving relations between them, for the contents consist mainly of five of the groups of pieces known to the world in later times as the French Suites. They were not called by that name then, possibly never at all by Bach himself. It has been suggested that they somehow got the name in view of their compactness and slightness; and it might be added that the dexterous delicacy of their artistic treatment in detail and spirit and even a little daintiness, have something akin to the traditional idea of French art. It is the latter qualities, indeed, which suggest the charming relations between Bach and Anna Magdalena, and it is difficult not to hope, at least, that the suites were actually written for her in this very early period of their married life. In this connection it might be, perhaps, objected that it is odd that the first three are in minor modes, D minor, C minor, and B minor. Bach's course in such a case would have been purely spontaneous. His instinct most subtly and rightly told him to offer what was serious and interesting first of all, and to come to the sparkling and the gay last. It seems almost superfluous to recall that human creatures do not take kindly to the grave after the gay, but they do very willingly turn from the grave to the gay. But at any rate the movements in minor mode are not sad or gloomy. The sarabande in the first suite is, no doubt, in a vein of acute yearning and passionate intensity which must be admitted to have an element of deep sadness in it. But surrounded as it is with movements of dainty and pleasing character, it might be taken that for a moment the composer was asking his wife-pupil to commune with him in deeper thoughts, and the gay little minuet that instantly follows conveys in the subtlest fashion a return to the normal standard of intercourse.

Many and various are the moods suggested in the first four Suites, all in the main gravitating in the direction of demureness; the fifth is of totally different complexion. It may be doubted if Bach ever wrote a work more completely serene, happy, and sparkling. The pure murmuring beauty of the allemande, the gay rush of the courante, the dignified strength of the sarabande, the sparkling vivacity of the gavotte and the bourrée (which has made the first one of Bach's most popular little movements), the truly wonderful and innocent tenderness of the loure, and the supreme merriment and animation of the gigue, make the whole series one of the most perfect little works of art in grouping, texture, spirit, and artistic finish ever produced by J. S. Bach. If the quality of these works truly prefigured Bach's feelings towards his wife at this time, their married life had indeed an auspicious beginning.

From the technical point of view the scheme of the Suites is of that particular type of orthodoxy which Bach himself did most to establish. The history of the gradual growth of the form by the process of elimination is at once complicated, interesting, and clear. Beginning with the pavans and galliards, in the Elizabethan and Jacobean times, progressing with the association of other movements with them, the gradual dropping out of the primitive couple (the pavan in the Restoration music in England being associated with the later group for a time as a kind of prelude, and then finally disappearing), and the sifting and survival of the fittest—this history must be read elsewhere. It may be added that composers adopted extremely divergent courses, either experimenting conscientiously with groups which gravitated towards assimilation, or trying wild experiments in the juxtaposition of erratic components, as in Rogers's "Nine Muses," or Couperin's most amusing "Fastes de la grande et ancienne Ménestrandise." Bach, in some ways one of the most venturesome of composers, was in other ways most deliberate and respectful to tradition in its deepest sense—that is, in the sense of its representing the efforts of a vast number of co-operating intelligences seeking the solution of interesting problems. The orthodox scheme, allemande, courante, sarabande, and gigue, had not as yet been propounded as a special revelation. Like everything else, it was in more or less of an inchoate and uncertain state when he came upon the scene. His studies of forms of art of all countries had brought him into contact with a variety of formulas more or less approximating to this, and evidently manifesting a greater weight of opinion in its favour than any other. So he himself submitted it to the test, adding only such little "Galanterien" as were always allowed before the final gigue, and gave it the fiat of his judgment in the vast majority of works which he wrote in the Suite form.

This series of Suites in the "Clavier-Büchlein" (to which Bach afterwards added another charming example in E major to make up the number to his favourite group of six) is, apparently, the first group of such works which he brought together. Their conciseness and the absence of any prelude in all the Suites may have been owing to a wish not to overburden his beloved pupil. It must be added that the work illustrates a trait of Bach's personal disposition which is less serviceable to posterity. He shared with Michael Angelo an aptitude for leaving things unfinished; and of extra pieces which are contained in the book over and above the Suites, a "fantasia pro organo" in C comes to an abrupt stop after a dozen bars; and a promising aria in C minor has only a slender accompaniment for about eight bars, and for the rest of a long movement offers nothing but the melody. Beyond these there is a charming little minuet, transferred from Friedemann's book, and a beautifully ornate "Orgelchoral" for the clavier on the tune *Jesus, meine Zuversicht*, and this completes the entire contents of the "Clavier-Büchlein" of 1722.

A few years later, in 1725, another collection was made, which was even more interesting than the first. Part of it was very likely made by Anna Magdalena herself, as no inconsiderable portion of the volume is occupied by a number of little minuets, polonaises, and other short movements in her own handwriting, which seem likely to have been favourites of hers. The more imposing works in the volume are two more Suites, the movements of which were ultimately included in two of the Partitas which Bach himself printed in the first volume of the "Clavierübung" (see p. 456). These, as a matter of fact, are rather more difficult and are on a larger scale than the Suites included in the first book, and both of them have preludes, of which that to the E minor Partita is on a very extensive scale, suggesting progress in Anna Magdalena's efficiency as a performer. The collection also contains the first prelude, in C, of the "Wohltemperirtes Clavier," which, in a much shorter form, had already appeared in Friedemann's "Büchlein," the whole of the first so-called French Suite, and part of the second, which breaks off in the latter part of the sarabande, leaving it, like two of the pieces in the first book, incomplete.

But most interesting of all are a number of little songs for soprano voice, most of which Bach probably wrote for his wife. About one, the beautiful simple air *Willst du dein Herz mir schenken*, there has been much difference of opinion as to whether it is by Bach himself, or (as is for some reason argued) by an almost unknown composer Giovannini. Of the others there is little doubt that they were by Bach. The beautiful aria "Schlummert ein" presents a curious enigma. It was evidently written for Anna Magdalena herself, but though there are two copies of it in the book, one has no accompaniment at all, and the accompaniment of the other stops and becomes a blank long before the end of the song. But the strange fact is that it is not lost, for in a fine cantata for bass voice of many years later it makes its appearance again, with the accompaniment completed for strings (see p. 433). To two of the songs a personal interest is attached; for one is about his pipe and his tobacco; and the poem, most probably by the composer himself, combines with a playful mood a serious reflection,—a process very characteristic of the author:

So oft ich meine Tabaks-pfeife
Mit gutem Knaster angefüllt
Zur Lust und Zeitvertreib ergreife
So giebt sie mir ein Trauer-bild,
Und füget diese Lehre bei,
Dass ich derselben ähnlich sei.

The other is a tender little poem addressed to his wife:

Bist du bei mir, geh' ich mit Freuden
Zum Sterben und zu meiner Ruh',
Ach, wie vergnügt wär so mein Ende,
Es drückten deine schönen Hände
Mir die getreuen Augen zu.

The book also contains the sarabande which later served as the theme of the "Goldberg Variations" (see p. 474) and some songs, and concludes with the chorale *O Ewigkeit, du Donnerwort!*

But between the times when these two interesting little collections made their appearance Bach completed another collection which has been the greatest delight of musicians of after times. About the date of this there can be no manner of doubt, as it appears on the written title-page, which runs as follows:

"Das wohl temperirte Clavier oder Præludia und Fugen durch alle Töne und Semitonia sowohl tertiam majorem oder Ut Re Mi anlangend, als auch tertiam minorem oder Re Mi Fa betreffend. Zum Nutzen und Gebrauch der Lehrbegierigen Musicalischen Jugend als auch derer in diesem studio schon habil seyenden besondern Zeit Vertreib aufgesetzet und verfertiget von Johann Sebastian Bach p. t. Hochfürstl-Anhalt. Cöthenischen Capell-Meistern und Directore derer Cammer-Musiquen. Anno 1722."

This is the first half of the collection known in English-speaking countries as the "Forty-eight Preludes and Fugues," and the date shows that Bach must have been at work on it about the time of his second marriage. But it is not to be supposed that the composition of the pieces themselves belongs to that time, for everything points to the collection not having been written at one time, but having been the association of short movements, many of which had accumulated in the course of years. It has already been mentioned that many of the preludes made their appearance, some in a less developed form it is true, in Friedemann's "Clavier-Büchlein," and this also seems to justify the inference that many of the pairs of preludes and fugues were not deliberately written to belong to one another, but were brought together wherever there seemed a sense of fitness. Though, to consider the matter with full latitude of surmise, there seems no reason why, if the preludes had been in existence first, Bach might not have written the fugues afterwards to fit on to them. Several of the pairs, of which the preludes are known to have existed long before, still seem so admirably fitted to one another that it is hardly imaginable that their coming together should have been merely fortuitous. And in some cases again the amplifications of the preludes in their final versions undoubtedly fit them much more completely to be combined with the fugues; which seems to point to the composer's having had the suitableness of either for the other very clearly in mind. In any case the style of the pieces is always so far consistent that there is no mating of absolutely incompatible qualities or styles.

Bach made various experiments in different styles, and among them are some in the old simple style of choral counterpoint for organ and for clavier as well as for voices. But it is noteworthy that he did not mate a fugue in that style with a movement in the instrumental style characteristic of his time. Indeed, in the "Wohltemperirtes Clavier" there are not many movements which are not genuinely instrumental in style. This was but natural with the preludes, as the form had been cultivated for more than a hundred years, and since its first appearance as an instrumental form it had always been florid and well furnished with rapid passages. It would have been more natural for the fugues to be in a choral style, since the fugue was essentially a contrapuntal form, and counterpoint was a device of choral art. But even in the fugues Bach mainly adopts the genuinely instrumental style, vivacious with accent, rhythm, and free play of rapid

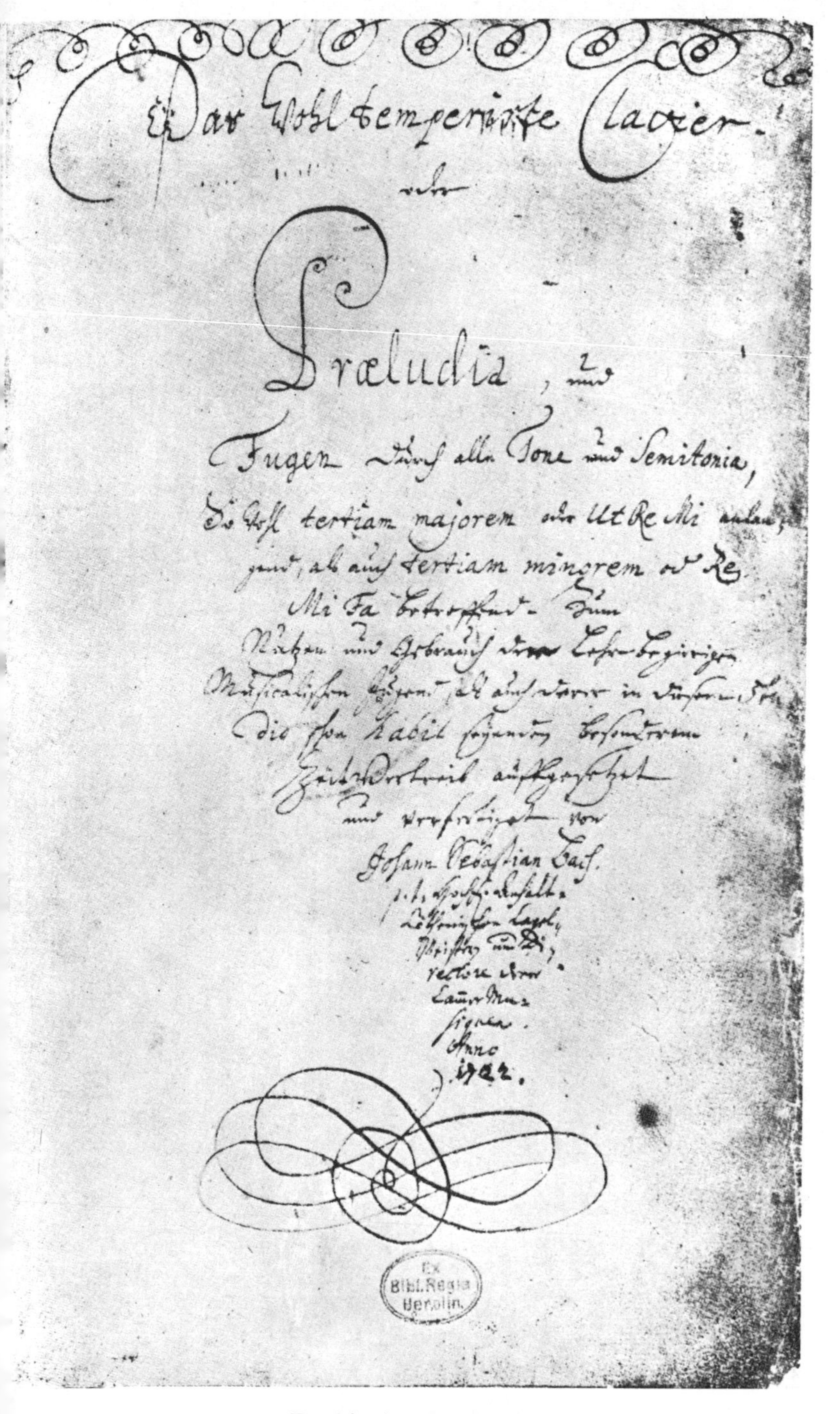

Das Wohltemperirte Clavier.
oder
Præludia, und
Fugen durch alle Tone und Semitonia,
So wohl tertiam majorem oder Ut Re Mi anlangend,
als auch tertiam minorem oder Re
Mi Fa betreffend. Zum
Nutzen und Gebrauch der Lehr-begierigen
Musicalischen Jugend, als auch derer in diesem studio
schon habil seyenden besonderem
ZeitVertreib auffgesetzet
und verfertiget von
Johann Sebastian Bach.
p.t. HochFürstl. Anhalt.
Cöthenischen Capel-
Meistern und Di-
rectore derer
CammerMu-
siquen.
Anno
1722.

Bach's Autograph

itle-page of "Wohltemperirtes Clavier." Reproduced, by the courtesy of Messrs. Breitkopf & Härtel, from the Leipzig Edition of *The Works of Bach*.

notes; and in this collection, brought together and completed in 1722, there are not more than two fugues at most which have the tokens of the choral style, and they both have peculiarly serious and sober preludes.

But this adoption of definitely instrumental style for fugues was no new thing. The early types of ricercare and canzona, which display the characteristic treatment of subjects which was more or less systematised in fugues, were written in a choral style, but that was because the instrumental style had hardly begun to exist. As soon as composers began to feel that the old choral style was not all-sufficing for instruments they began to write their fugal movements in a lighter and more rhythmic manner. Even Andrea Gabrieli in the sixteenth century occasionally ornamented his subjects and his instrumental counterpoint with turns and runs, and his nephew, the great Giovanni, extended the practice more generally. Frescobaldi at the beginning of the seventeenth century wrote little fugal movements in a vivacious and spirited instrumental style, and his pupil Froberger followed suit in the same direction. Every generation developed more fully the true instrumental type of fugue, for Pachelbel extended its freedom considerably, and Buxtehude, in his turn, showed his high instinct for instrumental style in fugues which were almost as rich in detail and as full of true instrumental effect and rhythm as Bach's own. But all their work had been done for the organ, and very few composers had addressed themselves to using the form for the clavier alone. In Kuhnau's suites and sonatas there had been some fugal movements, and the fugal type had been employed in the early Italian violin sonatas, but a scheme so large and comprehensive as John Sebastian's had never before been attempted, and even what had been attempted on a small scale did not show any recognition of the difference between organ style and clavier style.

But here, again, too much stress must not be laid on Bach's recognition of the style most apt for the clavier. The invention cannot be legitimately attributed to him. Music had arrived at the point of development when the clavier style was being generally discerned. Domenico Scarlatti was John Sebastian's senior by two years, and no one ever showed a higher or subtler instinct for the style of the harpsichord; and though he scarcely wrote any fugues, his concise movements are full of all the vivacious rhythmic contrivances which were perfectly suited to the fugal form. John Sebastian's pre-eminence does not, therefore, lie so much in the invention of the clavier style as in the extent to which he expanded it, and the marvellous scope and variety of the artistic material which he presented in that style in the fugal form. He did not, it is true, get entirely away from the organ style; for that permeated his whole artistic being, and it peeps out in nearly all his works, for whatever medium of utterance he wrote. But in all cases the general texture is, in its predominating qualities, thoroughly suited to the conditions of presentment.

So it may be said here that the fugues of the "Wohltemperirtes Clavier," though bearing traces of the influence of the organ style, which was the diction most congenial to Bach, are in a very large majority of cases quite unfitted to be played on the organ, and when they are fitted to be so transplanted they may be judged to have been works which belonged to an earlier time, before he had developed the full maturity of his powers; of which the fugue in A minor [No. 20] is the most obvious example. But it is not only a mere question of style. The composition of fugues for the domestic keyed instrument demanded a totally different conception of the form and radical differences of scheme and effect from organ fugues. The more intimate circumstances in which clavier fugues would be performed required more intimate treatment of detail. The lack of sustaining power in the instrument precluded the piling up of great masses of harmony and the processes which led to great climaxes of sound and the effects to be obtained by powerful suspensions on the organ, and this excluded one of the most familiar effects of the old type of fugue. Where the organ could keep on the notes of a chord or an individual part indefinitely, on the clavier it would be necessary to repeat the notes in some way or another. Hence the whole appearance of clavier music became different from organ music. For where the organ composer could write a sustained chord, the clavier composer had to find a formula which represented the continuance of a chord in an artificial manner. From this cause arose the conventional formulas of accompaniment, such as the so-called "Alberti bass," which, having been adopted long before Alberti because it lay conveniently under the hand of the clavier player, was ultimately transferred to other branches of art, where it had no reason of existence whatever, by composers who wanted cheap devices to save them the effort of invention.

But the qualities of the clavier in this respect had important results which could not have been foreseen by the early composers who divined the mere necessities, and these were manifested first of all in preludes. In the early stages of the development of instrumental music, the passages and figures which were used were unsystematic and indefinite; but by degrees composers realised that any formula of arpeggio which was adopted to represent the harmony which the harpsichord or clavichord could not sustain, must almost necessarily have some individuality of its own, and that this definite character having once been presented, the adoption of another which was inconsistent with it entailed incoherence, inconsequence, and an appearance like the helpless babblings of an undeveloped mind.

But the influence of this necessity was not merely negative; it soon suggested to the minds of composers a most valuable means of unifying a whole composition in a very decisive manner. For, as soon as it was seen that the figures devised to represent the harmonies could in themselves be made attractive and characteristic, artistic instinct began to divine that entire movements could be closely knit together by reiterating them in subtle variations of position, or with such variations of the actual contours as could be adopted without obscuring the initial idea. Out of the limitations of the clavier, therefore, grew the practice of preludising coherently on a series of chords; which was a very attractive form to the logically artistic mind, and has at certain times in the history of art been cultivated with remarkable concentration of artistic faculty; as, for instance, by Chopin; who in all probability got the idea from the very work under consideration, and expanded the conception to suit the capacities of the modern pianoforte in such works as his "Etudes" and "Preludes." It should also be noted in passing that the principle, having once been realised, spread through the whole range of music and is found in the works of men of all schools in various phases of usage, from Schubert and Mendelssohn to Wagner. Bach himself employed it very copiously at times in the instrumental accompaniments of his great choral works; which was the more natural when in the absence of the systematisation of harmony and key of the sonata type (which was not due to be understood till a full generation later), it formed one of the most practicable means of making a work of art thematically coherent.

Such a type of procedure was of all things most suitable to the conditions of domestic music. It is inevitable that the music of men's homes should be much more closely scanned than the music of public gatherings. It is inevitable that it should be more closely knit and more compact. It is also very natural that it should be on a smaller scale, for large paraphernalia are not wanted to present diminutive works of art. And inasmuch as the method of reiteration is liable to become monotonous if it be persisted in too long, a small circuit such as is appropriate to preludes for the clavier is the ideal ground for the employment of the type of procedure in its most unalloyed simplicity. Bach, indeed, was the first composer who seized on the principle with uncompromising thoroughness, and he seems to delight in exploring its possibilities. Out of the twenty-four preludes, at least fifteen are based on the principle, and several of the others bear conspicuous traces of its influence; but here, as elsewhere, he manipulates it with inexhaustible resourcefulness.

The actual manner of employing it is never identical in any two cases. It may be seen in its most absolute simplicity in the first prelude of all, which is so slender and so slight as to be little more than the texture of a dream. It represents the elemental principle of a succession of harmonies vitalised by reiteration of a single figure, which makes the entire movement coherent from end to end. Yet simple and slight as the principle is and unsophisticated as is its application, it forms the groundwork of a movement which has very few equals in the universality of the appeal which it makes to hearers gifted with any delicacy of feeling. And it is worth noting that there are an unusual number of versions of the movement; since, as before mentioned, it appears in Friedemann's "Clavier-Büchlein" in a short version and again, later, with modifications in Anna Magdalena's second book. So that the composer must have returned to it again and again, always trying to make its perfections more complete and more subtle.

The general scheme of the second prelude is the same as the first, but shows how the principle may be more richly elaborated; since the figure itself is presented in two closely related parts and the coda is much more extensive and more rich in detail than that of the first, as it needed to be in relation to the greater solidity and energy of the prelude as a whole. The third prelude presents quite a new aspect of the principle; as the type-figure is twofold, in parts not thematically related as in the second prelude, but contrasting; and its constituent ideas are bandied about from hand to hand and subjected to many variations. The fourth prelude in C sharp minor presents a much more highly organised variety, in which two type-formulas are discussed in a kind of earnest conversation between the "parts" throughout, with episodical passages. The fifth in D major is yet another type—the formula is strikingly definite, and therefore serves the better for the ingenious and effective interpolation of extraneous notes amongst the busy reiterations of the type-figure; which notes not only have the effect of sharp little flashes of sound but subtly suggest an independent melody. In this connection naturally follows the tenth prelude in E minor in which the type-figure is given to the left hand, and serves as an accompaniment to a long-drawn melody interspersed with ornamental adjuncts for the right hand. The prelude gains additional interest from the point of view of Bach's artistic revisions; since its germ appears earlier in Friedemann's "Clavier-Büchlein"—where it represents the primitive type of the first prelude, the melody in the right hand being altogether absent and replaced merely by short chords on the accents following the harmonic progressions of the left hand—it seems conceivable that Bach found the figure insufficiently interesting to sustain the whole responsibility of the movement, and added the melody, which therefore makes the figure in the bass purely secondary. But at the same time it serves as sufficient basis of coherence to allow the melody to range in freedom like an impassioned rhapsody; and the accessory interest thus obtained supplies justification for a much greater extension of the coda. The sixth prelude is an extension of the type of the first and second with more rapid changes of harmony and more importance in the moving bass.

Progressing still further, the eighth prelude in E flat minor supplies an altogether new type which seems at the outset to negative the very principle on which it is based. For the underlying basis of harmony is not presented in a figurate form at all but in simple chords. But the effect of coherence is attained by these chords being systematically grouped in threes in the metric form which is called a "molossus"; and this serves as the unifying principle throughout the long rhapsodical melody which is given to the right hand, on the same principle as the lively figure in the tenth prelude. Strangely enough, notwithstanding the extreme simplicity of the procedure, the prelude is one of the most impassioned and the most interesting of the whole series —a movement exceptionally full of deep feeling, and carried out with a consistency which is not surpassed in any of those in which the more obvious device of reiteration of a figure is maintained throughout. It is evident that Bach thought the movement worthy of exceptional care and consideration, as there are two versions, and twelve bars of the latter portion (which seem ideally to extend the mood of the main body of the prelude) seem to have been an after-thought—analogous to the enlargement of canvas which is sometimes found in the works of the most critically-minded painters.

The principle of laying so much stress on the metric element became of great importance. It is nowhere again so frankly presented as in this prelude—but its introduction offers an opportunity of enhancement of the interest of the type-formula, and in many cases

Bach uses it as a powerful element of definition, either in a single part (as in the seventeenth prelude in A flat) or distributed so as to appear to represent alternation of separate parts, as in the slow movement of the "Italian Concerto" and other works.

There is no need to take all the preludes in detail; a subtle variety of artistic application pervades them all. In only a few cases does the composer make experiments in a different order of procedure. The ninth prelude in E major appears in the guise of a free melody richly harmonised with flowing parts. A characteristic figure is very prominent but is more irregularly introduced than in the figurate preludes presenting a succession of harmonies. The prelude in G minor, No. 16, has the character of a violin solo of the type of slow movements found in concertos and sonatas of the time; such as Vivaldi's and even Corelli's. Bach very frequently attempted such adaptations, as in the beforementioned slow movement of the "Italian Concerto" for clavier, with very characteristic and beautiful results, which bring into prominence his great love of long-drawn, expressive, rhapsodical melody enhanced by subtle touches of decorative ornament. A few of the preludes bear strong traces of the organ style, such as the twelfth in F minor; and in the twenty-second in B flat minor he indulged his love of rich harmonisation, unifying the whole by the almost ceaseless reiteration of a metric formula.

Apart from these technical considerations, representing the intellectual side of the art, the great variety of mood and expression is most notable. The preludes are no barren expositions of purely technical devices; though some artistic problem is always embodied and happily solved, the intrinsic quality of the ideas themselves has a still higher value. There is not one prelude in the collection which does not appeal to the hearer's feelings as much as, if not more than to his intelligence, and with infinite variety; but the infinite variety is nowhere tainted with anything base or trivial, but is of the highest and purest quality. The composers who went before him had mainly to confine themselves to the development of technical resources, and it fell to the lot of John Sebastian to apply the technical resources to expression.

This is equally the case with the fugues. The mere fact that the conditions for which they were written made it desirable that they should be short, precluded their being made occasions for the display of what is commonly called learning or technical dexterity. And the composer, though his facility in canonic devices was unequalled, forebore for the most part to fill up even the measure of ingenuities which the learned pundits proclaimed to be necessary for any well-conducted fugue. A less orthodox series of fugues could not well be found. At the very outset the composer seems to give a little hint to those who take interest in such matters that he did not intend to be bound by the commonly received proprieties, as in the first six bars of the first fugue he makes his alternations of "Dux" and "Comes" succeed one another in an order which is not in accordance with the usual procedure. He makes no pretence of introducing episodes and counter-expositions, and set formalities of successions of keys. If the subject happens to lend itself to the usual procedure, he will avail himself of it. If not, it is of no consequence to him how unfugal the result may be. His object is to make an interesting and well-organised work of art, by the very widest interpretation of fugal principles, and it is of absolutely no consequence to him whether the subject is capable of being treated in stretto or not. Indeed, men possessed of a great taste for technicalities and little musical sense have found fault with some of the fugues because he did not avail himself of all the opportunities of technical display which his subjects afforded. But he had too much grasp of the situation not to know that if he extended the fugue unduly in order to bring in an extra piece of ingenuity the whole would have been marred by the sacrifice of the higher consideration to the lower.

When a subject invited ingenious strettos, like that of the first fugue, he packed the whole as full of such dexterities as it could hold, bringing in the stretto much too soon (according to the usually accepted conventions) in order to exhaust the opportunities of presenting the subject in a variety of lights; and hardly leaving a single moment from beginning to end without some part of the subject sounding. In other cases, where the subject is really not very adaptable, he allows it to drop into a secondary position. Thus in the fugue in E flat major he makes all his play with the figure of the codetta which comes between the statement of the subject and the answer; so that material which is purely parenthetical really establishes the whole character of the fugue. Again, in the fugue in F sharp major, the subject of which is quite workable, he makes use of a characteristic figure which comes in quite independently after the exposition, to give the cachet to the whole fugue. In the case of the peculiarly poignant and desolate fugue in B minor, one of the most striking features is a sequential episode which recurs three times, and which has nothing to do with either the subject or the counter-subject; but breaks the persistence of truly tragic melancholy with short interspaces of relief and beautiful contrast. An earlier employment of the same device has been referred to in connection with the organ fugue in D minor (p. 67).

A type of subject which is quite unfitted for the subtleties of strettos and such technical treatment is presented in the fugues in C sharp major and B flat, whose merry, light, and vivacious character would make the devices of the learned seem out of place. In both these fugues much play is made with accessory features, which in the first case are independent of the subject and in the second constitute its latter part. In the noble fugue in F sharp minor, again, the counter-subject is of far more importance in establishing the character of the fugue than the principal subject; and the same may be said of the fugue in F minor, the subject of which has a peculiarly stiff and monotonous crotchet motion, which, however, takes an entirely new significance when it is attended by the strongly contrasted and concise figure of the counter-subject.

From these considerations it follows that John Sebastian took an extremely independent view of the fugue form when used for the clavier; and the independence seems likely to have come upon him in the actual process of composition; otherwise it would seem illogical that in so many cases the subject should eventually occupy a subordinate position, and that the features which determined the character of the fugue should be after-thoughts. In theory, of course, the object of the fugue form is to deal with the subject which is propounded at the outset; but practice has the agreeable advantage of almost invariably proving theory to be ultimately inadequate. The abstract theory of fugue is as inadequate as theories in politics or philosophy which are not founded on antecedent practice but upon preconceived anticipation. The object of the many generations of composers who evolved the fugue was to find a sane and intelligible form in which to present their ideas; not a mere excuse for showing off technical ingenuity. No doubt, ingenuity being more plentiful than ideas, the result was rather deceptive; for a principle of the kind is capable of being dissected and analysed in cold blood till every progression and every point of procedure seems to be successively indicated as if by physical necessity.

But if such a point could really be arrived at with any form, its condemnation would thereby be pronounced. It can be of no further use to humanity. People who are under the impression that they can make works of art by applying rules of procedure are merely trying to pass off a framework as a living organism. It is in practice that the misconceptions of artistic law-makers are corrected. This may be applied to John Sebastian's peculiar manipulation of the fugue form. The truth must be admitted that human beings, especially the greater ones, have to warm up to their work in the process of working; and adapt themselves to the promptings of their inspirations as they reveal themselves. The greater minds often anticipate the whole scheme of whatever work of art they intend to complete before they begin to work upon it in detail. But this is more especially difficult with the fugal form, which is the gradual ravelment of long lines of concurrent melodies, the interest of which is constantly cumulative, from the single-part opening, till the knot is tied at the end. The effect of the form of procedure is to reveal to the composer unexpected possibilities in the relations of the subject to the context as the composition proceeds—and, as above suggested, an unexpected possibility which is frequently revealed is that the subject is intractable.

The fact that Bach, when he meant to make music in the form of the fugue, did not attempt to devise subjects which would serve to illustrate canonic devices is clear from the large number of them which do not admit of being treated in stretto at all. His incomparable facility in feats of skill justified his neglecting to prepare opportunities for its display, and encouraged him to project his mind in the direction of conceiving a subject which should have some characteristic feature, some characteristic suggestion of temperamental quality, or some general principle of motion which might form the basis or pervading type of mood in the whole of a movement; and it may be pointed out that he effected the objects which the theorists aimed at by much subtler means than they proposed. For the purpose of illustration the Fugue in D major, No. 5, is most apt. In this case the subject is admirably fitted to supply the pervading mood to the whole movement, but is quite unfitted for regular stretto work. Bach certainly brings the strikingly characteristic figure closer and closer as the work proceeds, till the reiterations not only touch one another, but are duplicated in two parts ; which is all, indeed, that the human hand could deal with under the circumstances. But as a stretto, in the ordinary theoretic sense of the word, it is a mere imposture. The root idea is made to pervade the mind more and more till it is so completely all-absorbed that the mental adjuster seems to say, "Hold, enough," and at the exact moment, which nothing but the highest degree of artistic instinct could divine, the wrought-up fervour of concentration ceases, and a few simple chords, cast in the form of the less characteristic features of the subject, seem, with a dignified courtesy, to close the book. But there has been no stretto. What stretto there is is a mental one. In this case the sudden rush with which the subject begins is the feature which rivets the mind and gives the cue to the development of the fugue. A similar device is found in the Fugue in E major, in which the incisively questioning little figure of two notes, with which the subject opens, gives the cue, and is made to flash out of the texture of flowing semiquavers throughout the movement; the last reference coming in the last bar but one, seeming like a playful mockery, for the question is left practically unanswered! The truth is, the composer seizes the material which is suggestive whereever he finds it. Sometimes it comes in the latter part of the subject, as in the exquisitely tender and pathetic Fugue in G sharp minor, one of the most humanly consistent of all; in which, though the first part of the subject is presented and developed with wonderful fancy, it is the little figure forming the latter part which pervades the whole fugue and quite puts the earlier part into the background at the end. In other cases, as before pointed out, he does not find the material which is to give character to the fugue till he has done his duty by the subject, and then it presents itself as it were by accident in the counter-subject or in musical material which is independent of the principal subject.

Even a comparative failure like the Fugue in A major shows what his attitude was. In this case he evidently anticipated much from the zigzag motion of the subject, which might be expected to lay hold of the mind decisively. But here the subject proved intractable; and, much as the skill of its manipulation may be admired, it must be admitted that it does not take possession of the mind like many another characteristic form of motion. It is capricious and wilful, but not attractive; and in the latter part of the fugue the composer resorts to the curious makeshift of presenting a variant of the subject, which moves more easily and suggests the ground idea of the subject, without being technically exact.

This leads to a consideration which is characteristic and important. The composer frequently resorts to the practice of developing the subject or its root idea into new and interesting forms, which give a fine aspect of continuity without reiteration of the exact concrete formula, adding interest while suggesting an expansion of the ground thought. This is illustrated by the very first fugue, in which the typical rising motion of the first four notes provides the cue for the final passage, wherein the rising process is expanded in more rapid notes, extending by gradations up the scale for an octave and a half, and reiterating the sense of the subject without ever actually quoting it exactly. A more highly organised example of similar development may be seen in the close of the E major Fugue in the second series. It is the underlying principle upon which the subject is based which is made use of, illustrating the spirit rather than the exact musical formula, and it is this larger view which gives the fugues such pre-eminent and unique interest.

When the subject is happy enough, within its confined limits, to suggest a principle which lays hold of the mind, it is persistently reiterated; when it is insufficient, other musical figures are introduced, sometimes to afford pleasant alternations of contrast, sometimes to form the real basis of the character of the fugue. But the character is always of vital importance. It is not merely a subject which appears at certain proper and logical intervals, but a mood or mental image which pervades the whole.

The fact is patent that the fugues individually represent various types of mood, from stateliness and severity and sadness, to the most unequivocal gaiety: and thus the value of this form of art is shown in its finest significance. The fugal principle is shown rightly to be a method of artistic organisation, and instead of being a stiff, prim, mechanical example of mere so-called science it becomes one of the most elastic and comprehensive means of conveying musical ideas. No doubt it represents an ancient and deep-rooted principle of art, and belongs to a stage which was almost purely contrapuntal in its inception, and the rules by which the exposition of the subject was governed give it a slightly conventional aspect; but when art had passed through the classical phase of the sonata and sought freedom again, though the formal exposition of the fugue has been dropped, the most modern phase of art again returns to the same treatment of subjects in polyphony which Bach illustrated in the first portion of the "Wohltemperirtes Clavier."

But there is another aspect of the question which must be considered, before all has been said, and that is suggested by the very name, the "Well-tempered Clavier." The adoption of this name by Bach was a public and deliberate recognition of a radical change in the construction of European scales, of such pre-eminent importance that it is no exaggeration to say that without it modern musical art would have been absolutely impossible. It need not be supposed that Bach was answerable for the acceptance of the new scale system. That was bound to come for the simple reason that the art could not get on without it. Things had been moving in that direction for a long while; indeed, it must ever remain a puzzle how some of the pieces in the virginal music of Queen Elizabeth's and James the First's time could have been endured at all except in the scale system defined by Bach as "well-tempered." And if the matter be looked frankly in the face it must be admitted that the appearance of extreme modulations in the works not only of such a rash speculator as John Bull, but also of such a serious-minded man as Orlando Gibbons, gives very strong grounds for thinking that a system at least approximating to "equal temperament" must have been recognised and even employed by musicians in certain quarters.

Equal temperament was certainly not employed in tuning organs, or in training choirs; but it could easily have been employed in such a simple matter as tuning the Virginals by adventurous virtuosi like John Bull; and it would have enabled him to astonish even the more intelligent musicians of his time by the execution of modulations which under the old system were quite impossible. In any case since such modulations are actually found in works of more than a hundred years before Bach's time, the inference is fair that the composers tuned their instruments so as to make them practicable.

But whatever had happened earlier, it was inevitable that, directly instrumental music began to develop, the scale system hitherto in use should require modification. In the old style of unaccompanied choral music there were hardly any modulations at all. Abstruse modulations were alien to the artistic objects of composers who wrote under the restrictions of the church modes. Even the idea of what is called a "key" was outside their range; and it only began to dawn upon the minds of musicians when the different modes were assimilated to one another by the introduction of a few sharps and flats. These sharps and flats were not introduced with any idea of defining a key, but in order to avoid disagreeable and harsh intervals which were alien to the passionless style of polyphonic church music. But when they were introduced, the effect was to obliterate differences between the Lydian and the Mixolydian modes, and to make even the Dorian and the Æolian sound like any commonplace minor mode of recent usage; and then composers, not in the least anticipating whither their road tended, found pleasure in the subtle gradations of melodic relation produced by using the same intervals of the modal scale in the different aspects which the "musica ficta" admitted.

This to a modern mind appears supremely elementary and almost childish. But if such an abstraction can be thought of as a musician who had never known a pianoforte with more than the white keys, and then had discovered a black one representing a new semitone between A and B, it would be easy to imagine the æsthetic joy which the melodic alternation of A B, and A B flat would present to him. And if to the scale of white notes with B flat added, another note between D and E were added, the E flat seems to extend the possibilities of music to a surprising degree. For not only does it offer the opportunity of ringing the changes between D E and D E flat, or between F E and F E flat, but it also admits of a totally new grouping of harmonies round the B flat.

Under the old unmodified system a chord could not stand on B because the fifth would be a dissonant. When the B was altered to B flat, it made a perfect fifth with F, but an ugly tritone with E natural. But when that was modified to E flat, composers soon realised that an entire new scale system could start from that B flat—a mode, indeed, representing the Ionic mode,—and then, by applying a modification of the scale which had been devised for one purpose to another which was in no way anticipated, a new feature of the utmost importance was introduced into music; and the effect of alternating passages consistent with the Doric mode starting from D, with passages starting from B flat and centralised round it, suggested the value of change of key as an element of design or organisation.

When instrumental music came to be cultivated, the fact that instruments could take many intervals which were not natural to voices unaccompanied soon made a larger number of accidentals desirable, and the increase of accidentals led to a wider range of keys. And thus it was that musicians began to realise the difficulties of tuning. As long as music did not require more than a scale which could be represented by the white keys of the organ or modern pianoforte, with an occasional accidental to avoid a disagreeable or unvocal interval, no difficulty was presented. But when the key principle was realised and composers found themselves impelled to modulate more freely, they found that the system of tuning which produced the most perfect and pure intervals for the limited range of sounds required by the old modal system entailed extraneous keys being painfully out of tune. And this must have been forced upon their notice all the more strongly because they had been accustomed to purer harmonies than are ever heard in modern times. Composers whose tastes lay in the direction of the old style of choral music thought that music might be restricted to a few keys, and were loth to abandon the system known as unequal temperament. But composers who realised instinctively that scales are purely artificial contrivances devised for artistic needs, and those who foresaw that when once the key-system was recognised it was impossible to restrict the range of modulation (since the relative range of modulations starting from different given points would be unequal), made up their minds that the system of equal distribution of the imperfections over all the components of the scale must be adopted, and that, in point of fact, all the semitones must be practically equal whatever they were in theory.

And this was the system of equal temperament to which J. S. Bach gave his unequivocal adhesion by putting together this collection of Preludes and Fugues in all possible keys. He was thus in the very forefront of progressive musicians of his time, and his action has been endorsed by the subsequent trend of modern music. For it is obvious that even the system of organisation upon which the sonatas of the classical sonata period are based would have been impossible unless the range of modulations was equal in every direction; and we owe the splendours of Beethoven's symphonies, as well as the excessive elaboration of more recent music, to the adoption of the equal temperament. Such circumstances, combined with the unique musical interest and beauty of the little works themselves, mark the first series of the collection known as the "Wohltemperirtes Clavier" as one of the most epoch-making productions in the whole range of the art of music.

Bach's energy in exploring the possibilities of secular instrumental music during the time when he was at Cöthen seems to have been all-embracing. His opportunities for hearing such music were plentiful, and, there being no special inducements to write choral music on a grand scale, his mind was more free to address itself to various forms of this large branch of art. There seems little doubt that most of his wonderful works for solo violin, whether unaccompanied or coupled with the clavier, date from this time. The works for solo violin unaccompanied may be said without exaggeration to be absolutely unique in the whole range of music. There are no compositions of the kind by any composer whatever which have such scope and interest, none which lend themselves in such a degree to the highest gifts of interpretation, and none in which such an amount of noble expression and such richness of thought have been rendered possible for the single instrument. Of Bach's powers as a violinist not much can be decisively asserted. It is worth remembering that music of some kind rendered upon the violin was one of his first artistic experiences, as his father had played on a stringed instrument and had taught him the violin when he was a child; and among his duties on his first appointment at Weimar was that of playing in the Duke's band. And we know that he expressed his liking for playing on the viola, because he was in the middle of things.

It must be admitted that the style of violin music was quite overwhelmed in him by the pre-eminent influences of the organ style; but for that there seems sufficient reason in the fact that in his boyhood the style of violin music was but slightly differentiated. The violin had been cultivated throughout the seventeenth century, but it was only by very slow degrees that its technical resources were evolved, that the particular passages suited for it were devised, and that its powers of expression in cantabile passages and its capacity for rapid passages were so far realised as to serve as the basis of the admirable exposition of its true capabilities which is shown in the works of Vitali, Bassani, Corelli, and Vivaldi, and the Italian violinists who succeeded them. Though it is true that some of Corelli's works were written early enough for Bach to have heard them in his boyhood, it is probable that most of the violin music which came under his notice was the product of an earlier generation, presenting but few traits of distinctive style, and that organ music, which was the one and only branch of instrumental music of which the style was decisively differentiated, was the only one upon which his developing sensibilities could be decisively nurtured.

Thus organ style became in all things the most persistent influence in determining Bach's procedure, even when he was writing for an instrument so radically and uncompromisingly different as the violin. The violin is primarily a melodic instrument, the organ is most emphatically not so; the violin has infinite capacity for expressive variation of tone, like a voice, the organ has none except such as is arrived at by mechanical devices; the violin is a single-part instrument, the organ essentially and necessarily a many-part instrument. Without entering further into their oppositions, the contrast between them is summed up in the analogy which their natures suggest. The organ has often been called the king of instruments; and if justly so the violin may fairly be called the queen.

But of these radical differences of nature Bach was neither unaware nor inapt to take advantage. No composer ever had a finer sense of the free and sensitively expressive type of melody, which the violin has a pre-eminent capacityfor presenting, than John Sebastian. He shows the type in many of the arioso recitatives for solo voices in cantatas and other great works of the kind. The melody of the violin, moreover, being free from words, left him more untrammelled both by association and by the constraint of submission to actual syllables to soar away from conventions and formulas into the region of introspective emotionalism which was dear to his Teutonic nature. Moreover, no composer ever had a happier sense of vivacious, merry, sparkling dance measures such as the violin is so ideally fitted to present, and for which the organ is so utterly ill suited. So the aspects in which the organ style is discernible in his violin music are, after all, confined to such as do not seriously affect its real appositeness; consisting mainly in the use of types of passages which were familiar in organ music but also capable of being rendered on the violin, and in the use of contrapuntal texture, and the suggestion of suspensions and large progressions of harmony, to which the attitude of a mind nurtured in organ music preferably resorted. The extraordinary difficulties which his solo music presents impelled violinists ultimately to develop a special phase of technique to conquer them, because the music is in itself so supremely great and noble that high-minded performers could not rest satisfied till they found the way to master it. And hence it has come about ultimately that these solo works are regarded as among the most convincing proofs of the powers of interpretation of the foremost violinists of later times.

The principal collection of these, which Bach in all probability completed during the time when he was at Cöthen, consists of six works, three of which are, technically, suites and three sonatas. The distinction between these two forms had been growing by degrees during the previous century, and found its complete establishment in the types of the *Sonata da camera* and the *Sonata da chiesa* of Corelli; the Suite or Sonata da camera being constituted of movements founded mainly upon dance forms, and the sonatas upon more serious abstract forms. In the grouping of these works which Bach adopted, sonatas alternate with suites: the sonatas coming first, third, and fifth, and the suites, here called "Partien," second, fourth, and sixth. Each of the sonatas begins with a slow movement in the free rhapsodical style which he made so essentially his own and illustrated so magnificently in the fantasia for organ in G minor. The second movement is in each case a fugue, the third movement in the first sonata is a Siciliano in the relative major, and in the other two a slow movement, and the fourth movement a brilliant quick movement—the last movement of the second sonata, indeed, is a "moto perpetuo." Bach's scheme, therefore, conforms to the grouping of movements commonly adopted by the Italian violin composers and the masters of other countries who followed them, the fugue corresponding to the canzona of the earlier composers.

In two of the suites wnich he here calls "Partien" he is also conservative in general lines; but all three have peculiarities. The first Partita has a "double" or variation to each of the main constituents, the allemande being followed by a "double," the courante in turn by another, and so also with the sarabande and bourrée, the latter of which has a brilliant "double" to conclude with. This suite, therefore, has the comparatively rare feature of ending with one of the group of movements which were technically called "Galanterien," on the theory of their being of lighter cast than the other movements. It is possibly a mere accident that the omission of the gigue is amply compensated for by the fact that the bourrée in question is one of Bach's most attractive and characteristic movements for the solo violin. The second Partita in D minor is quite regular in its first four constituents, having allemande, courante, sarabande, and gigue, after the most orthodox scheme; but the group is followed by the famous chaconne, a series of variations on lines parallel to the time-honoured "divisions on a ground," but laid out in such an admirable sequence, so far-reaching in musical interest, so copious in resource, that it holds its place as one of the most important of all movements ever written for the instrument; and has in recent times been one of the favourite works by which violinists of high aim endeavour to prove the extent of their intelligence and their technique to sympathetic audiences. The movement is often played without the suite, as it is of very ample length.

The third Partita, which is in E major and stands last of the set, is for the most part a speculative group. It begins with a brilliant prelude which was afterwards developed into the symphony at the beginning of the Rathswahl Cantata, *Wir danken dir Gott*, of 1731. The second movement is a loure, affording a happy contrast, as the slow measure of six beats in a bar has a somewhat languorous character, even in the hands of the strenuous John Sebastian. The third is the wonderful gavotte "en rondeau," which is one of the favourites with violinists and the public, and forms an admirable contrast to the loure; and the remaining movements are two minuets, a bourrée in E minor, and a short gigue to conclude with. John Sebastian did not often venture on a speculative group of this kind, because his invention and resources were equal to making something new without forsaking the old order. He was in the position of a man who found copious work to do, ready to his hand, and was content to grapple with that and not leave undone what needed to be done in order to gratify curiosity in regions beyond the field which remained as yet incompletely tilled. But nevertheless it is interesting to observe the scheme of a rare example of the speculative order, and to notice with what perfect insight he devised it; and it is worth noting also that it comes last in the series, where wholesome sanity would naturally place it, and that the only conspicuous parallel among his works in speculativeness of a similar kind is in the sets of movements for clavier, which he also called Partitas, and brought together in the latter part of his life.

In respect of regularity of order, the six superb suites for the violoncello, which were also probably written during his time at Cöthen, are conspicuous. Each has a prelude, sometimes of even vast expanse, and the remaining series are in the accepted order, like the clavier suites, and vary only in the lighter movements or "Galanterien," which are minuets in the first and second suites, bourrées in the third and fourth, and gavottes in the fifth and sixth. A noteworthy point is that the fifth suite is written for a violoncello unusually tuned in C, G, D, G—for special effect; and the last is written for an instrument with five strings, which is inferred to have been not a violoncello but a "Viola pomposa," an instrument which Bach himself is said to have invented.

A yet further group of very important compositions

which seem to date from the Cöthen period is that of six sonatas for violin and cembalo. The schemes of these are more speculative; and the plan and components of the movements themselves are often most characteristic. They all end with lively movements, all have slow movements last but one. But the typical quasi-fugal second movement representing the canzona of earlier times is either absent or transformed into a very rhythmic and vivacious contrapuntal movement; and the first movement is sometimes slow, in Bach's unsurpassable rhapsodical manner, as in the first sonata in B minor and the third in E major, and in other cases of various experimental types. The total impression conveyed by some of these speculations in grouping is not always convincing, but the first sonata in B minor is one of the composer's most perfect and delightful works of this class, the first movement especially being supremely interesting and beautiful; and those in A, No. 2 and E major, No. 3 are of superb quality. Bach produced many isolated works of the same type as these; such as a very fine Sonata for Violin and Clavier in E minor (Peters T. V. I. 696, etc.) and sonatas for flute and cembalo, which, as music, are thoroughly delightful and interesting, but do not exclusively show off the character of the flute, and are often played by the violin.

Among the most important of Bach's secular instrumental works are the four "overtures" for orchestra, which also were probably produced during this period. They are generally spoken of as suites, but the name overture, which Bach seems to have given them, gains in this case no little importance through what it implies. There can be no doubt, indeed, that Bach was experimenting in these works in the most extended form of the French overture.

This overture comprised several movements, the most prominent of which are the massive opening slow movement, and the movement of fugal or "canzona" type which followed it; and this sometimes constituted the whole overture, both in Lulli's case and in the large number of overtures by countless composers who employed the same form in connection with operas, stage plays, oratorios, and cantatas. But it may safely be inferred that when composers produced works ostensibly on the lines of the Lullian or French overture, to be played as instrumental works apart from operas or oratorios, they adopted the more extended form in which the two opening movements are followed by a number of dance movements. Admirable examples of this kind of work had been produced before Bach's time by Georg Muffat, who confessedly came under Lulli's influence in the earlier part of his career, and Bach evidently had this type in his mind rather than the suite type in composing the group of "overtures."

The result is in every way notable; for the treatment throws light on the form of art itself as well as on Bach's methods. In the first place, his treatment of the opening slow movement shows his attitude of mind in relation to the enrichment of an established scheme. He has, indeed, so expanded and adorned the primitive Lullian model that at first sight it is almost unrecognisable. To those who cannot easily make acquaintance with the genuine Lullian examples, the familiar slow movement of the overture to The *Messiah* will quite adequately represent the type; as, apart from the Handelian flavour and solidity of harmony, that movement is purely Lullian in its unadorned simplicity. It represents the massive, slowly moving harmonies and the weighty suspensions of the Lullian type without any attempt to disguise or adorn it with accessory features. In Bach's examples the same basis is present—the grand harmonies and the suspensions and forcible discords,—but they serve only as a framework upon which Bach elaborates the superb texture of fine instrumental passages, shakes, turns. and ornaments of all kinds, which make every moment and every progression alive with genuine instrumental effect and interest.

This method of treating the form also lends itself to more close consistency and coherence in the musical material. In the Lullian type there is little beyond the mere consistency of style to make the movement coherent in detail, any more than there is in the slow movement of Handel's *Messiah* overture. But with the method employed by Bach the figuration and use of ornament at once give definiteness to the texture, and suggest inevitably the use of something in the nature of a musical subject; and the use of definite ideas of the kind places the organisation of the movement at once on a higher plane. The process represents the familiar phase of differentiation and systematisation which is so characteristic of evolution, and shows the justness of Bach's sense of the requirements of instrumental music.

Thus, in the slow movement with which the first overture in C commences, the first few bars present a definite passage of long notes and semiquaver figures, which at once decisively attracts the attention, and becomes the musical type of idea which persists thereafter throughout the movement, and thereby definitely unifies it.

The opening passage of the slow movement which commences the second overture in B minor is even more definite as a subject, with shakes and a fine bold melodic character, which by reason of its very decisiveness cannot thenceforward be dropped without an appearance of inconsequence, and therefore makes the movement even more closely knit than the slow movement of the first "overture." The slow movement of the third overture in D (commonly known as the great orchestral suite in D and the most popular of the group of works) is fully as decisive in its opening phrases, and the movement is developed on a grander scale than the others. The fourth of the group, also in D, has a definite figure also in the initial slow movement, which prevails throughout and unifies it admirably, though it is not so striking as the formulas which serve as the governing ideas in the overture in B minor and the other in D. It must be observed, also, that the style of these movements must have been specially congenial to Bach through habits of musical thought begotten by early experiences of organ style, as the massive chord-basis linked by suspensions is just the type which finds most adequate expression in the style of organ music.

Bach's treatment of the quick fugal movement which comes second in this form of art is quite equally suggestive. At the outset the recognition of the kinship with the French overture is illustrated by the extreme shortness, amounting even to insignificance, of all the fugal subjects; a feature which had been conspicuous in Lulli's examples, in which they are little more than suggestions of types of motion, without regular fugal development. Bach could not help using his subjects more systematically than Lulli had done, but as fugues the movements are of a very unusual character. In the first overture in C major, for instance, the movement comes to a close in that key at the end of the exposition, and then follows a long passage in which three wind instruments toy with the subjects in a playful manner, which is actually marked "trio." Similar episodes recur throughout the fugue, sometimes slenderly accompanied by the strings, but so distributed that an excellent scheme of organisation is presented together with plenty of variety of a simple and definite kind. An analogous procedure is adopted in the second overture in B minor, but inasmuch as it is only scored for flute and strings a similar end is attained by episodes in which the flute has brilliant passages accompanied lightly by the strings, alternating with the passages in which the whole mass of the strings vigorously deals with the principal subject. In the third, the most important of these overtures, the scheme is more elaborate, because there are three groups of instruments, the brass consisting of three trumpets, with drums attendant, the wood-wind consisting of the two hautboys, and the third group being the mass of the strings. In this the alternation is made mainly by the manner in which the brass instruments come in at definite intervals, marking special parts of the scheme by exceptional fulness. In the fourth the band is even larger, for there are three hautboys and bassoons as well as the trumpets and the strings; and contrasts of fulness are obtained by one episode mainly for wind, and others for strings alone, and passages, like those in the previous overture, in which exceptional fulness is obtained by having many of the instruments playing at once.

In such treatment as this the notable difference between Bach's idea of using the components of the orchestra and the modern conception is conspicuous. He practically uses them less for their colour than for their fulness, and employs the effect of contrast between full passages and slenderly orchestrated passages as an element of design, much as he would use a similar alternation of passages for full organ with slighter passages for few stops in his organ music—or, again, similar in effect to the alternation of passages for the chorus in choral works with passages for the band. In other respects the treatment of the instruments is the same as that in the Brandenburg Concertos, which has been already discussed (p. 119), and need not be recapitulated.

The two first movements afford a very quaint illustration of a singular characteristic of Bach, who sometimes, it must be confessed, strangely lost sight of expediency in faithfulness to his models. For, though the quasi-fugues are of enormous length, he returns to his opening slow movement when each fugue comes to an end and then gives the direction for the fugue to be played all over again. It suggests to the mind that he did not very often hear these works played himself. With regard to the rest of the movements of the overtures, the kinship with the French model, and with Muffat's "Florilegia," is shown in the number of dance movements of the liveliest character which follow the two serious opening movements. In these Bach's geniality is shown in its very frankest guise, and it manifests itself in a singular and almost unique phase; for none of the movements however, gay and merry, ever lose the distinction of noble art. Nobody but J. S. Bach ever succeeded in presenting such sparkling gaiety and fun in such fine and manly terms. However freely they sparkle and play, they are never trivial, but bear even in the lightest moments the impress of the great mind and the essentially sincere character of the composer.

Among the works which show that Bach's attachment to the organ and to the music of religion was not extinguished during the Cöthen period, is the lovable little collection to which he gave the title of "Orgel-Büchlein," consisting of short movements for the organ based on chorales, which must have been brought up to the condition in which it has since remained, in spite of incompleteness, during the period when his opportunities were mainly in the domain of secular instrumental music.

In view of the nature of its contents it may be of service to point out here that the various ways in which German composers dealt with chorales in compositions for the organ were strictly classified by them into three groups, the "Choralfantasie," the "Choralvorspiel," and the "Orgelchoral." In modern times, for the avoidance of confusion and misapprehension, it has been usual for writers who address those who are not intimate with the German technicalities to speak of such works generally as "Choralvorspiele" or "Chorale-preludes." But to the exact German mind this would be misleading. The "Choralfantasie" was the larger form in which the phrases of their loved chorales were introduced bodily with infinite adornment of expressive polyphony. Their nature was more or less determined by the fact that they were independent works of art, whereas the "Choralvorspiel" was dependent as a prelude on the chorale which was to be sung in the church service, and therefore avoided the too obvious presentation of the melodies, so that they might come more freshly from the congregation. The "Orgelchoral" was a much smaller movement, merely taking a tune in its complete form straight through, and arranging it with parts in instrumental style, which emphasised the expression of the tune or the words to which it belonged by all the subtlest devices of harmonisation and of characteristic figure and ornament which the composer had at his disposal.

Bach produced an enormous number of exquisite little movements of this kind, and the "Orgel-Büchlein" was probably the first collection he made of such as had been written at various times; many, no doubt, at Weimar, others at Cöthen, and the whole representing his activity in this range up to about the year 1723. In the title-page it is implied that they were intended as educational pieces, for the enhancement of the powers of young organists, primarily, no doubt, Friedemann—and happy indeed the learner who should develop his powers in the study of such singularly attractive little works. Another point which is characteristic of Bach is that they were intended to follow the order in which the chorales would properly follow one another in the actual scheme of the Lutheran Church for the whole year; but here the mission of the series was not entirely fulfilled, for Bach did not actually complete it, and the number of movements does not exceed forty-six.

There are several blank pages in the MS., and in some of these the names of the chorales which were intended to occupy them are given, sometimes even with short passages of music indicating the character the movements were to have The variety of fancy and resource of the little movements is quite phenomenal. Every individual chorale is treated with some special characteristic figure in accompaniment, sometimes tender, sometimes mournful, sometimes animated and vigorous, in accordance with the sentiment of the tune or the words. Some have simple figures which persist throughout, after the type of many of the preludes in the first part of the "Wohltemperirtes Clavier," some are elaborately contrapuntal in the instrumental style, in a great many there are admirably contrived canons. In some the tune is given simply, in others in variation with appropriate adornments.

In every one some new artistic scheme is presented and worked out with the most delicate finish. There is hardly any work of Bach's which brings the hearer into more intimate relations with him, or one more suffused with his personality. His deep love of the national chorales made him deal with them as an artist might who had to make a casket for some inestimable treasure which deeply moved his romantic and imaginative faculties and through them brought into play his highest artistic powers. It is, indeed, not a work for the public at all, but for those who can enter into converse with a great mind in the things which meant most to him. The best of them are even more intimate than the movements of the "Wohltemperirtes Clavier," and reveal the deep-set nature of the composer in a manner which sometimes almost brings tears to the trembling verge, and at others raises the loving smile. For if, on the one hand, we see him overborne by his besetting temptation to emphasise an idea with a semi-humorous stroke of realistic suggestion—as in the quaint jumping-down passage given to the pedals in the chorale "Through Adam's *fall* is

all undone," on the other hand we see how universal is the rule that only subjects which appeal to his humanity most deeply bring out his most wonderful art works. The world does well to wonder at the scope of his great choruses and choral motets, but in them the idea of a public audience of some sort is necessarily implied. In the organ-chorale and kindred works, Bach seems to be communing with his own spirit, to be possessed with the soul-question which is embodied in the sacred hymn, and to discourse spontaneously in those terms of temperamental reflection which are the special prerogative of the musical art. For the study of the temperamental personality of Bach's "Orgelchoräle," which stand out from the rest through their exceptional interest and moving qualities, exactly confirms the clues which would be afforded by the special church cantatas which stand out from the rest on similar grounds.

Far in the forefront of the collection stands *O Mensch, bewein' dein' Sünde gross,* where the composer seems to have had his faculties at the highest pitch of insight and concentration from first to last. And among the most characteristic and personal of his works of this kind may also be put *Wenn wir in höchsten Nöthen sein, Mit Fried' und Freud' ich fahr' dahin, Das alte Jahr vergangen ist,* and the two rather unusual experiments, *Ich ruf' zu dir, Herr Jesu Christ* and *Komm, Gott Schöpfer, heiliger Geist,* the scheme of which last evidently attracted him so much that he expanded it later in life into very much more spacious proportions (see p. 538). It is evident that the writing of "Orgelchoräle" and works of kindred type must have continued throughout the whole of Bach's life, as a sort of undercurrent and, he brought many more together at various periods towards the close of his life, in which appeared some wonderful innermost human documents of the very greatest fascination, such as *Schmücke dich* and several in the third series of the "Clavierübung." And finally this form of art has most pathetic associations, for the last work that he touched upon his deathbed was in this form, as will be related in its place. Hence the "Orgel-Büchlein" has an accession of interest even besides that of its contents, as being his first manifestation of a line of art which reached from that time till the end, and whose methods, indeed, underlay a great deal of the most interesting portions of his church cantatas and oratorios.

CHAPTER V

LEIPZIG, 1723–1750

It appears from a passage in a letter of Bach's written in 1730 that about the year 1722 he felt that his master, the Prince of Anhalt-Cöthen, was becoming lukewarm towards music owing to his marriage with a lady who had no taste for it, and that the time had come for him to look for a post where his field of work would be wider and more productive of results. It was in this year that Johann Kuhnau, the versatile and distinguished cantor of the St. Thomas School in Leipzig, died, and John Sebastian was moved to enter for the post. However, he did not do so immediately, for the council actually appointed G. P. Telemann, a musician of very considerable repute, at the end of the year. But Telemann declined to accept some of the conditions which they imposed, and retired, and it must have been shortly afterwards that Bach definitely offered himself.

In February, 1723, he went to Leipzig in order to make some manifestations of his powers; and, after the conditions—which included giving certain lessons in Latin weekly to the lower class of boys—had been considered and accepted, the council elected him. The appointment was confirmed on May 8th and Bach was installed on May 31st. He did not entirely sever his connection with Cöthen, as the Prince desired him to be his honorary Kapellmeister, but his active connection with that court ceased, and a new and more comprehensive field of operations was opened to him in which he exercised his great powers in their highest maturity for the remaining twenty-seven years of his life.

The duties and responsibilities of the Leipzig cantor were peculiar, and had no doubt grown up by degrees as the requirements of the school to which he was attached presented themselves. In relation to the personality of John Sebastian himself it is worth observing at the outset that he was not technically or officially the organist of any church. His position was mainly to superintend the musical training of the boys in the school and the musical arrangements of several churches where they had to sing. The school was a very ancient foundation which, from the thirteenth century to the Reformation, had been under the control of Augustinian monks. If the cantorship was instituted and its duties defined in the early days of the foundation, this would explain the fact that no connection with the organ is indicated; as that instrument could have had but a very limited share in the music of the earlier centuries of the school's existence, and the chief musician would have been mainly concerned with training the choir in unaccompanied choral music. A few years after Leipzig adopted the Reformed religion, the monastic foundation of St. Thomas, including the school, passed into the hands of the town council. Apart from doctrine, as was generally the case in Germany, no very great changes were made. The school, which had had for its principal object the training of boys and young men for the adequate performance of the music required in the services of the church, was still maintained for that purpose; and the number of scholarships established was even increased till they amounted finally to fifty-five. The connection between church and school remained as close as before, and the cantor's most essential duties were thus to prepare the boys in the music which had to be performed, and to keep them in order; and to superintend and direct the performance of music in the functions of the church on Sundays, and on some other special occasions, such as a few saints' days and great festivals like Christmas-day and New Year's-day and Ascension-day, and also at funerals and weddings.

The scheme of the music for which the cantor was responsible seems to have been clearly defined. It is to be noted that he was not only responsible for the direction of the music at St. Thomas's Church, but also at that of St. Nicholas, which was the other most important church in the town, and in many cases the same choir served both churches in turn. It was a rule that a motet and church cantata should be performed every Sunday of the year, and to render this possible they were performed in each of the churches on alternate Sundays; only on such special festivals as the New Year, Epiphany, Ascension-day, Trinity Sunday, and the Feast of the Annunciation, the full musical panoply was presented in both churches, the choir performing the same music in the morning at one church and in the afternoon in the other. Such requirements had considerable influence both on the scope and character of Bach's activity in church music during his Leipzig time, as it was the necessity of providing musical works for so many occasions which caused him to

St. Thomas Church, Leipzig

From *Die Musik*, October, 1905.

(Courtesy of Messrs. Schuster & Loeffler, Berlin.)

produce such an enormous number of church cantatas in the latter part of his life.

The foundation of St. Thomas had actually to supply the choirs for four churches in Leipzig: as it had to provide for the "New" Church, which had been the Church of the Franciscans before the Reformation, but had apparently been disused from that time till 1699, and also for the church of St. Peter, as well as for the more important churches above mentioned, of St. Thomas and St. Nicholas; but inasmuch as the scheme of music in the less important churches was comparatively insignificant, the cantor's duties in connection with them extended no further than the choice of chorales and motets. For the music for special funerals and weddings the cantor was responsible, and probably no negligible portion of his income was derived from the fees payable in connection with them; and he was expected to attend the funeral processions in person. The cantor's income was very slender, and could hardly have amounted to more than £70 a year, even when funerals and weddings with musical adjuncts were plentiful, and when the curious custom of the scholars going round the town to collect money for singing (of which the cantor was allowed a small share) was productive of satisfactory results.

At the time of Bach's appointment the St. Thomas School had been for some time in a very unsatisfactory state. Inasmuch as it was a charity school for poor children as well as a nursery for choir boys, it drew on a low class of children for the supply. Till just before his coming, accommodation had been inadequate, illness frequent, and insubordination general. Some efforts had been made in the direction of amendment, but the evil traditions were not successfully extirpated, and it is evident that Bach had no very easy or pleasant task in dealing with his charges. This is illustrated by frequent references during his Leipzig period to his lack of success in keeping the boys in order, inadequate musical results, and distaste on his own part for the trying responsibilities which were imposed upon him. As a teacher of individual young musicians the remarkable list of his pupils proves him to have been pre-eminent, and his personal influence to have been powerful; but as a master of unruly choir boys, who were incapable of being impressed by his personality, he was unsuccessful, and his lack of success gave him a distaste for his work in that direction.

But his discomforts did not end there, for he was constantly at variance with the town council and other authoritative bodies and individuals on the subject of fees, on the arrangement of his duties, and even on such a subject, not unknown to modern organists, as the choice of hymns, which he maintained to be in his province, and which the subdeacon of St. Nicholas's Church claimed to be his prerogative. One effect of these differences and disputes is the existence of a large number of documents in the shape of letters and memoranda by Bach himself, which are of value as illustrating decisively some of his personal characteristics. As the points dealt with are comparatively unimportant, the letters need not be quoted in full, but they show a rather surprising amount of practical qualities, common-sense, power of forcible statement expressed in a quaintly clumsy style, and also a certain native liveliness of temper. Besides the above drawbacks to the even flow of his existence may be mentioned the fact that the instrumentalists available for the band accompaniments to the church cantatas and for the performance of such instrumental music as was required for the church services seem to have been but indifferent performers.

He himself drew up a remarkable memorial for the Leipzig Town Council in 1730, dealing with the whole range of the musicians required for the adequate performance of church music; in which he deals with the band at his disposal, and indicates what it ought to be. He defines the situation characteristically by saying:

> "The 'Numerus' of persons appointed for the church music consists of eight; as four town pipers, three skilled violinists, and one apprentice. Discretion deters me from revealing anything near the truth as to their quality and musical knowledge; however, it is a matter to be considered ('consideriren') that they are partly past their work and partly not in such 'exercitio' as they rightly should be."

He then gives the names of the performers and the instruments upon which they performed, which shows that he had at his disposal the singular collection of two trumpets, two violins, two hautboys, and a bassoon, and he follows up the list by remarking that "thus there are wanting the following instruments which are necessary, some for strengthening the tone and some for playing parts which cannot be left out, to wit, two first violins, two second violins, two who can play viola, two violoncellos, one double bass, and two flutes." When the standard of the instrumental accompaniments which he was accustomed to write for his church compositions is recalled, it may be seen that a band so grotesquely inadequate must have been a very sore trial to him.

In the same memorandum he refers to the manner in which he had endeavoured to supply the serious deficiencies of the band by having the scholars taught the missing instruments; and he further points out that such a procedure seriously impaired the adequacy of his choral forces, as the boys who were taken for the instruments were also badly wanted to sing. The choirs required for the respective churches were none too large to begin with, few of them were musically efficient, and several singers were frequently absent ill, "especially at this time of year (August), as can be proved by the recipes written by the 'Schul Medico' in the Apotheke." The council indeed seem to have had very inadequate ideas of what was required for the effective performance of the music in the churches, and grudged the expense which would be entailed by putting things on a proper footing.

The fact that the above report was written some years after he came to Leipzig does not justify the inference that the state of affairs had been better in the intervening years. The disorganisation of the musical forces which were at his disposal was from the very first most disheartening, and it is not surprising that he gave more of his time and energy to composition than to the hopeless and uncongenial task of endeavouring to coerce choir boys and mere units of a street band into singing and playing the loftiest and most exacting music. Composition was the higher duty of the cantor, and no cantor endowed that office with a greater radiance of glory than J. S. Bach. But the average contemporary official mind was not adapted to gauge the higher achievements, and only felt that he fulfilled his lower duties inadequately. Yet the impulse within him to develop his artistic personality by the constant exercise of his powers in composition was not checked in the least. The drawbacks of his position serve mainly to make the unabated spirit with which he maintained his life's work the more impressive.

It is conspicuously noticeable that from the very beginning of his time at Leipzig Bach attacked a comparatively new sphere of art with an energy and a productivity which are almost incredible; as it was on his taking up his duties there that the profuse outpouring began of the greater portion of the church cantatas, which, from the point of view of mere quantity, form much the largest part of all his compositions. And it is further to be observed that the cantatas of the Leipzig period represent, in the main, a different attitude of mind from that which is evinced in the earlier cantatas. One effect produced upon him by his being in a city of wider importance and wider connection with the world at large was that his style and method became in a sense more cosmopolitan, and lost for a time something of their unalloyed Teutonic quality and the subjectivity of the essentially personal Bach. Such an outcome is obviously quite in accordance with what would happen in other phases of human activity. The characteristic race-qualities naturally linger strongest and longest in those towns and localities which are least in touch with the outer world. The surroundings of his earlier posts and the attitude of mind of the people with whom he had lived were more absolutely Teutonic in respect, at all events, of church music. But Leipzig was not only a place which attracted foreign ideas. It had long had opportunities to develop operatic tastes. It had had an opera house of its own since 1693, and apparently the wealthier inhabitants availed themselves also of the opportunity to attend the opera houses at Dresden and Weissenfels as well, and the taste for the Italian style thereby insinuated itself. And once rooted it began subtly to creep into the style of church music, as it had done in Roman Catholic places.

Moreover the contamination, for such it was in Teutonic church music, was assisted by G. P. Telemann, who, before Bach came to Leipzig, and before he himself was very near being appointed cantor, had been organist and director of the music in the New Church, which has been referred to above. Telemann, a facile and commonplace composer, totally devoid of the fervour of religious thought which was the characteristic of the out-and-out Teutons, was quite in sympathy with the taste which gravitated in the direction of Italian style. He used his opportunities at the New Church to introduce that style into the church music, with notable success as far as the public was concerned. The easy-going, flimsy music attracted the unthoughtful crowd, and the services became popular; just as in modern times services have become popular in which vapid and sensuous sentimentalities have been performed. The demoralisation, moreover, spread in a manner particularly awkward for the cantor of St. Thomas's, for, as before said, that school had to supply the choir boys for the New Church, and though only the lower division of the scholars sang at the New Church, the boys who began in the lower ranks of the school would in due time rise to the upper, and then join the choir of St. Thomas's. So the likelihood was that by the time they were artistically fit to serve under the cantor's direction they had become thoroughly imbued with the taste for the operatic style. Its gaiety and *insouciance* naturally appealed to young minds much more than the severity and deep feeling of the style which is more appropriate to devotional purposes and more consonant with the true spirit of the Reformed Church in Germany.

This style was evidently labouring under very serious disabilities at the time when Bach came to Leipzig, and it is probable that but for the depth and persistence of his artistic convictions the music of the Churches of St. Thomas and of St. Nicholas would have become Italianised altogether. But, nevertheless, it must be recognised that the principles of Italian art, in its broader and more substantial aspects, influenced him considerably; and in the first few years at Leipzig he endeavoured to accommodate his church cantatas to the prevailing taste in Leipzig. The superficial aspects of style and diction could not make any appeal to a disposition so spacious and inwardly dignified. He regarded the Italian opera as a sort of light amusement. His view of it is summed up in the tradition of his asking Friedemann if they should go over to the Dresden opera and hear the pretty little tunes. That a style with such associations and, indeed, of such flimsy character, could be employed for such exalted purposes as the services of the church appeared to him, as must be seen even by superficial minds, to be impossible.

Nevertheless, John Sebastian was not above learning from anyone whatever. If someone else in a light mood which was uncongenial to himself could hit upon an artistic device or process which he saw could be adopted with advantage in his more serious work, the fact of the attitude of mind being uncongenial would not hinder him from profiting by whatever was good in the product. Though the Italians took their music much more easily than the Teutons, their native musical aptitude enabled them to be pioneers in many respects, and whatever the actual intrinsic quality of their operatic products, the principles of form and organisation, the modelling of melodic phrases, even the manipulation of tone quality of various instruments and the development of instrumental style were, in their earlier stages, almost entirely in their hands. The more serious attitude of Northern nations towards art caused them to be more particularly concerned with actual ideas, thoughts, and with the expression of the deepest emotions. For the general foundation and methods of the art itself the Northern races had to learn from the Italians. The essential problem for the Teutonic composer was to segregate the adaptable from the unadaptable; to adopt that which was of universal application and to eliminate what was purely Italian and local. The phraseology is always purely local. But the frequent temptation of a composer studying the works of a composer of another nation is to imitate and even reproduce the phraseology, together with such features as are common to the music of all people and nations whatever, and to drop those very things which are the indispensable guarantees of his sincerity, inasmuch as they are the tokens of the race to which he belongs.

German composers had been learning from the Italians for upwards of a hundred years, and in many cases they had failed to discriminate between the things of universal and the things of local application. They had adopted, for instance, the purely conventional ornamental flourishes in the solo portions of their church music, and they had not only adopted them but imitated their style and contours and even the verbiage of their details. The ideal function of ornament as an enhancement of expression quite escaped them, in observing that the purely barren use of ornament gratified superficial hearers. The same was the case with the texture of accompaniments and other secondary phases of art-work. The Italians being easily satisfied with broad general effect, and having but little disposition for dwelling lovingly on lesser details, accepted without any distrust the hundreds of formulas which served to give animation to the general aspect, which were common property.

There is probably no province in art which so strongly indicates the difference between Latin and Teuton as the attitude towards detail. The difference is perceptible in painting as in music. Even in degenerate forms the essential difference of mental and temperamental qualities is perceptible. For in degeneration the Teuton falls into the crowding of badly flavoured details, just for the sake of suggesting profusion of industry, and the Italian in degeneration falls into the complacency of conventional formalism and coarse and blustering vapidity.

The greater minds instinctively reject the superfluous and the ephemeral, and take counsel of the permanent and the universal; and in this sense Bach always assimilated the features and methods from types of national art which were of value. Just as he adopted the form of the French overture, and dealt with it so that the musical aspect of the work had a purely Teutonic ring, so he adopted from the Italians types of form and even some of the melodic types of contour without dropping into the weakness of imitating the phraseology. The difference between his works which were of the pure Teutonic mould and those in which he followed Italian models is that, in the former, the movements are not so clearly or decisively outlined, but follow the suggestions of the sentiment with more irregular disposition of the organic elements, aiming at what may be called psychological rather than mechanical form; in the works on the latter lines he throws his movements into very clearly marked divisions, and uses a less complex manner of building up the superincumbent lines of free counterpoint which represent the harmonic superstructure.

The feature which becomes most prominent in these cases is the type of form known as the aria, which had become over-familiar through the mechanical manner in which the Italian operatic composers had used it. Bach adopted it whole-heartedly, and managed in most cases to give it new significance and interest of variety; though it must be admitted that he not infrequently seems to use its conventions as a matter of course, and sometimes to adopt the *da capo* without due consideration, when the copiousness of his resources in extending the development of the separate sections causes movements to run to an almost impracticable length. It must be observed also that he applied the scheme of the aria now and again in choruses and even in instrumental movements; and also, often without actually adopting aria form, laid out his simpler choruses in definite and clearly indicated sections, which suggest harmonic bases in a manner more natural to Italians than to Teutons.

From this point of view it is interesting to compare the cantata *Du wahrer Gott*, which must have been written before he moved to Leipzig, and which he is said to have rejected on the occasion of his performing what is called his trial piece on February 7, 1723, with the cantata *Jesus nahm zu sich die Zwölfe*, which was actually performed on that occasion. The former occupies a peculiar position, as though of the Weimar type the period of its composition was probably separated from the Weimar time by the years at Cöthen mainly devoted to secular instrumental compositions. It has four numbers only. The first is a duet for soprano and alto accompanied by two hautboys and "continuo," overwhelmingly rich in expressive texture, and giving to the voice parts phrases which are essentially Teutonic in their tenderness and devotional expression. The movement is, indeed, very clearly designed, but the manipulation of the scheme is so deeply and individually thought out that it produces little of the impression of the Italian aria form. The stress that is laid on expressive detail distracts the mind from caring about the form. In the recitative which follows, the voice part expresses deep feeling in the manner of which Bach was supreme master; and a feature which is highly characteristic of the Teuton is the use of the short chorale *Christe, du Lamm Gottes* quite simply as the upper part of the harmonies which accompany the voice. It is done so naturally that it might be easily overlooked, but when observed it suggests an underlying thought which adds colour to the words: "*Ach, gehe nicht vorüber, du, aller Menschen Heil, Bist ja erschienen die Kranken und nicht die Gesunden zu bedienen.*" The device is Teutonic in that it makes use of a symbolic feature to widen and deepen the expression of the idea. The third number is a singularly melodious and flowing chorus, resembling in mood the beautiful chorus at the end of the "Matthäus-Passion," and the last number is founded on the same chorale, *Christe, du Lamm Gottes,* which had been used in the recitative. The chorale being, as before remarked, extremely short, is given three times: the first time with deeply expressive figures of accompaniment distributed between the two hautboys and the strings; the second time with different treatment of detail, including a canon in which oboes and violins answer the treble voices with the phrases of the chorale at the fourth below and third above; and the third time with yet further figures of accompaniment and new harmonisation of a very noble character, and the movement concludes with a richly polyphonic "Amen." As a subordinate feature it may be mentioned that the voice parts in the chorale are doubled throughout by trombones and cornetti. The whole cantata is exceptionally rich in feeling and interest, one of the most individual and expressive of all Bach's works of the kind, essentially and deeply devotional in the finest sense, and Teutonic and Protestant in the prominence of the chorale.

The cantata, *Jesus nahm zu sich die Zwölfe,* which he adopted in preference as his trial piece, is in five numbers. The scheme of the first movement, part of which at least is a chorus, is rather puzzling. After the short introductory passage, for one hautboy and strings, the tenor part makes the short declaration, which is the title of the cantata in ornate quasi-recitative, and the bass voice takes up the words of Christ, *Sehet, wir gehen hinauf gen Jerusalem,* in highly ornate style. There are no indications that it is for a solo voice, but it is obviously quite unfitted for a chorus to sing; and it is quite likely that Bach, as in many other obvious cases, either forgetting or ignoring in haste the fact that clear directions for the performance of his music would concern posterity as well as himself, omitted to write in the word which would have justified the personal character of the utterances. The solo itself is full of the feeling of foreboding induced by the thought of the last journey to Jerusalem, which is characteristically expressed by a figure in the accompaniment suggestive of wailing;—

Both parts are written on the chorus lines, but the sopranos and altos have nothing to do till the second division of the movement is reached, and then the style is completely changed, and, abandoning the rich characteristic treatment of the earlier portion of the movement, the composer adopts a style of the most simple character, and so totally devoid of independent instrumental interest that it might perfectly be sung "a cappella."

The impression the movement conveys, as a whole, is that Bach began it in one style, and that half way through he changed his mind and thought a simpler method more appropriate. But perhaps on account of the higher musical qualities of the first portion, and also perhaps for lack of time, he allowed the first portion to stand. The second movement is an aria constructed on the principles of the Italian form, with sundry apt modifications which tend at once to enforce the expression and infuse additional interest. The third is an accompanied recitative, of no great importance, but containing elaborate and rather conventional runs; the fourth is yet another aria for tenor with a characteristically lively tune, and the last movement is a chorale, *Ertödt' uns durch dein' Güte*, the harmonisation of which is in Bach's own unsurpassable manner. But unfortunately the voices are not left to produce their effect by themselves, but are accompanied by a flowing accompaniment of semiquavers which persists in a single part from beginning to end. The effect of a figure of the kind persisting without break or variety is often liable to become tedious, and in this case the situation is accentuated by the perpetual motion being maintained by the hautboy, whose poignant tones when long reiterated produce an effect of weariness, which in extreme cases amounts to physical distress. It is as though Bach had set himself to carry out a technical device, and the perfect mastery with which he consummated his object had afforded him the sense of justification to set his sign manual to it.

Full consideration of the two works suggests that when he realised, on coming to close quarters on the field of action, that the cantata *Du wahrer Gott und Davids Sohn* was unsuitable to be presented as his trial piece, he was driven to prepare another which would be better fitted for the occasion, but that his mind did not adapt itself at once to the more mechanical requirements of such a situation, and time did not serve to coerce it. The choice of a particular work in preference to another, especially when the work chosen was intrinsically inferior, emphasises his consciousness that a different type of art from that which he had hitherto adopted was needed for the new conditions. The two works throw light on two important phases in Bach's development. The earlier was spiritual in the deepest sense, and the second as far mundane as the occasion (which was not a cheerful one, being the Sunday immediately before Lent) would allow, and the ineffably spiritual John Sebastian could bring himself to be.

All highly organised musicians are deeply sensible of the temperamental affinities of their human environment; the difference between the higher and the lower types lying in the particular strata of that human environment which affect them. Like draws like. The lower order of artists of whatever kind seek the sympathetic response of human creatures of like standard with themselves, and the downward tendencies are enhanced by fellow feeling. The higher order of artistic minds, on the contrary, never cease the aspiration to rise, and find their cravings satisfied only in the sympathy of beings on a plane as high as their own; and that sympathy when it can be found beckons to ever higher flights and more perfect achievement. But there are a few rare individuals who cannot find the equal standard of insight, because, indeed, it does not exist in their own branch of mental activity. But it does not follow that they are conscious of the reason of their own isolation; for there is a great difference between being aware of a thing and being conscious of it. Such very rare beings only become aware that there is some cause which prevents the people with whom they are in contact from understanding and being in touch with the standard of their work, and it sometimes begets rage, and sometimes the disposition to ponder. In the latter case the temperamental question is whether it is worth while addressing deaf ears, either out of sheer individual pertinacity or in the hope that they may somehow come to hear in time; or whether it is possible so far to change the venue without besmirching that sacred thing, the artistic conscience, and approach the lower stratum of humanity in the terms that they are able to understand.

It is not necessarily lowering to a great poet to address an uncultured crowd of ignorant yokels in simple and direct terms, though his true mission may be to present the subtlest problems of human experience in terms which would be intelligible only to the cultured and the highly trained few. The deliberate choice of a low type of audience would certainly militate against the maintenance of the high standard of expression which is necessary for the utterance of higher thought, and, as is commonly observed with artists, poets, musicians, it before long atrophies the higher gifts. Still, if the situation be given and if it is necessary for the higher type of man to address himself to those masses who could not in these circumstances follow his higher flights of suggestive discourse, practical common-sense and instinct alike approve such approximation to the standard of insight as the situation and the nature of the man allow.

It can hardly be denied that the average quality

and style of Bach's cantatas after he went to Leipzig became different from his earlier style; and it must be admitted that in many cases they became less interesting. It might be argued that *Ich hatte viel Bekümmerniss, Gottes Zeit, Du wahrer Gott,* were the production of more spontaneous youthful fervour, and the later works the production of the mature artistic mind, and in some ways better balanced and more practically designed. It might, on the other hand, be argued that the necessity of writing new cantatas incessantly to meet the demands of the Sundays and the festivals rendered his work more mechanical, and made spontaneous poetic feeling less constantly available. In truth, both causes were no doubt operative, but it is well to try to see (mainly as a study of the personal disposition of the great John Sebastian) if the influences of the new environment had not a great deal to do with the change. And it is well also to keep in mind the fact that, even if in these church cantatas he adapted himself to the attitude of mind of the audience which he was bound to address, he in nowise abrogated his mystical Teutonic romanticism, and was yet destined to rise far higher than he had ever done into the regions of the very ecstasy of spiritual devotion in the "Matthäus-Passion," the B minor Mass, and some of the latest cantatas and works for the organ. The cosmopolitan influence is mainly to be looked for in his cantatas and church works which were written in such profusion for the services of the church at Leipzig before 1729.

The first works which, as far as can be ascertained, he presented before the congregation at Leipzig after he actually came into the active exercise of his duties as Cantor, tend to confirm the impression conveyed by his choice of his trial piece. Unfortunately the extraordinary uncertainty with which he wrote in all accessory directions and records, such as tempo marks, marks of expression, indications for manner or means of performance, and all such mechanical details as were superfluous as long as he was superintending the performance of the music himself, extended lamentably to the omission of details of the dates when any of his works were written. The date of his first appearance as Cantor-composer is supplied by the "Acta Lipsensium Academica" of 1723, which states that "The New Cantor and Collegii Musici Director, Herr Johann Sebastian Bach, who came from the Ducal Court of Cöthen, performed his first music here with great applause on the 30th of May on the first Sunday after Trinity." A later entry in the same records indicates that the performance took place in the Church of St. Nicholas.

It happens that there is no work which has that actual date, but there is a very imposing cantata, *Die Himmel erzählen die Ehre Gottes*, which is dated as for the second Sunday after Trinity of that very year, 1723; and there is also a cantata, *Die Elenden sollen essen*, which is marked for the first Sunday after Trinity, but without date. Conspicuous coincidences indicate that the date was 1723, and that the latter cantata was therefore the first of his works which was performed after he settled down to his duties. The undated cantata is not only on precisely the same scale as the dated cantata, and very similar in style, but the scheme is the same and the constituent numbers are almost identical in character and order; and, lastly, the trumpet has a part in each of such exceptional and prominent brilliance as is scarcely to be found in any other works by the composer. Both cantatas are divided into two portions, commencing with introductory choruses on a grand scale, of similar design; proceeding with alternate recitatives and arias; concluding the first half with a chorale; recommencing the several parts with an instrumental sinfonia (which in the dated cantata is marked to begin "nach der Predigt"), and, after further alternate arias and recitatives, concluding the whole with a repetition of the chorale which came at the end of the first part with different words. The instruments employed in the orchestra are also almost identical. Together with the strings there are parts for two hautboys. The oboe d'amore is employed in both—in the undated cantata in the aria "*Ich nehme mein Leiden mit Freuden,*" in the dated cantata, in the sinfonia at the beginning of the second portion of the work, and in the aria *Liebt, ihr Christen, in der That.* The trumpet, as before mentioned, has parts of exceptional prominence in both works. In the undated cantata it is used in the sinfonia at the beginning of the second portion of the work, and in the aria *Mein Herze glaubt,* in which, indeed, it has one of the most elaborate and brilliant parts to be found in any movement in the whole range of music, and more to do than the voice itself. In the dated cantata it has a brilliant and conspicuous part in the first chorus, in the aria *Fahr' hin,* and in the chorale which concludes both parts of the work. The instruments which are not common to both cantatas are the bassoon in the undated cantata, which has a subordinate part to play, and the viol da gamba in the dated cantata, which, both in the sinfonia of the second portion and the aria *Liebt ihr Christen,* has an important part in a duet with the oboe d'amore.

These many points of similarity in the two works make it extremely probable that they were written at the same time. It is common for all composers of any vigour of mind to work out methods, schemes of organisation, even types of melody, which have occurred to them as propitious, in different works which belong to one particular period of their lives; and, on the other hand, it is very unlikely that if Bach had written *Die Himmel erzählen,* in 1723 he would have written another cantata so similar in plan, type, and orchestration in another year. In any case there cannot be the least doubt, as the one cantata is dated, and the undated one is so like it in many respects, that the features they contain represent the standard of style and form which he thought suitable to the people of Leipzig; and it remains to take note of those qualities which are significant.

The first chorus in *Die Elenden sollen essen* begins in expressive style, evidently meant to be slow, though without tempo mark. There is an Italian flavour about the introduction, especially at the close, from which the chorus takes its beginning. The movement is practically in two portions: in the first the voices are mainly used in masses; and the second consists of a long and brilliant fugal portion, liberally furnished with semiquaver runs of truly portentous length and expressing vigorous jubilation. The polyphonic writing is, of course, superb, but, especially in the latter part, it bids for effect on the score of this brilliancy rather than of expression. The first movement of *Die Himmel erzählen* is all brilliantly jubilant, and its brilliancy is enhanced by the trumpet part. A tuneful passage is enunciated by bass solo and taken up by the chorus, and then as in the other case the movement comes to a decisive point in the middle, and solo voices take up a brilliant fugue, which after the complete exposition is joined by the chorus. It is splendidly rhythmic and vivacious polyphony of the most elaborate kind, such as Bach alone could produce; but it is also direct and straightforward, and makes its effect by the richness of combined passages, rather than by any actual interest in the thematic material. In both cases these movements are the most important, by reason of their grand scale, of any in the two works.

In both cantatas there are four arias. The first in *Die Elenden sollen essen* is on a very extensive scale with a complete *da capo* on the Italian principle; but the material is very melodious, and it is singularly simple in the treatment of the accompaniment. Among Bach's tenor solos it is quite exceptionally singable! The second, accompanied by the oboe d'amore, is plaintive and tuneful, and also has a complete *da capo*. There is a short and simple aria of charming quality in the second half, for alto with violin accompaniment, and the brilliant air with trumpet obbligato before alluded to. In the other cantata the first aria is a remarkable example of close consistency of material: as the figure to which the words *Hört, ihr Völker* are wedded in the voice part forms the main staple of the accompaniment throughout

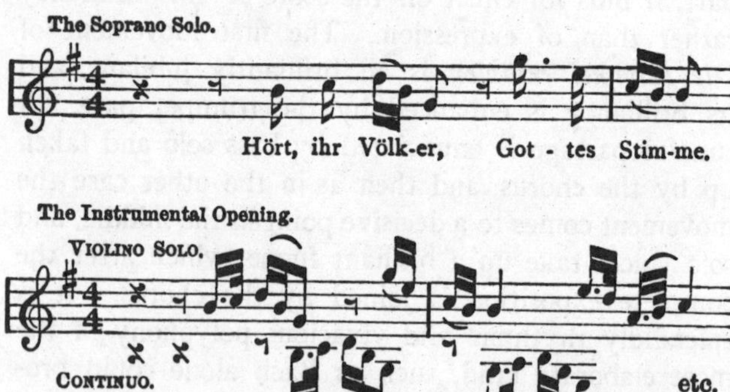

thus strengthening the essential meaning of the exhortation. The movement has yet again a complete *da capo*. In this case it is the second aria which is on the largest scale, being also made prominent, as before mentioned, by its brilliant trumpet part. Neither of the arias in the second part is of great importance, whether as regards material or development; though the effect produced by the duet of the oboe d'amore and the viol da gamba is decidedly picturesque and interesting. In both cantatas there are several recitatives which are for the main part in Bach's unique manner. They are not of equal interest, but the elocutionary sense, which with him ministered in the highest degree to the expression of the sentiment, is in many cases supremely displayed. In the second cantata recitative is twice combined with arioso, the form which is on the borderland between recitative and regular melodic aria, and in Bach's usage always supremely expressive.

In both cantatas the chorale which concludes both portions is fully accompanied with free parts for instruments. In the first cantata the sinfonia of the second half is made significant by the use of the same chorale tune, *Was Gott thut, das ist wohlgethan,* which had concluded the portion before the sermon.[1] This is given to the trumpet, with elaborate fugal accompaniment of the violins, thus at once happily establishing the connection of the part after the sermon with the part before it. In the second cantata the trumpet anticipates the chorale by playing a certain portion of it each time before the voices enter and then joining with them while they sing it. The sinfonia of the second portion of the second cantata is a very quiet but elaborate trio for oboe d'amore, viol da gamba, and continuo, containing a short adagio and vivace, and consisting of a continuous interlacing of characteristic figures after Bach's familiar manner in such a style.

The predominant impression of the two cantatas is that of immense technical mastery, brilliancy, directness, and power. The number of arias indicates the tendency towards decisive and clearly marked principles of design, and even the choruses show the same quality by reason of their division into two distinct portions. In such characteristics the influence of the new Leipzig environment seems to be expressed. The definiteness of the form, the brilliancy and directness of the manner, bespeak Bach's consciousness of new conditions. It need not be inferred that he abandoned

[1] This elaborately accompanied chorale was transferred later with various interesting amendments to the third cantata beginning with the words *Was Gott thut.*

his mystic devotionalism, or his gift of characteristic melody and harmonic progression, but he accommodated them in a manner which would make them more readily intelligible to the new kind of audience.

A cantata, *Ein ungefärbt Gemüthe,* which Bach appears to have produced a fortnight after the last of the preceding cantatas—that is, on the fourth Sunday after Trinity,—is of smaller scope and not very striking. The words, as Spitta points out, are not suggestive, and the movements, though masterly in detail, are not particularly sympathetic or characteristic in thematic material. It begins with an alto Aria, and there is a fairly extensive chorus in the middle in two distinct portions, the latter half of which is introduced by solo voices, and the chorale movement at the end is finely planned, with alternations of the vocal utterance of each phrase of the chorale with elaborate instrumental episodes. There are fine passages of recitative and arioso, and the trumpet is again made use of, as well as two oboi d'amore. The general features are manifestly similar to those of the previous cantatas.

Yet again, three weeks later, he produced the very extensive cantata in two parts *Aerg're dich, o Seele, nicht* which is more interesting and expressive, especially the first chorus, the words of which evidently appealed to him strongly. He uses the voices on an elocutionary principle similar to his methods in recitative, obtaining admirable expression of the sentiment in the manipulation of the independent parts. There are no less than three remarkable examples of arioso endings to recitatives in this cantata; which shows the persistence of Bach's personal gravitation.

This is borne out also by the Chorale which concludes the first part, as it has elaborate instrumental episodes between the Choral phrases, as well as imitative treatment in the voice parts.

A similar attitude of mind is indicated by the Cantata *Ihr die ihr euch von Christo nennet,* which was probably written for the thirteenth Sunday after Trinity in this year. The words are by Franck and are set for Solo voices, with no choral movement except the Chorale at the end. The most beautiful solo is the first for Tenor, which is in a more elastic form than the usual systematic Aria, and seems to be suffused throughout by the tender appealing phrase allotted to the first words. A solo for Alto accompanied by two flutes is also very expressive. The final duet for Soprano and Bass is in simpler style, and is founded on a phrase which has close affinity to the leading phrase of the Tenor solo.

The Cantata *Preise, Jerusalem, den Herrn* was probably written in 1723 for a "Rathswahl" festival, the day when a newly elected town council took up their official responsibilities,—a day which the municipalities of Europe in most countries used to celebrate with great pomp. Bach had already had experience of the kind of function, as one of his very first works on a grand scale for voices and orchestra had been the "Rathswechsel Cantata," *Gott ist mein König,* which had been written in 1708 for the festival of the change of town councillors of Mülhausen. (See p. 52.) The occasion was one which admitted of but one simple direct kind of treatment. And the admirable device of employing the form of the French opera-overture for the first movement was adopted again by the composer as it had been before in *Nun komm, der Heiden Heiland.* The grandiose manner of the slow opening passage is most eminently suitable for a big municipal function, and Bach's use of it on this occasion shows in a marked degree his power of adaptation. The slow passage moves with a singularly stately stride, with passages for four trumpets and drums interspersed with the long-drawn succession of ornamented suspensions allotted to the rest of the orchestra. The spirit of Lulli, who presided so often at the magnificent courtly functions of Louis XIV., seems to be not far away. But he takes his departure when the vocal portion begins, as his gift for making up a little imitation fugue with a snap subject is as far removed from Bach's supreme mastery of that form as the child's game of soldiers is from the duties of an active general. Bach, however, in this case scarcely makes any pretence of writing a genuine fugue. There is just the lead of a brilliant ornate subject by the basses, and it is then immediately taken up by the sopranos in the same part of the scale, the other voices having congenial lively passages to sing simultaneously. The procedure illustrates the common-sense of the composer. To have worked all through the technicalities of the exposition and other regulations of the fugal form, on such a civic occasion, would have been just the point in which the submissive follower of conventional responsibilities would have gone astray. Bach's clear recognition of the validity of adapting the artistic treatment to the situation is happily manifest, just as it is in his comprehensive rejection of the accepted regulations of fugue in the "Wohltemperirtes Clavier." The part which corresponds to the fugal portion of the

French overture is indeed quite short. It is jubilant and vigorous with rhythm and movement, such as clearly suggest the healthy animation commonly displayed by the masses of the public on such occasions; and, after due shouting by the crowd of ordinary folk, the slow and dignified portion—which seems to represent the distinguished burgher councillors—is resumed, and fitly completes a very suggestive movement on a scale which would have filled Lulli's soul with amazement.

As far as solo music was concerned, an occasion of the kind did not invite poetic fervour and deep feelings of loving devotion. The solo movement which strikes the attention most vividly is the recitative for bass, *So herrlich stehst du, liebe Stadt,* with brilliant flourishes for four trumpets—essentially a striking piece of appropriate declamation, of which the tradition most certainly runs back for centuries, and which also presents itself frequently in modern operas. There are two arias which are not especially significant, except in the fact that they are happily devised for contrast; and the last chorus, after a long introduction in which the four trumpets are very much in evidence, is effectually contrived of alternations of energetic passages for the voices with characteristic passages for the orchestra—all of it rich in texture, but direct, simple, consonant with the purpose for which it was written. The final Chorale is simple. The work is, indeed, carried out with quite remarkable adaptability to the conditions, and it seems as if the decorum of the procession and the formalities of quaint municipal self-complacency could be read through the lines of the music. But it represents Bach even more than the earlier cantatas of the Leipzig time in his public capacity—the lovable, tenderly poetic, personal Bach is necessarily in abeyance. The insistent prominence of his individual personality at such a moment would be clearly unsuitable; he accepts the situation and applies his comprehensive mind to enrich the work with the highest artistic resources that are appropriate.

Another work of similarly festal character can be also identified as belonging to this year. This is the cantata, *Höchsterwünschtes Freudenfest,* which was written for the opening and dedication of a new organ in the church of Störmthal, a place near Leipzig. The cantata is on very broad and extensive lines, divided like *Preise, Jerusalem, den Herrn* into two portions to enable the sermon to be preached in the middle. Yet again Bach adopts the form of the French overture for the opening chorus, allotting the portion corresponding to the adagio to the orchestra, and the fugal portion (which on this occasion more nearly resembles the Lullian type by having a very short subject) to the chorus, and then resuming a modified version of the opening passage with different distribution of keys after the choral portion, and bringing in the chorus for a final burst of three bars at the end with great and appropriate effect. There are three arias and a duet for soprano and bass in aria form, and several recitatives, one of which is for soprano and bass duet in the form of question and answer, after the manner of some of the dialogues of Hammerschmidt and Bach's own examples in the *Ich hatte viel Bekümmerniss,* etc. The first question will sufficiently indicate the manner of the procedure. The bass asks, "*Kann wohl ein Mensch zu Gott gen Himmel steigen?*" and the soprano answers, "*Der Glaube kann den Schöpfer zu ihm neigen,*" and so on. The treatment is quite simple, and the effect is obtained by the inflections of the voice parts without any enhancement by accompaniment.

For the rest, the materials almost throughout the work are of most appropriate type. The opening instrumental adagio is powerful and rhythmic with trochaic energy; the fugal chorus most brilliant, with flowing melodious episodes; the first aria for bass is exceptionally fine in its broad and characteristic melody and in the fulness and richness of the accompaniment; and the soprano aria, which is in gavotte rhythm, has also a beautiful, flowing melody with a natural grace which Bach was always happy in assuming. The duet in the second part is in minuet rhythm and has a graceful and pleasant flow. It is noticeable that a different chorale is given for the end of each part; and on this occasion Bach adopts the simple procedure, so often met with in his later cantatas, of merely doubling the voice parts with the instruments, thereby enhancing the volume of tone without further enhancement of the effect beyond the characteristic polyphony.

The cantata is worth dwelling upon, if only to observe how little Bach was inclined to relax the exercise of his powers in works written for special occasions. The multitude of empty conventional works which have been made for special occasions induces the world to look askance at works of this type and to anticipate that they will have little genuine value. But this cantata vindicates Bach's absolute sincerity in such matters. The occasion can hardly have been a very important one, or one on which a high degree of artistic interest would meet with appreciation. But the work gives the impression that he was not only in a happy vein but spared not the most strenuous exercise of his powers to make it worthy even of the most important of occasions, thereby disarming the anticipation that more frequent contact with a big public would lower the standard of his interest in his work. To a man of Bach's rare calibre the responsibility of being true to himself was of higher cogency than any consideration of the importance of the occasion; and though he was impelled to adopt a somewhat different attitude with regard to the presentation of his thoughts, the matter and the employment of artistic resource are always of the highest quality which the strenuous and loyal exercise of his faculties could provide.

This cantata was performed in November, and it is considered probable that before the end of the year Bach not only produced another cantata, *Christen, ätzet diesen Tag,* but also one of the most imposing and most famous of his church compositions, the Latin *Magnificat,* both of which works were written for Christmastide. It is obviously a very plausible inference that he would have made an effort to present works of exceptional calibre before the people of Leipzig at Christmas, on the first occasion when he was responsible for the music for that much beloved and joyous festival. The cantata is splendidly adapted for the occasion, being scored for a band which gave the finest opportunities for brilliant effect, with four trumpets and drums, and three hautboys and bassoon and strings. Moreover, much of the choral work is brilliantly jubilant, especially the first chorus, and both first and last choruses are cast in a very definite form, nothing less indeed than the aria form with full *da capo,* which is far more suitable for the expression of energetic joyfulness than for more introspective devotional purposes. The solo movements which occupy all the central portion of the cantata are also, for the most part, consistent in mood; a duet for soprano and bass being made especially brilliant with elaborate ornamentation. The whole work is strong, vigorous and masterly, in the style most characteristic of Bach's earlier Leipzig period. An exceptional feature is that it contains no chorale.

The *Magnificat,* which is the most important church work Bach had produced up to this time, is on lines for which the recent Leipzig cantatas above described might have served for preliminary studies. The scheme is indeed very much like an expanded cantata of the Leipzig type. There are no less than six regular arias in it; the two grandest choruses are reserved for the beginning and end of the work, and the subordinate choruses, *Omnes generationes* and *Fecit potentiam,* come in as contrasts and serve to break the monotony of a succession of arias.

One thing must be admitted at the outset—there is no femininity about the work. There is hardly a bar which could be taken to suggest that Bach intended to emphasise any personal aspect of the hymn of the Virgin. His purpose seems rather to be to suggest the feeling that Christian worshippers in a body adopt the hymn as an expression of praise, gratitude, and joy for themselves. This had, in course of time, become the effect of the usage of the hymn for ecclesiastical purposes in the Roman Church. The multitudes of composers who had set it had all treated the original source and personal intention of the hymn as a negligible quantity. Such a subtle idea as the musical presentation of the humility, the proud joy, the exultation, the womanliness, and the wonder of the unique position which the Gospel narrative gives as the occasion for the hymn, would probably be too modern for any composer before the twentieth century to concern himself with. As a matter of fact the *Magnificat* had become a very special expression of congregational adoration—an act of worship, illustrating in a high degree the manner in which the religious attitude discards external anomalies or inaptness of mere verbal details and accepts the spiritual meaning, the devotional mood, the general mental tone of symbolic utterances as its own. Such a momentary detail as the personal expression, "respexit humilitatem ancillæ suæ," passes almost unnoticed, while the rest of the words of the hymn suggest nothing that is inappropriate to a male worshipper. An analogous situation is frequently met with in the recitation of the Psalms, and though the personal aspect is more in evidence in the *Magnificat,* the fact that Bach accepted the conventional usage is consistent with the large-minded and liberal common-sense which was one of his characteristics.

It is not to be supposed that Bach consciously adopted any particular attitude towards the works which he set. It seems to please a lightly thinking world to assume that both vicious and virtuous courses of action are deliberately adopted with full and careful weighing of each step; but the consistency of conduct which is often observable is generally the result of mere deeply rooted qualities of disposition. When a man works quickly and spontaneously, the little predispositions which are always pulling in special directions have the fullest opportunities to act.

It may not be in accordance with the usual conception of Bach's powerful and independent character, but countless small traits in his music indicate that he was very susceptible to external influences, both small and great. Among other things, he was extremely susceptible to the style and meaning of the words he set. When the sentiments they expressed were noble, pathetic, devotional, or tender, and were put into adequate language, his music revealed the complete concurrence of his mind. When the words were dry and mechanical, he sometimes saved the situation by putting into them far more meaning than was intended by the authors—more often by making his setting of them ingenious or interesting from an artistic point of view. Analogously, when he was writing music to German words his style was most frequently Teutonic, and when he was setting Latin words he was influenced by their familiar association with music in the Italian style. He had studied the works of many distinguished Italian composers and had even copied them out, and, as he was always ready to learn from anyone who could teach him anything, he not only adopted from them principles of form, such as are shown in the aria, but he also occasionally allowed the style of their treatment of voices to influence him (p. 349). But in this connection it is to be observed that his polyphony was always much richer and more free and forcible than anything which the best Italian composers could produce; and it must be admitted that he allowed himself characteristic roughnesses and angularities which they would have regarded both as unsingable and artistically inexpedient.

The change which has been indicated in the cantatas of the first year at Leipzig was in an Italian direction, and this tendency, combined with the Latinity of the hymn, caused the music of the *Magnificat* to gravitate even more strongly in the same direction. This is apparent in the conspicuously diatonic character of the choruses. The influence comes especially to a head in the massive conclusion of the chorus *Fecit potentiam,* which is, in principle, just like the familiar device of the slow closing passages of massed harmonies in Handel's works. It is also obvious in the quasi *a cappella* chorus, *Sicut locutus est.* It may also be frequently felt in the solos. The romantic and humanly expressive Teutonic sentiment is hardly ever apparent in them, and they are for the most part built up with polyphonic complexity, of clearly marked melodic figures. The character of the first chorus is most strangely free from any suggestion of the personal implications of the hymn. The rushing passages of the violins, which form such a striking feature both at the beginning and end of the work, are quite conspicuously multitudinous—as if he wished to suggest the exultation in the word "magnificat" to be the utterance of vast numbers of worshippers. The vein of vigorous and healthy exultation was one which was most congenial to him, and he makes the several voices alternately express it in florid phrases, and in short, incisive and joyous shouts, the whole being worked out on splendidly broad and satisfying lines. The solos often express the sentiment very happily, as, for instance, the *Exultavit* and also the soprano solo

Quia respexit, where the occurrence of the word "ancilla" perhaps induced for the moment a more personal quality. And again he shows himself curiously susceptible to the suggestion of a conspicuous word. He interprets the word "deposuit" by a downward run, which becomes one of the most persistent features of the aria commencing with that word. The duet *Misericordia,* in spite of the soothing effect of the beautiful accompaniment of the two flutes and muted viola, seems to be in a strain of rather excessive melancholy, as if he had been more influenced by the individual word than by the hope and confidence which the unquenchable mercy promised to all generations might inspire. So also the word "Gloria" in the final chorus seems to have inspired him with the idea of the expansion of all-embracing splendour of glory, which he suggests by piling up the voices in superincumbent passages of triplets, from low bass notes upward to the high soprano entry, which completes the mighty final chord—a process which he repeats twice with interesting modifications, so providing for the three clauses—that is once for each person of the Trinity. The second half of the *Gloria* aptly links the end of the whole work to its beginning, by reverting to the multitudinous figures, which, combined with the new passages adapted to the final words of the *Gloria,* makes a splendidly rich and vigorous conclusion.

It may perhaps be said that he was right in not endeavouring to associate the Latin words with an essentially Teutonic style of music. At that time it would certainly have seemed unnatural. Even much later, Beethoven himself was influenced by Italian style when he set Latin words. But in neither case is the individuality of the composer sacrificed.

The *Magnificat* is Bach's first work on a grand scale illustrating an expansion which was being manifested in some of his work, and ultimately bore even nobler fruit in the colossal B minor Mass. In some senses it may be regarded as a preliminary step in that direction. The highest possibilities were only to be obtained by the fusion of Italian methods with German earnestness. The mission of the Latin races in such matters had been mainly to supply those externals which are serviceable for practical purposes; the mission of the northern races has been to attend to the spiritual. The parallel is found in the forms of religion which have proved congenial to the Northern and Southern races respectively. The Roman Church made use of every possible resource which can appeal to the eye by ceremonial, and by all the panoply of vestments, jewels, gold and silver, banners, processions, histrionic disposition of gaily bedizened priests and functionaries, and such things as dazzle and intoxicate the senses. The typical Northerners were so ardent after the spiritual that in many cases they ruthlessly swept away everything that could appeal to the senses at all. They rejoiced in the ascetic triumph of making their places of worship bare of even the mere courtesies of devotion and of ornament. The reaction from the excess of materialism of the old order impelled them to forget how much the spiritual is capable of being helped by the association of externals; what romantic and poetic and emotional vistas are opened up by concrete symbols; what trifling concessions to the cravings of the physical nature can enhance susceptibility to the spiritual. But to the highest achievements attainable by man in any products of art or intellect diverse orders of human disposition must minister.

The Italian and the Teutonic artistic dispositions are, after all, merely two types out of many, but they embody the most extreme and strongly marked differences in artistic bias. And for the attainment of the highest manifestations of artistic quality as presented to the world in the works of such masters as Handel, Bach, Mozart, Haydn, Beethoven, and Wagner, it was inevitable that the predominating racial instinct or temperament should admit a considerable fusion of alien qualities. Just as the opportunities of Bach's earliest posts had favoured his gifts in the direction of organ music, as the appointment at Cöthen had favoured the latent powers which bore fruit in secular instrumental compositions, so now the Leipzig appointment, with its more copious opportunities of public performance, brought out those qualities in the composer which enhance the spiritual by the resources of the practical.

The "Magnificat" marks an important point in the process of assimilation which was, in course of time, to bear such phenomenal fruit. But it also presents the Italian phase of Bach's development more strongly than the German; the active and formal more than the reflective and spiritual. It is grand and imposing as a work of art rather than as a sympathetic manifestation of the individual John Sebastian.

Before leaving the subject reference must be made to curious interpolations which one of the manuscripts shows to have been made in the performance with special reference to Christmas-tide. No less than four different numbers seem to have been introduced. After the *Exultavit* there is a note: "N. B. Alhier folget der Choral *Vom Himmel hoch;* and after the *Quia Fecit*, "Hierauf folget '*Freut euch und jubilirt*'"; after the *Fecit potentiam*, "Hierher gehört das '*Gloria in excelsis Deo*'"; after the *Esurientes*, "Hierauf folget '*Virga Jesse floruit.*'" The first of these is absolutely Teutonic. The version given is a perfect counterpart of the ideal Teutonic form of the Choralvorspiel, only transferred to four voices. The chorale is sung in long notes and the other voices accompany it in free counterpoint, mainly contrived out of passages based on the figures of the tune. The second referred to is a joyous little chorus for five voices. The *Gloria in Excelsis* is also a chorus in five parts, and the *Virga Jesse* is the first four lines of an ancient Latin hymn set for duet between soprano and bass.

It was an ancient custom to bring home to the worshippers by realistic devices the events which became prominent at certain festivals of the year. Such had especially been notable in the performance of the Passion in Holy Week. But they had also been customary at Christmas, when such histrionic effects were adopted as the bringing of a manger into church, making the choir-boys proclaim the advent of Christ in the guise of angels, and priests or grown-up members of the choir represent shepherds. It was in consonance with this spirit that these strange and somewhat inconsistent interpolations were made. That they would be apt to the season of Christmas may be readily admitted, but their use can only be taken as illustrating Bach's disposition rather than his artistic sense. They can in no sense be taken as forming part of the work, but as things which at a certain season were introduced from outside with reference solely to that season and having no inherent connection with the work itself. Spitta suggests that the four numbers were sung by a small choir in the organ loft of the second organ of St. Thomas's Church—if so the effect would have been picturesque and interesting. But while it is quite possible that this procedure was adopted, there is no direct evidence in its favour, and the circumstantial evidence is of the very slenderest.

Unsubstantiality of evidence unfortunately prevails also in connection with most of the compositions which are attributed to this period of Bach's life. It is thought probable that the important cantata *Dazu ist erschienen* was written for the second day after Christmas, and even that another, *Sehet, welch' eine Liebe,* was written for the day after that. If that was so, Bach's activity must indeed have been preternatural; as it implies his having anticipated long beforehand so completely as to get the three large works ready, and also to copy the parts and get the forces required adequately prepared for the performance of three extremely difficult works in the space of four days.

The two cantatas are distinguished by the peculiarity that several different chorales are introduced into each of them at various points; which is noticeable because Bach generally identified each cantata with one chorale only, to concentrate and intensify the impression and the spirit of the words associated with it. The first chorus in *Dazu ist erschienen* is especially fine, comprising a massive, almost homophonic, opening portion and an elaborate fugue in the middle, and there is a fine solo for bass, *Höllische Schlange*, and also a very interesting recitative for alto solo, with elaborate accompaniment, and a joyous aria for tenor, *Christenkinder. Sehet, welch' eine Liebe* is not intrinsically so interesting or elaborate, but the chorales are beautiful; and the last, wherein the words *Gute Nacht, O Wesen* are sung to the tune of *Jesu, meine Freude*, is peculiarly touching in its suggestiveness. The first version of *Sie werden euch in den Bann thun* also contains two different chorales for Tenor Solo and the usual Choral ending, respectively. The two initial Choruses are very strong and interesting, especially the second.

The outpouring continued unabated at the beginning of 1724. A very imposing work, *Singet dem Herrn ein neues Lied*, is attributed to New Year's day, which would be only a few days after the performances of several of the cantatas above referred to. The score is incomplete, as there are lines prepared in the first chorus for trumpets and drums and hautboys, but no parts for them. However, in other respects the composition is adequately presented. The first chorus has a massive opening and a fugue, ending with a vigorous "Alleluja." The second number is a chorale, *Herr Gott, dich loben wir*, for the chorus in unison, with passages of recitative alternating with its phrases. There is a gay aria for alto with a charming tune, and other solo movements, and a full and grandiose chorale with a blaze of trumpets (here written out in full) to end with. The cantata appeared to Bach important enough to have it reproduced with some enhancements in 1730 for the Jubilee of the Augsburg Confession. The cantata *Schau', lieber Gott* for solo voices interspersed in an unusual manner with chorales, of which there are three, is attributed to January 2d; *Sie werden aus Saba,* a cantata of large dimensions, with very elaborate work for the voices in the first chorus, is attributed to January 6th; yet another, *Mein liebster Jesus,* which contains several beautiful and expressive arias, to January 9th, and a cantata of even exceptional beauty and interest, *Jesus schläft,* to January 30th.

The last indeed is so highly characteristic of Bach's treatment that it deserves fuller consideration. It is closely connected with the Gospel narrative of the day, and the sleep of Jesus in the storm-tossed boat on the Lake of Gennesaret, the terror of the disciples, the awakening, and the words "O ye of little faith!" and the grand assertion of the ever-present power to save, are dealt with in a symbolical sense, as applicable to all Christians. The cantata begins with a pathetic aria for contralto expressing the trouble of the soul while the Saviour seems to sleep, ending unconventionally on a discord.

A tenor recitative expresses the anxious question of the soul in perplexity, *Herr! warum bleibest du so ferne.* A brilliant aria for the same voice, with rushing passages for violins, gives suggestion of the disturbance of the elements, obviously intended figuratively. Thereon follows a very noble and serious arioso for bass, conveying the reproving words, "O ye of little faith!" and an aria for the same voice commanding the elements to be still. A short recitative for alto conveys the meaning of the words, "Wohl mir! mein Jesus spricht ein Wort," and the cantata is completed by an exceptionally beautiful and elaborate version of the chorale tune *Jesu, meine Freude,* the aptness of which to the symbolism of the work as a whole is obvious.

It would seem to trespass on the limits of credibility to suggest that Bach would have another important work ready by February 2nd. But the arguments seem valid enough to justify the attribution of the first performance of *Erfreute Zeit* to that date. It is not so interesting as the previously mentioned work, but full of vigour and decisiveness, and manifests kindred features with the "Magnificat." Speculative enterprise as well as the influence of Leipzig may have impelled him to make use of the form of the Italian concerto in the first chorus of the cantata.

The first of the three Cantatas beginning with the words *Was Gott thut* probably belongs to this period. Its scheme is peculiar. It has no final Chorale; but as the first Chorus resembles a type frequently met with in final Chorale-movements, it may have been an experiment in transposition.

Over and above the colossal amount of production

in the special line of church cantatas, the year 1724 is notable (if the arguments and inferences in favour of the date are valid) for the first performance of the "Johannes-Passion," Bach's first essay in the form of "Passion Music." It is true there is no proof positive of the date; but if the arguments in favour of its having been 1724 are somewhat intricate and unconvincing, the arguments in favour of any other date are not forthcoming.

The first composition of J. S. Bach of this kind is of very great interest for many reasons. The most obvious reason is that he achieved the one great work which stands absolutely alone and unapproachable as the ideal of this form of art, and that this achievement was, as in so many other cases, the fruit of the gathering up of previous experiments, of which the "Johannes-Passion" is the penultimate in point of scale and style. Another reason is that this branch of composition is the most copious manifestation in any form of art of the essential qualities of pure Teutonic devotionalism; its sentiment, its love of symbolism, its reflective absorption in mystical fancies, its human qualities, and the peculiar conception which Teutonic Protestants had established as their ideal of the relation between man and Christ. Of the long growth towards this idea Bach was the product, and after the long development of his own powers by the study of the music of other nations in other phases of art he proved that he had forgone none of his own birthrights as a Teuton, but had so completely assimilated and absorbed the methods of art into his own power that they minister without traces of anything incompatible to the ultimate triumph of the Teutonic ideal.

The reformation in Germany was, among other things, an attempt to purge religion from the crude traces of primitive superstition which, though sanctified by an immense tradition of years and highly interesting as showing the continuity of successive forms of religion, were better suited to Latin and Southern races than to the Northerners, whose intellectual perceptions and instinct for critical verification were so much more vivacious. The instinct of the Teutonic Protestant was to get away from all the hagiology and the paraphernalia and external accessories of the Roman form of Christianity, and to reinfuse the story of Christ's life and teaching with vivid reality, most especially in its human aspect. In some ways the difference between the two forms of the religion may be summarised in the sense that Southern imaginativeness was projected to the idea of the Godhead which was made man, and Northern earnestness was inspired by the idea of the manhood which manifested the Divine. In the one conception the multiplication of an infinity of supernatural artificialities is entailed, in the other the unlimited brooding on the ideal possibilities of the ideal human character. The one suggests abasement before the infinite magnificence of the Godhead, the other the deep love for the manhood.

The growth of the "Passion" form shows the bent of the race. The Reformed Church inherited from the Roman Church the tradition of presenting the story of the "Passion" with sundry slight histrionic devices to bring it home to the minds of the worshipper. In the week devoted to the contemplation of the final episodes of the tragedy which touched the souls of humanity so deeply, the story as told in the Gospel was broken up into the component elements of narrative and actual words spoken by individuals and distributed to various members of the officiating priests and the choir. So that the mere narrative portion was taken by one person, and the words used by various individual characters were taken severally by others, while the words of groups of people of any kind were taken by the choir, which in that aspect was known technically as the "Turba."

The tradition of the employment of music in the performance is so ancient that it reaches back into the ages where tangible records cease. Such music was inevitably of the same description as all the rest of the "plainsong," consisting mainly of monotone recitatives with archaic formulas of cadences, and occasional passages of more elaborate melody at special salient points of the story. Teutons have always found this type of religious art congenial, as is shown by their love of miracle plays, "Marienklagen," and kindred exhibitions in the middle ages; so the "Passionsmusik" form was retained, like many other features of the Roman Church, by the Protestants, and very soon characteristically amplified. The number of German composers who addressed themselves to the composition of Passion music is a striking proof of its congeniality to the race. Beginning as early as 1530, within six years of being called by his friend Luther to advise on the music of the Reformed services, Johann Walther produced settings of the Passion according to St. Matthew and St. John, and before the end of the century many German composers added compositions of the same kind, which became more elaborate and graphic as time went on.

Among those which followed soon after Walther's

should certainly be mentioned the "Historia vom Leiden und Sterben unseres Herren und Heilandes Jesu Christi," etc., by an otherwise unknown composer, Bartholomäus Gese, because it represents very artistically a scheme which must have been much in vogue. The story is told by the Evangelist in monotone, diversified by simple formulas like those of the ancient church, which are so consistently used that they give a faint suggestion of methodical form to the indefinite monotony of the intonation. The most prominent are the following:

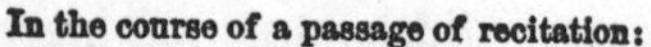
In the course of a passage of recitation:

Mit Fackeln, Lampen, und mit Waff - en

The close of the same passage being as follows:

Gieng er hin - aus und sprach zu ihn - en

And again corresponding to the first of the above in another place:

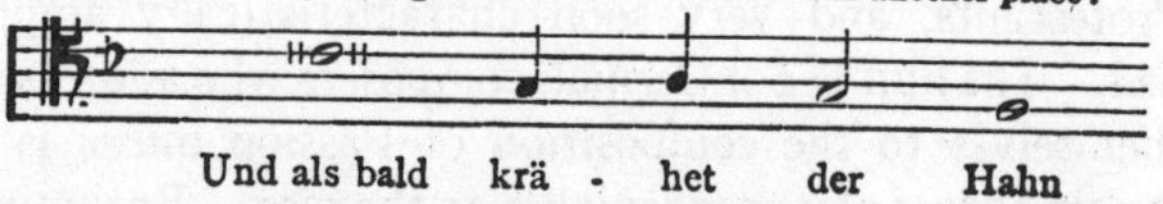
Und als bald krä - het der Hahn

And corresponding to the second of the above:

Sie antworteten und sprach - en zu im,

The work is peculiar in the use of the chorus for purposes other than the traditional "Turba," inasmuch as the words of Jesus and Peter and Pontius

Pilate and other individuals, as well as those of the Jews, are given to the choir in various numbers of parts. The proceedings are initiated by a very solemn prefatory chorus, to the words "Erhebet eure Hertzen zu Gott, und höret das Leiden unsers Herren Jesu Christi," etc. After the consummation of the tragedy with the words "Und neiget sein Haupt und verschied," the music is stopped for a time and silence enjoined for a sermon; after which the "Evangelist" resumes the recital and tells of the removal of the body to the tomb, where the story stops. And the conclusion is made by a simple final chorus, to the words "Dank sei dem Herren, der uns erlöset hat durch sein Leiden von der Hellen."

A striking landmark is the group of Passions according to all the four Evangelists by Heinrich Schütz, which must have been written soon after the middle of the seventeenth century. They represent the phase of development when the form had become thoroughly Teutonised and had not yet assimilated the newly expanding methods of Italian art. These works consist of archaic formulas of recitative, probably Teutonic, distributed to the various characters and interspersed by occasional unaccompanied choruses in five parts whenever the "Turba's" utterances come into the narrative; each work being prefaced and concluded by an unaccompanied chorus in more or less polyphonic style, to words which are either explanatory or commentatory. The range of artistic method is limited in the extreme, but the works nevertheless have considerable fascination through the consistency and sincerity of the style and the beauty of the expression. Schütz indicates the direction in which the treatment of the form is progressing by introducing occasional moments of dramatic feeling, as in the choruses representing utterances of the Jews and of the Apostles. This type of Passion music is more amply illustrated in the "Resurrection," also by Schütz, in which instruments and rather more elaborate solo music are introduced. It is to be noted that in these examples there are no chorales. They, indeed, waited till a very striking transformation of the form came about in the course of the succeeding century.

It is characteristic of Teutonic disposition to dwell upon things which appeal to the feelings, and, as it were, to contemplate them from various points of view. The old method of Passion music was merely to go through the story without pause. The practice of pausing and contemplating came in late in the seventeenth or the beginning of the next century, when arias for solo voices, forming commentaries on salient features of the story, were introduced; and about the same time chorales were also introduced to enable the congregation to feel that they were taking part in the solemn function. Then, as time went on, the contemporary types of artistic method came in more and more, the archaic plain-song formulas were transformed into recitative, the dramatic choruses expanded, and the points where pauses were made to contemplate and emphasise the salient situations were more effectively utilised as composers mastered the modern Italian types of solo and found out how to make the chorale movements more effective and interesting. By the beginning of the eighteenth century the standard of art had become very comprehensive.

One of the earliest examples of the century was

Handel's first "Passion," which is, on good grounds, held to have been written in 1704. It is peculiarly interesting as illustrating his musical character and style before he felt the full measure of Italian influence and transformed his art to suit the taste of thoroughly un-Teutonic audiences. It might, indeed, serve as a touchstone for the standard of Passion music art before John Sebastian gave his mind to it. We find from it that the special type of expressive recitative, which was used with such supreme effect by Bach, was really founded on traditions of some standing. For Handel in this early work employs precisely the same peculiar type, which often hovers on the verge between the melodious and fully accompanied arioso and the purely elocutionary recitative. Indeed, in the early works, some of the quasi-recitatives are quite strikingly Teutonic in the fervour of their devotional and genuinely emotional expression. Handel's "Passion" also shows the full recognition of the aria in its contemplative aspect, as we here find several solos following essential points in the narrative. For instance, at the very outset of the work, after a very expressive recitative of the Evangelist to the words "Then Pilate took Jesus and scourged him," the soprano solo follows with the aria, "Sins of ours of deepest stain." After the recitative, "Then delivered he Him unto them to be crucified," follows the alto solo, "Take courage, soul, the love divine embracing." Handel even anticipates Bach in giving as the final chorus the words "Schlafe wohl, nach deinen Leiden." The only feature of the full panoply of the final form of Passion music which is not conspicuously in evidence is the use of the chorales, otherwise the scheme is quite complete, and the work is one of very great interest and full of expression.

In 1712, that is, some few years after Handel wrote his first "Passion," Reinhard Keiser composed music to text by B. H. Brockes, which was considered very admirable, and it was performed at Hamburg in that year and the following. The same text was again set by Handel later; and Kuhnau produced yet another "Passion according to St. Mark," in 1721, the last year of his life. The latter is said to have been more archaic in style, but contained many chorales.

The "Passion" form had thus expanded from simple beginnings to a very elaborate and subtle form of art before Bach came to Leipzig. Since he had been there he had developed his methods in church music, and though the date cannot be fixed with certainty, it is argued with much plausibility, as has been before mentioned, that the first version of his first "Passion," that according to St. John, was first performed in Holy Week in 1724. It is an interesting fact, as showing the manner in which Bach considered and reconsidered his great works when opportunity served, that the first version of the "Johannes-Passion" began with the noble and pathetic chorus, *O Mensch bewein' dein' Sünde gross!* which was afterwards transferred to the "Matthäus-Passion," where it concludes the first part. As it stands there it represents a very elaborate expansion of the chorale-fantasia type; the orchestral instruments having expressive figures which are maintained throughout, the trebles having a chorale tune in long notes, and the other voices supplying the choral polyphonic texture. The sentiment is absolutely Teutonic in its deep sincerity and pathos, and represents the composer in a most characteristic vein. He possibly removed it from the beginning of the "Johannes-Passion" because of its intimate and reflective character and its extreme elaboration of texture, and substituted the chorus which now stands at the beginning, *Herr unser Herrscher*, which is more massive and direct, and is therefore more suitable for the outset and point of departure of a work on such a grand scale. This chorus, like the initial choruses in earlier "Passions," stands apart as a sort of introductory comment; and is noticeably cast on the broad lines of an aria with a first part and a contrasting part and a complete *da capo*.

When it is over the actual story begins, the Evangelist, according to ancient practice, being the tenor soloist, whose office is to tell all narrative portions in true recitative, without a trace of the old plain-song or other archaic type of chanting; the characters of the tragedy, Jesus, Peter, Pilate, Pilate's wife, the false witnesses and others being allotted to various suitable singers. The voices of many people (after the ancient tradition) are allotted to the choir, which has many incisive outbursts in forms of utterance which are graphically realistic. Over and above the offices of merely dealing with the story, both choir and soloists have now the important duty to perform of keeping the mind occupied with the salient situations—the choir in the numerous chorales and the occasional commentatory choruses, and the soloists in the various arias which have the same function. The scheme, indeed, was not new, as the same distribution of solo movements is found in Handel's early "Passion"; but Bach was, even in the first example, importing a deeper devotional tone, a greater richness of expression, and a wider scope than had hitherto appeared in this form of art; and he was, moreover, speaking in the Teutonic manner which was natural to him, in recitative, aria, and chorus alike.

His resourcefulness in enforcing the meaning of the words by artistic devices is illustrated constantly, as, for instance, after the Evangelist tells of Jesus carrying the cross to Golgotha, follows the commentatory aria for bass, *Eilt, ihr angefocht'nen Seelen aus euren Marterhöhlen, eilt nach Golgatha* and the chorus break in with short ejaculations "Wohin? Wohin?" coming to the perfect application of the scheme when the pause on the word "wohin" throws the answer of the solo voice, "nach Golgatha," into poignant relief. So, again, in the bass aria which follows the words of the short recitative, *Und neigte das Haupt und verschied*, the choir make a kind of affirmatory comment with the chorale, *Jesu, der du warest todt*, on the words given to the soloist. And the whole work ends with a tenderly expressive chorus, *Ruht wohl* in the simple and definite form of an aria, and a final chorale.

In considering such a work as the "Johannes-Passion" Bach's use of his instrumental resources calls for some notice. The resources which he had at his disposal were, without doubt, the same as he would have had for any of his cantatas, among which three trumpets and drums and horns had frequently been prominent. But the attitude of composers of that time to the orchestra was altogether different from that of later times. It was usual then, as has been before mentioned, to choose particular groups of instruments for particular movements, and to spread the tone colour over wide spaces, when in modern music there would have been a constant shimmer of variety. A composer who really gave his mind to his work would choose the particular instruments which were most appropriate to the sentiment of the words and the character of the movement. This is obviously shown in the manner in which Bach as well as other composers reserved the trumpets for brilliant occasions, and for movements in which there is exuberance of rejoicing or praise. It is also illustrated by the fact that Bach omits them as well as the horns altogether from the score of the "Johannes-Passion." It was natural that, for a function, the object of which was the devout contemplation of the central mystery and tragedy of religion, he should choose instruments of more subdued tone, and he distributes them with evident consideration for the enhancement of the sentiment.

For the ordinary full work of accompaniments to choruses and chorales, flutes and hautboys join with the strings and organ, sometimes having separate parts, sometimes merely doubling the voices, and sometimes doubling the strings. Bach's habit in that respect must be admitted to be puzzling. It can only be inferred that he accepted the usual course in this matter, and it is strange that its many anomalies should not have arrested his attention. The flutes are often too weak for the work they have to perform when they wrestle in the polyphony on equal terms with the strings, while the flutes, hautboys, and strings, being doubled or even trebled in unison, only spoil one another's tone, and the persistent sound of the piercing hautboy becomes, as has been before remarked, positively distressing. But the distribution of the solo instruments in accompanying the arias is evidently carefully considered, both with the view of aptness to the sentiment and to the general plan of the work. Thus the first aria, which is in a tender, sad strain, is accompanied by two hautboys and figured bass; the second, in a bright and loving vein, is accompanied by the flutes doubled in unison passages. The third aria, in which much use is made of slow, expressive polyphony, is happily allotted to the strings; the solemnly pathetic arioso, *Betrachte, meine Seel'*, is accompanied by the unique and suggestive combination of two viole d'amore and lute, which must have had a sense of twilight stillness and quietude, truly admirable for the contemplation suggested by the words; the aria which follows is connected with the arioso by continuing the use of the viole d'amore, but the appearance of the lute in the work is restricted to the arioso. In the aria relating to the Crucifixion, *Es ist vollbracht*, the viola da gamba is employed; in the arioso, *Mein Herz*, following the reference to the earthquake and the veil of the temple being rent, the natural expedient is employed of strings tremolandi and rushing in rapid unison passages below chords for the flutes and oboi da caccia, and in the last aria *Zerfliesse, mein Herze* the two oboi da caccia are combined with flutes and the throbbing bass of the lower instruments. Thus each aria is accompanied by a different group of instruments, not only inducing contrasts in wide spaces, but, as it were, allocating a special colour to each reflective sentiment. The system presupposes long continuance in one vein of feeling, which is not altogether natural to modern audiences, and requires some revival, at least in imagination, of the conditions in which the work was produced.

It may also be said that without some such help it is difficult for a modern audience not to feel puzzled by the absence of a definite plan in the work as a whole. The work is Teutonic in its absence of quasi-architectonic features. Teutonic feeling was satisfied when each successive movement was full of meaning, and did not require any dramatic developments to crises, or formal and mechanical distribution of the components of the scheme, to satisfy the desire for form. It is noticeable that the mood and style show but little trace of the special line of work which Bach had done in the Leipzig cantatas and "Magnificat" which had preceded its production, and this may add weight to the theory that this "Passion" had been written before he left Cöthen. But, on the other hand, it is to be remembered that in this work he was on absolutely Teutonic ground, and that the great "Matthäus-Passion" which came later is equally free from traces of the Italian influences which sometimes peep out in the cantatas.

In the period which intervened between the production of the "Johannes-Passion" in 1724, and the great "Matthäus-Passion" in 1729 no conspicuous works on a similarly large scale can be proved to have come into existence. It can only be guessed with approximate certainty that Bach was mainly occupied in pouring out church cantatas with ceaseless activity; and, no doubt, a considerable portion of his time was spent in grappling with the awkward situations induced by the disorganisation of the St. Thomas School, and the inadequacy of the band which was at his disposal, and with periodical differences with the authorities.

The year 1724 was, without any doubt, a specially prolific year in respect of church cantatas, and new ones made their appearance immediately after the "Johannes-Passion." The first work which is surmised with fair measure of likelihood to have followed is the deeply impressive cantata, *Christ lag in Todesbanden,* which is allotted to the second day of Easter, 1724. In some ways it stands out from the usual scheme of Leipzig cantatas, and reverts to an earlier and more individual manner, for it is more archaic and severe in style, but of that archaicism and severity into which Bach could infuse so deep a meaning. And the meaning is intensified a hundred-fold by the fact that every movement is a kind of variation or fantasia on the tune of the chorale, wherein it is an isolated foretaste of the type of cantata which Bach adopted most frequently in his latest years, and indicates its essentially Teutonic character. The scheme is devoid of arias, but after the first chorus (which is a superb adaptation for voices of the form of the organ chorale-fantasia, ending with a vigorous "Hallelujah" as a sort of coda), two single voices (the soprano and the alto) take up a new treatment of the chorale broken up into short phrases; then follows the single tenor part with a more flowing treatment of the tune of the chorale to the words, "*Jesus Christus, Gottes Sohn, an unser Statt ist kommen, und hat die Sünde weggethan, damit dem Tod genommen.*" Then follows a chorus giving the chorale in short notes, fugally, then another movement for bass gives the tune in three time instead of four with a swinging gait, then the soprano and tenor take up the choral argument, developing it into exuberant flow of ornamental passages, and the whole is rounded off by the simple concrete presentation of the chorale in four-part chorus. The persistence of the chorale throughout, in constantly changing aspects, implies the concentration of the mind upon the central idea which is embodied in the tune, and its presentation as the theme, at the conclusion, welds the whole into a decisive conclusiveness. The manner in which this concentration upon one basis is carried out is the more noticeable inasmuch as the cantata was written for the second day of Easter—a day of supreme gladness to the Christian—and it is all in a minor mode. It recalls the noble sentence suggested as a motto for the Leipzig Conservatorium by Mendelssohn, "Res severa verum gaudium," and presents the exultation of the Christian in a far deeper sense than any brilliant musical equivalent of the mere exuberance of superficial joy could do. It may be permissible to remark parenthetically that Bach was fond of introducing suggestions of sorrow in the midst of joy—as for instance the quotation of the chorale *O Haupt voll Blut und Wunden,* at the outset of the Christmas Oratorio.

Among noteworthy cantatas which are surmised to have followed soon after the "Johannes-Passion" is *Erwünschtes Freudenlicht,* which is speculatively assigned to the second day of Whitsuntide, 1724. It is the very strongest possible contrast to *Christ lag in Todesbanden,* for it is in quite a singularly cheerful vein, in many respects even secular in style. The recitative with which it begins affords one of the most singular examples of Bach's use of realistic suggestion.

The word "Freudenlicht" evidently caught his imaginative attention and he gives to the two flutes in the accompaniment a quick little figure which suggests the recurrent leaping of a little flame, and is reiterated in various positions throughout the whole of the first movement. The duet aria which follows for soprano and alto is also characteristic, being genially and cheerfully tuneful, but carried out to such truly portentous length by a fully marked *da capo* that the world in general is almost precluded from being aware of its charms. It is a significant instance of Bach's curious attitude in such matters. The fascination of working out the inspirations of artistic development seems at times to have been so strong with him that it obliterated all practical considerations of expediency, and, like Schubert, he put an almost prohibitive penalty on many lovely inventions by ignoring the average capacity of human attention. An analogous situation is presented in the last movement of this cantata, which, oddly enough for a sacred work, is in gavotte rhythm, and on the lines of a gavotte with an alternative quasi-trio. The tune of the first gavotte is quite simply harmonised and very attractive, and carried out within the limitations of a dance movement. The alternative portion corresponds to a trio; and, no doubt, Bach had the conception of a trio predominant in his mind, for through the whole of it the altos and tenors are silent, and the trebles and basses make a long winding trio with the instrumental bass, which runs about after Bach's familiar manner on equal terms with the voice. Bach afterwards introduced the first gavotte into a secular cantata, "*Lasst uns sorgen,*" put together and composed for a royal birthday in 1733, and in that case dispensed with the singular second gavotte.

The cantata *Leichtgesinnte Flattergeister* may be fitly coupled with the preceding, as it is also in peculiarly light vein, and has even engendered the suspicion that it is a transformation of a secular work which has disappeared. It begins with solos and ends with a lively chorus in aria form.

Among the cantatas which are referred to the year 1724 several are specially notable. *Erschallet ihr Lieder* was probably composed soon after Easter. It has a characteristically ornate and animated chorus on a very large scale in *da capo* form to begin with, a bass solo accompanied by three trumpets and drums, a tenor solo *O Seelen-Paradies!* and a fine duet for soprano and alto, which is notable as combining a "ground bass" with an ornate version of the chorale *Komm, heiliger Geist* in the accompaniment.

Of very high importance and quality is the cantata *Weinen, Klagen, Sorgen, Zagen.* Its greatest interest lies in the depth of tragic sorrow which is expressed in the first part of the first chorus, which Bach afterwards transformed with truly marvellous insight into the "Crucifixus" in the B minor Mass. It is rather strange that in the cantata this most affecting music constitutes only a portion of a chorus in aria form, the second or middle portion of which is by no means so impressive as the first. And it must be admitted also that the deep feeling expressed in the first part makes it unsuitable to be given again *da capo.* The cantata has a very beautiful introductory sinfonia, and several interesting arias. There are good reasons for believing that some of the music was written earlier, probably at Weimar.

In the strongest contrast stands the imposing cantata, *Lobe den Herrn, meine Seele,* which Spitta surmises, with likelihood, to have been written for some great municipal function. Its special feature is the opening chorus, which is on an immense scale, and illustrates in a high degree the scope and certainty of handling to which Bach had by this time attained. It sets out with a typically jubilant passage of trumpets, the rest of the instruments joining in by degrees to the full measure of rich polyphony. The voices enter with rushing passages of semiquavers, alternating with shouts of emphatic chords to the words "Lobe den Herrn," giving a superb effect of exultant energy. A most happy contrast is obtained by the much quieter character of the subject of the central episode which is afterwards interwoven with delightful effect with the subject of the praise. There are two fine solos in the cantata for alto and bass. Of another Cantata of the same name nothing is known except that it was written for New Year's Day. The first Chorus is most brilliant, and has important parts for three horns, which are also conspicuous in a fine Bass Aria. The Tenor Solo has a Chorale in the accompaniment, and an elaborate bassoon obbligato.

Though it is not very easy to fix the exact dates of many cantatas which were written between the production of the "Magnificat" and that of the "Matthäus-Passion," it is safe to group a large number of them as representing that period; and it is fortunate that it is so, as their character throws so much light on Bach's personal development. The features which reveal themselves are the expansion and prominence of the first chorus and the more frequent adoption of the aria form not only for solo movements but also for choruses. As illustrating this phase, *Es erhub sich ein Streit* will be copiously suggestive. The cantata was written for St. Michael's day, and refers to the strife in heaven between the hosts of the archangel and Satan and his forces. The chorus springs without preliminary into the fugue, which is made to represent the sense of huge turmoil, with rolling passages of semiquavers and an overwhelming sense of rhythmic accent. The presentation of the idea is superb, but it affords one of the most unfortunate examples of Bach's indiscriminate use of the *da capo*, for the middle portion of the chorus necessarily carries the suggestion of the action forward, and the *da capo* takes the whole thing back to the beginning and goes over the ground again in the portion of the fugue describing the fight. The solo portions of the cantata are rather overwhelmed by the volume of the first chorus.

An exceptionally fine cantata which was written about the same time as the last is *Alles nur nach Gottes Willen.* In this, again, there is a most vivacious first chorus, with semiquaver runs and insistent emphasis on the world "alles" to which parallels are presented in the opening phrases of the great motet, *Singet dem Herrn.* The movement is in a free kind of aria form, in which the middle section is most admirably devised for contrast. The arioso for alto, *Herr so du willt* is one of Bach's most exquisite and subtle pieces of supreme simplicity. Of almost equal beauty is the aria for soprano, *Mein Jesus will es thun,* the close of which is quite extraordinarily human. It brings to mind the strange personal fascination the name "Jesus" had for Bach, and also (in a new aspect) the fact that Bach made such a specialty of fine endings!

The cantata *Erforsche mich*, again, has a very imposing first chorus in a solid style, with a conspicuous horn obbligato. It has only two solo movements, of which the second (a duet for tenor and bass) offers an instance of Bach's favourite use of massed violins in accompaniment, with a delightfully characteristic tune.

Bringet dem Herrn has a big free chorus at the beginning with a trumpet obbligato. The voice parts are at first massed harmonically with a tuneful upper part, and the middle part of the chorus is fugal. So the order of proceedings is just the reverse of that in *Alles nur nach Gottes Willen*. The cantata contains a very tuneful alto solo.

The general scheme of *Siehe zu* is similar, but it differs from the above mentioned cantatas in respect of the style of the first chorus, which is in the very plainest and severest counterpoint without any independent accompaniment except the bass line of the continuo, to which Bach has not even added figures.

These cantatas, together with those of the pre-Magnificat time, suggest that Bach, under stress of circumstances, had become rather over-systematic. The actual quality of the artistic work is almost always splendid, but there seems for a time to be less of the romantic element. No doubt the Leipzig congregations were not favourable to the higher imaginative qualities, and preferred good strong workmanship and well planned arias with nice tunes to them. But there was a strong reaction coming on Bach's side, of which the first chorus of *Weinen, Klagen* and the group of songs in *Alles nur* were a premonition. An example which shows how easily things might take another turn is *Ihr Menschen, rühmet Gottes Liebe.* It is really a solo cantata, and contains admirable solo music, especially the first tenor aria in $\frac{12}{8}$ time; but the point that is peculiar is the final movement. It is almost invariably the case that cantatas for solo voices end with the plain four-part chorale in which the congregation could join. But in this case the movement is worked up to the extent of being quite an important feature, having an elaborate accompaniment in which a very gracious and flowing semiquaver figure is constantly presented. It is, however, also one of the odd cases in which Bach has indicated that the oboes are to double the violins in this charming adornment of the chorale. A moment's consideration would show that the introduction of these instruments would ruin the effect. Probably Bach was so accustomed to hearing his beautiful phrases mangled by the players that he did not mind.

The fact that the poetic fire still burned as steadily as ever is shown by the character of several cantatas of probably slightly later date than those just mentioned. An excellent illustration is the singularly genial cantata, *Du Hirte Israel.* It is evident that the word which influenced Bach in composing was "Hirte," and that his mind was projected by it into a pastoral mood. The quiet, tranquil style is maintained throughout, with many subtle suggestions of the shepherd's environment, such as the prevalence of hautboy tone, and of musical figures suggesting the shepherd's pipe and a general air of innocent rusticity. Even the first chorus breathes an air of peace, and both the solo arias are of great beauty, especially the second, *Beglückte Heerde,* for bass voice; and the mood is even maintained in the final chorale *Der Herr ist mein getreuer Hirt.*

In marked contrast stands the earliest of the two cantatas, beginning with the words *O Ewigkeit, Du Donnerwort,* which belongs to this period. The "thunder word," Eternity, was well calculated to stir Bach's imagination, but he makes no attempt at histrionic effect; the impression is made by the manner in which the chorale is sung by the voices in the first chorus, in measured steadfast motion, contrasting with the rhythmic energy of the phrases in the orchestra. Here again, as in *Nun komm', der Heiden Heiland* and the Rathswahl cantata, *Preise, Jerusalem, den Herrn,* Bach casts the chorus in the form of the "French Overture," and the effect of the slow introductory movement is admirable in relation to the subject. Each movement that succeeds presents fresh attitudes of contemplation of the overwhelming idea, the first half of the cantata ending with the chorale associated with the words *O Ewigkeit.* The second half of the cantata begins appropriately with a powerful bass solo, *Wacht auf,* with a brilliant trumpet accompaniment. To this succeeds a duet for alto and tenor, and the whole concludes with a repetition of the chorale of the first half.

The cantata *Herr, wie Du willt* is a very remarkable example of the depth of insight which is so often shown in Bach's musical interpretation of words. If superficially interpreted, these particular words may be seen to be beset with pitfalls. They do indeed actually suggest an incomplete submission to the Divine will, as the soul is made to express itself in the words "Ach! aber ach! wie viel lässt mich dein Wille leiden," etc. The danger obviously is to accentuate the harshness of "the Lord's will" in order to enhance the credit of submission. In the text each pair of lines of the hymn relating to the divine will is followed by a passage in which the soul, in a sort of aside, expresses its real opinion. Therefore, if the words were quite frankly interpreted in musical terms, they would express but a formal and superficial attitude of submission. Bach had, in a sense, to accept the situation which was provided for him, and to write in a minor mode rather than the major which would have expressed more frankly the loyal and unstinted submission to the will of the Supreme Being whose wisdom passes all understanding. But all the same he adopts on the whole a cheerful vein. What may be called the energising figures, which at the outset are given to the hautboys and unify the whole movement by their persistence, are really almost gay in their innocent and modest simplicity. To suggest the insignificance of the human creature in relation to the Divine will the music is at first confined to the highest part of the scale, the bass being supplied by violins and violas pizzicato. But this procedure is constantly interrupted by the recurrence of the rhythmic group of notes which represents the words "Herr, wie Du willt."

* The Voices.
Herr, wie Du willt!

This figure (which might indeed be called a "Leitmotiv") is given at first to the continuo, and now and again to the horn or organ obbligato. The scheme then works out as follows:—The instruments having prefigured the musical materials and the mood, the chorus sing two lines of the chorale, and the tenor voice takes up the plaint of the soul in recitative, while the instrumental forces still keep the idea of the Divine will present in the mind, by reiterating the musical formula of the "Herr, wie Du willt," coupled with the innocent little hautboy figure. This procedure is followed throughout, the full choir alternating lines of the submissive hymn in terms of the chorale, and single parts making commentaries on the Divine will in recitative, and it is actually not till the end of the chorus that the voices take up the musical formula of the "Herr, wie Du willt," which is then repeated three times as though to emphasise the affirmation—but as a last touch of humanity the chorus actually leaves off on a discord, subtly suggesting that the submissive attitude is still left questioning!

But the following tenor aria is in quite a cheerful and contented vein, breathing "Freudigkeit" and "Hoffnung." A bass recitative begins by suggesting the futility and blindness of our will, and then comes the supreme stroke of the whole scheme, as it concludes with the words "Allein ein Christ, in Gottes Geist gelehrt, lernt sich in Gottes Willen senken und sagt," and the aria following completes the sentence with the words "Herr, so Du willt." The suggestion is that even Christ Himself at the supreme moment had uttered the words of submission to God's will, "Herr, so Du willt," setting them at once before the devout worshipper as enforced by the example of Jesus Himself. The aria which begins with these words is given to a bass and is in the style which Bach always instinctively adopted when he was trying to express Christ's own words in musical terms, or make Him, so to speak, utter them in His own person. It is, musically, of exceptionally tender, touching beauty, combining resignation with inexhaustible devotion. When it is over there is nothing more to be said, except for the congregation, with hearts full of the lesson the music has enforced, to sing the final chorale, which, as usual, is set, with sundry very subtle progressions, in a manner which is perfectly in consonance with the mood which the cantata is calculated to induce in the sympathetic worshipper.

One of the few Cantatas of which the date is certainly identifiable is *Ich lasse dich nicht*, which was performed in February, 1727, at a funeral ceremony. It begins with a duet for Tenor and Bass with an intricate accompaniment mainly woven of a tender phrase which occurs frequently in the voice parts. It contains also two fine Arioso passages for Bass.

In the remaining cantatas which can generally be referred to the years before 1729 the like readiness to grasp every musical opportunity is seen, and the manner in which the opportunities are used is generally characteristic of the man. In the fine cantata *Halt' im Gedächtniss Jesum Christ*, we find an interesting example of a dialogue between Christ and the soul, the words of Christ being given to the bass voice, as usual, and the words of the soul to the chorus. There is no verbal indication that the solo part represents the personal Christ, except that the words "Friede sei mit euch" are His, and that the mood and style of the music are again exactly consonant with the singularly characteristic manner Bach always adopted when setting the words of Christ; as in the settings of the Passion and in the cantata previously alluded to. In this case the manner in which Bach thought out the musical scheme is notable.

It may well be perceived that it struck him that there would be no ostensible point in Jesus' saying "Peace be with you" unless the state of mind of the persons to whom the remark is addressed was such as to make peace desirable. In other words, it would be superfluous to offer peace to those who already enjoy its blessings. We are therefore presented with the superficially illogical situation of an extremely serious, dignified, and tender aria, conjoined to and introduced by a very agitated, bustling, uneasy introduction. This introduction has no words; it just stands there in its unmistakable agitation, and then suddenly a change is made to a flowing $\frac{3}{4}$ time, and the words of Christ are heard. It is a far-reaching and suggestive touch. Its very superficial inaptness makes the mind pause to ask what such abstractly incompatible proceedings can mean. And the arrest of the attention gives the situation, when it is grasped, a greater hold on the mind; for when the agitated exclamations of those to whom Jesus addresses the comforting words are expressed in the terms of the music of the superficially incompatible introduction, the glimmering inferential explanation which occurred to the mind is vindicated. The case might indeed be taken as a test one in discussing the relations of absolute form and relative form; of the types of the preordained classical sonata and the type of interpretative music. The musical phenomena of mundane agitation and divine calm as here juxtaposed would, on purely abstract grounds, from the point of view of the musical classicist, be almost preposterous. But the instant the internal cue is seized, the psychological interpretation justifies the method of organisation, for peace contrasted with agitation in such a sense seems to be fully as justifiable a basis of musical design as the familiar device of a subject in the tonic and a contrasting subject in the dominant key!

Among personal peculiarities which cannot fail to catch the mental eye in this cantata are the sharp shouts of "halt, halt," which punctuate the polyphonic texture of the initial chorus and the characteristic device of interpreting the word here and there by a long holding note. *Nimm, was dein ist,* begins with an austere Choral Fugue unaccompanied, which is very suggestive of the words. The Arias for Alto and Soprano respectively are delightfully melodious. The Cantata contains two different Chorales.

The cantata *Thue Rechnung* is perhaps most notable as illustrating the manner in which Bach not infrequently found himself at the mercy of the words he had to set. An aria for tenor actually begins with the words "Capital und Interessen."

Herr, gehe nicht in's Gericht is noticeable for the first chorus, in which ejaculatory utterance of the beseeching sentence contrasts effectively and humanly with the solemn and dignified motion of the instrumental parts; suggesting the anxious disquiet of the soul before the steadfast impassivity of the Divine Judge. The aria for soprano, *Wie zittern und wanken,* is also noticeable, as the treatment of the accompaniment is unlike Bach's usual polyphonic methods and much more harmonic, thereby throwing the pathetic phrases of the hautboy and the voice into relief. The final chorale, *Nun, ich weiss,* is also in an unusual vein and very interesting.

The words of the cantata *Schauet doch und sehet* evidently moved the composer deeply, for it is a work of even exceptional beauty and pathos. The first chorus is interesting not only intrinsically, but also on account of a portion of it having been transformed with almost incredible aptness into the chorus *Qui tollis* in the B minor Mass. In this cantata it appears in much larger proportions, as it has a very beautiful orchestral introduction, which Bach omitted in the Mass, though it is mainly based on the figures of accompaniment which form such an attractive feature in the portion transferred thereto; here also it has a long and powerfully expressive second part, a movement almost wrathful in strength and severity of feeling. The recitative which follows, for tenor, is of very great beauty, with a characteristic accompaniment for flutes. A powerful aria follows for bass with trumpets, in which the treatment of the accompaniment seems to break unusual ground for the composer, though he makes it emphatically his own. A short recitative for alto is followed by an aria of exceptional beauty for the same voice to the words *Doch Jesus will,* which were sure to inspire the composer. The accompaniment gives it a peculiarly unique character as it is restricted to two flutes and oboe da caccia, so exquisitely woven round the voice that the ensemble makes a kind of delicate quartet. Even the final chorale is rather out of the ordinary scheme, as it is fully accompanied throughout, and interspersed with beautiful commentative orchestral episodes between the lines.

A point which is very characteristic of the composer in *Du sollst Gott* is that the words of the chorus being one of the commandments, the trumpet plays the chorale *Dies sind die heil'gen zehn Gebot'* on and off through the whole movement answered by the Basses of the accompaniment in augmentation. It is not, as it might seem, a mere witticism. It suggests that the movement is enveloped by the Chorale representing, symbolically, the Decalogue. The first Chorus of *Ein' feste Burg* contains a similar device.

The scheme of the first chorus of *Liebster Gott, wann werd' ich sterben* is very interesting, with novel points of orchestration. Slow pizzicato notes for strings and a singular feature of rapidly repeated notes for the flutes probably typify the shuddering at the thought of death. The bass solo, *Doch weichet*, has a very fine melodic phrase, and the final chorale, *Herrscher über Tod und Leben*, though quite unelaborated, is very strikingly put, in consonance with the fine symbolism of the words.

The conspicuous feature of *Gottlob! nun geht das Jahr zu Ende* is a chorus of vast extent "quasi a cappella"—pure unornate choral work—which comes in the middle of the cantata, the voices being doubled in archaic manner by cornet, trombones, hautboys, and strings. Among Bach's choral works this occupies a niche almost by itself. But when it is performed its effect would be greatly enhanced by leaving out the doubling instruments, which Bach had the habit of indicating without much consideration.

The cantata *Herr Gott, dich loben wir*, which was probably produced early in 1729, is noticeable as rather a curiosity. The first chorus is attractively obscure in tonality, owing to the archaic character of the chorale tune, which is given to the trebles in long notes, the rest of the choir having bustling passages of free counterpoint after the manner of an organ chorale-fantasia. It is difficult to say whether it begins in A minor or E, and the movement, which is quite short, ends on G as the dominant of C. There is a second chorus in the latter key, combined with a bass solo, in Bach's very liveliest vein—so festive and jovial, indeed, that it seems scarcely within the range of religious music. The subject of the chorus is one of Bach's most unblushing examples of realistic suggestion, all the choir partaking in a figure which is rather like a Tyrolese jodel, in consonance with the words "Lasst uns jauchzen."

This merriment is maintained by voices and instruments throughout, and the bass solo which alternates its strains with passages of chorus seems to be urging them to ever-increasing joyousness, which is achieved with quite extraordinary brilliancy in the culminating conclusion of the chorus. A note of seriousness is touched in the alto recitative, *Ach treuer Hort,* and a tenor solo which follows is so flowing and sweet that it might be referred to the *Mein gläubiges Herze* class, from the best known example of that familiar and delightful type. Indeed, there is a passage in it which anticipates that popular aria.

One special work stands out with some little prominence in the period between the St. John Passion and the St. Matthew Passion, about the date of which there is no doubt. Queen Christina Eberhardine, wife of the King of Poland who was also Lord Paramount of Saxony, was regarded with affectionate admiration by the people of Leipzig because, when her husband had gone over to the Church of Rome in order to qualify for the elective throne of Poland, she had remained faithful to Lutheranism. She died in 1727, and the solemn funeral ceremony took place on October 17th, for which occasion Bach wrote a "Trauer Ode." It is on much the same lines as a church cantata, though a little longer than the average, and divided into two portions, for a funeral oration to be delivered in the middle, in the same way as a sermon was often delivered in the middle of cantatas on special occasions. It differs from the cantatas mainly in style. The first chorus is quite unlike the first choruses of the cantatas, and most admirably conceived for its occasion in a nobly broad and massive style, with a sense of dignified sadness, the treatment of the voices being frequently ejaculatory, but without any fugal passages. There are two more choruses in the body of the work, one of them fugal and another melodious and homophonic. The solos, which are very fine, are also in a sense massive, and more akin to the solos in the "Passion" than to those in the cantatas.[1] It is said that several of the movements were embodied in the St. Mark Passion, which has been lost. A curious interest also attaches to the manuscript, as it is written on paper with a special water-mark, which also appears in the paper that Bach used for over forty cantatas, and by this means the approximate date of the cantatas is supplied.

The cantatas written by Bach after his arrival at Leipzig, in the years preceding 1729, represent a special phase in his development. The period is as well defined in its character, and its function in completing Bach's personality, as the other periods of his life. It was the period in which he was working most consciously under the influence of an audience, and was accommodating himself, as far as his nature allowed, to the necessity of addressing people who had somewhat lost touch with the primitive poetry of religion, and developed more aptitude for taking pleasure in purely artistic skill. It was the period in which Bach was aiming at being practical. But, in spite of pres-

[1] A detail which is interesting and significant is that in the short recitative *Der Glocken bebendes Getön* reiterated notes for the flutes with pizzicati strings and gambas and lutes serve to suggest bells. Parallel effects occur in *Komm du süsse Todesstunde* and *Herr Jesu Christ wahr'r Mensch und Gott;* but this is far the most elaborate and interesting example of such devices.

sure of work and the necessity of addressing an unsympathetic audience, the fervent poetry of his nature was not affected. Occasional cantatas, such as *Schauet doch und sehet,* and *Herr wie Du willt,* and *Weinen, Klagen,* show the full richness of Teutonic devotionalism in the midst of more cosmopolitan types; and it is shortly to be seen that his nature had lost none of its freshness, its poetic imaginativeness, or its perennially youthful fervour through the stress of these years. For when the constant labour of producing cantatas is brought to a pause, the work which presents itself, and which no doubt was the cause of the cessation of the outpouring, is the richest in human feeling, the most copious in all high qualities of art, of all his splendid achievements.

CHAPTER VI

THE MATTHÄUS-PASSION

THE records of the circumstances and conditions of composition which led to the achievement of the great "Passion according to St. Matthew," which is the richest and noblest example of devotional music in existence, are all as utterly blank as the other records of Bach's life. The work happily exists in all its lovable beauty, but how Bach lived and how he worked, how those in daily touch with him watched and possibly participated in the gradual unfolding of its inspiring pages, is unknown, and all the little incidents which would throw light upon his methods and habits of work are utterly vanished. Except for the manuscript score, which bears the tokens of the patient and steadfast labour of the composer, it might almost as well have been a supernatural accident.

Of the nature and quality of this unique form of art, for which unfortunately no other name has been discovered but "Passion music," sufficient has been said. Its source, growth and expansion have been outlined till the time of Bach's production of the "St. John Passion." It has further been indicated that after Bach came to Leipzig he not infrequently adopted a cosmopolitan style in his cantatas, temporarily allowing the romantic elements to be superseded by Italian modes of treatment. But the process of assimilation of the foreign methods did not in the least impair the fundamental qualities of his disposition, and from the outset of the "Matthäus-Passion" he shows that they were in no degree affected by the study and use of Italian forms. Indeed there is no work, even of the most fervent romantic style of his youth, which breathes more consistently the romantic temperament of the race whose best qualities he represents so nobly.

The first chorus, which occupies the position of a prologue, is on the very grandest scale, requiring two orchestras of wind and strings, two choirs of four voices apiece, and a separate treble part which sings with steadfast gait, against the multitudinous polyphony of the rest, the chorale, *O Lamm Gottes, unschuldig.* The first words of the chorus, *Kommt ihr Töchter, helft mir klagen,* suggest indirectly to the mind of the worshippers the attitude worthy of the subject. The alternation of the utterances of the two choruses, rising at times to almost dramatic intensity, and the rich flow of sad phrases and harmonies punctuated by monosyllabic interjections, lay a groundwork of the utmost dignity and solemnity. Then the voice which takes the part of the Evangelist (the counterpart of Historicus in Carissimi's little oratorios) takes up the story, plunging at once into the midst of it with the words, "When Jesus had finished all these sayings, he spake to His disciples," and then follow the words of Christ, "Ye know that in two days will be the Passover, when the Son of Man will be betrayed." The passage is given to a bass solo accompanied by strings in harmony, as is invariably the case where Christ is made to speak in His own person. The story is made to pause for a moment while the pathetic chorale, *Herzliebster Jesu, was hast du verbrochen,* is sung.

Then the Evangelist tells of the meeting of the high priests and scribes in the palace of Caiaphas, and their plan to take and kill Jesus. There follows the first chorus of what was technically called the "Turba," being the words of the assembled priests, "Not on the feast-day," in a vigorous and decisive vein, such as characterises nearly all the choruses which belong to the action of the story, and makes them stand out in clear and unmistakable contrast to the reflective choruses and the chorales. The episode of the woman with the vase of precious ointment is fully dealt with, and is followed by the commentatory recitative *Du lieber Heiland du,* which presents a characteristic procedure frequently adopted by Bach in the Passions; as the movement is accompanied throughout by a sad and tender figure played on two flutes, almost always either in thirds or sixths, below which the chords, filled in by pizzicato strings and "continuo," recur in absolutely strict and regular slow beats. The movement is really out of the category of recitative; for, though the melodious voice part is free and elocutionary, the unbroken persistence of the figures of the flutes and the recurrent chords on the strings establish a principle of expression and coherence of an invaluable kind which differentiates the type both from the purely informal recitative and the aria. It is the more serviceable in this Passion, as it distinguishes the quasi-recitative of commentaries from the unaccompanied recitative of the Evangelist who relates the story.

The relation of the treacherous compact of Judas with

the high priest is followed by a very pathetic aria, *Blute nur, du liebes Herz* in full *da capo* form, but with no other trace of Italian influence. The warning of Christ to his disciples, that one of them should betray Him, is followed by a graphic little chorus of the disciples asking, "Lord, is it I?" the voices rapidly alternating one with the other, a scheme which had been anticipated with the object of suggesting actuality by Schütz in his Passion. Closely following upon this is the solemn episode of the symbolical offering of the bread and wine, which has that singularly tender and solemn feeling before described as characterising the music put into the mouth of Jesus by Bach. This in its turn is followed by the recitative *Wiewohl mein Herz* which is a counterpart of the quasi-recitative *Du lieber Heiland*, the accompaniment this time being given to a duet of plaintive oboi d'amore. The confidence in his own courageous loyalty expressed by Peter invites a pause for reflection, which is afforded by an appropriate chorale; and thereafter follow the poignant episode of the Garden of Gethsemane, and the words of Jesus, "My soul is exceeding sorrowful even unto death," which naturally suggest further reflections. And these Bach most amply presents in two movements of extraordinarily tender beauty, in both of which his favourite device of alternating the solo voice with chorus in intercommunion of sentiment is most aptly used. The tenor voice in the first of these movements expresses the anguish of the thought, *O Schmerz, hier zittert das gequälte Herz*, with accompaniment of two flutes and two oboi da caccia and organ. The choir answers with the first phrase of a soft unaccompanied chorale; then the solo voice takes up the plaint again and is answered by the second line of the chorale, and so on throughout. The movement does not come to a definite end, but merely turns to the dominant of the coming key, C minor, and so makes way for a movement in which the scheme of alternation of solo voice and chorus is similar, but the voice part is of more definite character, as befits its designation as an aria. The words make an innocent attempt at comfort, as the solo voice utters "I will watch my Jesus," and the chorus answers referring to his sleep, "So may our sins be put to sleep," with a singularly characteristic and innocent tune. The wide expansion of this group of movements was probably deliberately made with the view of keeping the mind occupied with this mournful episode of the tragedy proportionately to its significance.

The whole story of the betrayal follows in detail with many remarkable instances of emphasis on the situations; for instance, the choir bursts in upon the tender flowing lament which is given to the soprano and alto, "So ist mein Jesus nun gefangen," with the sharp, angry interjections "Lasst ihr, haltet, bindet nicht," which, as it were, punctuate the whole movement with reiterated protests, thereby in some measure preparing the ground and the mind for the tremendous rush of the chorus, *Sind Blitze, sind Donner in Wolken verschwunden,* an example of graphic and raging energy such as had never been heard before. The strides of the sequences, the explosion of the sudden chord of F sharp major after the central close in D, the alternation of the choruses seeming to contend with one another in their shouts: "Eröffne den feurigen Abgrund, O Hölle," (first Choir) "Zertrümmre," (second

Choir) "Verderbe," (first Choir) "Verschlinge," (second Choir) "Zerschelle," seem to typify a perfect cataclysm of nature at the horror of the betrayal of the sinless Son of God. Thereafter follows in Bach's version the relation of the episode which ends with the words "And all the disciples forsook him and fled."

This is as far as Bach takes the story in the first half of the work, and the commentatory chorus which follows and completes it (in the existing version) is the marvellously rich and expressive movement which originally stood at the beginning of the Johannes-Passion, *O Mensch bewein' dein' Sünde gross* (see p. 238). It is practically a noble adaptation of the form of organ music known as the "Chorale-fantasia," but almost incredibly enriched by every known resource of art to intensify the expression and bring men's relation to the tragedy home to their minds. The beauty and aptness of the Passion form could hardly be more exquisitely displayed, but in order to realise it, it is necessary to consider the innermost meaning of the situation. The regular rotation of routine which is inevitable in ecclesiastical functions has the tendency to deaden the impression of what is related in sacred narrative or offered in the abasement of devotion; and so it comes about that such a poignant moment in the story might pass almost unnoticed. The disciples, the friends, the intimates, the choicest flower of those to whom He had daily revealed the treasures of His mind, those whose belief in Him had been so absolute and heart-whole and should be the means through whom His message was to be conveyed to mankind, are close at hand; but the moment which tests their loyalty comes, their courage fails, and He, sinless and betrayed, has not so much as one friend left to comfort Him. The contemplation of a situation so utterly forlorn, in which the cruelty of public injustice is accentuated by the refined torment of the disloyalty of beloved friends, suggests the condition of stupefaction in the minds of those who hear the story with complete perception. The music, which in this chorus summons the mind to concentrate itself on the poignant episode, seems to express the kind of pain that comes on the mind when something happens which transcends man's power to estimate and express. It floats like the subtle suggestion of a mood of sorrow filled with remembrance. The instruments—flutes, oboi d'amore, strings—discourse their tender phrases for a while, till, as though human contemplation had arrived just at the point of utterance, the trebles of the chorus quietly begin the chorale, *O Mensch bewein' dein' Sünde gross*, to which the other voices respond by taking up the same words and amplifying the expression of the sentiments with those intimate touches of realistic suggestion of which Bach always availed himself. The implication is, of course, a figurative one, as the men who are exhorted to bewail their sins are not the disciples who had fled. Their transgression is here but a type—the reminder of the universal inadequacy of mankind,—and the devout address their admonition to themselves; as much as to say: "It was for us that this was endured, and yet we are as little steadfast in our loyalty as the disciples in the time of need."

The form of the "Chorale-fantasia" is especially apt for the contemplative state of deep sorrow. Each phrase of the chorale is followed by a short interval in the vocal utterances, during which the instruments maintain their plaintive discourse. And the effect is essentially true of the human state in such conditions. It is as much a fact of experience as of theory that short sentences interspersed with pauses have a very powerful effect in impressive situations. As examples of Bach's insight in the matter, reference may be made to the strangely fragmentary chorale at the end of the motet, *Der Geist hilft uns,* and the chorale at the end of the dialogue cantata, *O Ewigkeit*. The profound effect of the sentences "Man that is born of a woman," etc., in the English burial service, may be also recalled in this connection. The effect in this case was obviously not Bach's invention, but a property of the form. But the manner in which he manipulated the details shows how deeply he was moved by the words. They seem to govern and direct every progression and every melodic phrase. Type-figures there are no doubt—as an example may be quoted the type

which Bach very often used to express a kind of sympathetic wail, as for instance in the *Farewell Capriccio* to his brother (p. 43), and the sonata in B minor for violin and clavier, and the fugue in F sharp minor in the first twenty-four preludes and fugues. But the figure is only one out of many, and is not only subjected to many variations, but is, indeed, itself a variation, which seems to reveal itself as an afterthought.

As an example of the extent to which Bach's mind is alive to the emotional undercurrent of the words, the treatment of the chorale phrases in this movement may be pointed out. In almost every case the treble voices anticipate all the other voices in leading off each phrase, till near the end. They fall behind a little in the penultimate phrase, and in the last of all the subordinate voices have several bars to sing before the chorale phrase is uttered. It is as though the soul found it difficult, through sheer distress, to utter the final words "Wohl an dem Kreuze lange."

But in truth the extent to which Bach was moved in this case and the thoughts that crowded in upon him as he wrote make the chorus almost impracticable. It is so full of expressive details that even conductors who have not surrendered to the entirely gratuitous theory that Bach's deep meditations are to be set going like a lot of noisy machinery in a factory, are driven to abandon in despair the attainment of a performance which will adequately represent what any sympathetic person can see that Bach intended. So far the amplest experience conveys the impression that the ideal expression of the chorus must remain unattainable till conditions of rehearsal and the attitude of those who lay stress on barren tradition are entirely changed. Meanwhile those who are capable of understanding derive some consolation from the contemplation of the exquisite devotional poetry of Bach's personality which is here so amply revealed.

This chorus completes the first half of the work, and undoubtedly sundry religious exercises were gone through before the second part was entered upon. This begins with the tender plaint of an alto solo, evidently prefiguring the Church, in the words "Ach, nun ist mein Jesus hin," to which the chorus answers with the question of the Song of Solomon "Wo ist dein Freund gegangen, O du Schönste unter den Weibern?" The movement obviously supplies an additional prologue for this act to make each part of the work complete. Then the story is resumed: Jesus brought before the high priest, the false witnesses, the high priest's verdict "He has spoken blasphemy," the chorus of Jews "He is worthy of death," the insults, the mockery, each episode with attendant reflections tenderly expressed in chorale or recitative and aria. Then follows the episode of Peter's denial of his Master, and the affecting episode of the cock-crow, which recalled to Peter the words of his Master, "Before the cock crow shalt thou three times deny me," and Peter's instant remorse, expressed in a melismatic passage of recitative, which is one of the most touching passages in the whole work, and one of the most remarkable examples in existence of the use of such a device for the purpose of expression. This is followed by one of the most beautiful movements in the work, the soprano aria with violin solo in Bach's most expressive vein, *Erbarme dich, mein Gott,* which symbolically transfers the remorse of Peter to the worshipper. It is a notable proof of the completeness of Bach's assimilation of the Italian form of the aria, as the whole is most deeply Teutonic both in its sentiment and in the richness of the artistic treatment of instrumental and vocal melody for the ends of expression.

The tragedy proceeds with the binding of Jesus and His being sent by the high priest to Pilate as a malefactor, and the dialogue between Pilate and Jesus, the appeal of Pilate's wife, Pilate's question to the Jews: which should be liberated and handed over to them,

Jesus or Barabbas the murderer? and the immediate and spontaneous shout of the Jews: "Barabbas!" the absolute realistic terseness of which is so overwhelmingly effective; Pilate's question: "What then shall I do with Jesus?" and the fierce answer of the crowd: "Let Him be crucified!" and Pilate's answer, "Why, what evil hath He done?" which is followed by the tender recitative, accompanied by two oboi da caccia, *Er hat uns Allen wohlgethan,* and an aria with an accompaniment, which seems to hover in the air, for two flutes and two oboi da caccia, *Aus Liebe will mein Heiland sterben.* A repetition of the fierce chorus "Let Him be crucified!" follows. And so the tragic story proceeds step by step, each individual taking his part and the "Turba" vociferating dramatically till the final scene is reached.

This gives rise to a singularly touching alto recitative, *Ach, Golgatha, unsel'ges Golgatha,* with an accompaniment of two oboi da caccia and violoncello, which is one of the most perfectly apt pieces of colour in the whole work, and is followed by the aria *Sehet Jesus hat die Hand* for alto, which is interspersed with the questioning cry of "Wohin" by the chorus, the scene of the Crucifixion, and the bitter cry of the Crucified: "My God! My God! Why hast Thou forsaken Me?" the rending of the veil of the temple, and the earthquake, graphically suggested in the realistic manner which Bach's sincerity generally made convincing, the application of Joseph of Arimathea for the body of Jesus, and a solo for bass, *Am Abend, da es kühle war* (which Bach headed as a recitative, but which is in reality an exquisitely expressive and melodious arioso), and the story ends with the burial and the watch set over the grave. The work itself is completed by the reflections of the worshippers in the recitative, *Nun ist der Herr zur Ruh' gebracht*, with the pianissimo answer of the chorus, *Mein Jesu, gute Nacht*, breathing that touching intimacy which was characteristic of Teutonic feeling towards Jesus; and the marvellously noble and tender double chorus, *Wir setzen uns mit Thränen nieder und rufen dir im Grabe zu*, which again bespeaks the loving sorrow of those who have listened to the unfolding of the world-moving story and taken it to heart in all its deeply impressive and suggestive meaning.

The genius of Bach has so enriched it with every device of expression, dramatic force, variety and aptness of musical material, and interest of artistic resource that, notwithstanding the pauses at every episode for reflection and contemplation, the whole story seems to proceed with constant speed, even for those who can only partially realise in imagination the circumstances for which the work was written and the peculiar fascination of the conditions in which it was originally performed. There are frequent cases where the glamour of surroundings suffused with ancient associations and deeply rooted sentiments lends special enchantment to works of comparatively little intrinsic value, whose aptness to the surroundings is fortuitous, and which, when removed from them, manifest no traits which recall them. Bach's "Matthäus-Passion" is at the extreme opposite pole from such works. Though it is absolutely impossible to revive the conditions for which it was intended—chiefly because the particular type of worshipper's mind to which it was addressed, as well as the material surroundings, are gone forever from the world—it suggests the sublimation of all the finest traits of those conditions and surroundings in every page. It is probably the most beautiful expression of a beautiful phase of religion. It need not be supposed that a devotional attitude so supremely ideal could have ever had a general practical existence. Even in Bach's time the majority of the congregation would have been quite unworthy of the work as a scheme of religious art. It can at least be said of them that they put themselves in a position to afford Bach the opportunity of knocking at the door of their hearts and offering his view of the manner in which the story of the Passion might be profitably taken. And there can be no manner of doubt that most people who have ever heard the work with any attention, were they ever so little in touch with the devotional attitude at the outset, would be touched with some glimmer of the divine light of love before the work is over. For truly the keynote of the whole, as has been said in connection with the "Johannes-Passion," is the divine manifested in man. The beautiful conception of the supreme sacrifice of self willingly undertaken by the Supreme Being in taking the form of man and voluntarily submitting to suffer every indignity and cruelty, and even death at the hands of man in order to redeem him, puts the ideal of absolute self-sacrifice at the very highest point the human mind is capable of conceiving.

Bach's "Matthäus-Passion" presents the recognition of this conception by Teutonic religion in very marked guise, inasmuch as the Godhead of Christ is scarcely anywhere apparent. The tragedy is unfolded in its purely human aspects, as the sacrifice of the man who was ideally adorable as man rather than on account of his divine descent. The situation recognises, as it were, the absolute abnegation and the full acceptance of the brotherhood of man; it sets aside the glamour of the divine origin and appeals to men's hearts direct, to look upon the story of unsurpassable human goodness, patience, endurance, loving-kindness and suffering, to dwell upon every moment of it and set it before mankind as the highest state to which manhood can attain, redeeming humanity itself by the proof of its supreme possibilities of selflessness, and winning the title to divinity by a life and a death which surpassed all the experiences of mankind.

It was probably not intentional, but in the very first short passage of recitative this situation is suggested, for when Jesus predicts the coming betrayal and crucifixion he speaks of himself as the "Son of Man" not as the "Son of God," and the answering chorale echoes the same feeling, "Deeply loved Jesus, what law hast Thou broken that man should such judgment pass on Thee?" The same attitude persists throughout, with the rare exceptions of such movements as the "Thunder and Lightning" chorus, the portents at the time of the Crucifixion, and the quotation of "Surely this was the Son of God" near the end, which are just sufficient to keep the superhuman element in sight without disturbing the concentration upon the human aspects of the tragedy. It is indeed in such regions that Bach was so pre-eminent. His music is almost invariably intensely human in its expression, and, notwithstanding the enormous amount of church-music which he wrote, unecclesiastical. It is intensely spiritual, deeply devout, nobly and consistently serious, but with the largeness of temperamental nature that reaches out beyond the limitations of any four walls whatever into communion with the infinite. The story of the Passion as told by him would appeal not only to the Christian but also to a pagan who had but the slenderest knowledge of the traditions of Christianity. It was the outcome of Teutonic Christianity of the time, and yet it transcended it in the far-reaching power of the music and makes an appeal which can be answered by humanity at large.

Of the power and variety of art which it displays it is hardly necessary to speak. After passing through the various phases which have been described, his mastery of all the methods of art then cultivated was supreme. He had, indeed, extended their range far beyond the standard of any composer of his time, and brought all that he had mastered into exercise for the first time in this work. For however great many of his previous works had been, they none of them range so widely and so richly as this; and at the same time the unity of the whole work in style, spirit, and texture is almost incredible. The strength and consistency of the man's nature, completely matured, make every page glow with his personality, and with a humanity so noble and far-reaching that it stands alone and unique without any works which share a place with it, or anything which in its peculiar qualities and scheme could follow it.

It appears that when the "Matthäus-Passion" in its first form was first performed on Good Friday in the year 1729 it was not fully appreciated. It could hardly be expected that it would be. Whether he had it performed in succeeding years cannot be verified. It is only ascertainable that the original version was considerably altered by him, and that the final version as it is now known to the world was performed under his directions in the year 1740 or soon afterwards. It continued to be performed in Leipzig even after Bach died, but did not become known to the world outside till, just a hundred years after its first appearance, it was performed at Berlin on Mendelssohn's initiative and under his direction on March 12, 1829.

The complete survival of the "Johannes-Passion" and the "Matthäus-Passion" is probably owing to the fact that at Bach's death they came into the hands of his son Philip Emanuel. He is known to have written three other Passions; but they are all lost, apparently beyond rediscovery; and it is supposed that it is owing to their having been in the hands of Wilhelm Friedemann, the eldest son, and the irregular and ill-balanced member of the family, through whose carelessness they were lost. Parts of the music of a "Passion according to St. Mark" are said to be preserved in the "Trauer Ode" written for the funeral ceremony of Queen Christina Eberhardine in 1727 (see p. 262).

There is also, strangely enough, a complete "Passion according to St. Luke" in Bach's handwriting; but it is evidently not by him, as it does not bear any resemblance to his musical personality at any period of his life. A vivacious letter of Mendelssohn's to a man who had been so unlucky as to give a large sum for the manuscript, under the impression that it was Bach's work is worth quoting. He says:

> I am very sorry you have given so much money for the "St. Lucas Passion." True it is that, as an undoubted manuscript, it is not too dear at the price, but, all the same, the music is not by him. You ask "On what grounds is the

Lucas' not by Sebastian Bach?" On intrinsic grounds. It is hateful that I must maintain this when it belongs to you; but just look at the chorale, "Weide mich und mach' mich satt"! If that is by Sebastian, may I be hanged!—and yet it is unmistakably in his handwriting. But it is too clean. He has copied it. "Whose is it?" say you. By Telemann, or M. Bach, or by Alt Nichol, Jung Nichol, or plain Nichol? What do I know? It 's not by Bach!

This verdict must be emphatically endorsed.

CHAPTER VII

THE MOTETS

On October 16th of the year 1729, which had been so splendidly signalised by the appearance of the "Matthäus-Passion," the aged rector of the St. Thomas School, Johann Heinrich Ernesti, died. As it seems most probable that the disorganisation of the school and most of the unpleasant circumstances in which Bach found himself in the earlier years at Leipzig were ultimately owing to the decrepitude of the said rector, it would be natural to anticipate that the cessation of official incapacity would change the situation considerably for the better, as far as Bach was concerned. In the end, no doubt, Bach's position did improve very considerably, but as no new rector was appointed for eight months, the effect in that direction was not apparent for some time; and the most important immediate outcome of the death of the head of the school was a new work by Bach, which, for once in a way, can be definitely located both in time and in connection with definite mundane occurrences. Ernesti's long tenure of office made an imposing funeral almost inevitable; and for that function Bach wrote the first of the great motets of which the date can be identified; this is known by its initial sentence as *Der Geist hilft unser' Schwachheit auf.*

The actual form of art which was signified by the name motet had varied considerably at different times, under the influence of changing taste. In very early days it had been used for the crude attempts to combine different tunes together, before the elementary principles of counterpoint were evolved, and in those days a motet was often a secular composition. In the days of pure choral music the name was used to signify a sacred composition for voices unaccompanied, very often of considerable dimensions and in several well defined sections, rather like movements joined together in a series. Later the name was used for compositions on a large scale, including accompanied solos and choruses in the Italian style, and mainly homophonic. This form, however, is of no concern whatever in connection with J. S. Bach. The earlier, purely choral form, after being cultivated with great success by the composers of the old church, proved also very congenial to the composers of the Reformed Church; and many noble and dignified works of the type were produced by them, of which the most recent of high quality had been produced by John Sebastian's uncle, John Christoph Bach. Another uncle, Christoph's brother Michael, had also been favourably connected with this form of art, and so also had Buxtehude. So a number of influences, hereditary, local, and racial, combined with intrinsic qualities to make the old form of motet peculiarly congenial to John Sebastian. He is known to have written a large number of such works, for various groups of voices, but several of them have disappeared, and several of those which are attributed to him are manifestly by some obviously inferior composers. The few that remain are far above anything else of the kind produced by any other composer whatever in scope, intrinsic interest, texture, artistic resource, and nobility of expression, and stand high even amongst Bach's own greatest achievements.

It need not be pretended that the motet which he wrote for the funeral of Ernesti is among the most attractive examples of its kind, but its qualities throw much light upon his attitude in artistic matters and even upon his disposition. There is nothing actually to identify Ernesti personally with the disagreeable relations of Bach with his official superiors, but the known circumstances make it obvious that Bach must have felt that it would have been quite superfluous to pretend that the rector's death would be any loss to the school, and that depth of feeling could not honestly be displayed. He evidently had all the circumstances clearly in his mind, and among these were the conditions of the performance. In this respect a clue is said to be afforded by the existence at the St. Thomas School of a set of band parts to double the voices, from which it is inferred that the choir went to the house from which the funeral procession was to start, and sang the motet in the open air, and that the voice parts were doubled by the instruments to give them support. But besides these instrumental parts there is also a figured bass part for the organ, and as the organ was certainly not carried round the town with the funeral procession, the inference founded on the existence of band parts seems somewhat weakened. But again, on the other hand, the existence of an organ part is not absolutely conclusive proof that Bach contemplated performance in church, as the said figures might have been added for use at practices, when the choir was learning the work, or at some other time. On the whole, the character of the work is unfavourable to the theory that the motet was sung in procession, and the existence of instrumental parts suggests to the open mind that such adjuncts were called in to give the motet exceptional effect, and one distinguishable from ordinary motets at ordinary services, in view of the exceptional nature of the occasion.

At first sight it seems strange that the first movement has by no means a funereal aspect. It is, indeed, rather matter-of-fact and business-like, in a major key, with an animated rhythm, and ornate, energetic semiquaver passages in $\frac{3}{8}$ time. The eight parts are distributed into two choirs of four parts each, which answer and mingle with one another in the masterly fashion which Bach alone among composers had absolutely at his command. No personal feeling can be identified at all, unless the singular experiment in realistic suggestion of breaking up the first syllable of the word "Seufzer" to imitate the broken utterances of grief can be counted as such—a device which Bach had employed in the early cantata *Aus der Tiefe* (p. 56). The work as a whole may be more safely taken as a fine official document, representing, in a sense, doctrinal music. Bach was theoretically very keen on doctrinal matters, but he was far too full of human temperament ever to produce a fruitless and barren piece of pure technical disquisition; and just when the doctrinal vein seems specially strong in the second section of the first chorus, *Sondern der Geist selbst vertritt uns auf's Beste mit unaussprechlichen Seufzer*, where the time changes to $\frac{4}{4}$, the warmth of human expression breathes for a while in the statement of the fugue subject and its strange realistic accompaniment of broken utterances above referred to. The official aspect seems to be suggested again in the four-part chorus which follows, *Der aber die Herzen forschet,* which is a kind of fugue in archaic style with the typical minims and crotchets and quavers of orthodox counterpoint. But of its peculiarly reticent and severe kind it is a fine and satisfying example. The final chorale maintains the standard of the whole. Instead of being sentimental and touched with the sweetness of human regret, as are so many of Bach's most beautiful arrangements of chorales, it is peculiarly untender. The tune itself, *Lass' freudiger Geist,* is made up of very short phrases, and the lack of swing which results is emphasised by the pauses which occur at the end of each. But the effect in relation to the occasion is peculiarly impressive. Each little phrase comes to represent a short ejaculation with a pause of reflection after it (see p. 272), and this combined with the reticence of the harmony causes the qualities of dignified severity amply to make up for the absence of human feeling which would in this case have been out of place.

The contrast of the whole with the *Actus Tragicus —Gottes Zeit* of the Weimar time—is most striking. In that cantata personal feeling and the contemplation of the relation of the human creature to death is emphasised to the utmost. Bach's own temperamental feelings in the matter were engaged and all the sweetness and the beauty of that side of his nature are exquisitely expressed. But in this case we are face to face with a work which is devised in relation to a public ceremonial funeral, and in that sense must have been quite strikingly appropriate and effective. What seems a paradox throws vivid light upon Bach's character. The essence of Bach's art is that it is not make-believe. Men in official positions have not infrequently to make a pretence of being deeply concerned in things which have not the smallest personal interest for them. In many cases they have a kind of ready-made scheme which presents the appropriate trappings of woe or joy in a conventional manner, adequate to satisfy the external requirements which strike the public eye. The greater and more independent natures have to find a better way out of the situation. Bach was not personally concerned in the demise of Ernesti, and he chose essentially the right course in avoiding emotional and tender feeling, and making a great work of art worthy of a public occasion; which treated the funeral of the rector as an official matter rather than a personal one, and with distinction of phrase and aptness of dexterous handling discussed the aspects of death as it presents itself to one seeing it from afar off. In this way a motet which is in a sense singularly ungracious for the most human of composers gains a peculiar and exceptional interest. And when all the circumstances of the case are reconstructed in imagination—the funeral procession, the attendant crowds, the respectful recognition of the closing of a long official career—the scheme as worked out by Bach seems almost ideally impressive in its very aloofness from tender considerations.

As has before been mentioned, a new rector was not appointed for eight months, and then a man of very different calibre from Ernesti was chosen. Johannes Matthias Gesner, who came into office in June, 1730, was a man of enlightenment and culture, full of energy and devotion, and unsparing in his efforts for the furtherance of whatever good was possible in any phase of life to which he was called. He was, moreover, an old friend of Bach's, who had met him in the Weimar time, and his receptive mind was fully capable of appreciating Bach's great powers. How sympathetic and appreciative he was may, indeed, be judged from a note which he appended to an edition of Quintilian which he brought out in 1738, in which he says, with reference to the praise which Quintilian bestowed upon the skill of a certain player on the lyre of ancient times:

> All this you would think of small consequence if you could return from the other world and see Bach playing with both hands and all his fingers on an instrument which seems to combine many citharas in one — the organ of organs,— running over it hither and thither with both hands and with swiftest motion of his feet, eliciting many varied passages of sounds diverse and yet unified. If you could see him, I say, doing a thing which several citharists and innumerable tibicines could not do, and not like a citharœdos playing only his own part, but equally watchful of all the performers to the number of thirty or forty; calling this one to attention by a nod, another by a stamp of the foot, the third by threatening finger to rhythm and beat. He, doing the most difficult part can discern any mistake and the defaulter, and keep everybody right. Though I am a great admirer of the ancients as a rule, yet I think this Bach of mine combines many Orpheuses and twenty Arions in one.

The mere fact of having so warm and intelligent an admirer at the head of the school must have made Bach's position much easier, and Gesner, while exerting himself to get the school generally into better order, paid special attention and consideration to the better allotment of the duties of the cantor, and relieved Bach of some of his more unpalatable work, such as teaching

Latin to the lower classes of boys, and at the same time gave him more control and authority over the actual musical work of the school. But the improvements took time to effect, and there is one conspicuous proof at least that Bach felt the worries of his position most acutely just about the time of Gesner's appointment; for the only letter of Bach's extant which expresses decisively the desire to leave Leipzig if congenial work could be found for him elsewhere, dates from some four months after Gesner's arrival. But there are a few trifling indications which help to explain such apparent perversity as his trying to abandon his position as cantor just at the time when there were the most promising signs that its circumstances would speedily improve. There are proofs that Bach was on the worst of terms with the authorities just before Gesner arrived on the scene, and that the fact was very strongly present in the minds of the council who elected Gesner is shown by the remark which is recorded to have been made by a member of that body, referring to the Rector-elect, that "he hoped they would have better fortune in the appointment they had just made than they had had in that of the Cantor." And this state of affairs is accentuated by the fact that the notorious remark of a councillor that Bach was "incorrigible" was made on August 2, 1730, nearly two months after Gesner's appointment. This would tend to show that it took time for Gesner to make his influence and authority felt; which was no doubt the safest way in the end to make it permanent. But meanwhile Bach may have been rather discouraged than not, at finding that things were not speedier in mending, and this appears the most likely explanation of the fact that the letter he addressed to an old friend, Erdmann, who had been appointed agent of the Emperor of Russia in Dantzig, is dated October 28, 1730.

Apart from the circumstances of the case, the letter is one of the most interesting of Bach's personal documents outside music which has been preserved, as it not only throws light on his impressions with regard to certain important episodes in his life, but it is also quaintly characteristic in style. The greater part of it is worth quoting. After the usual high-flown address, Bach goes on:

Four years have passed since your Highwellbornness gave me the pleasure of receiving an answer to a letter of mine, wherein, I remember, you desired me to give you particulars of what had been happening to me (Fatalitäten), which shall here be set down. From my youth up you have been well acquainted with my "fata" until the time when I went to Cöthen as Capellmeister. There I had a kindly and music-loving and music-understanding prince, with whom I was minded to complete the measure of my life. But it is to be observed that when his Serenissimus wedded a princess of the House of Berenburg, his musical inclinations seemed to wane, as the new princess appeared to be somewhat unmusical. So it pleased God that I should be called to the musical directorship and cantorship of the Thomasschule. But it was not congenial to me at first to become a Cantor after being a Capellmeister. So I deferred my resolution for a quarter of a year. But since the position was described to me as favourable and since my sons seemed inclined to pursue their studies here, in the name of the Most High I ventured and came to Leipzig, passed my "Probe" and made the change. Here I am by God's will thenceforward established. But now I find that the situation is not so advantageous as it has been described to me: that many of the emoluments are withheld, that it is a very expensive place, and that the authorities have wonderfully little sympathy with music: so that I must live in spite, jealousy and annoyance. It has become inevitable (genöthigct) that with the help of the Most High I should seek my fortune elsewhere. In case your Highwellbornness should wish or find another convenient post for an old and true servant, I seek a recommendation on my behalf; and if that be not lacking to me, it will be my best effort to give satisfaction for so high a recommendation and intercession.

My present position represents about 700 thalers and when there are more funerals than ordinary the emoluments increase in proportion. But the air is healthy, so it falls out that last year I had 100 thalers less than ordinary from funerals. In Thüringen I can live better with 400 thalers than I can here with twice as much, through the expensiveness of living. Further, I must dwell with some little detail on my domestic circumstances. I am now for the second time married, and my first wife died in Cöthen. Of my first marriage there are still three sons and a daughter living, as your Highwellbornness may graciously remember (to have seen). Of my second marriage there are one son and two daughters living. My eldest son is a "Studiosus Juris"; of the other two, one attends the first class and the other the second class, and the eldest daughter is yet unbetrothed. The children of the second marriage are yet small, the first-born is six years old. But they are all instinctively born musicians, and can provide that I can make up a vocal and instrumental concert in my family, since my present wife sings a clear soprano and also my eldest daughter strikes in not weakly.

And so the letter ends with some more complimentary phrases. Nothing is known of any answer to it, and it had no outcome. Bach made no sign, at any other time that can be traced, of wishing to leave Leipzig, and the letter is chiefly noticeable for the clear light which it momentarily throws on the writer's history and his feelings about his position. From the fact of his not following it up, it may be hoped that the conditions of his life and opportunities for the exercise of his powers improved, but the much-desired evidence is not forthcoming, and the only course left open is to resume consideration of the works which mark indubitably his constant exercise of his powers.

As has before been pointed out, motets formed part of the regular scheme of the church services at Leipzig, but of the many which Bach is known to have written only very few remain, and it seems that those that have survived were written soon after that which was written for the funeral of the Rector Ernesti.

The only motet of his for five voices which survives is *Jesu meine Freude,* and this is especially interesting as an illustration of Bach's characteristic practice of making the sentiment of the words the guiding principle in developing his scheme of design—that is, of using design as a means for conveying to, and impressing upon the mind his conception of the inner meaning of the words. The pivot on which the work turns is the chorale, *Jesu meine Freude,* a tune for which he seems to have had a great fondness. The tune was familiar to Teutonic Protestants, and as the central feature of a sacred work of art was far more effectual to them than it could be to a modern people of any other persuasion. Bach's scheme is to alternate the verses of the chorale with contrasting and commentatory episodes. The principle is the same as that of the rondo, one of the types of form of widest distribution in art, and one adapted to the lightest of gaiety as well as the deepest abysses of passion. The chorale hymn constitutes a kind of sacred symbol, radiating suggestions which are taken up with loving earnestness in the episodical portions which are interposed between the recurring verses of the hymn. Bach gives the first verse of the tune in four parts, harmonised in his own uniquely expressive manner. The first episode which follows serves at once as a parallel and an artistic contrast, being a typical motet chorus to the words *Es ist nun Nichts Verdammliches an denen die in Christo Jesu sind.* Rhythmically disposed harmonies alternate with richly contrapuntal passages, affording the effect of comparative informality in contrast with the metric definiteness of the chorale tune, the second verse of which follows the first episode. Another and much more extensive episode follows, in three movements. The first of these is a trio for high voices (affording very valuable contrast and relief), the second a chorus of severe character for five voices, *Trotz der Gruft der Erden,* and the third a brilliant fugal movement, which passes into a meditative adagio with the words *Wer aber Christi Geist nicht hat, der ist nicht sein* at the end. The group makes a substantial centre to the motet. After it yet again the chorale comes, its fourth verse much more highly elaborated after the manner of the "Orgelchoral" and brimming with expression, with its answering commentary *So aber Christus in euch ist,* this time a trio for low voices, which happily balances the trio for high voices in the previous episode. Yet again the chorale, but most subtly dealt with! A quartet without bass begins in a new key, and is so far from suggesting the music of the chorale that it seems intent upon bidding "Gute Nacht" in tender and gentle accents; and in the midst of the flowing grace of the quaver-motion enters, with quiet insistence, the metric tune of the chorale in the alto, with the words "Gute Nacht, O Wesen." The other parts are not distracted from their particular line of thought, but continue weaving lovely phrases into polyphony on the "Gute Nacht," while the alto part, still faithful to its text, continues to sing right through the metrical hymn. Simple as the procedure really is, it affords an excellent example of the manner in which real music concentrates a vast number of phases of thought simultaneously, exactly analogous to human mental or psychological states.

After this subtle presentation of the chorale, Bach reverts to the music of the second number of the work, altering the words from "Es ist nun Nichts" to "So nun der Geist," etc., and also altering a good deal of the musical material. This return to the first episode is obviously of great value as an element of artistic organisation, and is enhanced by the aptness with which the chorale is again introduced in its sixth verse to conclude the whole work; and the sense of completeness is happily enhanced by the fact that in this final recital of the chorale Bach resumes the simpler harmonisation of its first presentation.

The most difficult problem in a work on such a large scale as the choral motet, apart from the humbler problems of mere technique, is the attainment of adequate variety. The resources in that direction are reduced to a minimum, both by the limited range of variety of colour, and by the actual limitations of the human voice as a means of performance. For though the human voice is more capable of expression than any other instrument, the mere physical effect of sound too long continued within a limited range becomes wearisome. Bach in this case attains the necessary relief from monotony by limiting the number of voices employed in three of the movements, and by the contrasts of style between the metrical form of the actual chorale and the free contrapuntal style of the other numbers. Where most works of this period appear to the modern mind to take inadequate advantage of opportunities is in the distribution of the keys. The situation is illustrated in suites of that time, all the movements of which are, as a rule, in one key. It is obvious that composers and public did not feel wearied with the persistence of one key so much as people in later times; that not having experienced the pleasant relief of frequent and apposite shifting of central points they did not realise that it could be of any advantage. To a modern audience the excessive recurrence of E minor in this motet gives a certain sense of monotony. It is felt that if the recurrences of the chorale tune only had all been in the same key, and the episodes in other keys, the effect of those recurrences would have been so much stronger. But Bach, writing for his own generation, put eight out of eleven movements in E minor. However, the changes in this case are most apposite, the first being to G major for the fugue, which enhances its brightness, the second to C for the trio of alto, tenor, and bass, which enhances its innocently flowing character in $\frac{12}{8}$ time, and the third for the quartet to A minor, which emphasises its tender sadness.

There are, unfortunately, great difficulties in putting to practical tests the scheme and the beauties of this poetic motet: the music is so wedded to the German words and so dependent on ready grasp of mystic suggestion that it is hardly possible to find a choir which could perform it with sufficient sympathy, or an audience capable of adopting the attitude of mind which is necessary for the full reception of its qualities. It must be regarded rather as a fascinating revelation of the personal character of the composer and of the depth of his devotional disposition.

The same must be said, indeed, of the rest of the known motets, though the fact of their being in eight parts is not so much of a bar to their being performed as might be assumed on the surface. At least one of them must be always regarded as the greatest test of pure unaccompanied choral singing in existence, and choirs which have reasonable claims to being in the first rank are bound to attempt its performance now and then as a *tour-de-force*. The motet for eight voices which is made out of the 149th. Psalm, *Singet dem Herrn*, is indeed a *tour-de-force* of the kind which appeals to a large public, as it is essentially fit to demonstrate the volume of tone of a great choir, their spirit, agility, and endurance—all invaluable and easily appreciable traits in human beings. The object of employing such a large number of parts is mainly to make available the great variety of superb effects which can be produced by the apposition of two complete masses of voices. The basis of the idea is the contrast of two choirs, commonly held to have been originated in the two organ galleries on either side of the choir of St. Mark's at Venice, which Adrian Willaert is said to have utilised for two bodies of voices answering one another. The effect has always had great attractions for the human mind, both with accompaniment and without, and has been employed by most of the great composers of serious music from the latter part of the sixteenth century to the present day, the most familiar examples in Anglo-Saxon countries being the double choruses in Handel's "Israel in Egypt."

The advantage Bach enjoyed over all other composers in employing this type of art for unaccompanied motets lay in his unsurpassed power of characteristic part-writing for the voices, which produces such profuse interest of detail and linear texture. Through it he is enabled both to obtain sharp contrasts in the work allotted to each choir when they are required to be independent, and to make their agreement decisive when they have to answer one another in different levels of the scale. A very simple and effectual illustration is offered by the beginning of the motet, where the second choir shouts lustily the word "Singet!" in spondaically rhythmic chords, while the first choir sings ornate melodic passages, which gradually fill in with rich linear complications the interstices between the chords of the second choir; and by the time the process is completed the second choir in turn by degrees takes over the ornate melodic passages in different parts of the scale, while the first choir in its turn resorts to the jubilant shouting of the chords to the word "Singet!" the climax being the close "capping" of one another in vigorous alternations of short phrases. Of the alternations of long and of short phrases and the variety with which they are apportioned there is no need to speak; but one passage may be described as illustrating Bach's almost incredible facility in wielding multitudinous parts. The words "Die Kinder Zion sei'n fröhlich" are given in a brilliant fugal subject to the sopranos of the first choir; but at the same time the second choir is in full swing, all parts being busy with the musical material of the section; and in this occupation they persist, as if quite unconcerned with the doings of the first choir, while it goes through the complete fugal exposition. But when that is finished and all eight parts are busy, the second choir seems to become aware of the jubilant fugue subject which the first choir has been singing and begins on its own account on the same subject, but beginning this time from the bottom with the basses, the other voices answering step by step upwards till the whole of the two choirs are engaged in the same brilliant jubilation, which ends with rhythmic phrases of the utmost possible vivacity. Though the description is necessarily technical, Bach's intention is not technical any more than it is in the many other cases where he uses similar resources. He has not here to convey any tender or emotional meaning but the enthusiasm of human beings competing with one another in the very exuberance of their utterance of the words "Sing unto the Lord a new song," and in this sense the incisive shouts of "Singet!" "Singet!" are positively dramatic. Yet this would be impossible and utterly barren in effect but for the immediate answer of the other choir in its more continuous phraseology. In all such things Bach's treatment, though necessarily discussed in its technical aspects, has behind it some human interpretation and human purpose.

The contrast of the procedure which follows the first movement is altogether admirable, as the second movement is based on the simple melodies of a chorale. It is an old friend in a new guise, for here again we have the alternation of the familiar phrases given to one choir, and answering passages with different words and in more free style for the other choir. The whole is charmingly natural and tranquilly devout, and forms an episode of great value as a contrast to the movements at the beginning and end; and after it the vigorous jubilant style of the opening movement is resumed, at first with passages in which the two choirs answer one another, with the words "Lobet den Herrn," and finally with an extremely brilliant fugue, *Alles was Odem hat, lobe den Herrn! Hallelujah!* in which both choirs join, with rushing volume of sound suggesting the utmost exuberance. One little touch at the end is almost quaint in its sincere humanity, for the uplifting of the human feeling in the last phrase of the "Hallelujah!" as given to the sopranos, almost bursts the bounds of exact decorum:

yet its sincerity and aptness to the situation make it genuinely inevitable.

The eight-part motet, *Fürchte dich nicht,* for two equal choirs, has only one movement, but that movement is of colossal proportions, and is divided very clearly into two distinct portions, after a manner which has often been pointed out as being a favourite with the composer. The first portion is characterised by the rapidity with which the choirs answer one another in short phrases, and the second half by the amalgamation of the two choirs into one of four parts in a fugue with a long chromatic subject, which, by its continuity, makes a marked contrast to the somewhat restless and broken character of the first portion. A chorale is not introduced separately, but the tune of *Warum sollt' ich mich denn grämen* is given to the treble voices in the fugal portion of the movement.

The motet *Komm, Jesu komm, gieb Trost mir Müden* is of very different character. The first portion is in Bach's expressive vein and marked "Lento." There is no flashing of quickly answering phrases, but the choirs respond to one another in quiet, pleading, melodious passages which are maintained in the pathetic fugal portion, *O lass mich nicht in Todespein.* A short and more animated episode, *Komm, ich will mich dir ergeben,* leads to the most elaborate portion of the work, a finely flowing allegretto to the words "*Du bist der rechte Weg,*" and the whole is rounded off with a short melodious aria for four voices, which is not a chorale, though harmonised after the manner of one.

As has before been mentioned, many motets are attributed to Bach which are doubtful. Indeed, several manuscripts have his name written on them which are certainly not by him. This is possibly accounted for by the fact that the motets were among the very few works of his whose fame still lingered on during the time just after his death, when the world in general arrived at the complacent opinion that his achievements in general were no concern of theirs. The motets, however, were among those mysterious shibboleths which hum in the public ear, and somehow stir men's fancy with the tradition of something great and imposing, without their ever having actually heard or seen anything of them. The motets continued to be sung at Leipzig. There was a sort of mystery about them. Wiseacres who occasionally heard them reported to a curious world how wonderful they were. As Bach's works were then almost entirely unknown except to the small circle of the intimates of his lifetime, and as the latter left Leipzig after his death, there was no one there sufficiently in touch with his style to judge what was and what was not his, and whenever the manuscript of a motet came to light without a name, it was natural, simple, and convenient to write that of J. S. Bach on it.

In these days it may be a matter of surprise that it should be possible to have any doubts whether a work was by J. S. Bach or not. His personality is so exceptionally decisive that it would be thought that while no one else could pose in his garments, neither could he long make believe to be anyone else. But happily the tendency of mind to think of any man as superhuman is passing away; and men are getting to realise that it is more wonderful to think of supremely great works being achieved by human beings in spite of their human weaknesses, than to account for them by the pretence of a supernatural character which relieves them of human disabilities. The occasional moments when a great man lapses into incoherence or indefiniteness only enhance the interest of his fully matured works. All the master minds whose personality is most conspicuous yet leave the world in doubt at times as to the genuineness of works attributed to them, and in Bach's case further explanations are possible. One of the motets attributed to him by Spitta might without doubt have been produced quite early in his Mühlhausen period, before he had so comprehensively enriched his powers by copious study and practice in every form of art. In other cases there seems no doubt that motets have been made up of works by different composers, just as so many operas and other works were made up in the latter part of the eighteenth century; and it is possible that some motets attributed to Bach have some of his work in them, combined with work by Telemann or some other fairly efficient composer. And yet again it must be recalled that Bach trained a remarkable group of very able pupils, and these had the most favourable opportunities of saturating themselves with his style, and might very easily have produced motets which approximated to his personal manner in his least personal moments. In one case, at least, that of the famous *Ich lasse dich nicht*, the decision is especially difficult, because, while many good judges think it is by his uncle Johann Christoph, the fact that that composer greatly influenced his nephew in his most impressionable days, and that there was racial and temperamental kinship between them, would account for its being difficult to say decisively that it is not by John Sebastian. However, it clearly is unnecessary to discuss works which are doubtful, since their being doubtful is sufficient proof that, if authentic, they are not fully illustrative of the composer's powers. Among the likeliest is the eight-part motet *Lob und Ehre*, most of which, especially the final chorale, might pass muster as Bach's with the obvious qualification that he sometimes tried experiments which were not wholly successful.

The four-part motet *Lobet den Herrn*, which has a figured independent part for organ, is also confidently attributed to Bach. It is a boldly written fugal movement, with sufficient vigour and expression to be possibly his, but it is of scanty importance as illustrating his personality compared with the works above discussed.

It must remain a matter for wonder how such phenomenally difficult works could have been performed with such resources as Bach had at his disposal at Leipzig. That they were performed, and sufficiently well to have been impressive, is incontestable. Taken together with the analogous difficulties of many of the choruses in the cantatas, it implies that a great deal of stress must have been laid on special departments of technique in the singers in the church choirs, which now, especially in ecclesiastical choirs, have ceased to be cultivated Notwithstanding the unfavourable record of the boys at St. Thomas's School, it is difficult not to feel some respect for them when it is considered that they must have been able somehow to get through such a supremely difficult work as *Singet dem Herrn.* It has naturally been surmised that some accompaniment might have been supplied to these motets. But, apart from the fact that the essential beauty of this form of the motet lies in its being for unaccompanied voices, there is the fact that no organ part is in any way indicated in the score of most of these works, and that among the parts of *Singet dem Herrn* which were used by Bach for performance at the St. Thomas Church and are still preserved, there is no trace of anything in the nature of such a part. The case is different with the motet provided for the funeral of Ernesti, for which, as before mentioned, figured bass as well as instrumental parts are in existence, but the fact that this was for a special occasion, and that it is the only one of the group of motets which has this feature, militates against the view that any accompaniment was used for the other motets.

CHAPTER VIII

THE MASSES

THOUGH the religious spirit of the northern portion of the Teutonic race found its most congenial expression in the chorales, church cantatas, and such other forms of art as belonged essentially to the Reformed Church, it is well to remember that a very large portion of German principalities and powers continued loyal to the Roman Catholic Church, and that German composers had to supply music for the Roman ceremonial as well as for Protestant services. Moreover, the haphazard distribution of Catholic and Protestant centres, which resulted from the purely fortuitous preponderance of ruling family creed or local tradition, complicated the question of allegiance at times very capriciously; since a man might live in a town which was mainly of one form of faith and owe allegiance to a ruler who was a conspicuous representative of the other. Such a situation was notably illustrated in the person of John Sebastian Bach, and it was probably due to the difficulties which the divergent claims of the two forces induced that the world owes one of the greatest musical works in existence.

Bach was in the employment of a Protestant institution, set up in a Protestant town, and devoting his life to the glorification of Protestant services by thoroughly German Protestant music. But he also owed allegiance in the higher degree to the Roman Catholic ruler of Saxony, and whenever there was any serious question at issue between him and his immediate Protestant superiors at Leipzig, the ultimate appeal lay to the Roman Catholic power. The circumstances of Bach's official life constantly tended to make it important for him to stand well with the higher power. Uneasy relations with his immediate official superiors began at the very outset of his time at Leipzig. The independence of his character combined with the high level of his musical and temperamental standard to put all the lower natures in the town council and the consistory against him; and the anomaly that the theoretic scheme of the cantor's duties was hardly compatible with the actual standard of work which was required of him gave an appearance of substantiality to the criticisms of those who were unfavourable to him. Things were easier during Gesner's short tenure of the directorate of the St. Thomas School, and in him Bach found the liberal mind and generous temperament which could take in the situation in all its bearings and alleviate the strain between the large and the petty natures. But even while Gesner was still in office Bach had occasion to be conscious of the lack of appreciative sympathy among the powers that were at Leipzig, and of the advantage of standing well with the ruling Duke of Saxony; and in July, 1733, when he went to Dresden to see his son Friedemann installed as Organist of the Sophienkirche he bore with him a portion of a mass which he presented to Friedrich August, together with a letter which de fines his object. After the usual complimentary preface the letter proceeds in terms of modest deference:

> I lay before your kingly Majesty this trifling proof of the science which I have been able to acquire in music, with the very humble petition that you will be pleased to regard it, not according to the meanness of the composition but with a gracious eye, as well befits your Majesty's world-famed clemency and condescend to take me under your Majesty's most mighty protection. For some years, and up to the present time, I have had the direction of the music in the two principal churches in Leipzig; but I have had to suffer, though in all innocence, from one or another vexatious cause, at different times a diminution of the fees connected with this function, which might be withheld altogether unless your kingly Majesty will show me grace and confer upon me a predicate of your Majesty's Court Capelle, and will issue your high command to the proper persons for the granting of a patent to that effect. And such a gracious accedence to my most humble petition will bind me by infinite obligation: and I hereby offer myself in most dutiful obedience to prove my indefatigable diligence in composing church music, as well as in your orchestra, whenever it is your kingly Majesty's most gracious desire, and to devote my whole powers to your Majesty's service, remaining, with constant fidelity, your kingly Majesty's most humble and obedient servant,
>
> JOHANN SEBASTIAN BACH.
>
> Dresden, July 27, 1733.

The ultimate effect of this letter, reinforced by renewed applications, was that Bach was in 1736 made Hof-Komponist to King August III. What is of much greater importance is that the movements he offered to his sovereign were the Kyrie and the Gloria of the B minor mass; and this was the first intimation the world received of the existence of part of the mightiest choral work ever written. That he had not completed the work at that time is certain, and it is almost certain that it was never presented to the monarch as a whole, since its colossal proportions rendered it unfit to be performed as part of the Roman Catholic ceremonial of the mass.

The whole story of its coming into existence is indeed enigmatical to a fantastic degree. The enigma might be soluble as far as individual portions of the mass were concerned, since the Kyrie, Gloria, and Credo were still frequently, and the Sanctus occasionally, sung in Latin at certain seasons in the Lutheran churches in Leipzig, but they were not sung as parts of a whole consecutive work, but as insertions in the regular scheme of the Lutheran service. As, therefore, the complete work is unfitted for practical use in either Roman Catholic or Protestant churches, the only possible inference seems to be that Bach was moved by devotional impulses to complete the music to the Latin of the Roman mass, portions of which may have been written for use in the Lutheran service at Leipzig; and the fact that the composition was spread over many years at once confirms the inference and helps to explain the singular qualities of the work. But the enigmas are by no means exhausted by these considerations. Not only were the movements not composed consecutively, but in a large number of cases they were adaptations or expansions of movements taken from other works, such as church cantatas, and in one case even from a secular congratulatory cantata, written for some royal visit to Leipzig. And among the amazing features of it all, not the least amazing is the aptness of the transference from the German words to the Latin. In all cases the connection of the music with the meaning of the words in the respective languages is very close, and the result not merely justifies the apparently anomalous procedure, but, in the particular instances, entirely stultifies abstract criticism.

It is clear, then, from the outset that Bach went to work in an altogether different spirit from any which could have been adopted by Roman Catholic composers. They had, as a matter of fact, two different ways of dealing with mass music. When they wrote for voices unaccompanied they endeavoured to assimilate their style to that of the devotional composers of the latter part of the sixteenth century. But when they had an orchestra and solo voices as well as a choir, their style became essentially mundane. The passionate words of prayer served mainly as syllables for vocal music which would gratify a gay and thoughtless throng. Bach, though using the same Latin words as were employed in the Roman Church, took them to heart with a depth of earnestness which was essentially Teutonic. And this attitude was the ultimate source of the unique qualities of the work as a whole; for as an example of the setting of the mass it stands quite alone, even Beethoven's great mass appearing artificial and operatic by comparison.

The mere fugue subject of the *Kyrie* would be quite sufficient to show that the work was on a different plane from all other works of the kind; for the melody of the melismatic passage on the second syllable of the word "eleison," even in the single part, suggests an urgency of almost painful pleading; while the manner in which the passage rises to successively higher points affords opportunity to give vivid individuality to each several voice part, as the singers vie with each other in the eager urgency of the prayer. The scheme of the whole chorus is built up so as to make the pleading subject mount to successive points with more intense and more moving harmonisation till the whole of the five voices roll with devotional fervour into the final cadence. The *Christe* for two sopranos which follows, affords a very effectual and tender contrast, as it is in the major mode and free from the almost gloomy sadness of the *Kyrie.* It is as though the *Kyrie* implied the recognition of the faults which needed forgiveness, and the *Christe* breathed confidence in the infinite mercy which would pardon them; the effect of the voices being enhanced by the melodiously flowing accompaniment of massed violins after a favourite manner of the composer. After the *Christe* the *Kyrie* is, as usual, resumed, but not with the same musical development. Bach's instinct was in this case signally just: for music which closely represents and follows the course of human emotion does not admit of restatement. Beethoven instinctively indicated the simple principles which govern the question of repetition in his instrumental works; wherein it will be observed that in those which are pregnant with human feeling, such as the first movement of the "Sonata appassionata," and that of the Sonata in A, Opus 101, the first half of a movement is not repeated, but only in such cases when the charm or interest lies mainly in the qualities which represent absolute self-dependent music. The second *Kyrie* is much shorter than the first, sterner, simpler, and reduced to four voices instead of five; and the clue is supplied by its being in F sharp minor instead of B minor, thereby supplying a singularly effective anticipatory counterfoil to the *Gloria in excelsis* in D major, which instantly bursts in upon the close with brilliant animation. The greatest contrast is effected by vivacity of rhythm, and the exuberant energy of the principal subject is intensified by its being first presented by the trumpets, producing the effect of a dazzling light shed upon the multitude singing their fervent jubilations. The rush of sound after a while comes to an abrupt and arresting close, and the mood changes completely with the words "et in terra pax," a contrast of subdued wonder, tranquil, and meditative: into which is infused by slow degrees an air of serene joyousness as the subject of the "bonæ voluntatis" flows in among the quietly moving phrases. The initial subjects of the *Gloria* do not make their reappearance, but the music warms as the two subjects of the "peace" and the "good will" are interwoven into a close of perfect contentment.

After such an extent of choral work the *Laudamus te* is aptly allotted to a solo soprano, associated with a solo violin, a favourite combination with the composer. The style is extremely ornate, but never degenerates into mere conventional floridity. It might be suspected that Bach was following out the traditions of Roman Catholic composers, who in their mass music were so fond of writing elaborate roulades and flourishes for the operatic singers to show off their voices for the delectation of the faithful. But he had other objects in view.

It may be admitted, indeed, that Bach was one of the

most ornate composers who ever lived, but his profusion of detail was not a thing aimed at for itself, but the outpouring of the superabundance of his musical nature upon a musical groundwork which was brimming with vitality. Ornamental composers, as a rule, regard themselves as excused from presenting anything but the baldest and most conventional successions of harmony, and possibly eschew any interest of melody on the plea that the decorative adjuncts would be spoilt by it. With Bach, ornament becomes available to add force to the meaning of the words at the same time that it ministers to the claims of style. The solo movements in the mass afford the singers more than ample opportunity to display their technique, but they demand a very high power of interpretation as well, and without it in this case the technical facilities are purely futile. The power of the highest order of interpretation is also needed in this case by the solo violinist, for the part for him in this solo cannot be played by anyone whose mind has not been adequately nurtured into the completest sympathy with Bach's type of musical thought and phraseology. Here as elsewhere Bach's work demands a high elevation of mind, which makes an adequate presentation of the solos in the mass quite as difficult to obtain as the interpretation of the choruses.

Bach's sense of style is finely shown in the adoption of the very simplest possible diatonic procedure in the chorus, *Gratias agimus tibi,* which follows the solo, *Laudamus te.* The music, indeed, is borrowed from a slightly earlier cantata, *Wir danken dir, Gott,* wherein the German words have the same meaning and spirit as the Latin. The transplantation is, thanks to the consistency of Bach's style by this time, entirely conclusive, and ministers with singular value to the general scheme of design of the work, suggesting the atmosphere of quiet and steadfastness most grateful after the elaboration of previous movements. So far as motion may be compared to stillness, it serves the same sort of purpose as the plain spaces in the midst of ornate structural features in architecture, restoring the sense of stability of which the mind is liable to lose hold when constantly excited by profusion of details; and in this chorus the sense of stability is confirmed by the type of the subject used in its fugal complexities, which suggests a most ancient lineage.

The duet for soprano and tenor soli, for which the words *Domine Deus, rex cœlestis* serve, is not so ornate as the *Laudamus te,* but it resumes the richer elaboration of texture. The melodic material is in a singularly tender mood, the cue to which is a short descending figure of four notes from tonic to dominant which Bach used rather frequently when in that vein, as in the solo *Sehet, Jesus hat die Hand uns zu fassen angespannt* in the Matthäus-Passion, and in the cantata, *Süsser Trost mein Jesus kommt,* and the mood is emphasised by the accompaniment for flute, violins and violas *con sordini* and pizzicato basses. Such a mood might not seem obviously appropriate to the words unless it be remembered that the name "Jesus" always suggested to Bach, and probably to the majority of German Lutherans of that time, a feeling of tenderness and love. The activity of Bach's mind in pondering over these things is illustrated by the fact that in the earlier part of the duet the solo voices always alternate the words "Domine Deus, rex cœlestis" and "Domine Fili unigenite Jesu Christe," overlapping, so that they are practically almost simultaneous, evidently employing the available means to suggest "the unity of the Persons." In the final passage which links the duet to the succeeding chorus the voices join together in thirds and sixths in the appeal to the "Agnus Dei" in a vein of tender sadness.

The *Qui tollis*, a four-part chorus which follows, is one of Bach's most concentrated and deeply felt movements. The scheme is a fugal exposition and free developments proceeding therefrom with independent figuration for the accompanying flutes and strings. The vocal subject seems even to spring spontaneously from the verbal syllables, and every individual note has its meaning and function in the scheme of melodic expression, of which fact the pathetic little phrase of the "Miserere nobis" would leap to the memory as a spontaneous stroke of genius.

But the fact is that the movement was not composed to the words, but is borrowed from the cantata *Schauet doch und sehet.* True it is that there is the closest kinship of meaning between the words of the cantata "Behold and see if there is any sorrow like unto My sorrow" and the Latin "Thou that takest upon Thee the sins of the world, have mercy on us," but it would scarcely be believed that music could be so aptly transferred from German to Latin unless it were here seen. The phrase which serves so ideally for the "Miserere" stands as follows in the original:

Apart from the perfection of the transference, Bach improved the movement in the process. He made its texture a little richer and transposed it a minor third lower, thereby giving it a more mournful character. The clue to the alteration of the opening phrase

is found in the forty-fourth bar of the original version of the movement, where in order to make the relation of the choral bass part to the instrumental bass more perfect he modifies the phrase so as to present the subject in the form in which it appears in the *Qui tollis*. The two succeeding movements, the *Qui sedes* and the *Quoniam tu solus*, are solos for contralto and bass respectively: the former having an accompaniment for oboe d'amore solo and strings, and being in a vein of tender pleading, laying special stress on the words "miserere nobis"; and the latter in a bolder and more strenuous style, with a very striking horn solo and two bassoons in the accompaniment.

To the latter succeeds without break one of the great choruses of the work, the *Cum sancto Spiritu*, a movement in which all Bach's resources of brilliancy are brought into exercise, showing the ripe fruits of all his experience in this particular style, which is all his own; combining the devices of fugue with the mighty procession of harmonies, which march from climax to climax and fitly close this portion of the mass.

There seems no possibility of identifying the time when the Credo was written, but judging from the overwhelming effect of the change of style which it manifests it would be natural to suppose that it was written on purpose to follow the *Cum sancto Spiritu*. The Credo is indeed in what may fairly be called a Latin style; a powerful adaptation of the style of the Roman Church, which is partly owing to the use of a phrase of ancient plain-song as the most prominent feature in the music. But it is the accompaniment which Bach weds to it which gives to it the character of affirmation which is positively fierce in its intensity. This character, severe, simple, and direct, lays, as it were, the foundation of the musical setting of the creed; a character which is maintained unflagging throughout the whole of the opening movement, presenting Bach's resources of polyphony in constant measure of dignity and power. It must be admitted that after so decisive an opening the passage to the words *Patrem omnipotentem* is much less striking. It is indeed an adaptation, with characteristic changes of detail, from the first chorus in the cantata *Gott, wie dein Name*. The movement is animated, but indeed a little formal. It is followed by a duet for soprano and alto, *Et in unum Dominum*, which again is rather formal in character, the doctrinal statement not appealing to Bach's humanity in any suggestive manner. Far otherwise is it with the chorus *Et incarnatus est*.

The reference to the mystery of the Incarnation always appealed to composers, and even in early choral masses it frequently stands out from the rest of the music by reason of its solemn and tender feeling. Bach's treatment suggests the stillness of wonder tinged with sadness. The voices move slowly and quietly through strange harmonies, and the violins have a characteristic figure of accompaniment throughout which supplies an element of poignancy. It is interesting to find this figure employed again in the cantata *Nimm von uns* (see p. 407).

The "*Crucifixus*" which follows is the most deeply emotional chorus in the whole work. It is a slightly amplified version of the first part of the first chorus of the cantata *Weinen, Klagen, Sorgen, Zagen,* and is knit into the closest unity by the employment of a chromatic ground-bass, the persistence of which adds to the tragic intensity of the expression. Each voice enters separately as with an amazed soul-stricken ejaculation of the single word "Crucifixus," and then, all joining together in the reflective "etiam pro nobis," warm to a passion too deep for tears. Bach's supreme mastery of the expressive harmonies which are obtainable by polyphonic treatment here finds its highest manifestation. Even colour lends its aid to the effect; for the bass voices, having a part which is mainly independent of the true bass, descend near the end to a low part of their scale and produce an extraordinary effect of sombre depth. The final passage to the words "sepultus est" is one of the supreme moments in music. Its wonder lies in its combining, like a psychological condition, many different phases. While the rare harmonies and the melody descending to the lowest available notes in the voices express the depths of overwhelming sorrow, the subtle alteration of the progression of the bass from the long reiterated formula which has persisted throughout the movement suggests to the mind mysteriously the sense of something great that is coming. So the very passage which embodies the utmost exhaustion of despair suggests at the same time the premonition of the triumphant *Resurrexit*, which seems to leap from the very close of the *Crucifixus*, and is sustained with a perfect blaze of jubilant exhilaration throughout. A very striking feature of this chorus is the fine passage for the basses alone to the words "et iterum venturus est," which is, as it were, intruded out of sheer exuberance, and not only shows Bach's characteristic vein of melody in a very forcible aspect (which every singer who has enjoyed singing the passage will confirm), but is also a stroke of genius of a high order from the psychological side.

After a movement which is so supremely triumphant, reaction is inevitable. Bach allots a series of clauses of the Creed, which are for the most part not at all inspiring from the musical or emotional point of view, to a solo bass voice. The series of doctrinal statements have very little inherent cohesion, so Bach contents himself, as elsewhere, with relying on the artistic effect of pleasant flowing melody and the interest of development to carry the movement through. This tranquil movement is very happily placed and serves as a comparative pause and a moment of quietude between the *Resurrexit* which precedes it and the rugged severity of the *Confiteor* which follows. In this chorus Bach adopts an archaic manner in close kinship with the opening phrases of the *Credo*. The counterpoint of the voice passages is almost unadorned except by such simple and familiar devices as are recognised even in theoretic counterpoint. It would not be exceeding fair limits of conjecture to surmise that Bach was impelled by the prominently doctrinal aspect of the clause to adopt a style which strongly suggests academic orthodoxy. The effect of purely contrapuntal treatment is to give the impression of richly interlaced lines without much decisive definition of general design. This, in such forms as the fugue, is indeed one of its charms and excellences, since it ministers to elasticity. Bach's mind, always awake to the subtlest artistic purposes, made use of this character here in a very striking manner; for from the maze of the five- and six-part counterpoint suddenly emerges with almost savage insistence the ancient plain-song intonation of the *Confiteor*, first given to the basses and then in augmentation to the tenors. To the hearer it suggests almost dramatically the assertion of orthodoxy on the part of the typical priest, standing out in its uncompromising decisiveness from the vaguer orthodoxy of the masses of the people.

One of the most extraordinary passages in the whole mass occurs in the middle of this chorus, which shows the extent to which Bach was influenced by the suggestive qualities of individual words. At the arrival of the words "expecto resurrectionem mortuorum" the character of the movement changes so suddenly that it seems as if it was brought almost to a standstill. Orthodox counterpoint is abandoned; but it serves a purpose even when it is gone, for it throws into relief the surprising series of harmonies, which evidently presuppose the mystery of death being in the first place most prominently in his mind. And the sequence is just, for though the word happens to come last in the sentence, in fact death would obviously have to precede resurrection, so Bach rightly follows the order of ideas rather than the order of words. But every word is made to tell: the strange setting of the "expecto," suggesting wonder-stricken expectancy, the characteristic device of taking the basses up to their highest and brightest colour for the word "resurrectionem" and down to a practically dark and obscure note for the "mortuorum," are only a few of the points which are covered by Bach's comprehensive imagination; beyond them is the manner in which he conveys the sense of hesitating bewilderment and terror which suddenly vanishes as a cloud before the sun, and glides into the joyous light of confident belief in the resurrection which is vivaciously expressed in the final portion of the chorus;[1] as though the mind looked forward beyond the gate of death, and the soul of the worshipper were uplifted and absorbed in the contemplation of the promise of the limitless after-life, with which and the joyously confirmatory "Amen" the Chorus, and with it the *Credo*, concludes.

It would be natural to expect a considerable break between the *Credo* and the *Sanctus*. The truly tremendous scope of the choruses at the end of the former makes a comparative rest from surging masses of sound and great exercise of physical forces almost

[1] The musical materials of this jubilant part of the *et expecto* are the same, with some amplifications, as the central Chorus in the Cantata *Gott man lobet dich.*

imperative to both listener and performer. If the work had been constructed all in one piece, and there had been any choice in the disposition of the words, a very considerable contrast would have been desirable between the *Confiteor* and the *Sanctus* which follows it. As has already been pointed out, Bach wrote the various portions of the mass at long-spaced intervals. And the work is, in a sense, like a compilation of huge independent entities, juxtaposed rather than consecutive, and fused into one more by the consistency of the personality of J. S. Bach and his religious feelings than by any principles of scheme in an organic sense. It is unlikely that Bach ever conceived it possible for the work to be performed in its entirety just as it stands, without even the intervention of that rest and relaxation of the faculties which would be supplied by the portion of the service which is spoken or intoned. He may scarcely have contemplated its performance at all. The conditions of his life were not favourable for opportunities. It is almost inconceivable that performance in the secular conditions of the concert-room could have crossed his mind for a moment, and the result is that when performed in its entirety the sequence of great choruses presents practical drawbacks.

The first part of the *Sanctus* is indeed the greatest conception in the whole mass, but it labours, in ordinary mundane conditions of performance, under obvious disabilities. Yet it does so far soar into the empyrean above all that precedes it that even the average mind feels the grandeur of the conception. Moreover, apart from the fact of following such a series of massive choruses, the conception of supreme adoration expressed in it follows with fine intrinsic fitness upon the music expressing joy in the promise of life after death, when the glory of the Deity is presupposed to be no longer hidden from the worshippers. The music conveys in a superb fashion the suggestion of multitudinous hosts singing in adoration, and the rolling of tumultuous harmonies through the infinite spaces of heaven. The chorus is divided into two portions, after Bach's frequent practice, and the first half has a dignified and massive swing, well befitting the solemnity of the tenor of the words, and, after being developed up to the fulness of ripest vitality in every part, gives place to a brilliant portion, in much quicker time, to the words "Pleni sunt cœli et terra gloria ejus," which has a very spirited and rhythmic subject and serves well to complete the movement. The *Osanna* is also inevitably a chorus, and is very similar in style to the latter part of the *Sanctus*, besides being in the same key, which, when the performance of the work is without its liturgical context, is rather a drawback. The musical material is in this case borrowed from the first chorus of the secular cantata *Preise dein Glücke*. Its most striking feature is the animated effect of the two choirs, for which it is written, alternating and answering one another. Its vivacity is indeed dazzling, and lends most happy antecedence for the tender, contemplative character of the *Benedictus* which is given to a tenor solo, with violin solo accompaniment. The style here, as in most of the other solos, is ornate, dwelling very insistently upon the essential word "benedictus," as only Bach knows how to do, in decorative terms.

The *Osanna* is, as usual, repeated after the *Bene-*

dictus, and then comes another of the surprisingly apt transferences to the Mass, the deeply pathetic *Agnus Dei*. As is the case with the *Qui tollis* and the *Crucifixus*, the music seems to fit the words so ideally that it is difficult to realise that it was not originally conceived in connection with them. The words in the Ascension-tide cantata *Lobet Gott*, from which it is taken, are *Ach, bleibet doch mein liebster Leben*, and are obviously akin in feeling to those of the *Agnus*, though not bearing the same significance. The movement is subjected to much more expansion and development than the previous transferences in the Mass, and the result is the most beautiful solo movement in the whole work, breathing the tenderest melancholy, which the nobly melodious accompaniment of the massed violins, partly echoing the strains of the voice and partly giving play to independent figures, vastly enhances. The mass concludes with a repetition of the music of the *Gratias agimus* from the earlier part of the work, to the concluding words "Dona nobis pacem," the noble simplicity of style making a very fitting and solemn conclusion to the immense scheme.

The work as a whole is not only unique in its greatness and in the strange manner in which it was composed, but also as a vindication of the completeness with which it manifests the consistency of Bach's individual character. For while the music composed expressly for the mass spreads over several years, the *Kyrie* and *Gloria* having been written at latest in 1733, and the *Credo* possibly before that, the *Crucifixus* before 1729, and the *Sanctus* not till 1735 at the earliest, yet the consistency of the devotional personality of the composer welds the whole into a convincing unity. The borrowed movements are so admirably applied that, in truth, some of them are among the most beautiful and expressive in the work, as they are among the most perfect in the whole range of the cantatas. The borrowing may be explained by the surmise that Bach did not expect his church cantatas to be frequently performed, and that such music as he could not help knowing to be as noble and expressive as any he could produce might well be transferred to a place for which it was so ideally fitted. As it happens, these noble movements have more opportunity to be heard in the mass than they have in their original conditions, and the world has reason to be grateful for a procedure which brought such movements as the *Qui tollis*, the *Crucifixus*, and the *Agnus Dei* within the scope of a single work. But, whether the expressly composed movements or the borrowed movements are concerned, all alike show the fervour of intention and intuition, the depth of brooding thought, and the unsurpassable power to convey in the richest and most exalted manner the spiritual meaning which the composer felt to be embodied in the words.

Bach also wrote several masses on a smaller scale than the B minor mass, but they do not call for detailed consideration. Two of them, in G major and G minor, are compilations of movements and materials from various cantatas, such as *Es wartet alles auf dich*, and *Wer Dank opfert*, and *Halt' im Gedächtniss*, and *Gott, der Herr, ist Sonn' und Schild*—often more curious than satisfactory. It seems probable that both these works were written for the Roman Catholic service, probably to keep his Roman Catholic Lord Paramount, the Elector of Saxony, in mind of him, and this may have also been the case with the A major mass, part of which was borrowed from earlier works, and part composed specially. Of the latter the opening *Kyrie* is a very fine specimen of Bach's choral writing, and of his extraordinary mastery of technical feats, as no inconsiderable part of it is worked in canon.

The F major mass can hardly have been intended for the Roman Catholic ceremony, as the remarkable feature occurs in the *Kyrie* of a Protestant chorale, *Christe, du Lamm Gottes,* being introduced very conspicuously in the instrumental accompaniment to the severely contrapuntal voice parts. This would imply that if performance was contemplated at all it was intended for use at Leipzig at seasons when portions of the service were still sung in Latin. The suggestiveness of the particular chorale in conjunction with the *Kyrie* is obvious. It is also noteworthy that in this same chorus Bach introduces a canto fermo of the old church taken from the litany, thus combining traits of the older form of the religion with the new, as if to typify the continuity of the essential basis of religious worship. It seems probable that the masses were written at about the same period of his life as the B minor mass, that is, between 1730 and 1737, and it may be recalled that it was in 1736 that Bach was made Hofcomponist to the Elector of Saxony, who was also titular King of Poland.

CHAPTER IX

SECULAR CANTATAS

A LARGE number of secular cantatas, serenatas, and works of that kind which Bach wrote at various times are, it may be admitted, of less intrinsic interest than the rest of his works. But circumstances invest them with very considerable external interest. In the first place, curiosity is aroused to see in what way the mind which revealed itself most fully in art of the most elevated kind would comport itself in circumstances where loftiness of thought and deep feeling would be superfluous. And the interest of the situation does not confine itself to the simple question whether Bach was capable of gaiety, light-hearted merriment, and humour, for most of his secular works on a large scale were official productions, written to grace court functions of various royal or aristocratic patrons; and it would be hard to find any type of art which was less likely to appeal to him or elicit his finest inspirations. The high-flown extravagance which characterised poems written for such occasions was qualified to stupefy anyone but the most hardened of official composers, and it is very interesting to consider Bach's efforts to deal with them without belying his personality. Moreover the complications do not cease there. As has been pointed out, a great amount of useful work had been done before his time in the development of style and artistic methods, but this had been for the most part, especially in Germany, in the line of sacred music. The only branches of art on a large scale in which secular style had been deliberately cultivated were the Italian opera and the Italian serenata; but these types of art had not appealed to him, because the harmonic style which they represented was as yet in a much more elementary phase of development than the polyphonic or contrapuntal style in which he found his most congenial sphere of utterance. The cultivation of the homophonic style by Italian composers had already awakened men's minds to a lively perception of the virtues of design, and Bach, with his usual openness of mind, had followed their lead in such respects as approved themselves to his judgment.

But it is not in types of design that the differences between sacred and secular music are found. Elementary principles of construction are of universal application. The buildings provided for great gatherings of people at concerts or public meetings must have roofs and walls and means of access and egress like churches and cathedrals. The principles of form of some of the most deeply impressive choruses and sacred works by the greatest composers are the same as those of the most trivial songs in the cheapest of comic operas. It is in the style of detail, in texture, type of ornament, forms of expression, the features in which human and æsthetic interest is presented, that the main differences between secular and sacred art are manifested. Bach himself, in adopting Italian types of form, did not abandon the contrapuntal methods which were so deeply engrained in his disposition; but the Italians were tending to lay so much stress on the agreeable effect of well managed form that their attitude was reacting unfavourably on the intrinsic qualities of their music. They were passing into the hopelessly barren period, when people were satisfied with mere regularity and clearness of construction slightly adorned with meaningless and conventional ornamentation. There, of course, Bach could not follow them.

Hence the difficulties of his position in relation to secular art of this type were accentuated; for the contrapuntal style in choral music was so intimately and deeply associated with sacred music that it would be difficult to shake off the feeling of incongruity when it was used for secular words. In this kind of art the differentiation of style had hardly begun. The fact that Bach had given much attention to secular instrumental music did not afford much help. No doubt it lightened his hand and infused a rhythmic lilt into his secular compositions which was often of the greatest service; but the style of such instrumental music was not universally adaptable to the choral movements and vocal solos of the secular cantatas, though, as will presently be seen, he availed himself of dance measures in them with happy effect when occasion served. So it comes about that the greater portion of the music of the secular cantatas, especially those written for court functions, is not conspicuously different in style from his sacred music. The facts are confirmed by the parallel case of Handel, for the difference in style between his opera and oratorio airs is fundamentally very slight; and one of the most tender of his love songs from an opera has been adapted to sacred words of most serious import, and is sung in churches without conveying any sense of impropriety to worshippers who are unaware of its original intention, while many of the finest choruses in his secular serenatas and odes are identical in style with his oratorio choruses.

The secular cantatas of Bach do not, therefore, in themselves illustrate any special phase of development in the composer, but they do very strangely illustrate the adaptability of quasi-secular music to sacred conditions, and the fact that a good deal of very admirable music lies in the neutral ground, where kindred emotions are aroused which are only identifiable as sacred or secular by the words with which they are associated. The border line between the sacred and the secular must in any case be as indefinite and unstable as the border line in any other sphere. Though musical secularity tends away from the sacred type in the direction of gaiety and superficiality, the deeper secular emotions, in proportion as they become more serious, assimilate closely to religious emotions.

Bach was undoubtedly capable of ample gaiety and merriment, as the lighter movements in his suites and overtures show. On the other hand, his sacred music dealt with religious emotions which were not affiliated or restricted to any particular denomination, but were deep enough to be universal. And hence came about the circumstance which at first sight seems so perplexing, that many of the choruses and solo movements which Bach wrote for court functions were afterwards fitted with solemn words and transferred successfully to sacred works. If the music of these works had been exclusively secular, such procedure would have appeared almost revolting. But, in fact, the result shows how deeply sincere Bach could be even when he had to write music for a court function.

It is most probable that the earliest of these court-functional works was written in the Weimar days, for no occasion is known which would account for an earlier composition than the hunting cantata *Was mir behagt*, which was composed by command of Duke Wilhelm Ernst to words by Salomo Franck in honour of a hunting party which took place on the birthday of Duke Christian of Saxe Weissenfels in February, 1716. Like many other secular cantatas by Bach, the subject is treated semi-dramatically. The soloists impersonate Diana as goddess of hunting; Endymion, with whom she had been in love but whom she was temporarily setting aside while giving her attention to Duke Christian; Pan as god of the countryside, and Pales as goddess of agricultural animals. Diana begins with a recitative and a merry hunting aria, with suitable horn accompaniment. Endymion protests at being neglected, in a recitative and an aria, the former of which contains an ornamental passage on the first syllable of "Jagen" of almost incredible length. Diana and Endymion sing a duet, and then follow a recitative and an aria for Pan, the latter of which, in spite of the uninspiring words "A Prince is the Pan of his country," is a very fine and vigorous movement, which Bach inserted with a few revisions in the latter part of the sacred cantata *Also hat Gott* as long afterwards as 1735. Pales has a charming shepherd-song with accompaniment of two flutes, which is followed by a lively chorus and a duet. The most interesting feature in the whole work is the aria for Pales, *Weil die wollenreichen Heerden*, in which the whole musical material of the accompaniment of one of the most famous of Bach's sacred songs, *Mein gläubiges Herze frohlocke*, in the same cantata, *Also hat Gott*, mentioned above, makes its appearance with a solo voice part which is totally different from that well-known melody:

The melody in "Was mir behagt."

Weil die woll - en - rei - chen Heer - den

The melody in the Cantata "Also hat Gott die Welt geliebt."

Mein gläu - bi - ges Her - ze, Froh-lock-e, sing Scherze, Froh-

The Accompaniment.

durch dies weit - ge - pries - ne Feld

locke, sing Scher - ze, Dein Je - sus ist da.

The phenomenon of such an after-thought as the ultimate development of the sacred song on the secular foundation, and an after-thought which has every appearance of spontaneity, is surprisingly illuminative of Bach's tenacity in turning ideas over in his mind and trying them in various aspects. The cantata proceeds with an air for Pan and ends with a very lively and rhythmic chorus, with much horn-blowing and playing of passages suggestive of the exuberant liveliness of joyous people going hunting. The chorus illustrates a rather exceptional excursion into the region of secular choral music; the interpretation of secularity in this case being mainly the adoption of a franker connection in the music with the metre of the poem set, and a rhythmically homophonic treatment of the voices. Bach transferred this last chorus with considerable modifications to the sacred cantata *Man singet mit Freuden.* The cantata was indeed a conspicuous example of doing varied service, for besides the transfers above mentioned it was used again for a birthday of a younger member of the Weimar family, by changing "Christian" into "Ernst August" wherever it occurred in the music, and yet again it was used at Leipzig in honour of Friedrich August, King of Saxony.

The next secular work of the kind was probably the serenata *Durchlaucht'ster Leopold,* written in honour of a birthday of Prince Leopold of Anhalt-Cöthen while Bach was in his service before the move to Leipzig. The words were not calculated to inspire the composer, as they are formal and artificial, but Bach shows his sense of responsibility by artistic treatment. It is as though he made up his mind that, however dull the words were, his share of the whole should be worthy of him. The work is all for solo voices, and comprises a dignified opening recitative followed by an elaborate aria for soprano, extremely florid in style, and an aria for bass. Then come features which are interesting from the point of view of the special line of work which occupied him while he was at Cöthen. A duet aria for soprano and bass is marked "Al tempo di minuetto," and has the graceful and pleasing character of a minuet. It passes into a more vigorous movement, followed by an ornate recitative for soprano and bass, and this in its turn by a very lively aria in dance rhythm, after the manner of a bourrée. A very quaint solo for bass with flowing accompaniment for bassoon and violoncello, and a final duet marked "Chor," also in unmistakable dance rhythm, like a very tuneful and animated minuet, complete the work. The scheme is admirable; beginning in a solid and dignified style and ending with gay and happy measures, the texture and treatment of details being essentially in the manner Bach adopted in the lighter movements of his suites and overtures. In view of these qualities it seems singular that Bach used nearly all the movements again in the sacred cantata *Erhöhtes Fleisch und Blut.* Another cantata in honour of Prince Leopold, *Mit Gnaden bekröne,* remains only in an incomplete state in which it was recognised by Spitta in a private collection. Some of it appears to have been included in the church cantata, *Ein Herz das seinen Jesum lebend weiss,* which contains some brightly melodious solos and a lively final chorus.

Yet another cantata of the same order, *Schwingt*

freudig euch empor, was used in a variety of capacities. It served in 1726 as a congratulatory cantata for the birthday of the second wife of Prince Leopold, also for someone else's birthday celebration later. It was reconstructed with the insertion of chorales as a church cantata, and it also served as a birthday cantata for a popular professor of the Leipzig University, one Johann F. Rivinus. In this composition there are two choruses, one to begin and the other to end the work, and alternation of recitatives and arias for the middle portion. It is worth noting, in connection with the Cöthen associations, that the final chorus is in a dance measure and style.

One of the most important of these complimentary cantatas is that known as *Der Zufriedengestellte Æolus*, which went through an exceptionally humorous transformation. It was originally written in August, 1725, in honour of the birthday of a professor of the University of Leipzig named August Friedrich Müller. A little over eight years later, at the beginning of 1734, Bach had to provide a cantata in honour of the coronation of Augustus "the Strong" as King of Poland. The transfer of the cantata from Müller to King Augustus was facilitated by the fact of their having the same name, "August," and the dimensions and quality of the work were such a very high compliment to the former that it became more than amply adequate to the titular eminence of the latter. The work is indeed one of the most extensive of Bach's secular cantatas; for it is not only on a very large scale—requiring two flutes, two hautboys, two horns, three trumpets, drums and strings (including viola d'amore and viola da gamba), a very efficient chorus, and several soli for its rendering—but it stands high as an example of Bach's copious fancy and invention. The first movement, *Zerreisset, zersprenget,* is a Chorus of Winds, with rushing passages of the most brilliant description for both instruments and voices. The second number is a recitative for Æolus which is accompanied by the entire orchestra—a thing which is rare in Bach's works. The realistic suggestion of the rushing winds is again in evidence. The aria which follows (also for Æolus) is a good specimen of Bach's conception of secular music, being very rhythmic and jovial. Æolus announces that he "will laugh heartily" and the music, in a semi-humorous manner, amply confirms the statement.

A charming contrast is obtained by a tender and graceful air for Zephyrus. Pallas and Pomona also take part in the discussion in various admirable recitatives and arias,[1] and the work is completed by the

[1]The aria allotted to Pallas was transferred later to the sacred cantata *Gott, wie dein Name.*

jovial chorus "Vivat August," which in its direct rhythmic vigour seems to be akin to Lulli, a kinship which is not diminished by the excellent effect of interchanging groups of three and two bars.

Yet another cantata, *Vereinigte Zwietracht,* was written in honour of a Professor of the Leipzig University, Gottlieb Kortte in 1726. In this case the work goes by the name of a "Dramma per Musica." It begins with a march, which suggests the merry pretence of solemn processioning of students to pay their compliments to the professor. The music has a whimsically innocent air which recalls both Lulli and Purcell. Bach probably knew very little of the instrumental music of either of them, but the manner in which kindred impulses beget kindred results is shown by comparison of the opening bars of Bach's march with those of Lulli's march in "Theseus."

The march is succeeded by a very lively chorus, which calls the students to mind again. It is a singularly apt example of Bach's characteristic transferences, as the movement is devised by adding voice parts to the third movement of the first Brandenburg concerto.

A set of soloists take their turns in the capacities of the personified abstractions, "Industry," "Honour," "Happiness," and "Thankfulness," and the work ends with a robustly straightforward chorus which is homophonic almost throughout, and has a very hearty tune, in which Professor Kortte is wished long life and health.

Kort - te le - be,.... Kort - - - te blü - he,

In this case Bach's personal sentiments must have been much more genuinely engaged than in the complimentary cantatas to grandees. He seems to have entered into the spirit of the occasion heartily, and the music is frank, fresh, and unsophisticated, expressive of such secular joviality as would be inevitable on an occasion when young members of a university did honour to an esteemed professor. A great part of this cantata was used again in a "Nameday" cantata for King August, with the words *Auf, schmetternde Töne.*

In 1733 Bach had several times to produce secular choral works for complimentary occasions. *Die Wahl des Hercules,* which was composed for the birthday of an electoral prince, stands out in marked contrast to the foregoing. Here Bach was confronted with a scheme fatuous enough to extinguish the most ardent inspiration. The petty rulers of parts of Germany, taking Louis XIV. as their model in such matters, had grown so accustomed to their subjects literally grovelling before them on state occasions that to have omitted to compare them with gods and goddesses of ancient times would have been quite a gross breach of good manners, and a manifest neglect of what was due to social superiors. Everyone was quite aware in the secret recesses of his mind, where truth always keeps a dim and tranquil light, that it was all silly pretence and folly. The court trick is to disguise such things by the cleverness with which they are presented; to gloss the conventional by the intermixture of the lively play of mental dexterities; to show the expert's skill in what may be regarded as the purely ornamental part of social intercourse. Bach had not led the life which gave him any key to such a kind of existence. It may be admitted that when he addressed communications to grandees he duly abased himself even unto the ground in accordance with the unwritten law of his time, but that was not an attitude which he could adopt in music with any hope of doing himself justice. The course which he ultimately took in the latter part of his life was as surprising as, in a sense, it was heroic. He seems to have shut his eyes to the actual verbiage, and to the futile flummery of transparently ridiculous flattery which the verbiage expressed, and to have gone to the root of the conceptions, the ultimate primal abstract sentiment which underlay the accumulated rubbish of courtly convention. The course pursued in previous cantatas has shown the tendencies of his gravitation. Many movements set to secular words had, possibly accidentally, proved quite fit to be associated with sacred words and embodied in sacred works. *Die Wahl des Hercules* almost suggests that he here awoke to the full consciousness of the course which was best for him to follow in order to safeguard the sincerity of his art. His course was to merge the individual in the universal, the practical in the ideal.

The root idea of the poem is the indecision of the youthful Hercules whether to choose "Wollust" or "Tugend" as the object of his life. They are, of course, personified, and sing recitatives and arias to display to him the respective advantages they have to offer. Hercules consults "Echo," whose responses are in favour of "Tugend," and then Mercury announces that Hercules is really no other than their Crown Prince Friedrich, who is going to adopt "Tugend," and all that is necessary further is for the chorus, representing the public, to express their high appreciation of his decision and their good will. The musical scheme consists of an opening chorus, a succession of vocal solos and duets, and a final chorus. The opening chorus is quietly contemplative in a manner suggesting the frame of mind induced by the thought of youth and its infinite variety of physical and spiritual possibilities—youth that may expand into a glorious future—youth that may be cut off before its prime—youth that may be destined for suffering or for joy. It does not particularly matter about this Prince Friedrich. What will do for youth in the abstract as it presents itself to the contemplative mind will do for him. So Bach has written a very quiet and serious chorus to the words *Lasst uns sorgen, lasst uns wachen über unsern Gottes Sohn,* it being of no consequence whether they referred histrionically to Hercules, or immediately (as is inferred in the figurative procedure) to the young Prince Friedrich. The chorus expresses a sentiment which in itself is admirable, and expresses it admirably. So when, in the following year Bach was preparing his

"Weihnachts-Oratorium," this chorus, with the words changed to *Fallt mit Danken, fallt mit Loben vor des Höchsten Gnaden Thron,* was placed at the beginning of the fourth part. It may be worth pointing out in passing that the work, written for the birthday of a young prince (who, in theory at least, was worthy of the highest love and reverence), naturally suggests aptness of transference to the Weihnachts-Fest, especially with people who were disposed to emphasise the human side of the Christ-ideal rather than the Godhead. But more arresting than any other movement in the work is the exquisite slumber song, *Schlafe, mein Liebster und pflege der Ruh*, which is put into the mouth of Wollust. Here the ideal is manifest. Bach is not thinking of the individual instance, but of the general conception of the slumber song by the cot of an innocent child in all its beauty of sentiment. The ideal conception in this case laid hold of him in its fullest force and it bore fruit in some of the most exquisitely tender and touching music he ever produced. So, when at work on the same "Weihnachts-Oratorium" above mentioned, the movement was transferred to represent the slumber song at the manger-cot of the Holy Babe. And in that capacity it has become one of the best known of all Bach's solo songs.

The procedure so indicated was followed with most of the movements in the *Wahl des Hercules.* The song in which Hercules takes counsel with Echo becomes *Flosst, mein Heiland* in the Weihnachts-Oratorium; Virtue's song *Auf meinen Flügeln* is transferred to the same work as *Ich will nur dir zu Ehren leben;* the song of Hercules addressed to Wollust,

Ich will dich nicht hören, becomes the well-known *Bereite dich Zion*, and the tender duet between Hercules and Virtue, *Ich bin deine, ich kusse dich*, etc., becomes *Herr dein Mitleid*. There only remains the last chorus, which is just a lively expression of good will to the young prince such as was inevitable on such a complimentary occasion, in which case the individual could not be so easily merged in a type, and the chorus is founded on a gavotte rhythm and quite frankly metrical, so this one movement was inapt to be transferred to the sacred work.

Considering that the "Weihnachts-Oratorium" was produced such a short time after the complimentary *Wahl des Hercules*, it is just conceivable that the order in which secular and sacred words have generally been inferred to have been attached to the music was, at least in some numbers, really reversed. It is dimly possible that Bach had written some of the numbers for the "Weihnachts-Oratorium" earlier, and, having then to produce a complimentary cantata for the court people, had used up some of the movements intended for the sacred oratorio—as it were, by the way. It is not as if the complimentary work could be frequently performed; it fulfilled an essentially momentary function and was done with. If Bach had inserted music to different—even divergent—words in compositions which were likely to be performed again and again, the procedure would be questionable and the result most probably disagreeable. But the offering for a birthday of a royal prince is probably only half listened to when it is performed, and it is put aside if it cannot serve for any other purpose. So if Bach did write the music for some of the movements of the

"Weihnachts-Oratorium" first, he was taking a perfectly intelligible course in embodying them in a royal birthday ode, more especially as his treatment of the sentiments involved was so wide as to have general rather than individual application.

The case is almost identical with the fine "Dramma per Musica," which Bach wrote in honour of the birthday of the Queen of Poland, which was kept on December 8, 1733. The strong and jubilant first chorus, *Tönet, ihr Pauken,* readily transfers its joyful exuberance to the first chorus of the "Weihnachts-Oratorium," with the words "Jauchzet, frohlocket"; the middle part of the chorus, which is specialised in the secular version by the words *Königin lebe! dies wünschet der Sachse,* becomes in the sacred version *Dienet dem Höchsten mit herrlichen Chören.*

The aria *Fromme Musen! meine Glieder,* which is put into the mouth of Pallas in the congratulatory cantata, becomes *Frohe Hirten, eilt* in the "Weihnachts-Oratorium." The bold and strenuous tune *Kron' und Preis gekrönter Damen,* which is given to Fame in the secular cantata, becomes *Grosser Herr und starker König,* and admirably fulfils its function; and the final chorus, not having a dance rhythm in this case, is sufficiently serious in style in spite of its jubilance to serve as the first chorus of the third part of the "Weihnachts-Oratorium," with the words *Herrscher des Himmels erhöre das Lallen.*

In the following year, 1734, further royal visits to Leipzig entailed further complimentary cantatas. In October Bach had to supply a work of this kind, and, it is said, in the space of three days. The first chorus is a most brilliant example of his writing for two choirs, to the words *Preise dein Glücke gesegnetes Sachsen,* and this, with modifications, makes its appearance as the *Osanna* in the B minor Mass. It is impossible to say whether it was originally written for the complimentary cantata for the King; it seems highly improbable. Another movement in the work, the aria *Durch die von Eifer entflammeten Waffen* for soprano, makes its appearance also in the "Weihnachts-Oratorium" as the bass aria *Erleucht' auch meine finstre Sinnen.*

Yet another work on a still larger scale, *Schleicht, spielende Wellen,* was produced in honour of the birthday of King Augustus in the same month of this year. In this case Bach appears to have been ready beforehand, and the work is on an imposing scale. The poetic scheme is that the various personified rivers of Germany, such as the Danube, the Vistula, the Elbe, and the Pleisse, hold discourse and glorify the King. The work is on the usual lines with chorus at beginning and end and solos occupying the whole of the middle part. In this case Bach does not seem to have used the material in other works, though, indeed, it is not excessively secular in style; but the words are too decisively localised to be available for a general performance.

A secular cantata, *Angenehmes Wiederau,* written for the occasion when a certain Count Johann Christian von Hennicke received homage from a place called Widerau in 1737, had a somewhat different destiny. The words were written by Picander, and contained parts for Fate, Happiness, Time, and the River Elster. In this case Bach seems to have been fortunate in the impulse given him by the words, for the work contains some purely delightful music. The first chorus, which by the way serves also to conclude the work, is one of the most tuneful things he ever wrote of the kind. Several of the solos are fine, and one especially, *Ich will dich halten,* is among Bach's most notable bass arias. The music was afterwards transformed almost entirely into the cantata for St. John's Day, *Freue dich, erlöste Schaar,* with expansion of the recitatives, especially that before the bass solo, which is quite superb, and fuller instrumentation, and a chorale at the end of its first half. The joyous tune of the principal chorus fits with extraordinary aptness to the words, though, strange to say, in this case it is, for Bach, exceptionally secular in style.

Bach is known to have produced still further complimentary works for similar occasions, but they have been lost. He also had occasionally to write music for weddings. One of these, *Weichet nur, betrübte Schatten,* was probably written before the Leipzig time. It consists of a series of recitatives and arias for soprano solo, the last of which is a gavotte. Some of the materials were used again, for instance in the sonata No VI. for violin and clavier, in which a subject from one of the arias makes its appearance. Another wedding cantata, written much later, indeed near the end of his life, was *O holder Tag, erwünschte Zeit.* It is a work of exceptional beauty, rich in all the resources of art, and delicate in feeling, comprising four highly developed and melodious arias for soprano voice, all fully accompanied, and some fine recitatives. Bach evidently made this work serve in other capacities, as it is found also, with another setting of words beginning *O angenehme Melodei,* but unfortunately this does not relieve it of the disability of referring to special occasions, as the names of the people in whose honour it was used occur in it.

One other secular cantata, of such a peculiar character that it stands out from all the rest, is the so-called "Bauern Cantata," "*Mer hahn en neue Oberkeet.*" It was written in 1742 in connection with the reception of allegiance by one von Dieskau as "Gutsherr" of Klein-Ischocher in Saxony. The poem is in a burlesque vein and refers to rustic gaieties, which Bach interprets by adopting a pronounced rustic vein in the music. It has an introduction for violin, viola, and bass, in which several rustic tunes are knit together after a fashion which in later times would have been called a potpourri. There is no pretence of development or artistic treatment, and the tunes tumble into one another in a perfectly irresponsible and incoherent manner which implies that the movement was a joke. The whole work, which is for various solo voices with instrumental accompaniment, is carried out in the same merry spirit. There are two well developed arias which, for the time, pass out of the region of pure peasant tunes, but even they have a frank lilt which is very engaging, and of these one is borrowed from the Cantata "Phœbus and Pan," being no less, indeed, than Pan's own trial song. For the rest the movements are based on merry country tunes, some of which are known as folk-songs to the present day, some of which are also in dance rhythms. Bach occasionally touches on the province of humorous music, as in the delightfully frank tune which constitutes the final duet *Wir gehn nun wo der Tudelsack, der Tudel-Tudel-Tudel-Tudel-sack, in unsrer Schenke brummt.*

It suggests the inference that he had assimilated plenty of folk-songs into his musical personality and when they were wanted they readily presented themselves without showing any lack of consistency.

There are a few secular cantatas which were not originated by the requirements of special occasions of compliment. The most important of these is "The Contest between Phœbus and Pan," referred to above. The words were by Picander, with whom Bach so frequently collaborated in the Leipzig time, and it appears to have been performed in the year 1731 by the Leipzig Musical Society. In this work is probably presented Bach's view of secular music undisturbed by the conflicting claims of ceremony, and it also affords glimpses into his personal attitude in relation to subjects chosen for musical treatment. The conception is a happy one in that respect. Phœbus and Pan dispute over their respective pre-eminence in music. The former treats the latter's presumption with lofty contempt, and

Pan points out the influence of his music on the nymphs and the denizens of the woodlands. They each give samples of their art: Phoebus in a slow, melodious, and very serious song, which has something of the feeling of a sarabande; Pan in his turn sings a brisk, jaunty air, much of which is in a humorous vein, even suggestive of Beckmesser in the reiteration of a quaintly silly figure in the accompaniment, and the absurd device of reiterating part of the first syllable of the word "wackelt," in the form of "wack-ack-ack-ack," etc., on a high note which, no doubt, has kinship to a laughing syllable, or rather is an exaggeration of that procedure. The verification of this kinship is in fact supplied, for when Bach transferred this song to the "Bauern Cantata" (for which its rusticity befitted it) the syllable used for comic reiteration was the first of the word "lachen." Tmolus and Mydas act respectively as quasi-counsel for each party, and each sings a song.

Mydas's contention in favour of Pan meets with wrathful contempt on the part of Mercury, Phœbus, and Momus, who advise him to take his donkey's ears back into the woods, while Momus advises Phœbus to "grasp his lyre again," for "nothing is more lovesome than his song." The whole work is rounded off by choruses at opening and close; both of them in six parts, both directly and simply melodious, and both of them in aria form. Except in the humorous parts the style of the work does not really differ much from the style of the church cantatas. The choruses, it is true, are not so elaborate in texture as in the sacred compositions, and are more simply harmonised, but the arias of the more serious characters are quite of the serious cast; indeed, it may be admitted that they are in too serious a vein and too lengthily developed for a secular work of this kind. They overweight the work and even make it wearisome. The scheme is also the same as that of most of the church cantatas, lacking only the characteristic feature of the chorales. With reference to Bach's personal attitude in this work it must be admitted that he no doubt had in his mind in the person of Mydas, a reference to an actual individual, one Scheibe, who had a grudge against Bach and had written some galling remarks about him.

A cantata on a considerable scale, which displays more of a definitely comic musical mood, is that known as the *Kaffee Cantata* (Bach spelled it Coffe), beginning with the words *Schweigt stille, plaudert nicht.* It has reference to the growing appreciation of coffee, which at that time was a comparative novelty, but had become very popular and was in some quarters considered injurious to health. The subject of the work is the disapproval of father Schlendrian of his daughter's taste for it, and his determination to break her of it, which culminates in a threat that she shall not marry till she gives it up, to which she succumbs. But she in turn gets the better of the argument by causing it to be known that no suitor is likely to be acceptable to her unless he will allow her to have her coffee. The material is very slender, but Bach makes merry with it in a series of recitatives and arias which are happily characteristic of the personalities of the disputants; and the work concludes with a lively trio quite in a folk-tune style. In this case there are lightness and merriment enough to sustain the secular character.

Bach also wrote a few secular cantatas for single solo voices at various times, analogous to the Italian cantatas *a voce sola.* Indeed, he actually wrote three cantatas to Italian words, one of which, for soprano solo, is lost. Another, *Amore traditore,* for bass voice accompanied by harpsichord, is rather an unusual phenomenon, as most of the cantatas *a voce sola* were written with accompaniment of 'cello and figured bass; but in the last movement of this cantata Bach gives a full and elaborate harpsichord accompaniment, in which a rapid, broken arpeggio figure plays a very important part. The figure itself is rather commonplace but bustling and animated. It is, indeed, like everything else in the cantata, influenced by the Italian words. A composer of Bach's fine sensibility is almost bound to be influenced by the associations of the words he sets, both in style, texture, and phraseology The fact may be set aside as comparatively unimportant, that the musical melodic phraseology is developed in close association with characteristics of language, which causes all genuine lyrical music whatever, when sung to translations from the language with which the composer originally associated it, to labour under almost irremediable disabilities. But the fact that a composer hears all languages constantly associated with particular types of melodic formulas, particular procedures of harmony, and a certain rather limited range of musical figures, makes it almost impossible for him in setting foreign words to escape the usual musical concomitants of those words if he has at any time been familiar with them. Moreover it is difficult to avoid the importunity of the inference that Bach wrote this cantata just as he copied out such Italian works as Lotti's Mass in G minor, mainly with the view of enhancing his own artistic efficiency. It is quite possible that self-criticism may have made him feel that at times his highly wrought artistic instinct induced an overloading of texture and an uncompromising strain of melodic independence which tended at unguarded moments to become crabbed. He was also certainly aware that the Italians erred conspicuously in the direction of easy grace and smoothness, and that practice in their style might be a possible mitigator of angularity and of the ungracious assertion of his personality in unsuitable places. His attitude in this matter illustrates most happily the largeness of his nature and the genuine devotion which kept him always awake to possibilities of enriching his artistic powers and making his work more perfect. In this way he became one of the most notable examples of those types of humanity who go on learning to the end of their days, and a confirmation of the fact that when a man has surpassed all his fellow men he can still learn something from them if he is not blinded by self-complacency.

The third Italian cantata, *Non sa che sia dolore*, for soprano solo with accompaniment of strings and flute, was written for a different purpose, as it is inferred to have had special reference to the Italian tastes which were predominant at the court of the Margrave of Anspach. It is a work on a large scale, with a very long sinfonia for instruments at the beginning, which is graceful and flowing without any strong incisiveness of character. It has the peculiarity of being in the aria form without having an aria style. The rest of the work consists of two recitatives and two very long arias, all of which have something of an Italian flavour, though the texture of the accompaniments is richer than any Italian composer could have made it. It is not intrinsically very interesting or characteristic, but from the point of view of workmanship worthy of the master hand.

Of secular Cantatas there only remains to be mentioned a German cantata for soprano voice, *Von der Vergnügsamkeit,* beginning with the words, "Ich bin in mir vergnügt," which is on the plan of the Italian *cantata a voce sola.* It consists of four recitatives and four arias, the third recitative being developed, after a frequent practice of Bach's, into an arioso. The arias and one of the recitatives are accompanied by a small orchestra, which is employed in the same manner as in the solos of the church cantatas, and the style is in the main quite as serious as these works. It seems likely, as Spitta suggests, that it was written for Anna Magdalena.

CHAPTER X

THE ORATORIOS

THE custom of dwelling upon the incidents commemorated at certain festivals and seasons of the Church and enhancing their impression on the minds of worshippers by music and simple histrionic devices, was traditionally followed in the Lutheran Church at Christmas time and at Easter and on Ascension Day, as well as in Passion week; and among the latest of Bach's choral works on a large scale are those known as the "Weihnachts-Oratorium," or Christmas oratorio, the Easter oratorio, and the Ascension oratorio, which were composed for those occasions. They none of them accord with the usual conception of the term oratorio, which is most commonly associated with such types as those of Handel and Mendelssohn, and implies something of a dramatic character and an organically developed plot.

The Christmas oratorio, which is by far the largest of the three, cannot be said to have any dramatic development at all. The incidents and facts have no cumulative interest, but rather the reverse, for those which are of deepest interest come in the earlier portion of the work, and the story merely goes on to the point which is commemorated in the festival when the performance takes place, and then leaves off. Moreover, the work differs more conspicuously from most familiar types of oratorio in other respects, inasmuch as it was not intended to be performed all at once, but was divided into six portions, each of which was to be performed on a different day, beginning on Christmas Day and ending on Epiphany. It follows that each of the six portions was a self-contained and complete art-work; and such unity as there is in the whole lies in the continuity of the story, and in the composer's having adopted musical expedients which gave to the receptive mind the impression of consistency.

The type is evidently unique, and its full effect is obtainable only when the work is actually performed under the conditions for which it is most subtly devised. In a very diverse sphere of art it resembles Wagner's fourfold "Ring des Nibelungen," in which each of the four works is a complete work of art and yet each of the three earlier works leads on to its successor, and the fourth is dependent on what has gone before it for its intelligibility. The object of the Christmas oratorio is to keep the worshippers' minds occupied with the successive events commemorated through the whole Christmas season and make them ponder well upon them by the suggestive thoughts and reflections which are appended. The methods adopted are the same as those in Bach's examples of Passion music. The tenor soloist who takes the part of the Evangelist tells each incident simply in recitative, and a succession of reflections and thoughts suggested by it are embodied in arias, ariosos, chorales, even passages of chorus, which occupy a great deal more space than the narrative.

Each part covers but a small portion of the story. In the first day's portion the Evangelist has but two recitatives: the first relating the coming of Joseph of Nazareth to Bethlehem in Judea with Mary, and the second the birth of the child; and the rest of the nine movements consist of the opening chorus expressing the joy of Christmas time, and the various arias and other movements which supply poetic commentaries, ending with a chorale.

The procedure is the same throughout. The second portion turns on the announcement of the birth to the shepherds, and the heavenly host praising God. The third tells how the shepherds came and found Mary and Joseph, and the babe lying in the manger. The fourth refers to the Circumcision, and to the naming of the child, as had been foretold by the angel. The fifth tells how the wise men from the East came to Jerusalem asking where was the newly born King of the Jews, and how King Herod was alarmed and took counsel with the high priests; and the sixth and last relates how the wise men were guided by the star and brought their offerings to the humble manger-side, and that being warned in a dream not to reveal to Herod where they had found the child, they returned to their own country—and here the story, or rather the series of episodes, comes to an end.

It must be obvious that such a scheme would be impossible but for the sacredness with which the episodes are invested, and the depth of sentiment which is stirred by mere reference to incidents connected with the birth of Christ.

It is not the mere bald statement of each incident, but its copious implications and the manner in which it seems to set the imagination expanding in all directions, which give such initiatory vitality to the scheme, and it is in expanding and vitalising these implications and workings of the imagination by the power of music that Bach's genius reveals itself. And there are but few situations which throw more light on the sphere of the artist and the individual disposition of John Sebastian Bach. Primitive and undeveloped minds invest the incidents in the lives of human beings who excite their imagination and cause an exaltation of their faculties, with a vast tribute of miracle and mystery. It is their way of showing the ardent genuineness of their wonder and admiration. The supernatural is invoked, not so much to account for the words and deeds of their heroes and demigods, as to give them additional radiance, to glorify them even to super-humanity, and to justify the adoration of their worshippers by making use of the power which the suggestion of the supernatural exercises upon primitive emotions.

The function of art in analogous cases is to take the place of the supernatural for more highly developed minds, in whose temperament the spheres of emotion and reason are more equally adjusted. The incidents in the lives of beloved beings are invested with all the glory and beauty of form and colour and interest of detail, which the highest development of artistic power can effect. The supernatural features in primitive legends are akin to the exaggeration and extravagance which result, in everyday experience, from undeveloped powers of thought and expression, and from the incapacity of the human creature who resorts to such artifices to convey to his fellow-creatures anything approaching the strength of impression which the circumstances he narrates make upon himself, without representing all the inches as miles and multiplying all his figures by thousands. The functions of the highest art are very different. Its object is for the most part to impress its subjects upon human minds most deeply by displaying its facts under conditions which appeal to sensibilities as well as to the mind. And while primitive exaggeration was the fruit of the lack of technique of expression, the methods by which art glorifies its subjects become continually more and more convincing, as developments of artistic methods, going on by a cumulative process for generation after generation, make the technique of expression more and more copious.

Bach, as has before been shown, was at once the product and the co-ordinator of methods which composers had been building up for centuries. And he himself had enormously enhanced their efficacy. The adjustment of means to ends could hardly be more aptly shown than in the Christmas Oratorio. For the work, being a mere succession of incidents, depends for its effect upon the manner in which music enhances all the suggestions which radiate from them. The special art forms which were most suitable for such purposes had been found, perfected, and tested again and again. The moment was one where the sacredness of the incidents related was felt in a most fruitful manner, and Bach himself was one who would have felt it with the most entire sincerity. The Christmas Oratorio may therefore be taken as a very typical example of the device of glorifying cherished incidents by musical adornment and expansion. It is in every way a field in which the personality of J. S. Bach would find most congenial opportunities. He himself had chosen and tested the various art forms which were most apt for the occasion, and made them his own. The particular phase of religious sentiment which was represented was just at its best, and Bach himself as the embodiment of the new awakening of Teutonic music was ideally fitted to express it in the terms of his art.

In the design of the six portions it is inevitable that there should be some similarity, which produces an unsatisfactory effect when the work is performed all at once, but would help the listeners when performed on six separate days. It was practically inevitable that each part should begin with an introductory movement of considerable proportions, and five times out of the six this is a chorus. Three of these choruses are borrowed (as has already been said) from secular complimentary cantatas written in the previous year, 1733. All are eminently appropriate, whether traceable to other sources or not (see pp. 340 *et seq.*)

The two choruses which are not traceable as borrowed, namely, those which serve as introductory to the fifth and sixth days' performances, are on a larger and more generous scale, and of more interesting texture than the others. The one introductory movement which is not a chorus is the well-beloved Pastoral Symphony which stands at the beginning of the second day's music, in virtue of its dealing exclusively with the shepherds. Bach must truly have rejoiced in shepherds and pastoral folk, for the thought of them always seems to set his mind welling with lovely tunes of a folk-song order which vividly suggest the shepherd's life. And the Pastoral Symphony is indeed a piece of poetic characterisation of the first order. A certain element of uncouthness adds to the fascination, and the singular profusion of instruments with a rich reedy tone (the two oboi d'amore and two oboi da caccia) establishes the character of this portion of the oratorio with overwhelming emphasis.

As is almost inevitable, the second movement in all the six portions of the oratorio is a piece of recitative, relating in the simplest manner possible the incidents which serve as the text of the day's musical discourse. From this point the order of movements in the several parts most rightly varies. In the first, fourth, and sixth portions an accompanied recitative conveys the figurative application of the incident, its interpretation in terms of the worshippers' personal feeling. In the second the recitative relating the initiatory incidents is followed by a chorale, exhorting the shepherds not to be in fear, for the angels are telling

> "*Dass dieses schwache Knäbelein*
> *Soll unser Trost und Freude sein.*"

In the remaining two portions, the third and fifth, the third movements are most interesting, for in these a short dramatic chorus is introduced after the textual recitative. The type is found in the short choruses which abound in the Passions when a number of persons, such as disciples, Jews, priests, or other clearly defined groups, are made to utter their feelings or wishes. They might appropriately be classified as "Turba" choruses, as their character is so strongly defined, and the portion of the choir which from early times sang these passages was traditionally known as the "Turba" or crowd. The procedure adopted is vividly enlightening. In the first case, that is the third day's portion, after the initial passage of recitative, the chorus sings with bustling animation, "Let us go even to Bethlehem and see this thing which is come to pass," and a bass solo instantly answers, using the concrete sentence from the story as a cue for a metaphorical expansion, "Er hat sein Volk getröst't, er hat sein Israel erlöst, die Hülf' aus Zion hergesendet, und unser Leid geendet." (He has comforted His people, He has redeemed Israel, He has sent help to Zion, and ended our afflictions.)

It serves as the channel to direct the minds of the worshippers from the mere facts to the wider issues which are prefigured by them, and their bearing on the soul-condition of Christians at large. The device used in the fifth day's portion is even more interesting. The wise men are evidently impersonated in the short "Turba" chorus, when they sing with graphic eagerness "Where is the new-born King of the Jews?" and the alto solo breaks in for a moment with the words "Seek him in my breast"; the animated chorus resumes, "We have seen His star in the east [Morgenlande] and are come to worship Him," and the alto answers: "Happy are ye that have seen the light! it has appeared for your salvation. My holy one! Thou, Thou art the light, which shall also appear to the heathen, and they know Thee not yet!"

The untiring susceptibility of Bach's mind is illustrated by the fact that in no case does the third number in the several parts correspond in any two successive days. It happily becomes a point of divergence by which curiosity, begotten of the uncertainty as to what is coming next, is aroused; and strengthens the interest in the following movements. And the chorale with which each portion (except the third) concludes, restores the sense of unity.

There are hosts of noteworthy features in the various parts. In the first, the introduction of a chorale which has pathetic associations, the *O Haupt voll Blut und Wunden*, follows immediately after the aria *Bereite dich, Zion*, widening the meditation with a touch of pathos; and after the second passage of the Evangelist's recitative, comes one of those uniquely wonderful movements to which Bach seems to have the sole key, the duet between soprano and bass, *Er ist auf Erden kommen arm*. It is a development of the "Dialogues," which have been so often referred to in connection with the sacred compositions of Bach's predecessors, and with many of his cantatas, such as *Ich hatte viel Bekümmerniss* and *Gottes Zeit*. In this case the soprano solo is mainly confined to the singing of a chorale, each line of which has an answering comment in recitative by the bass voice, the whole being knit together by a lovely little figure in the accompaniment which has a quaintly pastoral flavour and hovers round the voices throughout.

The most delightful movement in the second day's music, after the Pastoral Symphony (which has been discussed), is the well-known slumber song, *Schlafe, mein Liebster*, which had made its appearance previously, as before mentioned, in the complimentary cantata *Die Wahl des Hercules* in 1733. The position which it occupies in the Christmas Oratorio must be admitted to be a little puzzling, for it follows upon an accompanied recitative in which the bass voice addressing the shepherds says: "So singet ihm bei seiner Wiegen aus einem süssen Ton', Und mit gesammtem Chor dies Lied zur Ruhe vor." But the "Wiegenlied" is fortunately not sung by the chorus but by an alto solo. Possibly Bach meant to convey the idea of the soul of man in the abstract singing the lullaby to the beloved babe in the manger. The impression it conveys to the average mind is that the shepherds have come to the manger side and hear the mother singing it. At any rate the effect it makes is supremely happy, for the accompaniment, being full of delightfully reedy oboe sounds, maintains the pastoral atmosphere, and it is worthy of note that the sounds in question are added for this version. The song as it stands in *Die Wahl des Hercules* has only strings for the accompaniment; in this version a solo flute, solo oboe d'amore, and a second oboe d'amore and two oboi da caccia are added with very characteristic effect. The version in the Christmas Oratorio is also interesting as illustrating Bach's constant self-criticism. The voice-part in the central portion of the aria, in the version in the *Wahl des Hercules*, is rather dull and monotonous. In the present version, Bach has given it a vast amount of additional vitality by introducing semi-quaver passages and syncopations and a variety of artistic devices to enhance its æsthetic interest. The case is such a happy illustration of his way of building up the artistic value step by step that it is worth while to put the passages in juxtaposition—remembering also that the version in the *Wahl des Hercules* is for soprano voice and a third higher than the version in the Christmas Oratorio.

"Die Wahl des Hercules."
Und er kenne keine Schranken, er kenne keine Schranken.

Weihnachts Oratorium.
Wo wir unser Herz er-freu - - - - - - en,

This second section of the work is full of fine and beautiful points. After the Slumber Song, a short passage of narrative for the Evangelist is all that intervenes before the chorus of the multitude of the heavenly host praising God,—a splendidly dignified and vigorous movement, in which it is especially noticeable that Bach does not resort to any of the histrionic effects which generally prove too seductive for the average composer to resist, but relies solely upon the absolute properties of fine melodic and harmonic progressions and splendidly strong contrapuntal complexities. A still further fascinating thought of the composer is to accompany the final chorale with the lovely tunes of the Pastoral Symphony, which are interspersed between each line of the hymn, at once rounding off the work into completeness, and maintaining the pastoral character up to the very last.

The third day's music is also devoted to the shepherds. In this section many of the movements are transferred from secular works written the previous year, and their transference is quite justified by the result (see p. 328). Of the new compositions, the alto solo, *Schliesse, mein Herze, dies' selige Wunder*, stands out for its conspicuous beauty as one of the most melodious and tender arias in the whole oratorio; a singularly fine chorale, the last line of which is almost unique even among Bach's examples for the extraordinary scope of its progressions, completes the music of this portion, but directions are given for the first chorus to be sung again.

The next portion also contains several borrowed numbers. Besides these there are two dialogues between soprano and bass solos; the bass solo having a recitative throughout, on which, half way through, a very beautiful melody is superimposed, quite independently, for the soprano voice. It has something of the character of a chorale, but is possibly by John Sebastian himself. The second dialogue duet is rather different in treatment, as the solo soprano sings a metrical melody almost throughout, the bass singing expressive unmetrical recitatives below it. The chorale at the end is notable for the scale of its independent instrumental accompaniment.

The fifth and sixth portions contain much less which can be traced to earlier works. Both the initial choruses are on a very large scale—that for New Year's day (the Circumcision) is in aria form, and of the familiar *Bachish* type in which harmonic structure is entirely hidden by the rich texture of animated polyphony, which is most appropriate for the words *Ehre sei dir Gott*. After it, follow the "Turba" chorus above discussed and its attendant metaphorical application (p. 359); a chorale, a fine bass solo, and an accompanied recitative (in which expressive instrumental effect is employed); a beautiful terzetto with violin solo and the chorale which concludes the whole.

In the initial chorus of the last portion, for Epiphany, the voices are treated fugally, in Bach's most energetic manner, with copious runs and ornamental passages; and the other outstanding features are the aria for soprano, *Nur ein Wink von seinen Händen*, and a very remarkable composite solo for tenor with accompaniment of two oboi d'amore and bass, *So geht! genug, mein Schatz geht nicht von hier.* In the latter, passages of free recitative alternate with short passages in strict time, ending, after a manner so familiar in Bach's cantatas, with an adagio passage in deeply expressive arioso style, which widens out the horizon most surprisingly with a touch of anguish, overshadowing in forethought for a moment the joy of the season (see next page).

This is followed by a kindly tenor aria, and that in turn by a recitative for four voices, which brings all the soloists who have been employed in the work together for once—a singular illustration of Bach's wide awakeness to the practical as well as the spiritual. And the conclusion of the whole is the same chorale, *O Haupt voll Blut und Wunden*, which had been introduced at the outset of the first day's music, and is this time enhanced by an elaborate instrumental accompaniment in which trumpets and drums are much in evidence.

The manner in which Bach uses his instruments is yet a further illustration of the extent to which his mind took in every phase of the artistic problem. There is in this matter a singular analogy to his procedure in individual movements, since each portion is characterised by a special tone quality, and has what would be called by painters a scheme of colour. The first and last, as would be instinctively felt to be appropriate,

Weihnachts Oratorium.
Du, Je- su, bist und bleibst mein Freund; Und werd ich
2 Oboe d l' Amore.
piano.
Organo e Continuo.
ängstlich zu dir flehn; Herr, hilf! Herr, hilf! So
lass mich Hül - fe sehn.

have the greatest and most complete array of all the instruments. There are trumpets and drums in the first chorus of all, and in the final chorale of the first portion, also in the first chorus, and in the final chorale of the last day's music, and there is also a solo trumpet in the aria *Grosser Herr* in the first portion. In the rest of the work the trumpets are in abeyance, except in the first chorus of the third portion. In the second portion the pervading tone is that of the oboes, which is obviously appropriate to the shepherds who are so prominent in that part of the narrative. In the fourth part, and in that part alone, horns are used. In the fifth part the scheme of tone is more composite, but tends to emphasise oboe tone again. So that even in the distribution of the colours there is evidence of design, each day having a special tone quality, and no two successive days having the same.

The emphasis which is laid upon the individual character of the music for each day is one of the hindrances to its being fully intelligible under ordinary conditions. The fact that Bach's mind was always so ready to adapt the artistic work to the actual conditions of presentment, militates against the Oratorio producing its effect when performed all at once. The choruses which begin five of the portions are essentially initial choruses, and the Pastoral Symphony is also an initial movement, and the more Bach realised the appropriate type and style of an initial movement the less such movements are fit to be assimilated into a continuous whole. It is an illustration of the value of that culture which is unfortunately sometimes rendered distasteful by the misrepresentations of some of its advocates.

There are numerous works of the very highest artistic quality which have been so perfectly devised to fit special conditions that when the conditions are unobtainable they appear almost unintelligible. In such cases minds of average vivacity are able to reconstruct the conditions for which the work was devised when they have sufficiently formulated them in imagination, and through that process they obtain the attitude which is indispensable to the enjoyment of deep phases of artistic expression. The perfect adaptation of artistic works to the conditions of presentment is the whole sphere of style, and in this department Bach's instinct was supreme. The Christmas Oratorio manifests evidence of it in a high degree, and for that reason becomes less intelligible in ordinary conditions of performance, whether in a church or a concert room.

The Easter Oratorio *Kommt, eilet und laufet* is a short work in a very joyous vein. The scheme is altogether different from that of the Christmas Oratorio. There is no Evangelist to recite the incidents of the narrative, and there are no chorales. The story remains in the background, the incidents being taken for granted and applied figuratively to the soul of the worshipper, which is suggested as running to the sepulchre and asking where the Beloved is gone; referring to the answer of the angel that He is risen, in the terms, "We rejoice that our Jesus lives, and our hearts, that were overwhelmed with sorrow, forget the pain and think in happy song that our holy one lives again," and then bursting into the joyous "Praise and thanks." It therefore consists of a metaphorical parallel or commentary analogous to similar portions of the Passion music, but without the recital of the story.

Among noteworthy features is the composer's adoption of a form he had not often used, at all events in choral works. It has been pointed out that in several of his cantatas he devised the opening movements in the form of the French overture. In this work he devises the opening movement in the form of the Italian overture, such as was used by Alessandro Scarlatti as a "sinfonia" to an opera. He possibly adopted the form because the weighty initial movement of the French overture would not be so well adapted to give the sense of joyousness which would be appropriate to a work for Eastertide as the allegro movement which commences the Italian overture. He actually calls the opening group of movements "sinfonia," and the purely instrumental portions consist of the lively allegro, corresponding to the familiar first movement of a classical sonata or symphony, and the adagio corresponding to the slow movement, which in this case suggests a momentary revival of the sense of bereavement in the minds of the disciples and lovers of the crucified Lord.

The third movement begins in the style of the lively third movement of an Italian overture or symphony, but passes very soon into a duet for tenor and bass, which is no doubt meant to suggest the running of Peter and John to the sepulchre (a tradition which is said to have been perpetuated in the histrionic presentation of the story in German churches at Eastertime); and this in its turn is carried on yet further with a chorus which typifies the eagerness of the souls of the worshippers to run to the sepulchre also and to contemplate the tokens of the resurrection. The idea of running after one another is very quaintly suggested in the following passage:

In a quartet-recitative, the imagined souls of devout Christians discuss the situation figuratively, and a soprano solo sings "Soul, thy spices shall no longer be myrrh, but thou shalt appease thy painful longing with a crown of bay." It is the soul that comes to the tomb and sings a kind of soothing slumber song, given to a tenor voice, implying that the believer's sleep in death will be sweet and relieved of its terrors through the "Schweisstuch" of Jesus. It makes plaint in a duet recitative and arioso that it "can no longer see the Saviour," and again in a solo for alto asks where it may find Jesus; to which a bass solo answers in recitative, expressing the joy that "Our Jesus yet lives," and a short but brilliant chorus expresses "Praise and thanks." The work does not contain any imposing choral features, and intrinsically is not very impressive. The tenor solo is highly characteristic of Bach in one of his most attractive moods, but unfortunately is so long as to be almost unpresentable. For the rest, Bach seems to content himself with the expression of joyousness on unusually slight and simple lines; and the work is notable for the extent to which the incidents of the resurrection are taken for granted and, as it were, transferred figuratively, with a great deal of sentiment, to the soul of the latter-day Christian, thereby illustrating the tendency of the Teutonic Protestants to re-establish the personal relation between the individual and Christ which has been so frequently referred to.

The Ascension Oratorio is on different lines, for in this are found again the features of the Passion-music type—such as the recitatives in which the Evangelist quotes the passages in the Gospel referring to the

Ascension, and the solos bringing the soul figuratively into immediate contact with the situation, and the chorales. It opens with a superbly vigorous and extensively developed chorus, *Lobet Gott in seinen Reichen*, whereupon follows the recital by the Evangelist of Jesus blessing his disciples. After this come a touching and tender recitative, *Ach Jesu, ist dein Abschied schon so nah*, and the pathetic solo for alto, *Ach, bleibe doch mein liebstes Leben*, which has been described in the expanded form in which it appears in the B minor Mass as the *Agnus Dei*. The work, which is not long, then proceeds with a chorale, and further relation of the incidents with commentatory movements referring them as usual to the soul, and ends with a superb chorus in which a chorale is introduced with brilliant accompaniment of orchestra and free contrapuntal treatment of the subordinate voices, after the manner of a Choralvorspiel.

The work is much weightier and more powerfully developed than the Easter Oratorio, and it is not so easy to guess its date. The form of the alto solo implies that it was written before the B minor Mass, as the form in which it appears in that work is more developed. At the same time, inasmuch as the composition of the Mass spreads over many years, it may have been written between the *Kyrie* and the later movements, since the first portion was finished in 1733, and it is considered probable that the whole Mass was not completed till 1737. The Christmas Oratorio is attributed to 1734, the Easter Oratorio to 1736; and the Ascension Oratorio may have been written about the same time, and yet have left time for the amplified version of the *Agnus Dei* to have been added to the Mass. It is even less like the ordinary conception of an oratorio than the Christmas Oratorio. The scheme and scale are those of a grand church cantata, and it is generally classed as one. Intrinsically it represents Bach's maturest standard, and contains some of his most characteristic inspirations, among which must be counted the wonderful aria for soprano, *Jesu, deine Gnadenblicke*, which carries the composer's methods of applying polyphonic counterpoint in solo movements to the very highest pitch of artistic intensity. It is, indeed, a quartet between the solo voice and the flute, oboe, and viola, in which the higher dignity of the solo voice is mainly recognised in its having the words which define the sentiment, to which the beautiful interlacing of the melodies, and the harmonies thereby induced, supply musical expression. A feature which must not be overlooked is that there is no deep bass in the whole movement, so that it seems to hover in the air and subtly to suggest kinship with the serenity of a cloudless sky. The scheme was peculiarly congenial to the composer, as may be observed in such types as the trio sonatas, and the solo *Bete, bete* in the cantata *Mache dich, mein Geist, bereit.*

CHAPTER X

THE LATEST CANTATAS

WHEN attentively considered, the manner in which Bach completed the spacious circuit of his life's work appears almost pathetic in its aptness. In some respects there can hardly be a doubt that he foresaw the inevitable end, and calmly projected his mind to the completion of schemes which required final touches to make them fully representative of his personality. In other respects the course he adopted was not deliberate or conscious, but merely the result of personal and temperamental bias. This latter condition is probably shown most conspicuously in the line he adopted in his church cantatas in the last twenty years of his life.

It is to be observed that nearly all his greatest sacred works, such as the "Johannes-Passion," the "Matthäus-Passion," the masses and the oratorios were produced in the course of the ten years between 1728 and 1738; and it would be natural to infer that their composition would have caused a temporary relaxation of the constant outpouring of cantatas. In any case the concentration on a number of great works, especially the "Matthäus-Passion," had some influence on the condition of mind in which he addressed himself to works written after it. Every great mind grows and expands by what it achieves, and it is found in this case that when the outpouring of cantatas is resumed, characteristics become obvious which show unmistakably that the Teutonic influences which had been so evident in earlier days before Bach came to Leipzig were regaining predominance.

It is a significant fact that in 1728, just before the period under consideration, an isolated cantata, *Wer nur den lieben Gott lässt walten,* the only cantata which is attributed to that year, prefigures the scheme of most of the later cantatas. It must have been written close to the "Matthäus-Passion," and its character confirms the inference that the attitude of mind in which he must have written that great work was influential in impelling him to revert to the Teutonic phase which is manifested in the later cantatas. It seems like the herald of that renewed impulse which was, after 1730, to find such copious expression. In this work no less than six out of seven movements have the chorale of the cantata as the most conspicuous feature. In the first chorus its steadfast phrases alternate with splendidly brilliant episodes for chorus and orchestra, thus anticipating the scheme of the later cantatas; the second and fifth movements are in a form in which Bach took great delight in his later days, in which the phrases of the chorale are alternated with answering phrases of recitative; the fourth movement is a duet of expressive character in which the chorale is played by massed strings in the accompaniment; the sixth movement is an aria for soprano in which the last two phrases of the chorale are introduced with impressive effect into the solo part; and the last movement is the usual simple version of the chorale. Even the singularly simple and tuneful aria for tenor *Man hatte nur*, which stands third in the order of movements, has close connection with the tune of the chorale, as its first phrase manifestly presents the identical melodic succession, though disguised by the three-eight tempo and the major key and the manner in which the melody is broken up into short phrases.

This revival of a Teutonic attitude of mind, which is manifested most conspicuously in the increased prominence of the chorales in the cantatas written after 1730, was partly due to the change of Bach's attitude in respect of his texts. It is obvious that one of his greatest difficulties in getting such a vast number of cantatas provided for the various Sundays and festivals of the year lay in finding adequate poems to set. He had been fortunate in having many good and inspiring poetical texts by Neumeister and Salomo Franck; but their cantata-texts were exhaustible, and for many urgent occasions he had been at the mercy of poets or versemakers who supplied him with little better than doggerel. He evidently revised and rewrote the words himself now and again, but there must have been occasions when he had not time for it, and he had to accommodate himself to what he could get from Picander or any other contriver of sacred verse. Alternatives of which he had occasionally availed himself had been the recognised hymns of the church; and among those he could at least find materials which were appropriate to special seasons, and much better and more genuinely expressed poetry.

The much more frequent adoption of hymns in the

last twenty years of his life brought certain interesting consequences. It was a drawback that their regular metrical arrangement made them less adaptable for setting as recitatives and arias. This was obviated to a certain extent by adding a great deal of poetical matter to the hymn, in the form of verses which lent themselves more easily for such purposes. But the very familiarity of the hymns and the impossibility of contriving extra verses which did not betray their extraneous sources induced the disposition to dispense with such interpolations where possible; and this had the effect of making more frequent the use of forms of art which were more genuinely Teutonic than the recitatives and arias which had been transplanted from Italian opera. But further than this, a more vital change was caused by the hymns bringing in their wake the chorales with which they were associated. And Bach's delight in them and his feeling for their devotional significance caused him to identify the cantatas with them by all manner of devices which quite transformed and Teutonised both their form and character.

However, it must not be inferred that this was a totally new departure taken in the later years of the composer's life. There had been some earlier examples of similar procedure, as in the notable case of *Christ lag in Todesbanden*, where all the movements are founded on the tune; and the introduction of chorale phrases into accompaniments, and in combination with recitatives and arias, was of common occurrence. It is merely the preponderance of such action which shows the revival of the Teutonic bias, and it also most happily shows the continuity of Bach's artistic life; as if some deepset impulse had lain dormant for long spells of time, and only occasionally gave indications of vitality, ultimately presenting itself as a distinguishing and conspicuous feature in the great mind's personality. The trait is not at all uncommon with great artists, who revert in their maturest periods to characteristic expressions and types of thought which have remained in comparative abeyance since early years. It is a most interesting verification of the genuineness of their utterances and the consistency of their personalities.

The German chorales may be regarded as among the most powerful influences in Bach's musical life. Few things had greater or more constant hold upon him. But in the course of his cosmopolitan explorations of artistic methods and forms in the desire to widen to the utmost the means for the expression of his own personality, they had sometimes been pushed into the background. But in the latest period the Italian phase of the cantata becomes less conspicuous, and the church hymns and the chorales renew their sway.

It is not, however, desirable to disguise some of the consequences. The forms which Bach had used for his great choruses which were not based on chorales had been cosmopolitan, and capable of variation and progressive development. The forms which were available for the expansion of the chorale were purely Lutheran-Teutonic, and that which Bach most frequently adopted was limited in capacity of development. It must further be admitted that in these later days Bach's procedure in a vast number of cantatas became, as far as design is concerned, mechanical. He had to provide a big work at short notice for a given Sunday or festival, the requirements for which were present in his mind; and having no time for pondering over new speculative designs, he filled in the measure of a scheme which he had tested and found adequate with art-work of the highest quality; probably not contemplating any wider issue than the Sunday or festival for which the work was immediately composed. His practice in this matter was analogous to that of the sonata composers of later days, who, in a large majority of cases, adopted precisely the same order of movements, and even the same order and disposition of the main constituents of the movements themselves; relying on their power of diversifying the actual musical material to insure variety and individuality to each work. And it must be admitted that Bach was quite as successful in giving individuality to his cantatas by the nature and treatment of his musical material as the best of the sonata composers were in their line.

In the chorale-cantatas the scheme becomes almost a certainty. The essential object of the first chorus, which is the most imposing feature in the work, was to build a grand movement round the chorale or develop one out of it, in such a way as to make the tune stand out like a solid and steadfast beacon from the elaborated details of polyphony which supply the artistic interest and the musical expression. The manner in which the chorale is dealt with becomes more and more decisively systematised into two clear types, which have their origin in forms of organ compositions based on chorales. These two types, singularly enough, represent two phases which are present at every period in which art has any vitality; the one form showing clearly its kinship with the past, and the other reaching out its hands to the future. In the former phase, in Bach's case, the fugal type is followed, in the latter the harmonic principle; the fugue being represented by continuity and the interweaving of strands, the harmonic forms by large blocks of diversified choral phrases like the solid masses of architecture.

In the large majority of these choruses Bach adopts the latter scheme, which it is advisable to consider more closely. The movement begins in this case with an introductory passage for the orchestra, sometimes founded on original figures by which the sentiment of the words is strongly expressed. Then the voices deal with the first phrase of the chorale, one of the parts having the tune in long notes and the rest of the voices singing passages which are sometimes independent figures, and at other times present some form of the figures of the chorale tune. After the first line of the hymn is completed there is a short episode for the instruments, and then the second line of the hymn is dealt with in similar manner to the first; and so on through the whole chorale, its phrases alternating with instrumental episodes throughout, and ending sometimes with an instrumental passage, sometimes more decisively with the last line of the chorale. The type of movement is obviously a specialty of this kind of church cantata, and besides its connection with the chorale-fantasia it also has close kinship with the traditional manner of dealing with a chorale when simply sung in the Lutheran services; when the organist was accustomed to extemporise episodes on the organ between the lines. The form has the drawback of being rather stiff and of scarcely admitting of any development to musical climax, for it almost inevitably maintains an equal level throughout.

Far more interesting and elastic is the other form of movement which, as has been said, was of a fugal type. In choruses of this order Bach followed with singular fidelity and felicity the type known as the Pachelbel Choralvorspiel. The chorus began, without instrumental introduction, with the successive entries of the several secondary voices in imitations founded on the tune of the chorale, but in quicker notes; and when they have all joined in, the voice to which the chorale is allotted, sings the tune in long notes, like a canto fermo in the older contrapuntal style, the others continuing the quicker motion. When the first phrase is finished the subordinate voices prepare the way for the second phrase of the chorale by anticipatory imitations dealing with the figures of that second phrase. Then the principal voice sings the second phrase in long notes like the first, and similar procedure is followed to the end. The first chorus of the cantata to Luther's words *Ach Gott vom Himmel sieh' darein* shows how closely Bach followed the same procedure as Pachelbel. In the Choralvorspiel *Gott Vater der du deiner Sohn* for the organ by that composer, the secondary parts, tenor, alto, and bass, enter successively with imitations founded on a diminution of the chorale tune, as follows:

When they have all in this manner made their entry, the soprano duly presents the chorale in long notes as follows:

In Bach's chorus the procedure is identical; tenors, basses, and sopranos successively make their entries with the first phrase of the tune in diminution;

rein und lass dich's doch
Bass.
Ach Gott, vom Him - mel.......
Ach Gott vom
Soprano.
.... er - bar - - - - - -
Basses.
sieh da - rein und........ lass
Continuo.
Him - mel sieh da - rein
men, und lass dich's doch er - bar - -
dich's doch.......... er - bar - -
Etc.

and as soon as they have all come in the altos sing the same tune in notes of double the length.

As soon as the first line of the tune is finished the subordinate voices proceed to anticipate the second line in the same manner.

And the second line is then sung by the altos in long notes as follows:

and the same process is maintained to the end. In this manner the whole movement is almost made up of passages from the chorale, and there is hardly a moment when some of its phrases are not heard. No other composer could hope to approach Bach in such a type, as his facility in the dexterous manipulation of single-part subjects, gained by such an enormous amount of practice superimposed on natural aptitude, enabled him to overcome the most extreme difficulties with such ease that they are never perceived; and it enables him also to use all his astonishing canonic combinations as means to the ends of expression.

After the initial chorus the solo voices come into requisition, and arias alternate with recitatives, and occasionally with movements of more Teutonic type, till the necessary measure of music for the church cantata in the service (somewhere said to be about thirty-five minutes) is completed; and then the whole is rounded off by the singing of the chorale in its simple direct form, the voices in characteristic four-part harmony being usually only doubled by the instruments. This ending with the simple chorale sung once through is obviously another specialty of the Reformed service; as, apart from intrinsic qualities of an impressive kind, so short and undeveloped a movement would not appear sufficiently spacious to serve as the conclusion of a large work for chorus, soli, and orchestra. It was the deep-seated veneration for the chorale and its devotional associations which gave it significance enough to serve such a purpose. In later times, when the works can hardly be heard at all except in the secular surroundings of a concert room, it is natural for those who undertake performances to look for such cantatas as have the chorales expanded by free instrumental accompaniments, or such exceptional cantatas as have free choruses at the end; and as these in the later cantatas are few and not by any means necessarily the finest examples, circumstances militate against their becoming known sufficiently to be appreciated. But on the other hand it may be said that Bach's unique manner of harmonising the final chorales gives them special fascination; and it may be further added that in such a case the advantages of musical culture are yet again manifested; for while those who are ignorant of the conditions for which these cantatas were composed would be puzzled at the apparent inadequacy of the finale, those who are more happily placed can, with the help of a little experience, so transfer themselves in imagination to the situation which Bach had in his mind, as to feel through the exercise of developed artistic perception almost the full meaning of the concluding chorale and its adequacy as an element of design.

Of the two types of cantata, those which begin with the instrumental introduction and alternate phrases of the chorale with episodes and those which begin with a chorus on the lines of the Pachelbel Choralvorspiel, it so happens opportunely that two of the finest cantatas written by Bach in the latter part of his life are remarkable examples. Of the first order is the cantata *Wachet auf* which belongs to the very outset of the period under consideration, as there seems sufficient reason to believe that it was written for the twenty-seventh Sunday after Trinity in 1731. The occasion does not seem to have been of sufficient importance to account for the exceptional splendour of the work, as it cannot be supposed that the mere fact that Sundays after Trinity do not often run to such a number could have been in the least inspiring. The source of the exceptional warmth and beauty of the work is more likely to have been that the poem was congenial and suggestive, that the subject of the Bridegroom and the Virgins appealed to Bach's imagination in the symbolical sense of its application to humanity at large, and that the chorale tune itself was exceptionally impressive.

The artistic scheme of the first chorus is in accordance with that above described, but it may here be considered in relation to expression and style. The passage which serves for instrumental introduction is rather shorter than usual, as though Bach wished to come to the point at once; but it is sufficiently long to establish the type of musical figures and the strenuous mood. Bach's instinct for style made him here, as in a great majority of cases, keep the musical material of the instruments distinct from that allotted to the voices. Their function is to supply the rhythmic element and the more vivacious details of the texture. The rhythmic element is manifested in a march-like character produced by the energetic trochees combined with the three stern beats of the molossus. The secondary voices on the other hand are almost unrhythmic; having passages with cross-rhythms, syncopations, overlapping melodic figures, and all such effects as suggest the individuality of the human creatures singing the various parts, at once independent and bound together by the unities of the art-work as a whole. The twofold scheme of the instrumental and vocal factors completes the scope of musical expression, the rhythmic and the melodic; the former representing the extra-ecclesiastical factors which had not presented themselves in church music before the Reformation, and the latter the primitive types of sacred music as transformed by being filtered through organ music. And over and above all the astonishing profusion of devices most perfectly assimilated the chorale soars in its long-drawn simplicity, as though undistracted by the hurly-burly of the other voices and the vivacity of the instrumental accompaniment. Yet its quasi-aloofness does not suggest indifference, but something above the rest—noble and tranquil, savouring of divine steadfastness.

The scheme of the whole chorus follows on the lines above described, the phrases of the chorale alternating with instrumental episodes. Bach probably felt the drawback of the form, in which the constant stopping and recommencement of the voices seriously hampers the development of climaxes; but he makes up for it by the realistic suggestion of the subordinate voices shouting, "Wohl auf, wohl auf! der Bräut'gam kommt, wohl auf!" "Steht auf, die Lampen nehmt, steht auf!" in short incisive phrases, as though suggesting of a verity the ardent elation of actual human beings in the realisation of the coming of the Lord; and by introducing a brilliant fugal "Alleluia," which disguises and bridges over the gap between two of the chorale phrases.

The enumeration of the various factors of artistic form and method might be pursued indefinitely. They all combine and assimilate in his hands to interpret that highly composite human phenomenon, religious devotionalism, as affected by association, tradition, imagery, sensibility, and mystery, directed in this case with deep poetic insight to the imposing conception of mankind stirred at the immediate advent of the Lord. Before leaving this cantata it will be well to observe the extent to which it presents essentially Teutonic qualities in other movements beside the first chorus.

After this movement a short recitative referring to the coming of the Bridegroom serves to introduce one of the dialogues between Christ and the Church which were so characteristic of Teutonic Protestantism and so sympathetic to Bach. The soprano, impersonating the Church, sings *Wann kommst du, mein Heil?* and the bass, impersonating Christ, answers *Ich komme, dein Theil,* in short and tender phrases, all held together in unity by the elaborately melodious solo for violino piccolo which is the main feature of the accompaniment.

Upon this follows another verse of the hymn, *Zion hört die Wächter singen,* the chorale tune being given to the tenors alone, with an accompaniment based on original figures which have quite an exceptional fascination. A highly sympathetic writer on Bach suggests that this singular and delightful passage has the intention of a dance tune; by which is indicated that Bach had in his mind the procession of the betrothed, and the joyous attendance of the virgins, whose gestures have a wayward grace which is suggestive of Botticelli. At first the quaintness of the suggestion rather balks acquiescence. But when the extraordinary vivacity of Bach's imagination is taken into account it may be admitted that among the many things which influenced the product, the idea of the virgins of allegory participating in the welcome of the heavenly Bridegroom may have had a share. Apart from its delightful intrinsic qualities the movement is interesting for affording such a conspicuous illustration of Bach's habit of transferring organ types of form to vocal music; as the movement makes its appearance as an organ Choralvorspiel in the collection known as the "Sechs Schüblerschen Choräle," with no alteration except the omission of the figures which indicate chords to be used as accompaniment in the present instance.

The movement is followed by a recitative for bass, evidently impersonating Christ, which serves as the preliminary to another dialogue between Christ and the Church, *Mein Freund ist mein, Und ich bin dein,* which breathes throughout a placid joy. The dialogue character is not so pronounced as in the first duet, for the phrases are longer and more melodious; moreover the movement is named "aria" and labours under the disadvantage of having a *da capo;* which Bach must have indicated without sufficient deliberation. The scheme of the whole work is completed by the usual process of singing the chorale, *Wachet auf,* simply harmonised in four parts. In this case it will be observed that the chorale appears in three forms—as the principal feature of the first chorus, in the form of the Choralvorspiel in the middle of the work, and in its noble unadorned simplicity at the end. It must not be overlooked, moreover, in this case that the reversion in the Teutonic direction is illustrated by the adoption of the dialogue form in the place of the Italian form of aria. For in spite of the *da capo* the texture and expressiveness of the so-called aria duet are much more Teutonic in character than the solo arias of the earlier Leipzig period.

In the depth and fervour of its Teutonic character the cantata *Ein' feste Burg* is fully equal to *Wachet auf* and, as has been mentioned above, it contains a very striking illustration of the Choralvorspiel type of first chorus, as compared with the harmonic scheme of the first chorus in the other cantata. It is even more than ordinarily difficult to fix the date of the work decisively. Its pre-eminent grandeur has inspired the belief that it must have been written for some great occasion, and the choice of Luther's words and the conspicuous use of Luther's tune as the prevailing musical feature have suggested the idea that it was composed for some Reformation festival. It appears possible that it was written for the two hundredth anniversary of the introduction of the reformed tenets into Saxony, in 1739. As the proofs are circumstantial rather than direct it is better not to lay much stress upon them, recalling the fact that Bach was of such a disposition that a subject which appealed to and aroused his imaginative faculties brought into play his highest artistic powers whatever the occasion.

The first chorus is of huge dimensions, and overwhelming energy, expressing in some indefinable way the strenuous confidence in the "feste Burg." Being, as has been said, in the form of a Chorale-prelude it begins at once, without instrumental preliminary, with the first phrase of the famous chorale, slightly ornamental in detail, and treated fugally by the voices, which enter successively. This must, of course, be regarded as anticipatory to the entry of the actual recital of the chorale, which comes in, in long notes, as the culmination of the opening passage of twenty-four bars; being presented, not as usual, by the voices, but by the accompanying instruments. This is such a striking departure and is carried out with such astounding skill and power of suggestion, that the scheme may profitably be considered in detail.

There is hardly any work which carries out with such amazing strength and consistency the problems which Bach set himself to solve. When he introduced the chorale in the trumpets and hautboys as the culmination of the initial part of the chorus, he must have welcomed the discovery that this phrase of the tune admitted of being treated in canon, because the brilliant sound of the trumpets and hautboys could be answered at once at the opposite end of the scale by the basses, thus enveloping the whole music from top to bottom in the chorale phrase, which is as it were the radiating symbol expressing the exhilarating confidence in the "Strong tower." But having once presented a phrase of the chorale in canon, Bach was bound by his sense of artistic responsibility not to drop so noticeable a feature, and he therefore faced the arduous task of treating all the other phrases of the chorale in canon on the same terms. And it may be frankly said that if he had not done so the effect made by all the latter part of the chorus would have been weakened. It was quite within the bounds of possibility that the later phrases of the chorale would not admit of being so treated. But some master minds seem to be able to disregard the ordinary laws of nature. Bach achieves the approximately impossible without having to take the smallest trouble about it. Every phrase of the chorale enunciated by the high and piercing instruments is answered immediately by the basses in the next bar, while all the voices go on vivaciously discoursing in elaborate polyphony; and not only so but the very device of the canon is made to minister to the intrinsic expression of the music itself. Such intimate detail is on the verge of present limits, but reference may be made to the simple procedure of the close, when the penultimate step of the final phrase of the tune entails, by the canonic procedure, a simple suspension of the final note in the treble, which is thereby forced momentarily downwards and takes its course through the expressive minor seventh of the scale, and begets the suggestion of the modification of the final phrase, which is sung fortissimo by the basses in their most powerful register over the final tonic pedal.

The scope of the chorus represents Bach's maturity at its very richest; the accumulation of resources through all the years of persistent labour provides a presentment of his artistic and temperamental personality in fullest measure, and in terms of the race of which in modern times he was the first great spiritual manifestation.

The only other movement in the cantata, *Und wenn die Welt voll Teufel wär'*, which was written at the same time with the first chorus, matched it in strength and impressiveness. It represents rather an unusual departure for Bach, as all the voices sing the chorale in unison with a most energetic and uplifting accompaniment, including trumpets and drums. The rest of the movements are borrowed from a much earlier Weimar cantata, *Alles was von Gott geboren.* The fact of this cantata having been written in the Weimar time is, however, fortunate in maintaining the Teutonic spirit of the whole, so no incongruity of style is perceptible. The chorale makes conspicuous appearance in the second movement, which, though called an aria, is a recital of the great tune, with elaborate variation of detail, by soprano solo, accompanied by independent solo for bass and brilliant passages for the instruments. The so-called recitatives are both amalgamated with passages in arioso form—the ideal Teutonic type lying betwixt the formal aria and the dry recitative. The final movement is the usual four-part chorale very strikingly harmonised. The Teutonic qualities are therefore amply spread through the whole work, and the famous chorale plays as conspicuous a part as in the cantata *Wachet auf.*

But perhaps it will be as well to recognise exceptions to such procedure at the outset. Bach seems at times to emphasise the Teutonic attitude of mind by distributing the chorale element in a different fashion, as is the case with the cantata *Gott der Herr* which appears to have been written for a Reformation festival in 1735. The difference is emphasised at the outset, inasmuch as the first chorus is not associated with a chorale. The share which the orchestra takes in the operations is unusually prominent. There is a long instrumental introduction with lively passages for two horns, and when the voices join in, it is at first in short emphatic episodes, asserting with vehemence *Gott, der Herr, ist Sonn' und Schild* in a sort of warlike spirit. The short bursts gather closer as the movement proceeds, and the general scheme of the chorus is rendered threefold, by a long brilliant polyphonic portion in the middle which is followed by a return of the opening phrase at the end to round off the whole. The musical qualities of the work, in which there are two arias, are rather mechanical, and its scale is not large, but the manner in which the use of two chorales is emphasised gives it a special character. That used at the end in the direct four-part form is *Wach' auf, mein Herz, und singe,* and the chorale in the middle of the work is *Nun danket Alle Gott,* which therefore occupies the same position as it does in Mendelssohn's "Lobgesang," and by a further singular coincidence is treated in the same way; the phrases of the chorale alternating, as in that well-known movement, with instrumental episodes. Apart from this coincidence it is to be observed that Bach uses horns and drums in the instrumental accompaniment, and gives them the principal instrumental subject of the first chorus to play, thereby uniting the opening and the middle of the cantata.

The use of several chorales in a single work, as has been remarked, is by no means common. In earlier years a few examples are found, such as the beautiful early cantata *Gottes Zeit* and *Schau', lieber Gott,* in both of which three different chorales are introduced; and also *Halt' im Gedächtniss, Wahrlich ich sage euch, Wo gehest du, So du mit deinem Munde, Der Friede sei mit dir, Sie werden euch* (No. 1), *Dazu ist erschienen* and *Sehet welch' eine Liebe.* A special position is suggested by the cantata *Schwingt freudig euch empor.* In cases where the chorale makes the central feature and radiating force, it is hardly necessary to observe that it must have been in the composer's mind from the first. But this cantata was originally composed without any chorales, since the first appearance of its principal movements was in a secular cantata in the honour of a birthday of the Princess of Anhalt-Cöthen. When Bach used up the materials of four numbers for the first Sunday in Advent, he could not convert the first chorus into a chorale chorus, but he enhanced the value of the work enormously for sacred purposes by adding several chorale movements. Immediately after the first chorus he inserted an elaborate and interesting duet for soprano and alto on the tune of *Nun komm', der Heiden Heiland;* then follows one of the movements borrowed from the secular cantatas, which must be admitted to be rather perfunctory in character, and another chorale is introduced to conclude the first part of the work. In the second part another new movement is introduced in the shape of a tenor aria which consists of the tune of *Nun komm, der Heiden Heiland* again, with lively accompaniment of two oboi d'amore, and the whole is made to end with the usual straightforward four-part version of the same chorale. From which it is to be observed that all the inserted movements are founded on chorales, and that the tune which ends the first half is different from that which ends the whole.

The most prominent instance of the use of many chorales in one work is *Christus der ist mein Leben,* which was probably written in 1732 and therefore belongs to the latest period. The first chorus consists of two different chorale fantasias with a discursive tenor solo joining them together. The first of these is on the chorale of the name of the cantata, which is presented simply in four-part harmony with fully independent instrumental accompaniment, in which a charming phrase for two oboi d'amore seems to hover ceaselessly in the background expressing tender longing and contentment. The most striking feature is a wonderful expansion of the beginning of the second phrase of the chorale to dwell upon the word 'Sterben." Those who hear with the understanding can feel how the words "Sterben ist mein Gewinn" gripped the composer. When the tenor solo which follows the first part of the chorus is going on the hearer sadly wants to know exactly what Bach meant by the lovable little phrase of the oboe d'amore above mentioned, for in the alternation of recitative and strict tempo it always ceases with the former and goes on with the latter. From the technical point of view the purpose is obvious, but from the point of view of expression the hearer feels that some beautiful poetic thought is there but cannot be formulated. The words here refer to the "Sterbelied" which he has made, "Would that to-day I might sing it," and then the music takes a totally new departure with the noble chorale, *Mit Fried' und Freud' ich fahr' dahin*, with a moving bass which no doubt came into the composer's mind at the suggestion of the words "ich fahr' dahin." The latter part of the movement is in the same form as the first part and has some exquisitely tender passages in it, but it must be admitted that the experiment of combining two different chorales in one movement does not appear to answer. It gives a sense of artistic incoherence, which is accentuated by the first part being very rich in material and in three-time, while the last portion is in four-time, and the tender oboe d'amore figure disappears entirely in the final portion, which therefore is not so interesting or suggestive as the first. A short recitative for soprano expresses the content of the Christian that he has done with the false world, and passes on into the chorale, *Valet will ich dir geben*, sung by the soprano with a beautifully intricate accompaniment. The following recitative for tenor solo refers to "Death the end of all trouble," and then follows one of the strangest arias Bach ever wrote—an adagio to the words "Strike soon, O blessed hour." The joy of the movement is the extraordinarily ingenuous accompaniment, most subtly thought out from the point of view of colour, with oboi d'amore and pizzicato strings; and in the poetic presentment of bells and tranquil lullabies suggesting an anticipation of some dainty French lyrical inspiration such as might even have visited Stephen Heller in his best moments. This music forms the basis of nearly all the movement, and on the top of it comes a declamatory tenor solo which is frankly impossible. The mere sight of it is enough to make any sensitive person's throat ache—and it is so angular as well as so high that it does not assimilate with the tender accompaniment. It seems in this case that Bach conceived the beautiful music of the accompaniment to express the words, and tried to put the tenor voice in afterwards, and did not get his faculties to take in the whole situation! Moreover the solo is of superhuman length, and if the singer ever got to the end he would have to sing more than half of it over again, if he was loyal to that direction—*da capo*, which was often written with such fatal ease and lack of consideration. A recitative for bass follows, the cue of which is "Mein Tod ist nur ein Schlaf" with a fine and characteristic melismatic close, and the fourth chorale, *Wenn mein Stündlein vorhanden ist*, is given to the words "Weil du vom Tod erstanden bist" in the usual form with an independent part for violin at the top making a fifth part. The chorale is a very fine one, and the harmonization up to the level of the finest and broadest that Bach ever achieved—in which every part, but especially the bass, is a joy to sing, for every singer feels he is a partaker in the noblest expression of the words.

Enough has been said to indicate that this is intrinsically one of the most interesting and poetical of

Bach's cantatas; so the experiment of using four chorales in a single cantata has the fairest of chances—especially as all four chorales are of the finest quality. But the effect is happily restricted to a very special occasion, the clue to which is not discoverable. For the cantata is evidently a funeral cantata, though it is specified only as for the sixteenth Sunday after Trinity, and Bach clearly felt that except for such special circumstances the impression was stronger, weightier, and more significant if the cantata centred on one chorale alone.

A striking example of the concentration of the whole cantata on a single chorale is the setting of Neander's hymn, *Lobe den Herren, den mächtigen König der Ehren,* which was probably written in 1732. The first chorus, which is of the exultant order with trumpets and drums, is in the chorale-fantasia form with the chorale in the soprano, and the subordinate voices echoing the tune. The second movement is for alto and is called an aria, but the voice part consists of an ornate version of the chorale. The third is an aria-duet for soprano and bass in which the voices have free variations of the chorale. The fourth movement is an aria for tenor with the chorale played by the trumpet, and the last movement is the usual presentment of the chorale, but with the addition of three independent trumpet parts. So every movement is associated with the chorale, implying clearly that "Lobe den Herren" is the text of the whole work.

There are certain types of procedure which Bach specially favoured in dealing with the chorale in the inner movements of the cantatas. The most remarkable is a combination of the phrases of the chorale with recitative. The process is sometimes carried out by two voices, sometimes by the choir singing the phrases of the chorale in four parts and the recitative for solo voice forming episodes between the lines, and sometimes a single voice deals with both the chorale and the recitative. There is a very remarkable example of the latter kind, in the second movement of the fine cantata *Ich hab' in Gottes Herz und Sinn*. The actual chorale which is used in the first chorus and in several other movements is *Was mein Gott will*. The second movement is a recitative and chorale combined for bass. It has only a figured bass, but the passages are so graphically suggestive in some parts, and so happily representative of the chorale in others, that the movement forms quite a striking illustration of the complex artistic personality of the composer. It is notable that whenever the chorale is going on the accompaniment is always closely connected with the first phrase of the tune, which commences as follows:

Es kann mir feh - len nim - mer-mehr!

and the accompanying bass of the introductory passage anticipates it in this manner:

but in all the episodal recitatives the bass follows freely the suggestions of the words; with runs in demisemiquavers and passages suggesting waves of the sea.

The voice part in the recitative portions is in Bach's most daring and graphic style, which entails marked contrast between them and the chorale portions. It is also important to note that in these combinations of chorale and recitative for a single voice the chorale is often represented by but a very small fragment at a time, which it would require the most intimate knowledge of the tune to identify. A short illustration will show to what an extent this close interchange is carried.

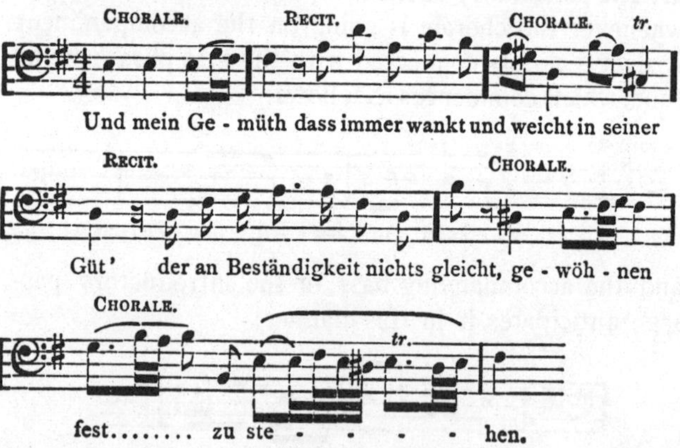

But everything in art depends on the context. In this case the combined chorale and recitative undoubtedly present a very restless and unquiet effect, though highly interesting. A forcible, even agitated, tenor solo follows, and then the chorale makes its reappearance in a totally different form, which reëstablishes the balance on the side of calm and placid beauty; for the alto sings the tune right through, quite simply, with one of Bach's uniquely flowing and soothing accompaniments. This cantata is indeed a perfect storehouse of chorale movements, for after a brilliant and restless solo for bass, *Das Brausen von den rauhen Winden,* follows an example of the other type of chorale and recitative mentioned above, in which the choir sing the phrases of the chorale in four parts and solo voices answer in recitative. In this case all the voices take a share. After the first two phrases, very subtly harmonised, the bass answers with recitative. The two phrases are repeated with slight variation, and the tenor answers; the next two phrases are sung by the choir, with answering recitative by the alto, and the two final phrases (which are fortunately in this case the same as the first) are sung by the choir, the soprano solo completing the whole with the final passage of recitative. The form in this case is undoubtedly most effective, and leads to a delightfully innocent and confiding aria for soprano, *Meinem Hirten bleib' ich treu,* ending with the touching words "Amen, Amen Vater nimm mich an!" the work being rounded off with the final statement of the chorale to words of solemn significance. The whole cantata is a remarkable example of the effect which Bach could produce by intermingling freely composed movements with movements based on chorales, and it is indeed of the quality which betokens that his powers and feelings were in their most vigorous condition.

Another most superb example of the combination of chorale and recitative is the bass recitative *O Wunder dass ein Herz* in the cantata *Mit Fried' und Freud' ich fahr' dahin.* The methods of treatment are here entirely different. The accompaniment begins at once with a discord, and presents a definite figure of striking character which persists through the whole movement and thereby unifies it completely—

therein showing kinship with the wonderful ariosos in the "Matthäus-Passion," such as "Ach Golgatha," while the solo voice alternates its contemplations in recitative and phrases from the chorale. This procedure obviates the restless effect which is produced by the elaborate movement above described in the cantata *Ich hab' in Gottes Herz und Sinn,* but the disposition of the alternative phrases in the voice part is much the same, and becomes close and continuous in the latter part of the movement. The manner in which the respective phrases are managed may be seen from the opening sentences. The recitative begins "O wonder that the heart is not in consternation at the thought of the pains of death!" and the chorale answers "That is through Christ, true Son of God, the Holy One!"

The position of this movement in the cantata is peculiarly happy, as it follows a slow aria for alto of the richest and most expressive texture; and its close (which consists of one of the melismatic passages of which Bach had the supreme secret, to the word "sterben") is most happily followed by a light and animated duet. The whole cantata is indeed of the very highest quality, for the chorale chorus with which it begins is full of the most exquisite poetry, and the close, *Der Tod ist mein Schlaf worden,* is one of the most pathetic and tender moments in all the cantatas. The singular fascination which the idea of beautiful death had for Bach is indeed a manifestation of a phase of his personality which is as wonderful as the supreme terms of art in which it is expressed.

Various circumstances have ministered to the making of the chorale *Vater unser im Himmelreich* one of the most familiar of the tunes outside Germany; and the cantata *Nimm von uns, Herr, du treuer Gott*—in which all the movements but one are either founded on or closely connected with that tune—brings home forcibly the spirit and purpose of the various fashions in which Bach makes use of the chorales. The first chorus is rather bald and is devoid of the usual interest of romantic detail. There is no great difference between the treatment of the instruments and the voices, so that one element of interest which is often of such conspicuous value with Bach is absent. The reason probably is that as far as the voices are concerned the movement is absolutely in the form of a Choralvorspiel. The first line of the familiar tune is prefaced by the successive entries of the lower voices singing it in imitation in minims; and, when they are all assembled, the sopranos join in with the tune in semibreves. The same procedure is followed with every phrase of the tune with absolute loyalty to the principle. But the movement differs from other choralvorspiel movements in the fact that it has an orchestral introduction, and that each phrase of the tune alternates with long orchestral episodes; so that the chorus is a rather rare and significant example of a combination of the two types of chorale-chorus. But it so happens that the other great choruses which are in the choralvorspiel form are in contrapuntal vocal style, and have no free instrumental accompaniment; and so, when Bach was moved to combine the two forms, the power of association made him forgo the instrumental luxuriance which would have distracted the mind from the beauty of the simple interweaving of the strands of the chorale tune. But in music the multitudinous implications of every phase distract the judgment from deciding which influence was foremost in the composer's mind. The sentiment of the verse set is peculiarly severe, and is expressed without any of the tenderness which saved so many of the Lutheran poetic utterances from harshness. So Bach's choice of a severe and unornate style is just as appropriate from this point of view as it is from the purely artistic point of view. The details might be followed out at great length; for though the instrumental accompaniment is so severe, yet in an inconspicuous manner Bach makes an almost ceaseless use of a short musical figure of this type:

to convey the suggestion of humbled sadness contained in the words "Die wir mit Sünden ohne Zahl verdienet haben allzumal," which are mainly the cue to the expression of the chorus. The figure is one which might be called a type-formula. It may have been more or less unconscious, but undoubtedly special definite sentiments very often suggested to Bach similar types of musical figures, as has been several times pointed out. The most familiar parallel in this case is the "Et incarnatus est" in the B minor mass, where the accompaniment is entirely knit of the following passage;

from this point of view it would be a very interesting inquiry what Bach means by the almost prostrate melancholy of that deeply emotional chorus. The clue might be found by comparing many instances of the occurrence of a similar figure. It may indeed be said further that some day the clue to a great many of Bach's instrumental works may be found in the identification of the types of figure which are always related in his mind to particular moods and phases of sentiment.

The only movement in this cantata which is not immediately associated with a chorale is the second, which is an aria for tenor, in which the intention is interesting, and—as is so often the case in Bach's tenor arias—the execution approximately impossible. The third movement for soprano solo is in the form so often referred to, of the combined chorale and recitative, the respective elements being almost continuous—like a man enhancing his conversation with fragments of poetry. The next movement, an aria for bass, is much the same in texture. The so-called aria (which has a very vivacious instrumental accompaniment) actually begins with a phrase of the chorale, to the stern words "Warum willst du so zornig sein," and the voice then proceeds to florid passages, only alluding once again to the same single phrase. But in the latter part of the aria the flute takes up the tune and plays it right through, the solo voice and the rest of the accompanying instruments continuing on their independent courses. The words explain the references, "Stelle doch die Strafen ein, und trag' aus väterlicher Huld mit unserm schwachen Fleisch Geduld." The next number continues similar considerations in the form of the chorale and recitative for tenor solo, in which a beautifully tender rhythmic accompaniment, closely related to the first phrases of the chorale tune, is especially attractive.

Yet another form is presented in the "aria duet" for soprano and alto which follows. It is actually described as "Mit Benutzung der Choral-Melodie." As might be expected, the words "Gedenk' an Jesu bittern Tod" inevitably engendered a tender mood in the composer. The movement is one of those in which Bach expends to the full his subtlety in enriching melodic phrase and expressive harmony with every kind of adornment, in the $\frac{12}{8}$ time which always seems to offer him such full scope. The chorale tune makes its appearance in every direction—with flute and oboe da caccia in the introductory part,—afterwards each solo voice takes its phrases in turn and then passes on to beautiful interlacings of expressively melodious passages, which hang round it as if echoing its mood —often with phrases which are no more than ejaculations such as this:

while the accompaniment, which, unlike the first chorus, presents the very richest features of instrumental style, is suffused with beautiful fragments of expressive tune, closely knit and supremely to the point. How closely knit they are may be seen from the fact that the ejaculatory phrase given to the voice as above quoted is borrowed from the first phrase of instrumental material:

The familiar chorale simply harmonised makes the usual conclusion to the cantata.

It may be worth pointing out, in relation to the period of Bach's life when they were written, that no less than four of these cantatas, *Ich hab'in Gottes Herz und Sinn, Christus, der ist mein Leben, Mit Fried' und Freud'*, and *Nimm von uns,* deal with the idea of death, and that the most beautiful of his early cantatas, *Gottes Zeit,* of the Weimar time, dealt with the same subject, with the same vein of mysticism, tenderness, and deeply religious sincerity.

Among further late cantatas in which the inner movements are very fully identified with the chorale is *Wo Gott der Herr nicht bei uns hält.* In this, the second number is a combination of chorale and recitative, in which the chorale is very clearly differentiated from the recitative, as nothing less than a whole phrase is given at a time; and it therefore stands out more decisively from the context than in many other examples. Moreover, this prominence is accentuated by a device suggested by the procedure of the choralvorspiel, as the accompaniment comprises imitations of each phrase in shorter notes. The fourth number consists of the chorale simply sung by the tenor with an accompaniment closely knit of characteristic figures. The fifth number is an example of the chorale sung by the choir in four parts with recitatives for the voices between the phrases, and a very striking and suggestive accompaniment of rhythmic character which knits the whole into unity. So there are only two movements out of seven which are not closely associated with the chorale.

It is to be observed that Bach generally treated the chorale tunes with great respect, as a species of sacred text. Yet there are a few cases in which he even modifies the actual scale or mode here and there for purposes of expression. One of the finest of such modifications is the end of the first chorus in the cantata *Mit Fried' und Freud',* where the melody is made to descend to the tonic near the close by a semitone (as in the third mode) instead of a tone, ministering thereby to the deeply pathetic effect of the passage (see p. 405). Such procedure is not altogether uncommon. Bach also sometimes ornaments the chorale tune, and sometimes he completely transforms it; making a kind of "metamorphosis of theme" to convey a special sentiment. Of this kind of process the cantata *Was frag' ich nach der Welt* supplies an exceptional number of illustrations. The tune of the chorale begins:

CHORALE.
Was frag' ich nach der Welt.

In the third movement, a combined recitative and

chorale (which appears under the welcome name of arioso), the melody appears in this variation:

Die Welt sucht Ehr und Ruhm......

The alto aria presents a much more complicated transformation in a *melisma:*

Be - thör - - - - - - - - te Welt.

In the recitative and chorale for bass the tune appears in this form:

Adagio.
Die Welt be - küm - mert sich

and in the soprano solo as follows:

Es halt es mit der blin - den Welt

This does not, indeed, exhaust the varieties of form and expression which Bach makes the tune assume, but it is sufficient to represent the facts. It seems as if Bach had deliberately adopted these devices in this cantata to give it special character.

The cantata *Ach lieben Christen, seid getrost* has but one inner chorale number, *Kein' Frucht,* in which the chorale is sung simply by the soprano solo with free accompaniment. But there is also an alto solo, *Du machst, O Tod,* the characteristic passage of which appears to have close connection with the first phrase of the chorale.

In *Gelobet seist du, Jesu Christ,* in which the first chorus is in the form of a chorale-fantasia, the second number is a combination of chorale and recitative for soprano solo in which the recitative is in each case an expansion of the sentiment conveyed in each phrase of the chorale.

In the cantata *Ach Gott, vom Himmel sieh' darein* there is the unusual feature of a passing allusion to a single phrase of the chorale in the recitative which constitutes the second movement. An example of similar fragmentary use of a phrase from the chorale as a sort of suggestion occurs in the great solo cantata *O Ewigkeit* (p. 428), and also in *Du Friedefürst, Herr Jesus Christ,* where the initial phrase is twice introduced into the accompaniment of an ordinary recitative, *Gedenke doch, O Jesu,* apparently recalling the designation of "Friedefürst."

The Chorale tune.
Voice.
Ge-den-ke doch, O Je - su
Continuo.

This cantata, which is one of the latest Bach wrote, has reference, like the cantata *Wär Gott nicht mit uns*, to recent wars in which the people of Saxony were deeply interested. The first chorus is in chorale-fantasia form, and the chorale is given quite simply at first, with evident intention of making it stand out strongly in a bold and simple manner. Later in the chorus it is accompanied by splendid elaboration of polyphony in the subordinate voices.

A much more subtle use of fragmentary and quasi-allusive reference to the chorale is in the third version of the cantata *Was Gott thut* (which was a copious revision of an earlier work). In both the arias for soprano and bass in that work the first phrase of the tune is a variation of the first phrase of the chorale, but very subtly disguised. The final Chorale movement in this work is an expansion of the Chorale movement in *Die Elenden sollen essen* (see p. 208).

In the larger of the two cantatas which begin with the words *Ach Gott, wie manches Herzeleid*, the second movement is a combination of the chorale sung by the choir with recitatives between the phrases. The interest is enhanced by the accompaniments being founded on a figure derived from the first phrase of the chorale in quicker notes, suggesting the persistent undercurrent of the idea of the "manches Herzeleid."

Chorale Tune.
Ach Gott wie man - ches Her - ze - leid.
Instrumental Episode.

In *Herr Jesu Christ, Du höchstes Gut* there are several inner movements which are connected with the chorale. The alto sings it simply with flowing accompaniment of massed strings; the bass aria suggests it in its first ornate phrase, and the same voice has also a movement in which chorale and recitative are combined.

Erhalt' uns, Herr contains a duet for alto and tenor *Der Menschen Gunst,* in which the phrases of the chorale are alternated with recitative. The first chorus is in chorale-fantasia form, and contains a quaint example of Bach's favourite realistic suggestions at the opening.

In *Schmücke dich, O liebe Seele* there is an arioso for soprano, *Ach, wie hungert,* which really consists of a variation of the chorale. The accompaniment of the first chorus subtly conveys, after Bach's favourite manner, the idea of graceful adornment. At the beginning of it there is one of the rare allusive uses of a chorale tune by the flutes.

Meine Seele erhebt den Herrn (which is not a setting of the Magnificat, but of a hymn by Joseph Klug) contains a duet for alto and tenor, *Er denket der Barmherzigkeit,* in which the chorale tune is introduced very aptly by oboe and trumpet, so as to present the scheme of a chorale-fantasia; in which guise it actually appears in the "Sechs Schübler'schen Choräle" for organ. (See p. 504.) The first chorus is also a chorale-fantasia, and has rather a special character owing to the archaic modal nature of the tune.

In *Das neugebor'ne Kindelein,* a cantata written for the first Sunday after Christmas, there is something especially attractive in the cheerful manner in which the secondary voices echo the phrases of the chorale in the first chorus. There is also a recitative in which the three flutes harmoniously play the chorale high in the scale, evidently following the suggestion of the word "Engel," and also a trio for three voices in which the chorale is sung by the alto voice and doubled by the massed strings.

In *Wo soll ich fliehen hin* there is a recitative for alto, *Mein treuer Heiland tröstet mich*, in which the chorale of the cantata is played right through by the oboe, and is almost exactly conterminous with the recitative, the meaning of the words of which is thereby emphasised with remarkable effect. This cantata also contains a tenor aria with a very brilliant accompaniment for viola solo. The chorale chorus at the beginning is notable for the profusion with which the phrases of the chorale are introduced, both in the instruments and the secondary voices.

Herr Jesu Christ, wahr'r Mensch und Gott is full of interesting features. At the opening there is an allusion to an extraneous chorale in the strings while the oboes play a phrase founded on the chorale of the cantata. The first line of the chorale being made the basis of the parts of the accompanying voices, seems to emphasize the idea conveyed in the first line of the hymn. The soprano aria *Die Seele ruht* is characterised by a striking accompaniment in which the oboe plays the plaintive melody while flutes keep up a ceaseless reiteration of quavers. The clue for this appears to be a sentence at the end, "Ach, ruft mich bald ihr Sterbeglocken," for when these words actually occur the suggestion of the bells is emphasised by the strings joining in the accompaniment with pizzicato chords.

The same device is employed in the Weimar cantata *Komm du süsse Todesstunde* and in the Trauer Ode. There is also a very fine bass solo with trumpet, *Wenn einstens die Posaunen schallen,* in which recitative and aria are closely and effectively intermingled. It contains some subtle allusions to the chorale of the cantata.

Besides these later cantatas in which the chorale is so variously employed, there is a large number in which the emphasis laid upon it is mainly or entirely confined to its elaboration in the first chorus and the harmonised version at the end; of which the following are examples.

Aus tiefer Noth is one of the few later cantatas in which the first chorus is of the Pachelbel choral-vorspiel type without independent orchestral opening. The correspondence of the melodic outline of the first phrase of the tenor aria *Ich höre mitten in dem Leiden* with the beginning of the chorale is likely to have been an unconscious result of subjective suggestion. *Christum wir sollen loben schon* also begins with a chorus in Choralvorspiel form. It contains a notably tuneful and florid aria for bass, *Johannis freudenvoller Springen.*

Mache Dich, mein Geist, bereit is especially notable for one of the most exquisite solos in all the cantatas, the soprano aria, *Bete, bete!* It is accompanied by a flute, violoncello piccolo, and continuo, intertwining divinely tender phrases, which plead against one another as if from the innermost depths of the soul; and into their company the solo voice seems to drop from the infinite with slow phrases expressing with the deepest urgency the words, "Bete, bete!" That Bach should have called such a movement an aria shows how completely the form had by this late period become intrinsically Teutonised.

The first chorus of *Ach wie flüchtig* is notable for the graphic manner in which Bach superimposes figures suggestive of the word "flüchtig" in the accompaniment to the chorale. It also contains a very fine bass solo, *An irdische Schätze das Herze zu hängen.*

Herr Gott, Dich loben alle wir was written for the Feast of St. Michael and is a wonderfully vigorous work. It has a special interest foı English Protestants, as it is written on the familiar tune known to them as the "Old Hundredth," and thereby affords them an exceptional opportunity to appreciate the form of the chorale-fantasia as superbly presented in the first chorus. The cantata also contains a most engaging tenor solo in gavotte rhythm.

Wohl dem, der sich auf seinen Gott contains among many other striking features a bass aria, *Das Unglück schlägt,* of immense proportions and of peculiar form, as it is broken up into alternating sections of quick and slow time and changes from $\frac{4}{4}$ to $\frac{6}{8}$. It also has a most elaborate accompaniment for oboe d'amore and solo violin.

Liebster Immanuel begins with a fine Chorale-fantasia Chorus in which the first phrase of the Chorale is very much in evidence in all parts of the accompaniment including Viole d'Amore. In the tenor Aria there is a very striking and characteristic example of poignant and forcible expression to the words "harte Kreuzesreise."

The first chorus of *Was mein Gott will* is notable for the fidelity with which the subordinate voices follow the phrases of the chorale in diminution in the first chorus, and the same is the case with *Ach Herr, mich armen Sünder*, in which the chorale *Herzlich thut mich verlangen* is given to the basses and the intertwining of its phrases in shorter notes has an exquisitely expressive effect.

Es ist das Heil has a fine chorale-fantasia for the initial movement, in which occurs a very strange passage which must have been the outcome of something which Bach had in his mind, but which it is difficult to guess. The soprano sings the long notes of the chorale phrase, *Der hat g'nug für uns all' gethan*, and the accompanying voices sing:

der hat g'nug, g'nug für uns, g'nug für uns

This cantata contains a duet which illustrates Bach's extraordinary facility in manipulating canon. The soprano and alto solo first sing a charmingly fluent canon at the fifth below, and then reversing the order of the proceedings sing a canon at the fourth above, and the flute and the oboe in the accompaniment also have a canon on their own account which they also reverse.

Wie schön leuchtet der Morgenstern has an initial chorale-fantasia which is in a radiant and joyous vein and most richly and copiously developed. Bach has somehow managed to convey the sense of the brightness of the "Morgenstern" just as he did the sturdiness of the "Feste Burg" by the general mood of the music. *O Jesu Christ* consists only of a single movement of very severe and simple character in chorale-fantasia form,—a striking aspect of which is the unusual constitution of the band, which consists only of two lituus (a kind of trumpet), a cornetto, and three trombones. The effect would certainly be very interesting.

In *Meinen Jesum lass'ich nicht* the treatment of the chorale in the chorale-fantasia is similarly simple, amounting to little more than a harmonisation of the tune with ornate accompaniment of "oboe d'amore concertante." The realistic effect of a reiterated-note figure in the tenor solo *Und wenn der harte Todesschlag* is notably characteristic.

Wär Gott nicht mit uns diese Zeit is a work of remarkable interest and beauty. The first chorus forms a parallel (with a vast difference of mood) to the first chorus of *Ein' feste Burg*, since, though it is in chorale-prelude form, the voices never actually sing the chorale, which is reserved for the horn and oboe.[1] The voice parts are extraordinarily elaborate, and the skill manifested in the manipulation of the chromatic subject with answers by inversion is as remarkable as the complete absence of any obtrusive appearance of dexterity. The movement is, indeed, a striking example of the extent to which Bach used the utmost dexterity merely as means to an end. According to Spitta the character of the cantata is due to the impression produced in Saxony by recent experiences of warfare (see p. 414). As is often the case, the solo music is not of equal interest with the first chorus. There are only two airs and they are of a straightforward and practical character, the first

[1] The same procedure is adopted in the first chorus of *Ich elender Mensch*, in which the chorale is played by the trumpet and oboe in canon.

having a very elaborate accompaniment for horn and strings.

In *Auf Christi Himmelfahrt allein* is revealed a work of superb quality. The chorale-fantasia chorus at the beginning is made characteristic by important horn parts, and it is happily followed by some fine solo movements, especially one of Bach's typical bass solos with brilliant trumpet "obbligato," the interest of which is enhanced by the unusual treatment of the close, where its vigorous animation abruptly merges in a splendid elocutionary recitative. This is brought within the circuit of the movement by repeating the introductory symphony at the end. The procedure is a reversal of the familiar device of ending a recitative with an arioso. The basis is psychological, the change in the attitude of mind suddenly induced being a source of revived attention.

Warum betrübst du dich, mein Herz illustrates another phase of Bach's experimental energy. The scheme of the first chorus is that of the chorale-fantasia, but so sophisticated that it might easily be misconceived. Each phrase of the chorale is anticipated by a long passage of expressive vocal melody, like an arioso, written in one of the chorus staves, but probably intended for a solo voice. The relative proportions of the passages are very irregular, and sometimes even long passages of recitative are introduced. Moreover, when the chorale has been completely dealt with once through, after a bass recitative the same process is resumed, though not so whole-heartedly. It is permissible to think that Bach got a little wearied of the scheme in which he had entangled himself before he got quite to the end of it, and had not time to recast the whole thing. In passing it is to be observed that the bass solo, *Auf Gott steht*, was transferred with modifications of detail into the Mass in G major.

Bach's fondness for trying experiments with diverse well-known forms is illustrated in some of these later cantatas. In *Christ unser Herr zum Jordan kam* he presents the opening chorale-fantasia in the form of the first movement of an instrumental concerto, and works the combination through with astonishing vigour and mastery of every requirement. Yet another parallel experiment is shown in the first chorus of *Jesu, der Du meine Seele* which is presented in terms of a solemn chaconne. The ground bass is mainly of the chromatic order, descending by semitones in a manner to which Bach was much inclined, the most impressive example being the Crucifixus in the B minor Mass. In passing it may be observed that the cantata contains a very beautiful example of the expressive order of arioso, and a fine aria for bass, *Nun, du wirst mein Gewissen stillen.*

A different kind of experiment is manifested in *In allen meinen Thaten*, where Bach compounds the French overture form with a chorale-fantasia on the tune of *Nun ruhen alle Wälder*.

In *Gelobet sei der Herr* the chorale-fantasia chorus is full of animation and vitality, and enjoys the distinction of being accompanied by an exceptionally full orchestra, including trumpets and drums. The final chorale is also fully accompanied.

Herr Christ der ein'ge Gottes Sohn, probably written in 1732, begins with a finely-wrought but rather monotonous Chorale-Fantasia and contains two fine Arias.

Ich ruf' zu Dir begins with a beautiful chorale-fantasia which has an exceptionally elaborate accompaniment, in which a violino concertante plays an interesting and conspicuous part. It seems to be carried out with even unusual concentration of mind, and is completed by a long coda for the instruments.

The second cantata which goes by the name of *Nun komm', der Heiden Heiland,* was written some twenty years after the first, and it is not so interesting. It is well to observe, moreover, that though it begins with the same words, the rest of the words are different. The first version had saliently interesting points which have been discussed (page 86). The present version is on the usual lines of the later chorale cantatas, with chorale-fantasia chorus in B minor and recitatives and arias in the usual order, all of fine quality but not demanding detailed consideration.

Allein zu Dir has a chorale-fantasia chorus of the usual type at the beginning, and a remarkable aria, *Wie furchtsam wankten meine Schritte,* for alto, with an interesting accompaniment of muted first violin and the rest of the strings pizzicati. It is generally of a purely normal type. In the chorale-fantasia chorus in *Sei Lob und Ehr'* the accompaniments are very elaborate and the voice parts very simple, so as to throw the fine tune into conspicuous relief. The four-part chorale is inserted in the body of the work, as well as at the end. The same treatment of the chorale is shown in the first chorus of *Ich freue mich in dir,* but the instrumental accompaniment is simpler. The soprano aria *Wie lieblich klingt es in den Ohren* is interesting. Bach seems to have some intention in relation to the words of producing echo effects, the same phrase being frequently reiterated first "forte" and then "piano."

The middle section of the aria is very strongly contrasted in style.

Wer weiss wie nahe mir mein Ende has an impressive and melancholy chorale-fantasia with recitatives interspersed between the phrases of the chorale and solo violin accompaniment—a very striking conception superbly carried out. There is an alto aria with an elaborate organ accompaniment, and an impressive solo for bass, *Gute Nacht du Weltgetümmel,* in which the tune begins very peacefully, and then the word "Getümmel" is suggested by an agitated accompaniment of strings with rapidly repeated notes.

As has been shown, the majority of the first choruses in these chorale cantatas are in the form of the chorale-fantasia. In one interesting case, *Jesu nun sei gepreiset,* Bach combines the two types of "Orgelchoral" in one chorus. It begins with a characteristic subject for trumpets in the instrumental introduction, and proceeds in an exultant manner with the chorale tune in the treble voices, the other voices singing brilliantly congenial counterpoint. After the whole procedure of the chorale-fantasia has been gone through, there is a pause in the animated proceedings and the voices sing very gently, *adagio,* the words "Dass wir in guter Stille das alt' Jahr hab'n erfüllet"—as though possessed for the moment with a sense of soul-subduing solemnity,—and then at once, *presto,* the voices dash into a movement of the Choralvorspiel type, to the words "Wir wollen uns dir ergeben jetzund und immerdar," and when that is completed, the style of the beginning of the chorus is resumed and the first two phrases of the chorale are yet again repeated in accordance with the episodal scheme. The treatment of the chorale at the end of the work affords a parallel: for the chorale is sung first right through in four-time with an instrumental accompaniment (which, be it noted, brings back again the jubilant phrase of the instrumental introduction to the first chorus, and thus establishes a fine unity of sentiment); then it is resumed in $\frac{3}{4}$ time; and yet again after that its two prominent phrases are repeated in $\frac{4}{4}$ time, and the orchestra rounds off the whole with the actual phrase with which the work began. The cantata is referred to the year 1735, and the words indicate that the date must have been just at the end of it. The exultant phrase which is repeated over and over again suggests the intention to inspire a strenuous outlook towards the coming year. The cantatas *Was willst du dich betrüben* and *Der Herr ist mein getreuer Hirt*, though not strictly chorale cantatas, illustrate the type; as the first chorus in each of them is in the chorale-fantasia form. In the latter case the accompaniment comprises extremely elaborate parts for horns.

There are many other features besides the copious use of chorales which show the renewal of the Teutonic impulse in Bach's disposition at this time. Among them may be mentioned the frequent use of the arioso form, a type which, as has been said, lies between the recitative and the aria, being much more rich in musical effect than the former and much less constrained than the latter; prefiguring the latest developments of purely Teutonic type. In this form Bach was wont to express things which moved him very deeply, and many recitatives culminate in passages of arioso. There is a beautiful and fully developed example in the cantata, *Schmücke dich, O liebe Seele* (see p. 415). Another feature which is essentially Teutonic is the use of melismatic passages for the expression of deep emotion (see p. 93). The type has been indicated in the wonderful close of the chorus *Es ist der alte Bund,* in the early Weimar cantata *Gottes Zeit,* and the well-known passage in which Peter's anguish is expressed in the "Matthäus-Passion." In these later cantatas they are of frequent occurrence. There is, as has been mentioned above, a very striking example on the first syllable of the word "Sterben" at the end of the choral recitative *O Wunder* in the cantata *Mit Fried' und Freud',* and another occurs on the first syllable of "Jammerthal" in the bass recitative in *Gelobet seist Du, Jesu Christ.* Two notable examples occur in connection with the words "Weh' der Seele" at the end of the alto aria in the magnificent cantata *Herr, deine Augen sehen nach dem Glauben,* which is referred to the year 1731.

Frequent reference has been made to the favour with which German Protestant composers regarded the form known as the "dialogus." It was of all things an essentially Protestant type, since, until the change of mental and emotional attitude in connection with the idea of the beloved Jesus, referred to in discussing the "Matthäus-Passion." the discourses between Jesus and the soul, which are the most striking of these dialogues, would have been clearly unimaginable. The most remarkable of these works is the complete cantata in dialogue form, *O Ewigkeit, du Donnerwort,* above referred to, which belongs to the latest period of Bach's life. Its essentially Protestant and Teutonic character is indicated by the fact that the first part of the dialogue turns upon a chorale tune. It is from one point of view what is technically called a solo cantata—though obviously an exceptional one. There are three solo voices, of whom the alto personifies "Fear," the tenor "Hope," and the bass, is specified as "Die Stimme des heiligen Geistes." In sober earnest the dialogue is yet another example of the dialogue between God and the soul, examples of which were written by German composers before Bach was born; but the deep interest of this example is that the soul speaks in two capacities, like (with a difference) the Florestan and Eusebius of Schumann. Fear and Hope alternate and intermingle, and the instruments keep up a restless motion in which the feelings associable with the "Thunder-word Eternity," such as awe, foreboding, gloom, tremulous helplessness, the sense of weakness in the face of the immeasurable power, are forcibly expressed. "Fear," the alto, begins with the phrase of the chorale which in its slow and measured motion so perfectly represents the state of the human creature subdued to awe by the consciousness of the immeasurable. Bach's true perception is shown by the fact that "Fear" goes on discoursing for some time before the other phase of the soul presents itself. It is not till after three phrases have been sung that "Hope," the tenor, begins to take a different view of the situation. There is only one sentence allotted to this personality, "Herr ich warte auf dein Heil," and this is repeated again and again, sometimes simultaneously with the measured phrases of the chorale and sometimes alone, emphasising the attitude of the devout Christian in relation to Christ; and it is to be noted that the accents have a plaintive tone, a touch of pathos like the well-known picture of G. F. Watts. It is indeed the single string that "Hope," as yet, is sounding here, and no better example could be offered of the kind of repetition of words which has ample justification. And it is to be noted finally that "Hope" has the last word, for the chorale which is sung by "Fear" dies away long before the final accents of the duet.

The second movement is a recitative duet in which the chorale only appears in a very suggestive fragment, like the fragments referred to in the tenor recitative of the cantata *Du Friedefürst Herr Jesu Christ* and in *Ach Gott, vom Himmel sieh'darein* (p. 413). It is quite clear that Bach meant to connect the recitative here with the chorale, and the combination of the æsthetic and the interpretative elements is charmingly illustrative of his disposition. The chorale begins:

and the recitative begins:

wherein the augmented interval naïvely and unmistakably represents the "schwerer Gang." "Fear" talks with agitation of the dread of death and "Hope" calls up thoughts of comfort. In the ensuing movements—a fine and spaciously developed duet and a recitative—"Fear" continues harping on the awesome aspects, and "Hope" clings to comforting reflections, and finally the bass, representing the Divine voice, brings the answer which has moved so many, and which mankind especially associate with such divinely endowed temperaments as Bach and Johannes Brahms, "Selig sind die Tödten die in dem Herren sterben." It is a very interesting illustration of Bach's psychological insight that there is quite a contest between the voice of "Fear" and the Divine voice for some time. "Fear" breaks in on the lovely phrase of the Divine voice which Bach-lovers know so well:

with the anxious words "Ach! aber ach, wie viel Gefahr stellt sich der Seele dar," etc. Finally the Divine voice takes possession of the agitated soul and completes the reassuring sentiment in an arioso. "Fear" thenceforth surrenders in a short recitative, answering "Hope" with a quaint air of satisfied complacency, and the whole cantata ends with the chorale *Es ist genug*, which has the peculiarity—like the chorale at the end of the motet *Der Geist hilft unser Schwachheit auf*—of being broken up into short phrases, producing a strangely reflective emotional effect.

Bach's justness of insight in departing from his usual practice of ending with the chorale of the opening is here fortunately manifested. For the essential idea of the cantata is the removal of the terror inspired by the "Thunder-Word, Eternity," by the promise of the Divine word, and as the terror is intimately associated with the chorale, it would have been a complete anticlimax if it had been brought back at the end. So in this case the use of a different chorale for the conclusion is more than amply justified and explained.

Another dialogue cantata which belongs to this period is a setting of the words *Ach Gott, wie manches Herzeleid*, which Bach also set on a larger scale with chorus (see p. 414). The characters or personified abstractions which the solo voices represent are not specified, but soprano and bass carry on a sort of controversy, the clue to which is presented in the first sentences of the opening duet. The soprano begins with the words "O God, how great my heartfelt pain!" and the bass, breaking in before the sentence is finished, sings "Only patience, patience, my heart!" From which it is clear that this cantata also represents a dialogue between two aspects of the same person, as in the *O Ewigkeit, du Donnerwort*. It is not carried on with anything approaching the dramatic intensity of that work, but the soprano expresses uneasiness and the bass consolation in several recitatives and arias, and the work is completed by a second duet. The soprano sings the chorale in both the first and last duet.

A third dialogue is *Selig ist der Mann*, which is specified as being between Jesus and the soul. The treatment is again much more lyrical than in *O Ewigkeit, du Donnerwort*. There is very little immediate interchange of sentences except in two short recitatives, and the various sentiments are conveyed in complete arias of fine quality, and in the chorale with which the work concludes. The character of the work suggests that it was not originally written for use in a church.

Besides these dialogue cantatas Bach wrote a considerable number of solo cantatas at this time. *Jauchzet Gott*, a brilliant and effective cantata for solo soprano, was probably written for his wife, Anna Magdalena. It contains several fine arias, and one beautiful movement which, though described as a recitative, is more of the nature of an arioso. In the last movement but one the solo voice sings a chorale, and the last movement is an *Allelujah* in a vigorous fugal style, in spite of its being for a single voice.[1] A point which illustrates Bach's habit referred to (p.272) of using types of figure to represent phases of feeling, is that near the end he uses the same type of figure to express the exuberant uplifting of feeling which he introduced at the end of the great motet "Singet dem Herrn" referred to on page 299.

Another delicate and beautiful cantata for solo soprano, which was probably written for Anna Magdalena, is *Ich bin vergnügt.* It contains two arias and two recitatives and a final chorale and is marked with unusual care and fulness, bearing all the tokens that the composition was a labour of love.

[1] The most complete example of such procedure is the first movement of *O heiliger Geist*, in which the solo soprano has to take part in a fugue on equal terms with the instruments.

Among several solo cantatas for alto voice, which were probably written for Bach's daughter, *Vergnügte Ruh'* is specially notable for the melodious beauty of the arias, and for the exceptional use of the organ obligato, especially in the second aria *Wie jammern mich*, in which the accompaniment is a kind of elaborate trio, with higher parts for organ and lowest for violins and viola massed together.

The cantata *Widerstehe doch der Sünde* is another for alto voice, and begins with a striking discord on a pedal, which Bach evidently intended to express the words;

and the melody given to the voice starts from an analogous chord:

It is possible that the short cantata, *Schlage doch*

gewünschte Stunde belongs to this period. It is for an alto voice and in a simply melodious and expressive style. It illustrates Bach's disposition for realistic suggestion, as it has a part for bells, which are introduced to suggest the striking of the wished-for hour.

Bach seems to have delighted in writing for a fine bass soloist in his choir, and there are many cantatas for that voice. Among them is a very long cantata *Ich will den Kreuzstab gerne tragen*, which contains many fine recitatives and arias, concluding with a chorale; which Bach himself designated as a "Cantata a voce sola e stromenti." Another cantata for bass voice, of great beauty, is *Ich habe genug*, consisting only of recitatives and arias. It is rendered especially interesting by the reappearance in the middle of the exquisitely tender aria, *Schlummert ein*, which had made its appearance twice (but both times incomplete) in Anna Magdalena's second book of 1725 (see p. 144).

For some unexplained reason Bach several times saw fit to begin solo cantatas with important instrumental movements. There may have been occasions when he resorted to such a procedure to make up for the absence of the usual initial chorus.

The cantata *Falsche Welt, dir trau' ich nicht*, for solo soprano, is noticeable for the extensive sinfonia for orchestra with which it commences, which is none other than the first movement of the first Brandenburg concerto. It contains a number of recitatives and arias laid out on a scheme similar to the Italian solo cantatas, and ends with a chorale.

Geist und Seele is a very extensive cantata for alto solo in which there are two instrumental movements to begin the two parts, which were probably transplanted from some lost orchestral work.

Gott soll allein mein Herze haben is also an extensive cantata for alto, which begins with a sinfonia, which is the same as the first movement of the concerto for clavier in E major; and one of the other movements, *Stirb in mir,* is a transformation of the Siciliano from the same concerto.

The cantata *Am Abend aber desselbigen Sabbaths,* has a grand sinfonia in D for strings, oboes and fagotto. In *Ich geh' und suche,* the last movement of the concerto in E for clavier serves as an introductory sinfonia. Bach entitles the latter work a "dialogue," and though there are no further indications, it appears to be intended as a dialogue between Christ and the Church. It is notable that there is no chorale at the end of the work as usual, but in the final duet the soprano sings the chorale while the bass sings *Dich hab' ich je und je geliebet.* The cantata is notable also on account of the extent to which organ obbligato is employed.

Ich liebe den Höchsten contains a conspicuous example of such instrumental introductions, as it begins with the splendid first movement of the third Brandenburg concerto in G; and the interest is enhanced by the fact that Bach added two horns and two oboes and "taille" to the score, which in the first version was written only for strings. The rest of the cantata is overweighted by having so grand a movement at the beginning. The copious employment of the organ, as in the above-mentioned *Ich geh' und suche* and *Vergnügte Ruh',* is a feature which frequently occurs in cantatas about this date, as Bach seems to be gladly availing himself of alterations which had been made in the organ at St. Thomas's Church in 1730 or so. The most conspicuous instance is the cantata *Ich habe meine Zuversicht,* which, in the shape in which it is known in modern times, has no instrumental introduction, but is proved to have been prefaced on its first performance in 1730 by the whole of the clavier concerto in D minor, transferred to the organ to show off the improvements. Another conspicuous example of the use of the organ is in the cantata *Wir müssen durch viel Trübsal,* which will be discussed later (see p. 446).

Ich steh' mit einem Fuss im Grabe also has an introductory sinfonia, though not of such spacious dimensions as those above mentioned. It is really a rhapsodical melody for oboe with accompaniment of strings. In the first aria (which is a duet for soprano and tenor), the tenor sings the above words and the soprano joins in with the chorale *Mach's mit mir, Gott, nach deiner Güt'.* The relation of the chorale to the sentiment of the words is obvious, and the scheme essentially Teutonic.

Es reifet euch ein schrecklich Ende is a remarkably forcible, even stern Cantata for Solo voices. The Aria for Tenor has a very animated voice part and an accompaniment which matches it in spirit. The other Aria is one of Bach's typical Solos for Bass with Trumpet obbligato, which is of the most brilliant description. It is so forcible as to be almost menacing. *Was soll ich aus dir machen, Ephraim* begins with a very impressive Bass Solo in which reproach is severely expressed. The accompaniment for two hautboys, horn, and strings is full of colour and character. The Tenor

Aria in the middle of the Cantata is not so spontaneous, but the final short Aria for Soprano has a most engaging tune.

The second setting of *Sie werden euch in den Bann thun* as a Solo Cantata should be mentioned as belonging to this period, though it is not very interesting.

'l he date of *Sehet, wir gehn* is not certain, but it was probably written after the "Matthäus-Passion." It is one of the most remarkable of Bach's solo cantatas. The first movement is obviously a dialogue between Jesus and the soul. The bass solo utters the words, *Sehet, wir gehn hinauf gen Jerusalem,* and the contralto representing the soul answers in loving dissuasion, saying "*O harter Gang! Dein Kreuz ist dir schon zugericht't wo du dich sollst zu Tode bluten.*" The second movement is a duet aria, in which the soul continues its plaintive burden, and the soprano sings a chorale, *Ich will hier bei dir stehen.* This is followed by a recitative for tenor, and a beautiful aria for bass, *Es ist vollbracht,* with accompaniment of plaintive melodious phrases for oboe, the strings mainly supplying the harmonies. The style suggests that the cantata was written about the same time as the *Wachet auf.*

The solo cantata *Bisher habt ihr nichts gebeten,* which has some beautiful qualities, was probably a late revision of an early work.

Er rufet seine Schafe mit Namen opens rather exceptionally with a short recitative for tenor accompanied by three flutes in flowing chord-passages of semiquavers. The aria which follows it maintains the character so produced, as the flutes continue a placid motion in triplets almost throughout. The effect is charming and suggestive. A strong contrast is produced later in the work by the accompaniment of two trumpets in a bass solo, *Oeffnet euch, ihr beiden Ohren.*

Siehe, ich will viel Fischer aussenden is a charming solo cantata, in which some characteristic traits of realistic suggestion are manifested. The gentle accompaniment of the first part of the first solo was evidently the result of Bach's thinking at the moment of gentle waves; and when the words change to a reference to sending also "Jäger" the horns are introduced, with happy effect. The cantata is on an extensive scale with two parts.

In *Meine Seufzer,* the first tenor aria is accompanied by two flutes and oboe di caccia and bass in a manner often referred to (as in the Ascension Oratorio and the cantata *Mache dich, mein Geist, bereit*), which makes the movement an elaborate quintet with the voice. In another solo, for alto, *Der Gott, der mich hat versprochen,* the voice sings the chorale *Freu' dich sehr* to a flowing accompaniment of strings.

Meine Seele rühmt is a rather uninteresting Cantata for Tenor Solo, which shares with barely a score of all the Cantatas the peculiarity of having no Chorale at the end.

Liebster Jes., is a dialogue between Jesus and the soul on a very considerable scale. The actual dialogue is less closely intermingled than usual, as the utterances of the soprano and bass, except in one recitative, are separated in complete arias and recitatives till the last of the solo movements, which is a duet.

Süsser Trost is a short solo cantata for Christmastide, which is chiefly notable for the use of a favourite melodic phrase of Bach's which may be taken as one of his type formulas (see p. 429), of which it is one of the most beautiful:

Süs - ser Trost, — mein Je - sus, mein Jesus kommt

In *Ich bin ein guter Hirt* the idea of the shepherd is consistently emphasised throughout. The first aria, a beautiful movement, is for bass, and seems to imply that Bach put the words into the mouth of Christ. The second solo, for alto, answers "Jesus ist ein guter Hirt," the soprano solo sings the words "Der Herr ist mein getreuer Hirt" to the chorale tune of *Allein Gott in der Höh' sei Ehr'*, in the form of a chorale-fantasia; an accompanied recitative for tenor refers yet again to the Shepherd and the sheep, and the remaining solo discourses on the words "Seht, was die Liebe thut." The final four-part chorale has the words "Ist Gott mein Schütz und treuer Hirt" to the tune of *Ist Gott mein Schild und Helfersmann.*

Though the conditions are not so favourable in solo cantatas as in choral cantatas Bach contrived to give chorales a prominent position in many of them. But in some cases the conditions practically excluded them except at the end, and this was also the case in a few of the greater cantatas of his latest period. A certain number of these bear traces of the impulses generated in the early Leipzig period between its beginning and the time of the "Matthäus-Passion." The scheme on which they are planned, and even the attitude of mind in which they are dealt with, show their affinities; but the power of development is enhanced and in not a few cases there is an element of characteristic poetry and a subtlety of insight which recalls the Teutonic aspects of the chorale cantatas. An early example of this group is the great cantata written for a Rathswahl festival in 1731, *Wir danken dir, Gott.* This belongs to a special class in which Bach was invariably most successful—the expression of praise and exultation. Perhaps the most conspicuous feature is the sinfonia, on a very large scale and for a big orchestra, which makes it an interesting subject for contemplation;—as it is the expansion into orchestral terms of the first movement of the solo sonata for violin in E major, with the solo violin part adapted for the organ. A more comprehensive expansion could not well be imagined! The first chorus comes as a surprise, for it is in a very solemn and noble vein, being no other than the chorus *Gratias agimus* in the B minor Mass. In the rest of the cantata the jubilant note is persistent with the exception of the soprano solo, which supplies a soothing contrast. All the soloists are engaged in singing Hallelujahs, and even the final chorale expresses the same spirit.

Erfreut euch ihr Herzen is in a kindred vein. The first chorus is extremely brilliant and elaborate, in aria form, with a strikingly contrasted middle portion. The characteristic figure given to the word "Erfreut" recalls the singular figure at the end of the great motet "Singet dem Herrn," in connection with which it was commented on (p. 299). The cantata shows the Teutonic impulse in a dialogue between Fear and Hope, which recalls the great dialogue cantata *O Ewigkeit, du Donnerwort.*

Ich glaube lieber Herr belongs to the same period,

and has the usual elaborate chorus at the beginning. Its Teutonic stamp is shown in the manifest intention to convey the sense of the words, for there is undoubtedly a great sense of effort in the phrase allotted to the word "glaube." The cantata is notable for the exceptionally elaborate development of the final chorale, *Durch Adams Fall.* It must be admitted that when Bach added instrumental parts to the final chorale he frequently seems, for some reason, to have done it rather indifferently. In this case the instrumental accompaniments are worked out with the utmost care and full concentration of mind, and a complete and beautiful movement is the result.

To the same order of cantatas belong *Es ist dir gesagt*, and *Brich dem Hungrigen dein Brod*. The former has a chorus in a massive style to begin the first part, and a characteristic and fine bass solo to begin the second part. The latter has a fine initial chorus of even unusually splendid proportions. After the orchestral introduction (the scoring of which was evidently suggested to Bach's mind by the idea of breaking bread) the voices are at first treated in an elocutionary manner, the whole phrase being quite a study in complex realistic suggestion. A tremendous fugal episode ensues, and then a return to the opening passage, making a group in aria form; but after that comes a sort of coda of the most brilliant description—a fugue which entirely eclipses the first part of the movement in power, directness, and expression, as Bach probably meant it to do in consideration of the words "Alsdann wird dein Licht hervorbrechen wie die Morgenröthe." All the cantáta is of delightful quality, comprising a charming aria for alto, *Seinem Schöpfer*, a rather melancholy bass aria *Wohlzuthun*, and a bright aria for soprano *Höchster was ich habe*.

Wer da glaubet was written for Ascension Day and is of imposing proportions. The first chorus is in a very solid style, more like the old conception of choral music before Bach's time, but splendidly effective. The manner in which the voices are introduced at their first entry, mounting up successively from the bottom to the top, is extremely impressive. There is a grand sense of firmness and strength about the whole movement. The second movement emphasises the word "glauben" again; the third is a chorale movement for duet of soprano and alto, in which the voices sing the chorale in a kind of free canon with vigorous figures of accompaniment, the bass solo which follows again emphasises the word "glauben" and the final chorale yet again refers to it. So the whole work seems suffused with one idea, which is amply enforced by the music.

Es ist ein trotzig und verzagt Ding has an unusually concise chorus at the beginning, which gives the sense of tremendous concentration of energy. A peculiarity in the cantata is that the tune of the chorale is exceptionally and delightfully obscure in tonality, and Bach seems to have been impelled not only to harmonise it in a fashion which emphasises the obscurity, but to bring the solo music into line by introducing the flat seventh of the key into the first phrases of both the arias. It is likely that he intended to convey the sense of the words "trotzig und verzagt."

One of the very finest of the non-chorale cantatas written after 1730 is *Herr deine Augen sehen nach dem Glauben*. The words in this case are partly from Jeremiah and the Epistle to the Romans and partly written for the occasion, which, according to Spitta, was probably the tenth Sunday after Trinity, 1731, and therefore early in the period under consideration. The great feature of the work is the opening chorus set to the severe words from Jeremiah, v., 3: "Lord, do not Thine eyes look upon the truth? Thou hast stricken them, but they were not grieved; Thou hast consumed them, but they have refused correction, they have made their faces harder than a rock." Bach has the word "Glauben" for the "Truth" in the first sentence and it has coloured his musical interpretation of the words; which becomes therefore a figurative exordium on the actual meaning of the passage in Jeremiah. The scheme is peculiar. The orchestral introduction serves its usual purpose, and then the voices enter (after an ejaculatory "Herr" and a short preliminary anticipation of the tune) in quite a cheerful though chastened spirit, in full ornate harmony, with an amiable metric and Bachish tune, which is reiterated and developed for a time, as if the fact stated was a very pleasant one to contemplate. Then comes a close and the aspect of things changes; "Thou hast smitten them" becomes the subject of an animated fugue in which Bach presents one of the frankest of his specimens of realistic suggestion:

wherein the short staccato notes obviously represent the blows; and the realistic effect does not stop there, for the orchestra has also a series of fierce blows on every beat of the bar throughout the greater part of this portion of the chorus. But in time it gives way to yet another fugue dealing with the words "They have made their faces harder than the rock," which Bach evidently interprets figuratively, and then gradually interweaves the thoughts of the earlier part of the chorus with the thematic material of this section and so completes the circuit again with the words "Herr, deine Augen sehen nach dem Glauben."[1] The usual arrangement of recitatives and arias follows, but it is notable that the so-called arias are for the most part very Teutonic in intensity of feeling. The first, *Weh! der Seele,* is peculiarly rich in expressive detail, and, as has already been mentioned, contains some wonderful examples of Bach's unique use of melismatic devices for the purposes of expression. The bass solo is actually described as an "arioso" and is rather exceptional in that class, as Bach's ariosos are generally highly subjective; but this has a most engaging melodic formula:

Ver-acht-est du den Reich-thum Sei - ner Gna - de.

which is presented in all manner of positions; thereby anticipating developments of solo movements in free form as manifested by Schubert, Brahms, Wagner and even the most advanced representatives of modern song. This cantata is divided into two portions. The second begins with a tenor solo

[1] This chorus was transferred by Bach to the G minor Mass, in which it forms the "Kyrie."

which suggests that Bach's mind was especially susceptible to realistic suggestion at the time. The examples in the first chorus have been referred to. "Langmüthigkeit" is illustrated by a note holding on for four bars in the bass solo; and in this tenor solo Bach undoubtedly arrives at one of the most uncompromisingly uncomfortable passages which he ever gave a soloist to sing in order to give the impression of the word "Erschrecke:"

Fortunately it is prefaced by a very familiar and melodious passage for the accompanying instruments and contains features of strikingly graphic expression in other parts of the solo. The balance is set even by a beautiful passage of recitative for alto in the meditative vein which is so full of fascination in Bach's work, the accompaniment for two oboes being managed as in the parallel recitatives in the "Matthäus-Passion." The whole cantata is rounded off by the singing of *Vater unser*.

Of absolutely different sentiment is the beautiful cantata *Bleib' bei uns*, which was probably written a few years later—perhaps in 1736. It illustrates a renewed tendency in the direction of the communing with the great mysteries, which has also been indicated in connection with the chorale cantatas. The words of this cantata refer to the meeting of the two forlorn disciples with their risen Lord on their way to Emmaus, which was related in the Gospel of the day, and

Bach of course interprets the words of the disciples, "Abide with us, for it is towards even," in the figurative sense of the Christian of later days appealing to Jesus for His constant presence. It is in Bach's tenderest vein. The chorus begins with a tuneful phrase with four-part harmony which might almost have been written by Gluck but for the apt manner in which Bach prolongs it by giving to the various voices successive imitations, as if pleading with the Lord, "Denn es will Abend werden." The central part of the chorus is fugal—an andante in Bach's more subjective style—in which a most striking effect is obtained by the frequent reiteration by various voices of the insistent

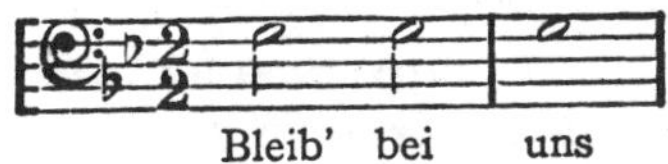

emerging from the fugal tangle of the other voices.

The chorus is rounded off by resuming the melodious and almost homophonic portion of the beginning, thus making a decisive form. The second movement, an aria for alto, carries on the figurative appeal,

> "Bleib', ach bleibe, unser Licht,
> Weil die Finsterniss einbricht,"

with a remarkably apt melismatic passage on the first syllable of the word "Finsterniss." In the centre of the cantata the soprano has a chorale, *Ach bleib' bei uns, Herr Jesu Christ*, with accompaniment of violoncello piccolo; a tender tenor solo, *Jesu lass uns auf dich sehen*, and the final chorale, *Beweis' dein' Macht*, to the tune of *Erhalt' uns Herr*, complete the cantata.

In several of these later non-chorale cantatas, meditative impulses seem to cause them to begin with sad reflections and forethoughts, which are gradually converted into happier moods. Among these is a comparatively early cantata of the period, *Es ist Nichts gesundes an meinem Leibe.* The first chorus has more affinity to those in the chorale cantatas; for it is a kind of chorale-fantasia in which the voices take the place usually allotted to the instruments and the wind instruments introduce the phrases of the chorale *Herzlich thut mich verlangen* at intervals. The chorale obviously stands as a kind of comment on the melancholy reflections, which the quality of the music associated with the words, and the figures given to the strings, so clearly express. The sentiment of the cantata, after a plaintive solo for bass, *Ach, wo hol' ich Armer, Rath,* becomes more cheerful, and it ends with the chorale *Freue dich sehr.*

Of the same kind, *Wir müssen durch viel Trübsal* is a very noble instance. It begins with the first movement of the finest of the clavier concertos, that in D minor, the clavier part being allotted to the organ—to which in truth it is not very well adapted. The interest is greatly enhanced in this case by the remarkably expressive chorus which Bach has contrived by adding independent voice parts to the slow movement of the same concerto. The third movement of the concerto is dispensed with, but the penultimate movement before the chorale, a duet for tenor and bass, *Wie will ich mich freuen,* is so lively that it might well have been taken from a similar source. It is to be noted that the cantata beginning with sadness and ending with joy, Bach sees fit to begin in D minor and end in F major.

A similar scheme is presented by the cantata *Ihr werdet weinen und heulen,* which belongs to the same period. The first chorus begins most expressively with rather a strange adjunct of "flauto piccolo solo." The interest of the movement is enhanced by a fine interruption in the shape of an adagio recitative, *Ihr aber werdet traurig sein,* which must be meant for a solo bass, though not so specified, and the chorus is resumed afterwards. In the sadder parts of the cantata there are some notable examples of the melismatic device, especially one on the first syllable of the word "schmerzen" in a tenor recitative. A strong contrast is presented in the latter part of the cantata by a brilliant tenor solo with trumpet obbligato, *Erholet euch, betrübte Stimmen.*

Of a different type belonging to this period is *Es wartet Alles auf dich,* which has a brilliant and vigorous chorus for the opening, with a splendid fugal middle portion. Bach's susceptibility to verbal impressions is illustrated by the manner in which the first syllable of the word "wartet" is always delayed. A similar feature may be noted in the chorus *Alle Augen warten, Herr, allmächt'ger Gott auf dich!* in the cantata *Du wahrer Gott.* An ornate soprano aria with oboe solo, *Gott versorget,* is an interesting and abstruse piece of expression. Materials in this cantata were used in compiling the Masses in G and G minor; as for instance the above mentioned solo, *Gott versorget,* which serves as the *Qui tollis* in the latter. Another fine cantata of the period, *Wer Dank opfert,* was also drawn upon for the G major Mass, the first chorus, which is of the normal type, being converted into the fugue in the final *cum sancto Spiritu.*

Among notable late cantatas which were not written to the words of hymns is *Unser Mund sei voll Lachens*, a work of pre-eminent brilliancy written for Christmas Day. The first chorus is one of Bach's most surprising transformations, as it is no less than the first movement of one of the D major orchestral overtures, with voice parts added. It is in the French overture form, and the slow portion of the movement is given to the orchestra alone, and serves as introduction and is repeated as the close. The voice parts are added to the central fugal portion—sometimes merely doubling the instrumental parts, sometimes presenting new voice parts. In this latter condition occur some of the most remarkable of Bach's realistic effects, as for instance in the tenor part:

Among the solo numbers is another borrowed movement, as the duet *Ehre, Ehre, sei Gott* is the *Virga Jesse floruit*, which was inserted in the Magnificat, according to Christmas usage, at the performance in 1723 (see p. 226). Most of the rest of the solos are of a very vivacious description, especially the bass aria, "Wach' auf." The cantata concludes with the chorale "Wir Christenleut."

A fine cantata in exceptional form is *O ewiges Feuer*, which was used by Bach at Whitsuntide, probably as late as 1740 or 1741. Its principal movements were taken from a wedding cantata of which only one incomplete set of parts remains. It contains but one solo movement of importance, the alto aria *Wohl euch, ihr auserwählten Seelen,* which, however, is a movement of remarkable beauty. The melody is characteristic of Bach in his tenderest vein, and is most happily enhanced by an accompaniment which is almost modern in the roundness and fulness of its tone. Its prominent position in the cantata helps to convey a special colour and unity to the whole. The first chorus is on a large scale and in aria form. The most characteristic feature is the quasi-realistic figure in which a long note is allotted to the first syllable of the word "ewiges," which suggests the meaning by its relation to the rapid polyphonic passages allotted to the other voices. The cantata has no chorale at the end, but there is a free and energetic chorus to the words *Friede über Israel* which begins with a couple of bars of massive harmony, *adagio,* that have quite a Handelian flavour. Both choruses present rather the aspect of supreme brilliancy of workmanship than of point.

Another cantata, the scheme of which differs slightly from the normal, is *Es ist euch gut, dass ich hingehe.* The words of Christ, allotted as usual to a bass, make in this case the starting-point of the sentiment of the two arias for tenor and alto, and of a noble fugal chorus, *Wenn aber jener, der Geist der Wahrheit, kommen wird,* which occupies the centre of the work.

One of the most important and imposing cantatas of the latest period is *Gott fähret auf mit Jauchzen.* The animation of the first chorus is almost barbarous in the vehemence with which it conveys the primitive idea expressed by the words—an idea at once musically picturesque and immense! God's going up seems to send all the elements whirling with tremendous convolutions, while from the midst of the turmoil the voices shout their elation in this headlong fashion.

Und der Herr mit heller Po-sau..........................
....
Etc.

The florid passage is so long that it cannot be given complete here; and it is a very quaint illustration of one side of Bach's character that he extends it in another place to such proportions that the Sopranos are expected to sing no less than twelve bars on a single syllable! Apart from such slight incidents, the chorus is carried out with certainty of control in the management of details, and especially in the laying out of the form, in such a way as to get stupendous effects of sustained climaxes in which passages on pedals play very imposing parts. The cantata is indeed full of fine movements. There is a tenor solo of a very animated description, to which a soprano solo, *Mein Jesus hat nunmehr das Heiland-Werk vollendet*, offers a quiet and tender contrast. The work is divided into two portions, and the second begins with a bass recitative of tremendously forcible character, *Es kommt der Helden Held*, and an aria which matches it in force, *Er ist's, der ganz allein*, and the alto soloist is also called into requisition for a flowing aria with accompaniment of two oboes. Both bass and alto arias have passages of deeply contrasted expression in their course, and the alto a notable emotional melismatic passage. The whole work is of that essentially strong character which suggests that Bach's faculties were at their brightest.

Yet another late cantata of imposing proportions is *Gott ist uns're Zuversicht*, a work written for some important wedding. The scheme is similar to that of the cantatas of the earlier Leipzig period, and two solo numbers, *O du angenehmes Paar* and *Vergnügen und Lust*, are borrowed, at least as far as material is concerned, from a Christmas cantata *Ehre sei Gott*. The first chorus is in aria form with fugal treatment in the first portion, and contrasting harmonic passages in the middle. There is a fine aria for alto, *Schläfert aller Sorgen, Kummer*, which has the first and last portions in $\frac{3}{4}$ time of flowing character, and a vivacious central portion in $\frac{4}{4}$ time. The cantata is divided into two parts with a different chorale at the end of each.

Among the very latest of the cantatas is *Also hat Gott die Welt geliebt*, for materials for which, as has been before said, Bach went back to the very first of his secular cantatas, *Was mir behagt*. The bass solo is only subjected to slight amendments, but the soprano solo, *Mein gläubiges Herze*, has a totally new melody given to the accompaniments of the original song, *Weil die wollenreichen Heerden*, and it has become in this form one of the most popular of Bach arias (see p. 331). To these movements Bach has added a chorus developed on the lines of a chorale-fantasia, and a vigorous final fugal chorus. The cantata has no chorale at the end.

Reference may fitly be made here to a solitary detached movement, the double chorus *Nun ist das Heil.* It presents the lineaments of a cantata chorus of the early Leipzig type, though there are none of that period which approach it in grandeur and scope. Nothing has ever been discovered about the purpose or occasion for which it was written, and it is useless to attempt to decide its date. All that can be said is that it stands there four-square, a massive achievement, almost unique in the thoroughness with which it represents Bach's personality in terms of exultant choral music. It has an affinity in style and sentiment to the great motet *Singet dem Herrn,* and must certainly have been written at a time when Bach's faculties were in their fullest vigour. The fugal subject illustrates very notably one of Bach's modes of enforcing the meaning of the words. For it is to be observed that each successive emphatic word is given a higher note as it occurs in the sentence:

Nun ist das Heil, und die Kraft, und das Reich, und die Macht

while the subordinate words remain at the same pitch, representing in musical terms an elocutionary *crescendo.* The emphatic crotchet motion is thrown into relief in the development of the movement by the animated rhythmic qualities of the countersubject and the polyphonic passages of accompaniment which surround the statement of the principal subject with a dazzling network of multitudinous melodies; choir answering choir, intermingling, contending, and all ministering to the overwhelming presentation of the spirit of the words.

In looking back over the wonderful array of these cantatas written in the last twenty years of Bach's life, the impression of supreme mastery is obtained. In some the standard of elevation induces a kind of aloofness from mundane emotions; but if there is not so much of romantic quality as in the earliest cantatas, the renewal of pure Teutonic devotionalism is shown in the manifold use of Chorales, and human tenderness, poetic symbolism, and devotional intensity are manifested in the highest degree.

CHAPTER XII

THE CLAVIERÜBUNG

THE number of important instrumental works which come into ken for the first time in the last few years of Bach's life suggests the inference that he pondered long and patiently over his works when opportunity served. The majority of his large choral works, such as the church cantatas, had to be completed for special occasions, so he was not in a position to lay them aside for further consideration and revision. But with the greater quantity of his instrumental works he was not tied to time, and when pressed by his official duties or hindered by an unready humour he could defer the final touches till a more propitious season. The position of his instrumental compositions is indeed altogether different from that of most of his choral works, for there was no claim on him to make them public property at all. When he took them in hand he did so because the spirit moved him, and when he offered them to his fellow men it implied that he regarded them as representing his highest standard of art, and his ideal of what such instrumental music ought to be. And indeed the instrumental works which are first heard of in these later years, such as the English Suites, the Partitas, the second series of twenty-four Preludes and Fugues, the Chromatische Fantasie, the Goldberg Variations, the "Ouverture à la manière française," and the Italian Concerto complete the long and splendid list of his clavier works in a manner which may well be called triumphant. For each in its way is among the finest examples in its respective line of art.

The fact that these works and several others less imposing but equally characteristic were revealed to the world so late in his life is no proof that they had not been written a long time before. Indirect evidence shows that many of the preludes and fugues of the second collection of twenty-four had been in existence in less complete forms long before he brought them into it. Of the Chromatische Fantasie and Fugue there is no kind of evidence to help to even an approximate date; but their intrinsic qualities, the warmth of imaginative speculativeness of the Fantasie, and the impetuous vitality of the Fugue point to an earlier phase in the composer's life. Chronological obscurities also present themselves in connection with the Partitas. The difficulty of identifying the periods to which so many great works belong is partly the result of the extraordinary fact that Bach never printed any instrumental compositions whatever until 1726, when he was forty-one years old. Indeed, but one of all his great choral works had been printed previous to this time; which was the fine cantata written in 1708 for the Rathswechsel at Mülhausen, when it was probably engraved in honour of the occasion. As far as his works were disseminated at all previous to this time they were so only by manuscript copies; and such copies do not fix the dates, because Bach rarely inscribed them on his works.

When at last he began printing in 1726, the dates at which the works were issued at least decided the latest dates which were possible for their composition; but, as will be seen in most cases, it left the limit very elastic in the other direction.

The publication consisted of a variety of works which were issued serially under the general inclusive name of "Clavierübung." It began with the first of the Partitas in the above mentioned year, and each year another Partita was added up to the year 1731, when, the six being issued, therewith the first series of "Clavierübung" was regarded as complete. Bach followed this up by publishing in 1735 the Italian Concerto and the Partita in B minor, which is also known as the "Ouverture à la manière française," as another instalment, and he brought out a collection of organ music as the third instalment about the year 1739; and the series was concluded with the fourth instalment, which consisted of the Goldberg Variations, published in 1742.

It is customary to regard the Partitas as the crown of Bach's works of the suite type and his last word in that line, and it is urged that they represent his ideal of German suites as distinguished from the suites of other nations. What was most probably in the mind of the inventor of this theory was that there were French suites and English suites and that therefore there ought to be German suites; and that as the title "Partien" had been first used by Johann Kuhnau, Bach's predecessor at St. Thomas's School, and so far only used at all in Germany, Bach's adoption of the title implied that he meant to identify them as German suites.

The name and the inclusive title of Clavierübung, which also had been used by Kuhnau, justify the inference that Bach was thinking of his predecessor's publication, but it does not justify the other inferences.

The intrinsic qualities of the Partitas seem to suggest that some of them at least were made up into sets in the final form in which they are now known, out of various movements, which, like so many others of Bach's works, had been laid aside for long periods of time. A feature which distinguishes the Partitas from the French and English Suites is the exceptional irregularity and diversity of the component movements. In the other suites he is most conspicuously loyal to the recognised scheme of movements, and, indeed, the consistency of his practice is mainly answerable for its being accepted as the most artistically satisfactory manner of grouping them. And as his certainty of infusing artistic interest into whatever he wrote, when his powers matured, precluded the uniformity of grouping being any drawback, there seems very little reason for his setting to work deliberately to write suites in speculative groups of movements so late in life. Indeed, it presents the appearance of stultifying his previous loyal adhesion to an admirable standard of grouping. But in these Partitas the lack of systematic uniformity is so aggressively in evidence that it is difficult to believe that they were deliberately written to present a new type of the art form. The fact that he introduces into them movements which had not before made their appearance in his clavier suites, such as a Scherzo, a Burlesca, a Rondo, a Caprice, and a Fantasia, is not the only thing which suggests that the Partitas do not represent his last word on the form, or his ideal of the German type of suite, for their intrinsic qualities suggest the same inferences.

One very prominent feature in Bach's constantly progressive career is that the scale and scope of development of individual movements expanded so enormously. This is illustrated by the huge dimensions of many of the first choruses of the later cantatas and by the first movements of most of his English suites. Moreover, as his years multiplied upon him, the tendency of his style was to become more and more serious and dignified. The case is parallel to Beethoven's last period. It is not that either of them grew incapable of gaiety, fun, merriment, humour, or even of tender sentiment. Their range was in no wise lessened, but whether a work was in a serious vein or in a light and merry one, the quality of the music conveys the feeling that it is the manifestation of a great temperament—the utterance of the strong and serious mind now at last provided with the full measure of artistic resources wherewith to express itself. The personality of the composer in the latest phase shines out more completely without any obscuring features unconsciously borrowed from other composers, or given as little concessions to the unintelligent.

But the Partitas are not developed on a grand scale: whatever average tendency is shown in them is in the direction of slightness and delicacy; the treatment is that of a great master dealing with small types of art, and fully aware of the kind of subject and the kind of work in detail which is most appropriate to small works. The very first Partita (in B flat) presents a number of features which are unfavourable to the idea of late production. The Prelude is on the scale of a miniature.

It is exquisitely finished in the minutest detail, tender, sensitive, and intimate; the veriest ideal of art which may be lived with at home every day. The Allemande follows it most happily. It is the most graceful and fluent of all Bach's numerous movements of the kind, but so slight as to have an almost evanescent delicacy, and in that quality showing very marked contrast to the weighty Allemandes in the English suites. The Courante is angular and uneasy, of an unusual type for Bach, and it has the air of an experiment, around which his mind was feeling and knocking without finding the way in. The Sarabande is great and weighty, and its severity is rather out of gear with the rest of the movements. The Minuets are so dainty and slender that they seem gone in a moment; and the Gigue points a very emphatic moral, for it is unlike any other gigue ever written by Bach. It is more akin in its humour to the brilliant Gigue in the French Suite in G, but it is much slighter. Its character is indeed Italian, and the device of crossing hands, which gives the whole movement its *cachet,* is closely akin to Domenico Scarlatti; but it is so very uncontrapuntal, so melodious, and so genially unpretentious, that it is even slender by the side of many of Scarlatti's Sonatas. So the theory of the Partitas being especially Teutonic does not seem to gain much encouragement from the qualities of the first.

The second, in C minor, is weightier. The first movement is an extensive Sinfonia with massive opening section, a melodious and ornate andante, and a fugal movement, probably meant as a transfer of the Italian "Sinfonia avanti l'opera" to the clavier.

The usual Allemande, Courante, and Sarabande follow, but the group ends with the unusual feature of a Rondeau and a Caprice; both of which latter movements are delightfully animated, rhythmic, and playful, but too similar to one another to come quite satisfactorily together, and not ostensibly adapted to their position in relation to the previous movements. The third Partita (in A minor) is one of those which had appeared a few years before in Anna Magdalena's second book. It is full of charm, but is, with the exception of the Allemande, rather slight and delicate. The two movements which are added to the original scheme, a Burlesca and a Scherzo, are both of a type extraneous to the usual suite scheme. The fourth Partita (in D) supplies further strong evidence against the sets being considered especially Teutonic, as the first movement is called an Overture, and it is actually in the form of the French opera overture, for which Bach had such fondness. This Partita must be admitted to be on a grand scale, with the exception of the dainty Aria and Minuet, and has a more homogeneous appearance than most of the sets. The fifth has the appearance of being a collection of movements written at various times. The first movement is called a "Préambule," which is not suggestive of Teutonic intention. It is quite unlike any other preludes to suites, being singularly sprightly and fanciful. The Allemande is strongly contrasted with it, as it is on a grand scale and very elaborate. The Courante, again, is quite unlike most of Bach's other courantes, being in the Italian form, in $\frac{3}{8}$ time, and very swift and fluent. Similarly the Sarabande is much slighter and less full of emotion than usual. The Minuet is an ingenious study in sparkling rhythms, and is evidently an experiment with the same artistic cue as the Gigue in the Partita in B flat, with the enhancement of captivating cross accents. The delightful Passepied is dainty and slender, but the Gigue is strong and highly organised in Bach's latest manner.

The sixth and last Partita (in E minor) is one of the two which appeared first in Anna Magdalena's book. The movements are nearly all weighty and elaborate. The fine movement with which it opens consists of an introduction and fugue, and is here called Toccata, whereas in Anna Magdalena's book it had been called a Prelude. The Allemande, Sarabande, and Gigue, are of splendid quality, the Courante slender, in $\frac{3}{8}$ time, with singular alternations of angularity and fluency. The Aria, the added movement, is rather slight. Bach evidently put it in to ease the work of its excess of severity, and possibly to counterbalance the effect produced by the transformation of the Gigue from the simpler form in which it appeared in Anna Magdalena's book, to the rather abstruse form here adopted—which is food for highly developed wits rather than for ordinary humdrum minds.

The general impression conveyed is that the sets were furbished very delightfully, with movements conceived at different times, and that their contents, so far from being demonstratively Teutonic, are, wherever racial leanings are apparent, either French or Italian. It is impossible to avoid comparing them with the so-called English Suites, which were not published in the composer's lifetime. If they had been they might not have attracted the favour which was awarded to the Partitas, as they are far more weighty, on a much grander scale, and at once more homogeneous and presenting more tokens of having been deliberately written as suites. They represent the difference between groups of movements which are necessarily coherent—products of the same mental impulse—and groups of movements which are merely juxtaposed. Why they were called "English" is not known. It is unlikely that Bach knew, any better than his famous biographer did, that nearly all the earlier part of the development of the form, from the tentative experiments of the time of Elizabeth and James I. up to the time of Purcell, had been the work of English composers. Long before any foreign nations had begun to think of music for the domestic keyed instrument, there was a colossal accumulation of English music of the very highest quality, in which the Suite form gradually took shape; and the evolution of the form went so far, before English composers were drawn from their mission by a wave of unracial levity, that even the final scheme, afterwards confirmed by Bach, presents itself in a large number of cases. Moreover Purcell's suites[1] are more nearly akin to those of J. S. Bach in strength and vitality of thought than those of any other composer, Kuhnau not excepted. It is just possible that Bach had come across them. As has been frequently said, he was always eager to make acquaintance with artistic works of any foreign nations which could produce them, and it does happen that (in view of the quality and scheme of Purcell's Suites) there would be ample justification for calling them English suites. But the invincible distaste which Germans have for genuinely English music has pre-

[1] See *Oxford History of Music*, vol. iii., p. 365, Purcell.

vented anyone from taking any note of the possibility of Bach's mind being more cosmopolitan than their own; hence the alternative proposal, obviously purely gratuitous, that the suites were written for an English nobleman. But there is one odd little bit of evidence which may be worth mentioning. The ultimate source of the title is clearly the fact that a manuscript copy of the suites, which was in possession of Bach's youngest son, John Christian, is said to have had the words "fait pour les Anglais" written on the first page of the first suite in A major. And the strange fact is that the little Prelude of that suite is an expansion of a Gigue in a suite by Dieupart, who was a popular teacher and composer in England and a little senior to J. S. Bach; and it is almost certain that Bach made acquaintance with the movement of which he made such use in an edition printed in England.

It is very improbable that the note referred either to an English gentleman (since the reference is in the plural) or to the English public. It is far more probable that the words "fait pour les Anglais" were written over the said first movement solely with reference to the movement of Dieupart's of which Bach had here made use; and that people who were not aware of the connection of Bach's Prelude with Dieupart's movement, which was written for the English, construed the remark erroneously as referring to the whole series of Suites; no doubt excusing their translation of the word "fait" from singular to plural on the ground that Bach's French was generally very slipshod.

The mysterious title seems to have hindered the acceptance of the view that the English suites are really Bach's last word in that form and the essential demonstration of the Teutonic ideal; but, if their intrinsic qualities are looked to, there can hardly be any question about the matter. They come into view only in the latter part of Bach's life, and they might have been written any time between the latter end of the Cöthen period and a long way on in the Leipzig period. They certainly represent his highest pitch of mastery. The immense scope of all the preludes (except the first in A major, founded on Dieupart's gigue) and the wide range of resource which they display, the weight, variety, and unvarying high level of material of the allemandes and courantes, the supreme dignity, pathos, and warmth of colour and expression of the sarabandes, the sparkling vivacity of the bourrées and the gavottes, and the superb texture of the gigues combine to make this series of suites stand entirely alone as representing the very highest examples of the type in existence. The two last French suites have a special charm and lightness, and admirable consistency of style; but the whole series does not give the impression of uniform high quality, certainty of resource, and nobility of expression which is given by the so-called "English Suites."

The actual title of the second instalment of the Clavierübung, which came out in 1735, throws much light on the works contained in it. It runs as follows: "*Zweyter Theil der Clavier Ubung, bestehend in einem Concerto nach Italiænischen Gusto, und einer Overture nach Französischer Art, vor ein Clavicymbel mit zweyen Manualen,*" *etc.* The works are commonly known as the "Italian Concerto," and the Partita in B minor or "Ouverture à la manière française." But the terms of the title referring to form and style and the information which it supplies as to both works having been written for a harpsichord with two rows of keys are of much service in helping to the full understanding of Bach's purpose. The Concerto is the only work of the kind which Bach wrote for the clavier alone, and is obviously an experiment, like many another, in transference of an orchestral form to a solo instrument. Some account has already been given of the characteristics of the early type of concerto in connection with the Brandenburg Concertos (see p. 120); and it was pointed out that the salient feature of such works was the alternation of passages for solo instruments and passages for the mass of the *tutti*. It is likely that the foremost incitement to the experiment may have been the earlier arrangements of the Vivaldi concertos for clavier; but it is also likely that one of the incitements was the opportunity which a harpsichord with two keyboards afforded to represent the alternation of *soli* and *tutti*. Bach indicates this intention by the use of the words "forte" and "piano," which are proved to refer to the respective keyboards, because one hand is sometimes marked "forte" when the other is marked "piano," and that would be impracticable on the harpsichord except by the use of different keyboards.

Bach is, as usual, very unsystematic in his use of the words: he leaves them out when they would be obvious, as at the beginning of the first movement, which clearly represents a *tutti* passage, but he puts them in sufficiently often to show what he means; and in the quick movements it is obvious that "forte" generally indicates a keyboard which represents *tutti* and "piano" a keyboard which represents *soli*. At the same time he by no means restricts himself to such mechanical consistency, but frequently puts "forte" to a melodic passage which he wishes to stand out strongly; as for instance, in the melodious passage for the right hand which follows the *tutti* passage at the beginning of the first movement in the thirtieth bar. Such strengthening of the melody is particularly notable in the beautiful slow movement; in which the right hand is marked "forte" and the left hand "piano." In this case the directions clearly refer to the difference of the tone quality of the two keyboards, as the character of the movement would not justify the extreme of difference in amount of tone which would be suggested by the usual meaning of the words. This movement is one of those outpourings of free rhapsodical melody which Bach alone could carry out on such a grand scale and yet give the impression of perfect artistic organisation. The type is the rhapsodical melody for violin which was occasionally attempted by Italian violin composers. The immediate forerunner may indeed have been a beautiful slow movement in a concerto in D by Vivaldi which stands third in those arranged by Bach. Bach's enhancement of Vivaldi's scheme lies not only in the much more spacious and emotional melody, but also in the treatment of the accompaniment. Vivaldi's accompaniment is nothing more than the repeated-note formula, which is one of the most elementary and lifeless forms of figuration. Bach makes the whole accompaniment consistent and full of vitality by basing it upon a short figure, which continues to be reiterated with constant variation throughout the whole movement, and supplies a principle of unity which allows the quasi violin solo in the right hand to soar into a greater freedom of range.

The type is a favourite with Bach, and presents itself in the ariosos and accompanied recitatives in choral works as well as in the preludes for clavier. In this case the consistency of the tender phrase is singularly apt to the expression of the melody, and the movement is one of Bach's most remarkable and personal outpourings, suggesting a strange sense of mystery—of groping after some indefinite object of desire, of longing and questioning, of the sadness which dimly tinges the vague sense of inevitable abnegation.

Such a movement seems rather strangely mated with the quick movements which stand on either side of it. They indeed are most vivacious, merry, bustling, even manifesting a sense of fun here and there. It is hardly possible Bach thought of them as in any way spiritually connected with the slow movement. The likeliest interpretation seems to be that in these he was thinking of the imitation of the movements in an orchestral concerto, with their contrasts of *tutti* and *soli*, and in carrying them out he was content to be gay, and indeed is so most successfully; but that in the slow movement he was carried away by the aptness of the form to his musical disposition and the expression of his deepest feelings

The Partita which kept the Italian Concerto company in this number of the Clavierübung is a parallel experiment in another line. In so far as it is defined as a Partita, it supplies a further argument to those adduced above, in connection with the six Partitas, that there was no intention to make these works representatively Teutonic, since this work is manifestly a transfer to the keyed instrument of the French overture which Bach had illustrated in his orchestral overtures. The first movement is on a very large scale and has a much longer fugue-subject than was usual in the French overtures of the Lulli type. Here, again, the two keyboards of the harpsichord come in serviceably to represent the *soli* and *tutti* of the orchestra. As the usual slow movement at the beginning obviously represents the full opening by the orchestra, Bach gives no indication, since it would all be obviously "forte," but in the Fugue the two keyboards are frequently indicated. There is no Allemande, but the second movement is a Courante of the French type; and nearly all the rest of the movements are in a lighter vein, delightfully frank, engaging,. and direct. Two lovely Gavottes—the second of which sounds as if it might have been written for the lute,—two charming and concise Passepieds, a dignified and noble Sarabande, two lively Bourrées, an unprententious Gigue, and a dainty Echo complete the series. The indications for the two keyboards only appear in the second Gavotte and the second Bourrée, which are marked "piano," and in the Echo. In the latter the influence of the two keyboards in determining the character is evident, for there can hardly be a doubt that Bach wrote the movement and put it in its conspicuous position on purpose to show off the echo effects producible by them. The alternations of "forte" and "piano" are indeed very close, representing the frequent answers of the echoes. But one of the most quaint and charming fancies in the presentment of the device is that the echo is often more ornate than the initiative passages, and sometimes even at a different pitch. It may be recalled that echo movements were very popular before Bach's time in many branches of art—Lasso having written some very ingenious examples for voices in many parts, and Sweelinck and others having written them for the organ,—but it is improbable that any composers thought of anything so subtly artistic as making the echo a variation of the passage it answered.

The third instalment of the Clavierübung consisted of compositions for the organ, and was engraved by 1739. Bach seems to have had a definite scheme in his mind in making the collection, for it begins with a Prelude in E flat of very spacious dimensions, such as would be apt to serve as the exordium to some important pronouncements; and the series ends with the Fugue (also in E flat), which is probably the most widely appreciated of all Bach's organ fugues, and is known in England as the "St. Anne fugue," from the similarity of the subject to a well-known hymn tune of that name. Between these two great works lies a series of twenty-one movements founded upon or associated with chorales (The four Duetti can be left out of consideration.) One can hardly suppose that Bach (in spite of the indifference which his indiscriminate use of the words *da capo* shows with regard to the lapse of time) intended the whole series to be played at a sitting. Moreover, if he had so intended he would not have ended the penultimate number, the Fugue on "Jesus Christus unser Heiland," on the chord of F. But still it is eminently characteristic of him to have given a general sense of unity to the whole series by the suggestion of a connection between the first movement and the last; which, indeed, has confirmed itself in the course of time to the extent of inducing men to believe that the first movement is meant as a Prelude to the last though separated from it by twenty-one movements and the irrelevant Duets. The Prelude is indeed massive and dignified, but unusually harmonic and melodious in style, and the details of the texture are by no means so characteristic as is usual in Bach's organ works. It was certainly written under Italian influences, and contains many traces of the Italian concerto type in passages which suggest alternations of *tutti* and *soli*. The Fugue is certainly one of the most perfect and finished of Bach's works of the kind. It has the peculiarity of being in three definite portions—all centralising on the same subject, though presenting different treatment of it, and at the same time manifesting a gradual growth of complexity and vivacity up to the majestic and imposing close.

It is an interesting fact that there is a Fugue in E minor written before Bach's time on similar lines, which is in three divisions and presents many of the same traits—even of texture. It has been commonly attributed to Frescobaldi, but does not appear in any of the collections published in his lifetime, and its style makes it almost inconceivable that it could have been written by him. It may possibly be by Muffat. Whether Bach was indebted to this work for the suggestion, or whether it was merely a coincidence, the fact is so remarkable that it could not pass unnoticed. Bach himself experimented in this threefold kind of fugue several times; one of his very finest fugues for the clavier, that in A minor beginning as follows

with a Fantasia preceding it, is in three distinct portions, but with different employment of the subjects and accessories. In that case the middle portion introduces a totally new and highly contrasted subject, which is worked out fully in that section; and in the third section the principal subject of all resumes its majestic prerogatives, and the subject of the second portion is interwoven with it. The scheme is at once simple, conclusive, and essentially musical, and, it is to be noted, very well adapted to the qualities of the clavier.

The methods of the E flat Fugue are especially adapted for the organ, beginning with the solemn dignity of the slow-moving style, without ornament, which is associated with all the deep sentiment of the old religious choral music. The fulness of tone produced by the five-part counterpoint is most appropriate to the opening section. After it follows the second portion, which is much more animated. It is practically a new three-part Fugue woven round the original subject, after the same manner as parts were woven round the chorale in the Choralvorspiel. The good, simple, and obvious device of refraining from the use of the pedals throughout this portion makes the volume of tone when the pedals reappear in the last portion extraordinarily impressive. The last portion is, moreover, another fugue on yet a further subject in $\frac{12}{8}$ time, the character of which lends itself to the increase of complexity of texture which is needed to maintain the sense of cumulative interest up to the end; and the subject of the first portion is duly reintroduced in combination with it, slowly rolling out its solemn and imperturbable phrase amid all the vivacious interchange of figure and rhythm which is being carried on by the other parts.

The Chorale movements that intervene between the Prelude and Fugue represent various types of treatment of such tunes and Canti fermi. The earlier numbers are in the severe if simple vocal counterpoint of the order of the Choralvorspiel. The two movements on "Aus tiefer Noth" are the only ones which represent completely what has been called the Pachelbel type, in which the respective phrases of the chorale are anticipated by the secondary voices in imitation before the chorale makes its entry in long notes. The first, in six parts, is, like the earliest numbers, in the severe contrapuntal style, and presents the rare feature of having the pedals written in two parts, the upper one of which has the chorale melody. In several of the movements the chorale is treated after the manner of the chorale-fantasia above described (p. 182), which is so often met with in the first chorus of the chorale cantatas, in which the whole movement is woven of interesting independent figures, with the chorale in long notes slowly taking its solemn way among them; as in "*Christ unser Herr zum Jordan kam,*" No. 1, "*Vater unser,*" No. 1, and "*Allein Gott in der Höh',*" Nos. 1 and 2, and "*Dies sind die heil'gen zehn Gebot'.*" In the last Bach indulges in a canon, as in the first "*Vater unser*"; the chorale being given in two inner parts generally answering one another at a couple of bars apart. Yet again the chorale answers itself in different parts by inversion, as in the second movement on "*Christ unser Herr.*" In some the chorale tunes are subjected to very elaborate variation in detail, which to one unfamiliar with them would make them almost unrecognisable; and they are sometimes used in such forms as subjects for fugues, or free fugal movements with characteristic independent pedal parts. Of this kind is one of the best known in the collection—the Choralvorspiel fugue in D minor on "*Wir glauben all' an einem Gott,*" in which the subject of the fugue follows the outline of the chorale melody, and the pedals answer in a delightfully frank passage striding up through an octave and down again, in sequences which have gained the movement the popular title of the "Giant's Fugue."

The most highly ornamental example is that on the well-known tune *Vater unser;* and as that is one of the most salient instances of the type, the subject founded on the chorale tune with which the movement begins may be taken as an illustration.

The actual chorale in this case is given by the treble and

tenor parts in canon, in unadorned simplicity, and the movement being in five parts presents the appearance of wonderfully intricate and interesting texture. The second movement on *Vater unser* is perhaps offered as a compensation for having disguised the tune so effectually in the first movement on the same tune, as it merely presents the simple melody in the treble with the other parts flowing smoothly below it. So it is what would be technically defined as an Orgelchoral. The inventiveness of interesting principles of treatment is mated with such incredible facility that the ingenuities never betray themselves unduly, but only minister to the purely musical and even expressive effect. They show how deeply the love of the chorales was engrained in Bach's disposition and how he delighted in giving to them the tribute of his supreme mastery in every kind of artistic adornment. And even beyond all this supreme exercise of his skill there was a further devotional purpose as there was in the "Orgel-Büchlein," for, as is indicated on the title-page, the chorales are all united by the fact that they belonged to the series which was recognised in the Lutheran Church as Catechismal hymns. Spitta even goes so far as to suggest that Bach's intention, in giving three versions of the chorale "*Allein Gott in der Höh' sei Ehr*'," was to symbolise the Trinity. It is not at all improbable, for undoubtedly it is difficult to exhaust the range and subtlety of intention which Bach manifests in every aspect of his creative work.

The fourth and final instalment of the Clavierübung consisted solely of the work known as the "Goldberg Variations," so called from Johann Theophilus Goldberg, a pupil of Bach's, who is said to have been a remarkably fine clavier player, and for whom they were written. Bach must have had a very high opinion of his abilities, as the "Variations" comprise a variety of difficulties for the performer both in the matter of execution and of interpretation such as are not to be found in any other of his works; and it is in every way one of the most extraordinary and interesting works he ever produced. It has been hindered from being generally known through being written for a harpsichord with two keyboards; since the devices of technique invented by Bach to utilise the two keyboards, in the way of hand-crossing and of passages passing one another, appeared for a long time to be almost impossible on the single row of keys of the pianoforte. But in recent days men with great grasp of technical devices have contrived ways of overcoming the difficulties, and the work is performed as often as its extreme length allows.

Since the very earliest days of clavier music the composition of Variations in one form or another has had a great fascination for composers. Indeed, they were cultivated more profusely in the early days than later, because of the lack of knowledge of principles on which long movements could be devised. For when composers of instrumental music wanted to keep their audiences engaged for more than a few minutes at a time, they were driven, through lack of knowledge of principles of development, to the expedient of playing popular tunes or dances over and over again; and the most hopeful way of making the process interesting was to introduce a variety of embellishments. Out of this grew up quite a special type of art, and the embellishment and variations of melodic phrases and the introduction of scales and passages were found to be useful in other spheres besides mere concise tunes. Thus it was transferred to the quaint form known as the "Ut-Re-Mi-Fa," which was popular from the time of John Bull till that of Froberger, and consisted of the reiteration of the first six notes of the scale up and down, with runs and arpeggios and all sorts of different fanciful devices added each time. To the same category belong the forms of the "ground bass" or "ground divisions," and its near relative, the Chaconne, which figures so frequently in Lulli's operas as the final number of a set of ballet tunes, and of which Bach left such a notable example as the Chaconne in the suite in D minor for violin solo. And closely akin to this was the Passacaglia, of which he also left such a magnificent example in C minor for the organ.

The profuse cultivation of such forms of Variations through several generations of distinguished composers caused this special branch to make considerable progress. The first effect of experience generated by practice was to make composers see the advantage of giving individuality to each variation by making one type of ornament or musical figure prevail through the whole of it, and from that the step was not far to making use of the character so obtained for purposes of contrast and affinity. The fascination of variation-making was thenceforward put on a high plane, as the respective individual variations could be made to express any condition of mood which was at the composer's disposal, such as gaiety, grace, tenderness, force, melancholy, fierceness, caprice, jollity, and so on, and the varying moods could be grouped in such a way as to make a composite whole of considerable interest.

A rather more than usual amount of groundwork had therefore been done before Bach came on the scene, and there was good foundation to build upon.

The Goldberg Variations are among the few instrumental compositions of John Sebastian's to which it is possible to allot a date with certainty. According to fairly trustworthy chroniclers, Goldberg's interests were taken in hand by a certain Baron Kaiserling, through whose instrumentality he became for a time the pupil, first of Friedemann Bach, and finally, in 1741, of John Sebastian himself. Then the Baron, who suffered from insomnia, asked Bach to write something for Goldberg to play to him when lying waiting in vain for sleep, and Bach thereupon composed this immensely long series of variations, which is said to have answered so well that, according to Forkel, the Baron gave the composer a snuff-box with a hundred louis d'or therein. History does not record what was paid to Goldberg for undertaking to play such difficult music late at night, but after generations will certainly think him more or less repaid by having such a work associated with his name; and it is through that circumstance that it is possible to identify the period when the variations were written. For, as Goldberg became Bach's pupil in 1741, and the variations were engraved by 1742, there can be little doubt about the period of their composition. The work may therefore be taken to represent the utmost development of Bach's powers in this particular branch of clavier music.

It certainly takes rank with the few greatest examples of this form of art in existence, its possible rivals being Beethoven's Diabelli variations, the variations in the "Modo Lidico," Brahms's variations on Handel and

Haydn's themes, and Bach's own Chaconne for violin. Bach anticipated modern developments, for the step is not far from the variation which, through a prevailing type of figure, can be identified with a characteristic mood, to the standard in which each variation is an organised little work of art, an embodiment of some æsthetic, modal, or artistic idea, only missing completeness sufficiently to take its place in a long series of movements whose mutual dependence is subtly disguised. So great by this time had Bach's mastery of the various resources of art become, that no two variations in the whole series of thirty resemble each other. Each variation unfolds some new and delightful aspect of musical expression, some new effect of sound, some new fascinating device of the higher artistic type. The variety of style seems inexhaustible, and yet each organic unit presents some necessary dependence on its neighbours and serves some artistic function in the whole scheme.

The technical vivacity is so great that Bach actually anticipated some of the favourite devices of the school of pianoforte virtuosos, of whom Liszt was the foremost type. And as if it were not enough to command all these resources, he subtly throws in a little item of playful dexterity in the shape of a series of canons at different intervals, beginning with canon at the unison in the third variation, and proceeding to canon at the second in the sixth, canon at the third in the ninth, and so on, giving a new canon a step wider at each third variation until the twenty-seventh, which has a canon at the ninth; and the technical device is executed with such perfect ease that the absolute fidelity with which it is carried out could hardly be divined till each example is closely examined, and the music is so purely and spontaneously delightful that there is hardly a moment anywhere when the smallest constraint is perceptible.

But even then Bach's resourcefulness is not exhausted, for he gives to several of the variations well-known art forms. The tenth variation is a concise and charming Fughetta, the sixteenth variation is expanded into a complete French Overture, including the slow introduction and the lively fugal movement, and the last of the variations is a "Quodlibet,"—in other words, a combination of folk-tunes built upon the original basis of the theme. Such absolute command does indeed tend to produce amazement. There is nothing like it in the whole range of Music.

Bach had set out on his journey with the overmastering instinct to express his personality in the terms of art, and, with an attendant instinct for what was lofty and pure which has never been excelled by any composer whatever, he toiled on without any relaxation of effort from the days of his youth till the time of his departure seemed almost in sight, developing his artistic powers by his unique methods of studying with the utmost closeness the artistic work of all composers who excelled in anything, and emulating each in his special province till the whole of what was of worth in the musical art of the world was assimilated into the copious but consistently characteristic range of his personality. If the Goldberg set of variations be not absolutely his most astonishing feat, it is one of the works in which he opens the door of his storehouse most frankly, that they who have understanding may see the fruitfulness of the loyalty of his lifetime.

CHAPTER XIII

THE SECOND SERIES OF TWENTY-FOUR PRELUDES AND FUGUES

It must have been about the time that Bach was busy completing the "Clavierübung" that he finally put in order and completed the second collection of twenty-four Preludes and Fugues which are generally looked upon as the second half of the "Wohltemperirtes Clavier," and thereby gave the excuse for the title of "The Forty-eight," by which the two series have commonly been known in England. But long since the days when they fortunately established their hold on the affection of English musicians and came to need an English title, careful consideration of the story makes it more than doubtful whether he intended the second series to be a continuation of the first. That he meant it to be a parallel collection cannot be doubted, in view of the number of the movements and their grouping. Unfortunately there is an absolute dearth of any evidence with regard to it. The first had a copious title-page with the date of its completion in Bach's own handwriting. Of the latter collection there is not even a complete manuscript, and only indecisive circumstantial evidence that it was completed either by 1740 or 1744. It is quite clear that it was brought together in much the same fashion as the first; for, as is the case with that, several of the individual movements exist in less complete forms, and some also in different keys. What especially distinguishes the second from the first collection is the quality, form, and proportions of the preludes. Their character strongly suggests that many of them were written independently, for their extent is often so great as to overbalance the fugues, and their style is not always consistent with them. Moreover, the peculiarities of design are so decisive in their significance as to make it almost certain that many of them were written as experiments in schemes of form which the composer had never once touched in the first collection.

How greatly they differ from the preludes of the earlier series may be judged from the fact that while in the first the considerable majority are in the old prelude-form described above (p. 150), which consists of a series of harmonies presented in terms of musical figures, in the second collection there is only one in this form, and the form in that case is subject to conspicuous modifications. And moreover while in the first series there is not a single Prelude which is divided into two distinct portions by a double bar, after the manner of movements in suites and sonatas, there are no less than ten Preludes in the second series which are so divided, with the usual indications for repeating the two halves; and many other Preludes are constructed upon principles which presuppose the scheme of design which induced this usage. In order to verify the fact that Bach was making experiments in distributing the components of movements of the type found in suites and early sonatas in various different ways, it is indispensable to have a just idea of the manner in which the evolution of the form of the typical first movement in classical sonatas came about; and it is necessary to disabuse the mind of the theory that the scheme of the typical first movement of the classical sonata was an evolution from the aria-form, as otherwise Bach's speculations in these remarkable Preludes become unintelligible.

When composers began to expand the concise types of dance movements into ampler proportions and to enhance their interest by artistic subtleties and delicacies of presentment, they soon found the advantage of producing the effect of coherence by making the musical material of the first few bars of the second half of the movement correspond with the musical material of the bars which occupied parallel positions in the first half, and the materials of the close of each half to correspond in a similar manner. The process is of the simplest type of orderliness — such as a methodical man might adopt in laying out a garden plot. And as the first half of the movement ended in the key of contrast, the second half, starting from that point, presented the initial phrases of the movement also in the key of contrast; and the final bars of the movement furnished a corresponding reversal by presenting the features of the close of the first half of the movement in the principal key. Taking capital letters to represent the musical materials, and numerals the keys, the order would be simply A 1, B 2, A 2, B 1, and this simple design Bach adopted from earlier composers in the large majority of his suite movements. The story of the evolution of the form of the first movement of classical sonatas from this point was, that as subjects and presentations of keys became by degrees more and more definite, the first subject took upon itself such pre-eminent significance that the mere reference to it at the beginning of the second half of the movement did not satisfy the instinct of proportion. So, when return was made to the principal key at the end of the movement, its effect was enhanced by introducing the first subject at the point where the principal key was resumed and repeating the second subject after it; and it will be seen presently that Bach in his speculative experiments anticipated this procedure. The result was that the first subject then made its appearance three times, and this was felt to be superfluous; so the reference to the principal subject at the beginning of the second half of the movement was dropped, and the period of rambling through various keys, which is called the "working out" or "free fantasia," began at once after the double bar.

The movements which definitely accord with the early type of suite movements are the Preludes in C minor, No. 2; D sharp minor, No. 8; E minor, No. 10; and G major, No. 15, and—with certain amplifications—that in E major, No. 9. The C minor is an interesting presentation of the suite type of movement in terms of the prelude type, often referred to, in which a simple little figure persists almost throughout. It is therefore one of the numerous examples of Bach's experiments in combined forms. In the Prelude in D sharp minor, a characteristic portion from the middle of the first part (bars 6 to 10) is repeated *in extenso* in the second half, and by a curious combination of circumstances, which seems almost chance, the first passage of the movement actually makes its reappearance at exactly the very place where the first subject would recur in a classical sonata movement, and has the passage with which the first half ended grafted on to it to conclude the movement. In the E minor Prelude, the figures of the opening suffuse all the earlier part of the second half of the movement without being stated in very definite terms, but a long passage of the latter part of the movement—no less indeed than twenty-eight bars—is a repetition, transposed and inverted with variations of detail and slight expansions, of the passage from the twenty-fourth bar to the end of the first half. The Prelude in E major—one of the most perfect—is an example of the suite type, with the enhancement of a most captivating Coda. The charmingly slight and gay Prelude in G major is exactly on the lines of a suite movement, and resembles some of the allemandes in its continuity and even in its style.

A step farther on come the Preludes in D, No. 5; F minor, No. 12; and G sharp minor, No. 18. These approximate more nearly to the sonata type, as the subjects stand out more decisively from the context. That in D major is to all appearances a counterpart or rearrangement of a movement from a concerto for orchestra. The well-marked first subject makes its appearance at the beginning of the second half of the movement (with melody inverted), and not only so, but after the period of wandering there is the characteristic halt which is so familiar in classical sonatas; the first subject is as deliberately presented as it would be by Mozart, and the process of turning subdominantwards is adopted, just as in classical sonatas, which enables the material of the end of the first half (beginning with the seventh bar from the end) to be presented in the principal key. So that with the exception of the dexterous modulation in the third and fourth bars, the last sixteen bars are a recapitulation (with incidental variations) of the same portion of the first half of the movement up to the double bar. The scheme is, therefore, exactly that of the first movement of a classical sonata.

The Prelude in F minor is even more remarkable, because the subjects are so strongly characterised and separated from the context. And also, be it remarked in parenthesis, that it is very Italian in style; which is the more noteworthy because, as a rule, Bach's experiments in Italian style are intrinsically inferior to his other works, and this example is decidedly not so. The two contrasting keys, F minor and A flat, are very strongly and clearly differentiated; and the movement is an example of the intermediate stage of evolution above characterised (p. 483) in which the principal subject makes its appearance at the beginning of the second half of the movement as well as the place where it would be expected in a classical sonata. But thereby comes a charming manifestation of Bach's readiness. Inasmuch as the movement is very short, every feature requires the most compact statement. Bach evidently felt that the full repetition of the first subject in the latter part of the movement would have had a purely formal effect. It is perfectly easy to verify the fact by inserting the first eight bars at the point where the key of F minor is resumed and dovetailing it on to the fourteenth bar from the end. Ordinary composers of classical sonatas would have done it in that fashion, but not Bach. The reference to the principal subject on the return of the principal key is reduced to a mere hint, like the mere word and nod of a man to an intelligent friend, and it is enough.

The wonderful Prelude in G sharp minor, one of the subtlest and most pathetically expressive of the whole collection, is more nearly akin to the suite type; but the return of the first subject ten bars from the end in the principal key is much more decisively and openly done than is usual in suite movements. It is rather its continuity of style which makes it unlike a classical sonata. On the whole, it may be taken as a combination of the sonata and suite types.

So far the management of form is fairly in accordance with well-known principles. But it is otherwise with the Preludes in C sharp minor, No. 4; F sharp major, No. 13; A flat, No. 17; A minor, No. 20; and B flat, No. 21. In all these it is apparent that Bach had the suite-sonata scheme present in his mind and was trying the effect of rearrangements of the components. The Prelude in F sharp major is, in some ways, the most remarkable, as it clearly indicates the idea of combining sonata form with the earlier type of prelude form, analogously to Bach's experiments in combining the chorale-fantasia with the French overture form in church cantatas, and other types. The first three bars present a very definite subject of the harmonic type, seeming almost to prefigure the manner of Philipp Emanuel Bach. The fourth bar introduces a new figure which, preludewise, is reiterated through a series of harmonies. Then the sonata type of subject comes back and, on arriving at the key of contrast, is interwoven with the prelude-figure. Thenceforward the two subjects carrry on an amicable discourse, being brought into prominence alternately. There is no double bar, so the course of things flows uninterruptedly into the portion which corresponds to the free fantasia, and so on until it arrives back at the principal key; when, in most deliberate fashion, with the veriest classical procedure, the first subject is duly recapitulated, and the prelude-figure, following on in turn, makes a charming little circuit of harmonies and ends with a remarkably fascinating little codetta. As has been pointed out, experiments in combining and assimilating two different types of art are quite specially notable features of Bach's disposition, but this stands as rather an isolated and unique example.

The Prelude in B flat is most suggestive. The ends of the two halves correspond, as in a suite movement, but there is no complete recapitulation of a first subject, and it is difficult to avoid thinking that Bach meant to play off a little trick on his hearers. For the course of events in the latter part of the movement arrives, as usual, at the presenting of arms to the principal key, where all people familiar with the type would expect the recapitulation as a matter of course. But Bach merely gives the faintest of hints and passes on to the recapitulation of the closing bars of the first half in accordance with familiar procedure. The main point of the feint is that Bach has the sonata procedure in his mind and gets his effect by defeating expectation.

It must be noted as a curiosity in speculation that in this Prelude, as in the Prelude in D sharp minor, passages which are highly characteristic in the middle of the first part are repeated also in the course of the second half; and the procedure in this case occurs twice over. The striking passage in bars 13 to 18 is repeated in bars 5 to 8 of the second half, and the passage in bars 9 to 12 in the first half is repeated in bars 21 to 24 in the second half; from which it appears that Bach was pleased with the constructive effect.

The extensive Prelude in F major is interesting on the ground of further combination of types. It is in the weightiest and most serious contrapuntal style, more like that of organ than clavier music, and seems to lead the hearer to expect something on the toccata lines. And indeed he might well be deceived for a time for the movement has no double bar and sounds quite like an organ toccata.[1] But when it is examined more attentively it is found that the whole of the first fifteen bars are repeated at the end with merely the change of modulation subdominantwards, as in the D major prelude, to make the latter part remain in the key. So the movement, in spite of its having no double bar, is an experiment in contrapuntal style in sonata form.

A suggestive parallel is offered in the C sharp minor Prelude, No. 4. For in this case, again, there is no double bar; but a strong point is made in the key of G sharp minor in the seventeenth bar, and the passage at the end of the whole movement is a repetition (with variations) of the five bars immediately preceding that close, as though the double bar had occurred there. A similar point is illustrated in the Prelude in B, No. 23. The singularly interesting and sinuous prelude in A minor is yet another speculation. The two halves are exactly the same length, but the correspondences

[1] Though it has no double bar, the place where it would occur is confirmed by the marked reference to the opening passage in the bass.

are all by inversion and in double counterpoint. Hardly any of the repetitions are exact; and yet almost bar by bar they seem to balance and to reproduce the musical purport. The subtlety of the artistic management is most characteristic, as it is more by the spirit than by the letter that the correspondences are suggested.

In all these preludes some definite intention is perceptible, showing how Bach's marvellous vitality of mind, fortified by the amazing amount of actual practice in writing, explored and sanely widened the range of his art. It brings to mind the story of his being asked how he achieved his wonderful work, and his modest answer that it was by assiduous application, and that anyone who applied himself as steadfastly could do as much.

The above survey does not exhaust all phases of experiment, but will serve to show the attitude of Bach's mind towards art's development. For the rest, the exquisitely tender Prelude in B minor, No. 24, is the most elaborately organised development of the old prelude type in a form which dimly suggests harmonic form of the sonata order. The tender melodious Prelude in F sharp minor, No. 14, has a complete recapitulation at the end, though it has no double bar, and some of the other preludes have passages which correspond with one another in various parts of the movements, and suggest speculative experiments, but of less decisive importance than those above considered.

From the intrinsic musical point of view, the amount of consideration devoted to these Preludes may seem disproportionate. But they are so important as showing the constant development of Bach's mind and the direction which this development had taken between the time of the bringing together of the first series and the second, that they demand the closest scrutiny. In some ways his cogitations and experiments in forms which had an Italian origin were not always entirely happy, as they somewhat obscured the Teutonic quality which was so essential a part of his personal character. In making his art more cosmopolitan these speculations occasionally lessened the depth of poetic feeling which was his greatest glory. But this is not observable in the preludes of this collection, as the prolonged revival of Teutonic impulse which has been described in connection with his later cantatas had re-established the natural bias of his mind.

The remarks which have been made about the fugues in the first collection apply equally to those in the later one. The proportion of fugues which fulfil the conditions laid down by the pundits is very small. There are some surprising *tours de force* in the matter of strettos here and there, as in the fugues in D major and B flat minor, and wonderful employment of canonic devices in the fugue in E major; but it certainly is a fact worth noting, that out of the twenty-four fugues twelve have no strettos at all, and three more only have them in a rather perfunctory condition. It also invites speculation when it is observed that most of the fugues which have strettos lie in one group, and those without strettos in another group; there being strettos in all the fugues from the second to the ninth, while all the fugues from the tenth to the twenty-first, with the not very decisive exception of the seventeenth, are strettoless. It is conceivable that this distribution was intentional; but it may also have been a singular accident. The reason why so many have no stretto is mainly that so many fugues in this collection are essentially instrumental in style, which is not favourable to the display of fugal dexterities of the old order. It may, indeed, be pointed out that the rule seems almost universal in this collection, as elsewhere in Bach's works, that fugues that lean in the direction of the old choral style are those in which the ancient prescriptions of fugue with episodes, counter-expositions, and various phases of strettos and canonic imitations are carried out, and that fugues which are frankly instrumental in character make little or no pretence of such features.

It so happens that in this collection the fugues which approximate to the old style of counterpoint are few in number. The Fugue in E major is the one which is most nearly vocal, and it happens also to be one of the most perfectly beautiful and the most perfect as a work of art, whether judged from the point of view of texture, closeness and coherence of treatment of the subjects, or of form. There are barely half a dozen fugues altogether which have the antique choral character, for those in D major, E flat major, G minor, B flat minor, and B major with the above mentioned would complete the most liberal list. Bach's object in using the fugal form here, as in the first collection, is to make fine pieces of music, not displays of dexterity. Where a characteristic subject invites dexterous manipulation of canonic devices, Bach sometimes makes liberal use of the opportunity; but where it does not, a higher kind of dexterity is exercised which more than compensates for the absence of strettos because the result is less formal. It is noticeable that in many of these fugues Bach makes great use of short, characteristic figures taken from the subject or the counter subject, interchanging them, and presenting them in a variety of phases just as a late modern composer of sonatas or symphonies would do in what is called the "working out" portion of sonatas, and even anticipating Wagner's use of the Leitmotiv and the stock in trade of the latter-day rhapsodists.

In this connection it may be observed that at the point where the learned pundit would recommend the docile composer to put a stretto, Bach, for the purpose of general artistic effect is usually busy making a specially fine succession of harmonies, which move with elastic strides to the final cadence, and minister not a little to that surprising sense of elation which so many of Bach's fugues convey. This is sometimes compatible with strettos, as in the case of the great Fugue in B flat minor, but it is much more effectually feasible in a majority of cases by taking characteristic figures out of the subject and building the whole texture of the progressions upon them. The latter half of the tremendously forcible Fugue in A minor, and of the delightfully characteristic Fugue in F minor supply obvious illustrations. The former is an admirable example of the freedom with which Bach treats the fugal principle. The subject is strongly marked and emphatic, and for that very reason Bach appears to avoid making it too obtrusive in its recurrences. It only makes its appearance five times altogether after the exposition, in the whole course of the fugue, and of those five times only twice quite literally; the other three times the first emphatic note is changed to half its value and sophisticated by actual alteration to a lower note so as to make its entry as unobtrusive as possible. And the observant mind in listening finds that the subject is going on without having caught decisively how it came in! But the greater part ot the business of the fugue consists of rapid repartees between the different voices quoting the figure of the second half of the subject

and phrases taken from the counter-subject, especially the little tail-piece,

as for instance the following passage;

The most striking feature in the fugue is the treatment of the little figure from the counter subject which, in the latter part of the fugue where concentration of interest is required, is made to mount step by step up two whole octaves and a semitone, giving thereby a splendid sense of scope[1]; while by finishing the passage on the flat second of the key it gives a vivid impulse to the final downward progressions of harmony. Similar qualities have been noticed in fugues of the first series, showing how little Bach thought it necessary to present an entire subject when he could make play with its component figures or "nuclei." The instance will serve to confirm what has been said of his anticipating the procedure of the "free fantasia" of classical sonatas and even of Wagner's and later composers' use of a "Leitmotiv."

In the F minor fugue a different surprise awaits the pundit; for the pre-eminence of the principal subject of the fugue is challenged at once by a quaint and attractive accessory which makes its appearance parenthetically in the first episode:

and is almost invariably introduced directly after the first subject has said its say, as if in playful mockery. It even has the last word. The whole thing is essentially human!

The types are many; and not a few are counterparts

[1] Compare the passage near the end of the central movement of the early fantasia in G for organ where the bass mounts up through an octave and a half.

of fugues in the first collection, treated with new artistic phases. A counterpart to that rare piece of delicacy and tender melancholy, the fugue in G sharp minor in the first series, is presented in the fugue in D sharp minor in the second; extending even to the subtle harmonies and the general scheme and tone-quality of the close. The familiar type of vivaciously rhythmic fugue, like that of the second and third in the first series, is represented by the first in C and the twelfth in F minor above alluded to, and the seventeenth in A flat and the last in B minor. Of the whirling type there are the fugues in D minor, C sharp minor, and F, which last suggests kinship with the gigue in the G major French suite. The fugue in G major stands by itself. It must certainly belong to the whirling group—but it is the whirl of a wraith or of a light moonlit cloud, so swiftly and lightly does it pass. And yet there is something singularly human in the scheme which begins so high and so brightly, and sweeps down into the depths at the end; from which point there is a rush as of sudden breath which wafts it abruptly into space. Meditative fugues are represented by those in F sharp major and F sharp minor, and that marvel of mystery, the fugue in G sharp minor, which might be taken as a very distant and slow-pacing progenitor of the last movement of Chopin's sonata in B flat minor. Of the weighty, massive types there are the fugues in D major, G minor, and B flat minor, all conspicuous for the amount of fugal devices displayed in them, as indeed befits their essentially dignified bearing. Of the quietly-moving, soberly-beautiful fugues there are the second in C minor, the seventh in E flat, the wonderful slow-pacing meditation in E major, and the melodious and soothing fugue in B major. The rest of the fugues are mainly studies in rather abstruse artistic problems such as the fugue in E minor, in which Bach endeavours to combine a number of different rhythmic units in one subject. The experiment is quite singularly out of the ordinary range of fugue, and the part-writing is at times very surprising; and among other peculiarities he helps himself out at the end by introducing a fourth part without reference to the subject, the fugue being really in three parts. The feature is not without parallel, as a fifth part is introduced at the end of the fugue in A flat after the pedalesque cadenza which is so like passages in the great toccata in F. The nineteenth fugue in A major is also a little abstruse in the same sense, and so is the twenty-first in B flat, the intention of which was to apply the characteristic quality of a subject which began on a note which is both rhythmically and tonally indefinite.

Consideration of the fugues in this fashion brings home to the mind how little space the mere ingenuities and conventions of fugue occupy. Bach happily distinguishes between the mechanism and the purpose for which mechanism serves. Mechanism is generally most aggressive with composers whose mastery of it is insufficient, which causes them to make it appear that they regard its dexterous management as an end in itself. The point of the story of J. S. Bach is that his enormous labour in mastering every field of artistic manipulation had given him such ease that even in the most difficult situations there is nothing to distract him from the full expression of his personality.

CHAPTER XIV

WORKS FOR CLAVIER AND ORGAN

THE prolonged maintenance of mental concentration upon a single great work, or a group of kindred works, is more characteristic of northern than southern races. It has rarely been more conspicuously manifested than by J. S. Bach. His life seems to be clearly parcelled out into periods during which he was directing his attention to various great works, or works which naturally fall into groups by reason of their affinities. Yet even he had moments such as any worker who has to undergo a prolonged strain of mental energy is aware of, when productive powers were temporarily diverted from a central object into side issues, and nature asserted her claims to relief by causing a distraction, and inviting the exercise of different mental muscles from those engaged upon the principal work of the time. This is proved by the huge mass of Bach's disconnected individual works of various kinds, such as isolated fugues, groups of preludes and fugues, suites, variations, toccatas, chorale preludes, sonatas, fantasias, and dance movements for all manner of instruments (including the lute and the viola pomposa), which must have filled up the interstices between his periods of absorption on the works of more conspicuous importance. The dates when they were written are for the most part beyond identification, and therefore they do not serve to illustrate the development of Bach's artistic resources in any particular period of his life. But it is undesirable to pass them by without recognition.

Among the most conspicuous is a fugue in A minor for clavier (P. T. V. I., 144–145), to which is appended, by way of a prelude, a series of chords, which are intended to be arpeggioed in accordance with the taste of the performer. The instances in which Bach has left a complete movement in such an unilluminated form are very rare, though there are parallel passages in the "Chromatische Fantasie" and in some parts of early versions of the preludes in the first part of the "Wohltemperirtes Clavier." It confirms the theory of the origin of the primitive type of prelude, and indicates that Bach devised such little works quite candidly from the point of view of mere successions of chords. It is unlikely that in this case (any more than in the passages in the "Chromatische Fantasie") he would have written anything specially characteristic as the equivalent to the chords. The passages were probably played as a series of simple arpeggios up and down. The fugue was almost certainly written first, and was purely a matter of impulse. It is the longest and most brilliant of all Bach's fugues for the clavier, and shows an affinity with the famous Weimar organ fugue in D major in the ceaseless motion of semiquavers. And there is, moreover, a characteristic feature which emphasises this kinship. In speaking of that fugue (p. 63) attention was called to the manner in which Bach developed a cadenza for the pedals at the end out of a characteristic feature of the subject. In this clavier fugue the conclusion is made exceptionally exciting in a similar manner by a culminating passage beginning low down in the scale and spreading out till it envelops the whole field of tone, which is developed entirely out of the first figure of the subject. The subject commences as follows:

And the Cadenza as follows

The kinship manifested in such fashion would give a plausible excuse to attribute this work to the Weimar period, but the extent and closeness of its development make it open to question whether it was not of later time.

A great many of these detached works were experiments, such as a detached fantasia in C minor in Italian style, and sundry brilliant toccatas; and not a few are short versions of works which Bach amplified and rewrote at some later time. Some few are collections of works which spread over a very long period of years. His life was so copiously occupied that it must frequently have happened that a promising beginning had to be left for a time undeveloped while he attended to something which was absolutely urgent. So, even in cases where chronology is not impenetrably obscure, it yet happens that it cannot be said exactly what period of his life is represented by some special group of works. This is the case with the works commonly known as the six Sonatas for the organ, which are nowhere authoritatively described as for that instrument, but on a title-page (which may be of Bach's time or soon after) as "Six Sonatas for Two Keyboards and Pedal," by which is most probably intended a harpsichord with two rows of keys and pedals.

Whether they were meant for organ or clavier, in any case they are quite exceptional among Bach's works. Their origin was, without doubt, the impulse to try how the type of the Italian violin sonata would answer as a work for a single performer. Since Bach was always prone to follow up a train of thought or a new line of work, it is very likely that these sonatas were begun at Cöthen, as a kind of sequel to the sonatas for violin and clavier or flute and clavier. In these works Bach had made quite a special point of writing in three parts, one for the solo instrument and one apiece for the hands of the clavier player; and it evidently struck him that something specially interesting might be achieved under the favourable conditions of putting all three parts at the disposal of one performer on a single instrument, and that if the two upper parts were made as independent as they would be with a flute solo and a clavier player, the soloist might have some interesting and profitable occupation in learning to play the works. And indeed, in transferring the type to the clavier, Bach made the most of this quality, for these sonatas gain quite a special character from the manner in which he makes use of the device of crossing the hands and interlacing the parts which are given to them. It seems indeed to be his cue in these works, and the effect is to make the works extraordinarily serviceable to develop independence of hands and feet. Bach delighted in combining the beautiful with the educationally helpful, and there is little doubt that the series of sonatas was written for Friedemann, to develop his powers of execution.

In adopting the Italian violin sonata form for such purposes, Bach took over the whole panoply. He followed the type in making each sonata of three movements—the first and last quick and polyphonic, and the middle slow cantabile. In passing it may be mentioned that the slow cantabile style upon which he laid so much stress is amply provided for. It may seem a little perplexing that he not only took over the grouping of movements and the name, but also the Italian style. This may have been owing to his extreme susceptibility even to words, so that the Italian name set his mind going in an Italian style. But it may also have been the much more subtle reason that, the type of sonata having been mainly cultivated by Italians,—and that with distinguished success,—the associations of the particular scheme were all mainly Italian. A similar peculiarity is noticeable in some of the sonatas for flute and clavier, especially one in E flat. In spite of the Italian flavour, however, the sonatas present a polyphonic texture of the very first quality, and there are few works of Bach's that are more delicately poised or more subtly finished.

Among the works of which it is quite hopeless to

attempt a chronology are the vast numbers of all sorts of movements based on chorales which are not included in any collections. Among those which are of very great interest are the few examples which remain of Bach's ways of accompanying the chorales when they were sung by the congregation. It is well known that it was customary for the organist to take advantage of the pause which was made at the end of each line to put in some decorous flourishes on the organ. This was certainly done for the most part extemporaneously, and no one was less likely than Bach to require to put down on paper what he would do on such every-day occasions.

But there probably were occasions when he would have written down what was to be done for someone else's benefit (and possibly also for the benefit of the congregation), when some insufficiently discreet or experienced performer had charge of the accompaniments. And it was probably for such occasions that he wrote down the accompaniments to be used for the chorales: *Allein Gott in der Höh' sei Ehr'* (B. G. XL. 44), *Gelobet seist du Jesu Christ* (XL. 62), *Herr Jesu Christ dich zu uns wend'* (XL. 72), *In dulci jubilo* (XL. 74), *Lobt Gott, ihr Christen allzugleich* (XL. 159), *Vom Himmel hoch* (ibid.). These are all interesting as primitive germs of the Chorale-fantasia (see p. 182); they are still more interesting as recalling the complaints of the consistory of the church at Arnstadt at the manner in which Bach in these early days put the congregation out with his harmonies! It is quite clear that the congregation sang the chorales in unison, as Bach's harmonies in these cases are incredibly rich and unconventional, and quite unsuited to vocal performance in parts. The ornamental passages between the lines are quite short, and in most cases are confined to the harmony upon which the previous phrase closed. In some cases the procedure is amplified and made more artistic by carrying on the forms of the ornamental passages into the phrases of the chorale which follow them, thereby softening the lines of demarcation.

As there are more than a hundred works on chorales it is not possible to consider them fully in detail. Moreover, it is not necessary, as a good many of these unattached items were experiments, by which Bach certainly did not set much store, for most of those which he thought worthy of consideration he brought together at various times. Still, among the scattered items there are some of fascinating quality, illustrating various types of chorale movements. Of the type of organ-chorales which were little more than arrangements (in which the metrical form was maintained), three on *Liebster Jesu wir sind hier* and one on *Herzlich thut mich verlangen* are most attractive. The last is one of the most beautiful of its kind, being arranged for two manuals and pedal so that the tune has a manual to itself, and is adorned with subtle use of accessory notes through which it is broken up into short phrases which were evidently meant by Bach to express the "verlangen"; and the harmony subtly ministers to the tender expression One of the three on *Liebster Jesu* is treated in the same way, but with a more liberal supply of ornament. The other two are simpler, hardly exceeding the limits of the ordinary harmonisation of the final chorales in the cantatas. Of more developed type are the movements on *An Wasserflüssen Babylon* and *Wir glauben all in einen Gott,* the first of which is specially beautiful, manifesting some of the qualities of the famous *Schmücke dich* to be considered later. Both are in five parts with two parts for the pedals, and a solo part for the tune. They would be properly described as chorale-fantasias, as the accompaniment wanders on as if reflecting on its own account, and the phrases of the chorale come in at intervals, just as they do in the first choruses of the chorale-cantatas. In passing it may be observed that the pedals are evidently meant to be restricted to stops of 8 ft.

Of more highly organised type making a complete and well developed movement is *Wo soll ich fliehen hin,* which is closely knit together by the genial little figure, probably suggested by the word "fliehen," which is reiterated almost incessantly in infinite variety of positions throughout with the chorale in the bass. *Wir Christenleut'* is a delightful example of similar treatment. The Vorspiel on *Allein Gott in der Höh' sei Ehr,* to which the name Bicinium is given, is only in two parts, and has the appearance of being an adaptation of a vocal solo with cello-piccolo accompaniment, like the Choralvorspiel from the cantata *Bleib' bei uns* in the "Schübler'schen Choräle" (see p. 536). There is a quaint waywardness in the accompaniment which is fascinating. *Jesu meine Freude* is highly organised and at considerable length, in two portions. The first three phrases of the chorale are given to three several parts twice over, with dainty accompaniment, in $\frac{4}{4}$ time. Then a total change of style is made in $\frac{3}{8}$ time, and a mysterious allusion to a phrase in one of the movements of the motet *Jesu meine Freude* presents itself, from which emanates a peaceful meditation marked "dolce" in which the remainder of the tune disappears. *Ein' feste Burg* is treated with great elaboration of the tune with copious ornament. In recalling Buxtehude's treatment of the tune and Bach's own treatment in the great cantata, one is tempted to think that some convention or habit of mind must have grown up in favour of ornamenting it in such a manner. This fantasia is a fine and strenuous example, and is liberally marked with directions for registration and changes of manuals. There are two beautiful chorale fantasias on *Valet will ich dir geben,* both on a large scale. In the first the phrases of the chorale are passed about from part to part with constant network of rapid passages woven around them, while the bass solemnly enunciates the tune. The second is in $\frac{24}{16}$ time, with the chorale in slow notes on the pedals, which makes the tune mysteriously intangible. Besides these chorale movements there are three beautiful and interesting sets of variations or "*Partien*" on *Christ, der du bist der helle Tag; O Gott, du frommer Gott,* and *Sei gegrüsset, Jesu gütig.* They have an air of ingenuous simplicity, which shows without doubt that they are very early compositions. Spitta even argues that they were written at Lüneburg. They are for the most part groups of fantasias on the chorale tunes rather than variations in the ordinary sense of the term.

The difficulty of dealing with the chorale movements, and indeed with the whole field of Bach's organ works, lies mainly in the fact that Bach attained to his full height comparatively early in this branch of art, for reasons which have been dealt with. It cannot justly be said that he ever advanced beyond the standard of his Weimar compositions in that branch of art. The Fantasia in G minor which probably belongs to that time (see p. 69) is one of the grandest of all his inspirations, and the well-known fugues in G minor, D major, and A minor and the first Toccata in D minor are so masterly in construction, so full of fire and vitality, and present the personality of the composer in such convincing terms that it is vain to pretend that he has ever excelled them; and the chorale prelude *O Mensch, bewein' dein' Sünde gross,* which appeared in the "little organ book," has no peer in the whole range of his compositions of that kind. The period when these works were produced is analogous to Beethoven's so-called second period, comprising all the works from about Opus 50 to Opus 90, in which the full fire and vitality of his still youthful temperament are displayed. For with men of such unquenchable spirit the youth of temperament often lasts a full decade and more after the physical youth is ended. In both men the works of this radiant period overflow into the latest period. So a man who would judge by intrinsic qualities is at fault. It can only be said that a large number of Bach's finest works for the organ, the dates of which are unascertainable, may have been written any time between the middle of his period at Weimar and the end of the first decade at Leipzig. To this category must inevitably be relegated the one great passacaglia in C minor, the superb toccata in C with the fugue in $\frac{6}{8}$ time, the prelude and fugue in C minor (P. T. V. I., 802, 803), and even the great toccata in F major.

The argument in favour of the Passacaglia being an early work is that it is written quite obviously under the influence of Buxtehude, who in that form manifested the highest flight of his interesting genius.[1] Buxtehude's influence upon Bach was undoubtedly great and permanent, but it must evidently have been more direct and conscious in the early Weimar time, as the D major fugue can be located in that period, and its connection with Buxtehude's fugue in F is unmistakable. The Passacaglia, as a matter of fact, resembles many other great experiments by Bach in being such an immense expansion of Buxtehude's scheme. Bach divined his cue, and made his effect by gradually building up the volume of tone and the enrichment of detail from the quiet opening to the sumptuous splendour of the closing bars of the passacaglia; and he makes that a point of departure for a fugue on the subject of the ground bass, for which there is an obvious æsthetic justification. For the rigid reiteration of a formula of a definite number of bars in length (which is the underlying basis of the Passacaglia), induces a sense of mechanical constraint, and in order to make the scheme complete a passage manifesting freedom of range is most desirable. Bach found this most aptly in the fugue, which vastly enhances the principle of the form. As the experiment is without doubt a great success, it is rather strange that he did not try it again.

But he must always have had his head as full of novel schemes as there was time for apart from his official work and one of these is the Toccata in C (P.T.V.I., 830)

[1] It should be added that it shows also the influence of Reinken; as the closing bars of the Passacaglia were probably suggested by bars 8 to 11 in the first movement of the first sonata in the "Hortus Musicus."

which is totally unique among Bach's organ compositions. The impulse that prompted it was related to that which prompted the composition of the splendid toccatas for the clavier in F sharp minor and C minor. They manifest the like peculiarity of being broken up into contrasting sections. They all commence with passages of bravura—which sounds unpromising,—but indeed the passages which Bach modelled in that style are almost sufficiently interesting to redeem a branch of art which has been more piteously discredited than any in its whole range, save and except the operatic aria. The bravura passages in all these cases are preliminaries to very serious and noble passages of slow and expressive character, and the scheme of each is rounded off by a long and extensively developed fugue.

The distinguishing features of the organ Toccata in C are that the effect of sectional contrast is so amply displayed, and that one of its four sections is unique among Bach's organ works. This section occupies the exact position which the nobly expressive adagio in $\frac{3}{2}$ time does in the F sharp minor toccata, and the parallel adagio in the C minor toccata, and even similar features in the early clavier toccata in D minor, and others too numerous to recapitulate. But in the organ Toccata the slow passage is a beautiful song movement, the long rhapsodical ornate melody of which recalls the slow movements for violin in which Bach poured out his soul so freely. It also resembles more completely the slow movement of the Italian Concerto, which, by a charming and serviceable coincidence, presents a characteristic parallel in its accompaniment to the constantly moving quasi-pizzicato quaver-figure for the pedals in the Organ Toccata. The beautiful air ends with short transition through one of the typical passages of truly tremendous suspensions which are so ideally fitted for the organ to display its remorseless persistence of tone, into the singularly gay and genial fugue which constitutes the finale. The composition reaches out its tentacles in all directions. If the songlike movement associates it with works of the latest period, the special interpretation of the toccata scheme links it to works of an early period. It is in every aspect supremely interesting and brilliantly effective.

The contrast which this work presents to the great Toccata with Fugue in F is too marked to be passed by without notice. For that is on quite a different scheme from those above referred to; being continuous from end to end. The spaciousness of its development suggests comparatively late production, and this inference is strengthened by its conclusion, which is one of the most overwhelmingly powerful passages Bach ever wrote. The fugue, as has been before said, is probably an addition belonging to a different period. It is quite overwhelmed by the toccata, and seems almost superfluous (see p. 68).

The only organ works which are referred with any confidence to the latest period of Bach's life are the Preludes and Fugues in C (P. T. V. I., 804, 805), E minor (P.T.V.I., 808, 809), and B minor (P.T.V.I., 810, 811), together with the Fugue in E flat which has been discussed in connection with the Clavierübung in which it appeared. The elements of brilliant effect which are manifested in works of the Weimar period are more or less in abeyance, but preludes and fugues alike give the impression of superb workmanship and seriousness. The prelude in C presents a continuous discourse between the three parts allotted to the hands, passing through a dignified circuit of keys and effectively punctuated by a decisive figure for the pedals

which recurs at intervals, as if commenting on the discourse of the manuals. The fugue is in five parts, but the fifth part, which is given to the pedals, does not enter till near the end of the fugue, when it enunciates an augmentation of the subject—a procedure which is very impressive. Prelude and fugue are closely allied in style, and have a singular concurrence in the fact that in both of them the closing passage is preceded by a succession of striking harmonies, which stands out powerfully from the context. The purpose is kindred to the device commented on in connection with the fugue in A minor of the second series of the "Wohltemperirtes Clavier" (p. 492).

The prelude in E minor is of a solid and businesslike type of which Bach made frequent use. The basis of the thematic scheme is mainly the alternation of two distinct subjects distributed in a broad circuit of contrasting keys. It is close in texture and in loyalty to its thematic material, and imposing in its scale of development. The fugue, on the other hand, which is the longest Bach ever wrote for the organ, is singularly loose in structure. All the central portion has the character of a fantasia, in which episodes of purely independent and irrelevant material, rather like cadenzas, alternate with short references to the subject. Bach clearly had some intention in this unfugal procedure, which is also met with in some others of his grand fugues. The problem is a subtle one, as in this case he certainly combines two different styles. It can only be said that he evidently aimed at relieving the extreme insistence on the striking subject, and that, in the frame of mind which happened to prevail when he was writing the fugue, the effect of purely decorative passages alternating with the fugal passages pleased him, and the leaven of boyishness which still clung to him in advanced age made him repeat the process again and again. Whichever way the ultimate verdict tends, there is no doubt that, after such procedure, consolidation is an urgent desideratum; and he attained it by repeating a long portion of the beginning of the fugue—no less, indeed, than fifty-nine bars—at the end, a procedure that has the same basis as the Aria form.

The great prelude and fugue in B minor may be the last which Bach ever wrote for the organ. The group is unlike any of his other organ works in the unmistakable sentiment of supremely noble and dignified melancholy which suffuses both movements. The prelude is superbly rich in texture, laid out on broad and grand lines, and illustrates Bach's methods in the rhapsodical type of movements by the alternation of ornate melody with progressions of massive harmony, which in this case are not presented in their bare simplicity, like the familiar elemental successions of suspensions, but decked with all the richest interest of figuration. It is, in fact, the order of tonality in which these imposing passages present themselves in connection with cadences of first importance which gives the clue to the design of the movement.

The fugue with its solemn, rolling subject clearly has some deep meaning. It seems to suggest a deep temperamental meditation on the remorselessness of destiny, and the helplessness of man in the face of it. The strange little ejaculations which are introduced as characteristic traits in the latter part of the fugue seem to represent gestures of acquiescence, especially when they come in with the pedals near the end.

As an illustration of the continuity of Bach's mental activities it may be pointed out that there is a dim kinship between the subject of this fugue and the subject of the fugue conjoined with the well-known early Toccata in D minor (see p. 64). The whole work is developed on grand lines and in the serious spirit characteristic of his latest period, and confirms to the last the presence of a great human soul expressing itself in the full mastery of artistic resources.

CHAPTER XV

THE "MUSIKALISCHES OPFER" AND THE "KUNST DER FUGE"

Bach is identified with several forms and types of art by the singular fact that he produced incomparably the finest examples ever achieved by man in their various orders. He produced the finest suites, the finest organ music, the finest church cantatas, the finest solo violin music, the finest choral motets, the finest chorale-preludes, and the finest "Passions." But with none of these forms is he more intimately associated than with the fugue and its close relations. It was the form in which he expressed himself most readily and most characteristically, and the form to which he gave a special kind of life, the possibilities of which were unsuspected until his time. Two of his very latest works seem therefore apt even to quaintness, for they frankly present, with little æsthetical circumlocution, the methods of his fugal procedure. It is as though, having completed all his wonderful achievements in that form, he set himself to make a final exposition of his artistic creed, and to offer to the world some examples of pure fugal construction which would define and make plain the lines on which he had proceeded in making his works of art. The two works, which hang together by community of principle, are the "Musikalisches Opfer" and the "Kunst der Fuge."

The first of these two is connected with Bach's visit to Frederick the Great at Potsdam, which is one of the most familiar episodes in his personal history, to which it is therefore necessary to give a little attention. The quiet tenor and persistent work of Bach's life at Leipzig are apt to convey the impression that he never moved therefrom. But as a matter of fact he made a good many journeys and tours in the north of Germany, both officially and of his own choice. He was, among other things, Kapellmeister at Weissenfels and went there occasionally; and he maintained also his connection with Cöthen. Dresden also frequently attracted him, for there, since 1733, his eldest son Friedemann had been organist at the Sophien-Kirche, and there also was a famous and well equipped opera establishment, and Bach's enquiring mind led him to attend the performances and to see friends, among whom the opera composer Hasse and his wife Faustina were included. His fame as a performer was undoubtedly great, and he was called upon to display his powers in other places besides Leipzig. So the impression of confinement in one place by ceaseless labour must be qualified by the recognition of occasional distractions. It happened that his son Philipp Emanuel had been appointed Kapellmeister in Frederick the Great's musical establishment in 1740, and that with him were many musicians who had friendly relations with John Sebastian. So it came about that the great Frederick was moved by interest or curiosity to see and hear him, and he was ultimately induced to visit Potsdam in 1747. The King, when not engaged in affairs of state or leading his armies in battle, usually had a little domestic concert in the evening, when he himself played the flute. Bach arrived just when one of these functions was beginning, and Frederick seems to have been so eager to see him that he insisted upon his being fetched at once in his ordinary dress with all the marks of travel still upon him. However, he was not then called upon to perform, but was allowed to defer the manifestation of his powers till the next evening. The King himself gave Bach a subject on which to extemporise; but as he was most anxious to hear Bach extemporise a fugue in six parts, in view of the difficulty of the feat, Bach is said to have supplied his own subject for that particular exhibition. But in the "Musikalisches Opfer," presently to be discussed, which puts on record various treatments, fugal and otherwise, of the King's excellent "theme," the six-part fugue is on the same subject as the other works. It is true that Bach, as a compliment, may have specially written a six-part fugue on the King's subject, but in that case he would most probably have made some allusion to it in the letter he sent to the King with the completed work, and as will be seen (p. 520) there is not the slightest hint of anything of the kind. So on the whole the preponderance of evidence is in favour of Bach's having extemporised both fugues on the King's subject.

How Bach tried the Silbermann pianofortes and played on the organ at Potsdam and visited the opera house at Berlin are all matters of secondary interest. The important matter in connection with this visit to the King is that it led to the production of the "Musikalisches Opfer," one of his very latest compositions; in which, as a compliment to the King, he settled down seriously to write fugues and canons and other examples of artistic forms based (with one exception) on the subject which the King had given him. The work is not of very great musical interest, but its general interest in connection with the personality of the composer is supreme. It is almost as if one could read between the lines the workings of Bach's mind! He possibly overrated the powers of the King for remembering the details of the extemporisations, and therefore reproduced more faithfully than he need have done passages which he would not have passed as adequate in a deliberately written composition. There are points which stand out unmistakably. It is evident, in the first place, that Bach, like other extemporisers, had some fixed schemes in his mind upon which extemporisations could be carried out—schemes rather more formal and conventional than he would use in seriously composing a fugue, but at the same time embodying essential principles: such broad outlines as the succession of different keys, the alternation of passages in which the subject is prominent with episodes in which the subject is absent except in the shape of fragmentary allusions. It may be seen also that Bach had such things always at hand as certain harmonic progressions, groups of suspensions, even phrases and formulas which could be used at special points in the process, just as practical extempore speakers have certain useful phrases and elocutionary devices always ready to help out their impromptus.

The two most important movements, which with the highest degree of probability may be taken as representing what he actually extemporised before King

Frederick, are the fugue in three parts, and the fugue in six parts. They may be said at once not to trespass at all in the direction of what is called fugal science. There is no stretto in either of them. The three-part fugue is naturally the one in which the subject is most frequently and variably presented; but it is subtly suggestive of the convenience of the extemporiser that the episodes in which the subject does not appear in its entirety are extremely long, and often contain purely conventional passages, such as Bach might have had always in mind for an emergency, and even passages of arpeggios which are quite irrelevant and unfugal. It is further to be noted that in the first exposition a show is made of presenting a definite counter subject, but it is entirely dropped in the middle part of the fugue, and only makes its reappearance in the latter part of it, where it is brought back and used in canonic imitation to save the situation, and also to present the effect of rounding off the fugue by giving the beginning and end some community of feature. For the rest the subject only occurs completely seven times in the whole course of the fugue after the exposition, and of these recurrences only two are in an inner part. These circumstances, together with the fact that Bach once slips into a reminiscence of the D minor fugue in the second book of the "Wohltemperirtes Clavier" (No. 6), all point to the record being as loyal a presentation from memory as he could recall of the actual movement extemporised. For the rest the work represents his typical readiness to base the interest of the fugue on other considerations than that of the principal subject, which is the more striking in view of the fact that the King might have been more flattered if it had been introduced in season and out of season.

The same feature is noticeable in the six-part fugue, for in that case the subject is not made much of or subjected to any great variety of presentment and combination. The distribution of its recurrences is so far systematic that it is given but once by each part in the course of the fugue after the exposition, and the order in which each part is favoured is based on logical principles. The use of thematic material is not at all close. New secondary subjects are introduced in each episode, and after being subjected to some little development are dropped and succeeded by further departures. And it is worthy of note that a reminiscent figure from the A flat fugue in the second collection of the "Wohltemperirtes Clavier" serves, in combination with a fragment from the King's subject, as the thematic basis of the last episode in the fugue. The main object of the work seems really to be to present a fine example of six-part work, without laying much stress on thematic development. The style is more strict and plain than in most of Bach's composed fugues, and does not really suggest necessary association with any special instrument or group of instruments. It might therefore be called an abstract fugue, and invites the same inferences as the three-part fugue, one of which is that Bach had developed the degree of mastery which enabled him always to produce work which was solid in sound and dignified in style, but that conditions favourable to concentration of attention and isolation from distractions were necessary to the production of music fully characteristic of his artistic personality.

It should be observed that Bach did not himself give the name of Fugue to either of these works, but the more ancient name of Ricercar. This title, which is frequently met with in the instrumental works of composers from the latter end of the sixteenth till far on in the seventeenth century, represented the form which was the immediate forerunner of the fugue, and attained at times, before it dropped out of usage, to its full lineaments. Bach clearly used the title because the letters served as the initials of a series of words which he gave as the title of the work, "Regis Jussu Cantio et Reliqua Canonica Arte Resoluta." The quaint symbolism is highly characteristic!

In some ways the sonata (probably ror flute, violin, and continuo) which is comprised in "Das Musikalische Opfer" is more essentially musical than either of the fugues or ricercars. But in this case it is quite obvious that Bach was not trying to put an extemporised work on record, but composed the sonata specially, on subjects derived (with copious variations) from the subject given him by the King. The work is on the usual lines of the typical Italian violin sonata, and is rather Italian in style, comprising an introductory slow movement, a long allegro, an expressive central slow movement, and a lively finale. It would not be expected that a work based on subjects which are not entirely of the composer's own initiation would attain the highest level of interest, but both the slow movements are beautiful pieces of work, full of delicate and interesting details, and the quick movements are developed in a most brilliant manner. Bach completed the compliment of the "Musikalisches Opfer," by adding a considerable number of canons on the "thema regium," including a "canon perpetuus" for two parts by inversion with free bass, and a "fuga canonica," which are mainly examples of the almost incredible facility which he had attained in technical feats of this kind.

The letter offering the work to the King was dated July 7, 1747.

To your Majesty I dedicate herewith in deepest humility a Musical Offering, the noblest part of which your own exalted hand supplied. With respectful pleasure I remember the altogether special royal consideration which I experienced at the time of my visit to Potsdam. Your Majesty yourself deigned to play to me the theme of a fugue on the clavier, and at the same time in a most gracious manner laid it upon me to develop the same in your Majesty's gracious presence. To obey your Majesty's command was my humble duty. But I soon remarked that owing to lack of necessary preparation the development was not so complete or so noble as the theme demanded. I resolved and hastened to work out the right royal theme more fully and to make it known to the world. This resolve has now been accomplished to the best of my powers, and it has no other object than the blameless one of enhancing in a small point the fame of a monarch whose greatness and strength in all the arts of war and peace, especially in music, everyone must admire and honour. I am bold enough to make this humble request, that your Majesty will deign to honour the present small work with your gracious acceptance, and grant your favour to your Majesty's obedient and most humble servant, the Author.

It is inevitable that the work known as the "Kunst der Fuge" should be coupled with the "Musikalisches Opfer," owing to the rare peculiarity which they have in common of consisting of a series of movements all based on the same subject. Indeed, with due recognition of the general futility of surmises, it is in a high degree probable that the later work was a consequence of the former. Since, having given a practical exposition of what could be done in such a series of movements with a subject given by the King, for the benefit of the King, it was natural to look for what could be done in like manner with a subject of the composer's own, for the benefit of musicians in general.

The second work is on a much larger scale than the first and covers more ground, and covers it also more systematically; the earlier fugues being simple and devoid of any very elaborate contrivances, while the complexity of the strettos and the more copious reiteration of subjects increase as the movements go on. For such special objects a special type of subject was needed, and it must be granted that the subject in its first form, as it appears in the first two fugues, is little more than a framework in vocal style, and has very little musical interest or character at all.

The first fugue is mainly a study in simple contrapuntal style, and, like the fugues in the "Musikalisches Opfer," only presents the subject a few times, without any stretto or manipulations of countersubjects. The second is a good deal more vivacious, having a preponderance of trochaic rhythm in the accompanying parts; but still there is little elaboration in the use of the subject. Things get more complicated in the third and fourth fugues, which are both of them on an inversion of the subject.

In the third the subject appears in the latter part in a form of variation which is used as the initial subject in some of the later fugues,

and in the fourth the subject is much more in evidence and is presented in more interesting lights, while the groundwork is ingeniously woven out of an insignificant germ of four notes which characterises the quasi counter-subject. The fifth fugue is on the variation of the subject which appears in the latter part of the third fugue, thus establishing a point of progressive coherence between the numbers. The exposition, moreover, is elaborated by the answers being given alternately in the inverted form and the original form of the subject, and there are several strettos, some of them very close. The sixth fugue is described as "in stile Francese," which seems mainly to imply a considerable prominence of dotted and short notes, again entailing a good deal of trochaic rhythm. The third-fugue variation of the subject is adopted and is answered by inversion in diminution. The style becomes more instrumental and the interest richer. Besides ordinary strettos there are strettos by augmentation, which are rendered the more effective by the liveliness of contrast between the trochaic metre of the accompaniments and the long notes of the augmented subject. The general result of amplified interest and expansion is to make this fugue appear to be a point of climax in the gradual growth of the work; and this effect was recognised and possibly intended by the composer, for the seventh fugue comes as a kind of extension or offshoot therefrom, as it is on the same form of the subject, which is answered at the same pitch, thereby calling the attention of the observant hearer to the connection between the two movements. From that point the movement is so crowded with allusions to the subject in diminution, inversion, double diminution, and triple diminution in variation, augmentation direct, double augmentation in strettos, and canonic imitation in every conceivable kind, that it is obvious that the composer means to take leave of the subject for a while when he has tied the knot at the end.

This proves indeed to be the case, for the eighth fugue leads off with an entirely new subject, a subject also which has much more musical significance than the original subject of the series:

Moreover after this subject has been worked for a while, yet another characteristic subject

is introduced, and the two are worked together in a great variety of positions of double counterpoint, and the proceedings culminate in interest towards the end of the fugue, when the original subject of the series again makes its appearance in a new and pathetic variation:

which is more apt to the somewhat sad expression of the two new subjects through being broken up into short phrases. The three subjects are happily intertwined in all manner of interesting combinations, thereby establishing a set of fresh starting-points for the second part of the series. The ninth fugue is in a new and lively vein, with a vivacious new subject, quite instrumental in style, to which, after a while, the original subject is added in augmented form, working out a complete exposition in which the contrast of the long notes with the vivacity of the quick notes of the actual subject of the fugue is highly effective. The tenth fugue presents an enigma which is almost insoluble, as it begins with a pathetic new subject, which, after being worked at some length, is displaced by a complete exposition based on the third-fugue variation of the original subject, which is interwoven with it. But from the point where this enters, the fugue, for the rest of its course, is the same as the fourteenth fugue, which thus only differs from it by being devoid of the exposition of the new subject at the beginning. It is quite inconceivable that Bach meant to have both these fugues in the series, and their being so is obviously owing to the fact that he did not live to complete and revise the work, and that no one knew what he intended with regard to them.

The fugue which stands as No. 11 is of great and salient interest, standing with fugue No. 8 by reason of much higher musical interest than the rest of the series. In most of the other fugues Bach either determined to restrain himself from the use of beautiful and characteristic ideas, and to write as mechanically as his habits allowed, or else he was quite out of his wonted musical humour. But here the native impulse was too much for him and the fugue No. 11 is worthy to stand beside the fugues in the "Wohltemperirtes Clavier" for spaciousness of development, depth and consistency of expression, and constant growth of interest from first to last. From the point of view of mere technical ingenuity it is most attractive. The initial subject is the inversion of the broken form of the principal subject of the whole series as it appears in the latter part of fugue No. 8. To it is added after a time the initial subject of that same fugue in inverted form, with a new chromatic kind of counter-subject. And then by degrees, as the wealth of artistic contrivance is increased, the second subject of No. 8 makes its appearance in various forms of inversion and variation, and from that time forward in the whole of the rest of the fugue (which is long) there is hardly a bar which is irrelevant; for every moment is used in presenting the four subjects in every kind of juxtaposition and combination, but always maintaining a noble and tender colour and a rather pathetic vein of sentiment. The richness and consistency of the texture throughout are as wonderful as they are spontaneous, and even where the three subjects occur simultaneously the uninitiated would perceive only a singularly beautiful piece of expressive music.

It may fairly be supposed that the remaining fugues were a kind of distraction, for the points that they illustrate have no bearing on practical artistic or æsthetic principles. Fugue No. 12 is written on the original subject inverted in $\frac{3}{2}$ time and with it is presented a

version in which everything is turned upside down,[1] even to the very turn in the cadence at the end. The least hint of the exposition will serve as an illustration of the procedure. (See opposite page.) The same is the case with the lively fugue No. 13 on a variation of the subject. Bach possibly wrote them just to see if it could be done; he certainly would not have classed them as musical works unless as extremely abstruse jokes.

The same may be said of several of the canons which follow the fugues. The ingenuity of the scheme and the perfect facility and dexterity of the execution of the first verges upon the absurd! The upper part begins with a variation of the subject of the fugues in quick notes, and the lower part answers by inversion in notes of double the length. This sounds ingenious enough, but it is not nearly so ingenious as the manner in which the anomalies of the procedure are accommodated. It is a case of the hare and the tortoise without the hare's mistakes, for by half-way through the canon the upper part is twenty-eight bars ahead of the lower part, and to proceed in the same manner would be merely ridiculous. So Bach makes a little break in the upper part and the lower part immediately resumes the outset of the canon in the quicker notes, in the same form which the upper part had at the beginning, and the upper part in turn is relegated to the tortoise-like procedure of augmentation and inversion. The result is an example of double counterpoint, which is rounded off by a very ingenious little coda in which, for a few bars, the upper part is allowed to resume the quicker

1 In the original the uninverted version and the upside-down version were given one over another, bar by bar.

motion. There are several more canons in various styles based upon ingenious and effective variations of the principal subject of the series, and they all have some kind of general scheme like the first, based upon a similar distribution of canonic inversions.

The canons are followed by two arrangements or enlargements of the quick fugues No. 13 and its inversion, for two claviers; and they, by the torso of a great fugue on three subjects, in the latter part of which Bach introduced the subject on his own name, which has become familiar in later times through the many experiments with it that have been made thenceforward by all manner of composers. This was probably the first of these experiments and it is possible that Bach meant to conclude the "Kunst der Fuge" therewith, as though in a whimsically figurative manner writing his sign manual in music at the end of his last fugal work.

As to the intention of the work, there is no possibility of arriving at any kind of certitude. The greater part of it does not come within the range of practical music at all, and Bach could never have intended it to be presented to an audience as a consistent work of art. What seems most probable is that he amused himself by experimenting on the possibilities of many of the different kinds of artistic devices which he had accumulated and assimilated in the course of his constantly active life—dexterities which afforded him pleasure in the exercise, and which in this case were, exceptionally, the aim of his labours.

In Bach's character there were obviously two divergent impulses—the emotional and the practical.

Any man endowed with immense strength must inevitably rejoice in its exercise, and the same is true of acquired dexterity; and however great the instinct for using such powers as means to serviceable ends, there must be occasions when, there being no ostensible object to which to apply them, they are used for the mere pleasure of feeling their existence and enhancing them. Bach's temptation to use his powers in such a way was twofold. The constant urgency to produce new cantatas for the various seasons and festivals of the church sometimes made it difficult to find a subject which appealed to his sympathies and awakened his highest inspirations; and under the stress of such urgency he often resorted to a display of superb skill to justify the work of art which had to be produced under uninspiring conditions. The frequency of this necessity fostered the readiness to take pleasure in the exercise of such skill, which, it may be admitted, was constantly enhanced thereby. And in this way the aptitude for producing abstract works of art which had no reference to specially interesting ends was engendered.

Of this impulse the "Kunst der Fuge" was probably the most conspicuous phenomenon. But no doubt his motives, as is usually the case, were mixed. The educational purpose, which is so frequently manifested in the titles which he gave to his works as well as in their intrinsic qualities, probably also weighed with him; and he most probably thought that the display of such a vast array of the devices and features of fugal art would help students of composition to realise what was worth doing, and how to dispose the various technicalities of fugue—the exposition and counter exposition, the various kinds of stretto, counter subjects, working of figures of the subject, and other phases of the mechanism. And this may have been the reason for his taking the unusual course of beginning to have the work engraved at once. As has been said, he did not live to finish it, and the final fugue on three subjects comes to an abrupt stop, no doubt far from its intended conclusion. No one was at the time sufficiently in touch with his work to know what was intended, and it is obvious also that the individual numbers are not entirely in the order which he would finally have adopted.

The engraving was proceeded with after his death, apparently under Philipp Emanuel's supervision, and he was the likeliest of the sons to know what his father's intentions were: but his own line of art was not of the nature to enable him to make up any gaps in his father's work, or to divine what to do when the order of the movements appeared inconclusive. The first edition is admitted to have been very badly edited, and its success when brought out in 1752 was far from encouraging. The work has always been spoken of by musicians as something most important, in its affording copious illustrations of Bach's fugal skill of the highest order. But no work of his is less known, and in its entirety it is not fit to be played as practical music. In this connection it is to be observed that it is not written in short score, as if for keyed instruments, but with the parts on separate staves, which makes it easier to read and to follow the ramifications of counterpoint and the strettos and canonic imitations. But this engenders no desire to hear the movements played by separate instruments, as the style is, for the most part, too abstract, and only in a few places suggests instrumental effect at all. And, finally, the work was not called "Kunst der Fuge" by Bach, and the movements were not called fugues at all, but "counterpoints," which points to abstract intentions and not to performance. The work contains, together with astounding examples of Bach's dexterity, a few numbers of great interest and moments of beauty, but beyond that it must remain more or less of a tantalising enigma.

CHAPTER XVI

THE END

THE hold which the German chorales kept upon Bach from first to last is the most significant token of the depth and steadfast earnestness of his nature, and the warmth and sensitiveness of his imagination. The strange love of symbolism which was deeply engrained in him made him feel them to be the embodiments of the religious sentiments which were expressed by the words of the hymns with which they were associated; and when he harmonised them or adorned them with all the subtlety of his art in the forms of "organ-chorales," "chorale-preludes," "chorale-fantasias," "chorale-fugues," or "chorale-variations" he was moved to give expression to the feelings of reverence and devotion which the hymns embodied. In the finest of his compositions in these forms the exquisite skill and sensibility with which he adorned the tunes was no vain display of artistic ingenuities, but the revelation of the deepest workings of his nature, the very musings of his inmost soul. This is apparent even in his unique treatment of the final chorales in the cantatas—where he presents a harmonisation of so strange and unconventional a kind that no other composer has ever had the temerity to venture on anything approaching it.

Such work is only possible under special conditions, when the man and the moment are consonant. Bach represented a phase of religious expression in music which cannot recur. All the finest qualities of Teutonic devotionalism and mysticism found their expression in him. Untroubled by the speculations of later philosophy, the central story of Christianity was to him a supreme and vivid reality, and constantly aroused in him the purest and noblest sentiments of which man is capable. And indeed such sentiments as trust, adoration, wonder, hope, humility, gratitude, contrition, submission, self-abasement and ideal love are most apt to be expressed in music. His imagination dwelt on the story of the supreme sacrifice and loved to meditate on the incidents of the life of One for Whom he felt a personal devotion. And these meditations are represented in his chorale preludes and works of that type, as though his mind wandered quietly on and the music welled out as the spirit moved him, kept just within the bounds of necessary artistic coherence by the presence of the sacred symbol of the chorale tune.

No doubt his attitude of mind varied, inasmuch as he was most essentially human. There are chorale-preludes and chorale-fantasias in which he seems to be bent on enriching the tune with the best out of the wealth of his artistic treasury, and paying it the highest tribute of his skill. Under the most favourable circumstances he combined the expression of feeling with the richest manifestations of his power. The types have been discussed in connection with the

"Little Organ Book" and the collection in the "Clavierübung." These, however, represent but a small portion of the enormous number of movements on chorales of different kinds which remain, representing every phase of his development from first to last. It is clear that his facility and the habit of directing his mental activity became so great that, as soon as the chorale was chosen and the mood engendered, the prelude or fantasia would spring forth complete in one jet.

The chorale movements were a constant resource to the composer, and a constant refreshment of devotional sentiment: somewhat analogous to the pencil drawings and studies by great painters, which have been executed sometimes for the mere pleasure of exercising skill or to record some fleeting artistic inspirations, sometimes with a view of solving some artistic difficulty which unexpectedly offered itself to the mind, inviting the pleasure of wrestling with it, oftentimes of perpetuating some thought of beauty in artistic terms. The circumstances in which such works were produced preclude the possibility of deciding the time of their execution, except in rare cases. A few tell their tale by intrinsic qualities, such as the primitive chorale-prelude on *Erbarm' dich mein* which is given in the Bach Gesellschaft Collection, vol. xl., p. 60. A fair proportion can be dated according to their appearance in collections made up by Bach himself, and of these a few make their appearance with pathetic aptness in the last ten years of his life.

It must be loyally admitted that in these last ten years the overwhelming torrent of production, which had lasted almost without intermission for over thirty years, came to a pause. It has been already related in what manner Bach made his farewell obeisance in the province of one of the two great influences in his life, the fugue. That took the story up to 1747. The other great influence, the chorale, takes the story up to the final moments.

There are three definite points at which the chorales make their appearance unmistakably in the last decade. A singular collection comes first, of which the title is as follows: *Sechs Choräle von verschiedener Art auf einer Orgel mit zwei Clavieren und Pedal vorzuspielen, verfertiget von J. S. Bach.* Bach seems to have been fond of drawing up title-pages, and the word "verfertiget" indicates that he was the author of this example. He had used it also on the title-page of the first series of the "Wohltemperirtes Clavier" (p. 145). The modest word "Choräle" as here used is unenlightening to people who are not German Lutherans. They are, in fact, a group of chorale-preludes and chorale-fantasias which in the majority of cases, if not all, are transfers or arrangements from movements in cantatas, illustrating the identity of such movements with the organ-chorale forms. The first of the series is the exquisite and dainty chorale-fantasia from the cantata *Wachet auf*, which has been discussed in connection with that cantata. (See p. 390). The second is not identifiable, but it is very probable that it is an arrangement of a movement from one of the lost cantatas. It is an illustration of a quaint fancy of the composer's (of which there are several examples in this collection, as elsewhere) for giving the tune to the pedals, though not in the bass, by the device of indicating eight-foot stops for the right hand, sixteen-foot stops for the left hand, and four-foot stops for the pedals. By this means the pedal part sounds above the part given to the left hand, and even at times above that given to the right hand.

The third number, *Wer nur den lieben Gott,* is transferred from the duet *Er kennt die rechten Freudenstunden* in the cantata of the name of the chorale; the parts for the voices and continuo are given to the hands, and the chorale tune (which in the cantata is given to the massed strings) is again allotted to the pedals, with the same device as in the second number of the series.

The fourth is a literal transfer to the organ of the duet for soprano and tenor, *Er denket der Barmherzigkeit,* from the cantata, *Meine Seel' erhebt den Herrn,* (see p. 415), the two voice parts being given to the left hand, the chorale (which in the cantata is given to the oboe and trumpet) to the right hand, and the continuo part to the pedals.

The fifth is an abbreviated transfer of the solo for soprano *Ach bleib' bei uns, Herr Jesu Christ* in the cantata *Bleib' bei uns,* in which the ornate part of the violoncello piccolo is given to the left hand and the voice part to the right. The sixth movement, *Kommst du nun, Jesu,* is a transfer of the alto solo in the cantata *Lobe den Herrn, den mächtigen König der Ehren,* in which the chorale, sung by the soloist in the cantata, is yet again given to the pedals, as in the second and third number of the collection, and the solo violin part and the continuo to the hands.

The collection is characteristic of the composer in many ways, especially of his noteworthy habit of trying his works in various different guises. It was evidently made with the intention of being engraved and published, and was so engraved in the composer's lifetime by Schübler of Zelle, from which circumstance the works are commonly known as the "Schüblerschen Choräle." And it may be observed, in view of the lack of discrimination which purists sometimes display in finding fault with the performance of sundry arrangements of Bach's works, that this collection gives an emphatic endorsement of that practice by the composer himself.

With this collection it seems most natural to couple the set of eighteen works on chorales, the title-page of which is an almost exact counterpart of that above described. But if the accepted story of the revision of the final movement of the series is true, it is obvious that the collection could not have been completed by Bach himself (see p. 542). But since nearly all the movements exist in fair copy in Bach's own hand in the Berlin Library it is probable that he began revising and bringing together what he considered the finest of his chorale movements, and did not live to complete the series, and that his son-in-law Altnikol added the last movement afterwards.

The collection contains many movements on chorales which are of most imposing proportions. Bach probably favoured them specially as representing the utmost limit of development of which the form seemed capable. Of such the long fantasias on *Komm heiliger Geist*, *Herr Jesu Christ dich zu uns wend*, *O Lamm Gottes unschuldig*, the second and third of the three on *Nun komm, der Heiden Heiland*, the second and third on *Allein Gott in der Höh'*, and *Jesus Christus unser Heiland* are examples. They nearly all consist of fine ramifications of characteristic passages in the accompanying parts with the chorale in long notes. Among these the second on *Nun komm,' der Heiden Heiland* and the third on *Allein Gott in der Höh'* are trios, dealt with in the same style as the trio sonatas (p. 500), in which passages which cross one another on the two manuals are special features. In strong contrast are two beautiful slow movements on *Von Gott will ich nicht lassen* and the first on *Allein Gott in der Höh'*, which are in a reflective mood, and exquisitely elaborated with subtleties of ornament and other details. The first of the two is a parallel example to those in the "Schüblerschen Choräle" in which the pedal is marked for 4-foot stops, and therefore plays the melody high among the other parts, the left hand taking the bass. The latter is marked adagio and the tune is daintily and reverently ornamented, the ornamentation culminating in a characteristic cadenza at the close. The movement on *Nun danket Alle Gott* is notable for the fidelity with which it follows the scheme of the so-called "Pachelbel Choralvorspiel," in the anticipation of each phrase of the chorale by the accompanying parts in shorter notes than the tune. The movement on *Komm, Gott, Schöpfer* is quite different from all the rest, being an expansion of the little movement on the same chorale in the Orgel-Büchlein (see p. 185). Bach must have been interested in the experiment and was possibly disappointed with the effect of its expansion. For the long passage which is added (being a repetition in the bass of the chorale tune which had first been in the treble) entirely ignores the characteristic figures of the opening, and adopts the scheme of spacious passage writing which was more sure of being effective. *An Wasserflüssen Babylon* is slow moving, quiet, and meditative; in a similar mood to the movement founded on the same chorale which has been before referred to (see p. 504). A special atmosphere is imparted by the manner in which the melodic passage in which Bach has presented the first phrase of the chorale seems to echo through the whole movement, as though he loved to toy with it in all manner of disguises. In this case the presentment of the chorale in the tenor part is not in long notes but in notes of the same value as those of the accompanying parts, which seems in the particular case to have a very happy effect.

One of the most beautiful of all, *Schmücke dich, O liebe Seele,* may be coupled with *An Wasserflüssen Babylon,* as it is in the same meditative vein, and has much the same tender devotional atmosphere. In this case the chorale tune is given in long notes in the treble and is only ornamented with moderation. The effect it produces on the sympathetic listener is indescribable, as if Bach could be felt to be communing with his own soul, which he had adorned with all the loveliest qualities a poetic imagination could supply. The story is told by Schumann in a letter addressed to Mendelssohn, how the latter played this movement on some occasion to the former, and it seemed as though "around the cantus firmus hung winding wreaths of golden leaves, and such blissfulness was breathed from within it, that you yourself avowed that if life was bereft of all hope and faith, this one chorale would renew them for you. I was silent and went away dazed into God's acre, feeling acutely pained that I could lay no flower on his urn."

The last of the series, *Vor deinen Thron tret' ich,*

is in the same vein, but consideration of it must be deferred till later.

Another work which belongs to the latest years of his life is the series of "Variations" on the Christmas chorale *Vom Himmel hoch*, which appears to have been written for the Leipzig Musical Society, possibly as a compliment, on his joining it in 1747. The so-called Variations are not Variations in the ordinary sense of the term, but chorale fantasias and chorale preludes. The collection has an affinity to the Goldberg Variations, inasmuch as each movement presents a canon of some sort. In the first movement the canon (at the octave) is between the accompanying parts which are given to the hands, the pedals having the chorale in its unadorned simplicity. In the second, again, the pedals have the tune, but the music for the hands presents the interesting quality of being on the lines of the Pachelbel type of the chorale prelude, the musical figures anticipating the chorale in quicker time—as in the first chorus of *Ein' feste Burg,*—and out of these figures Bach makes a fluent and tuneful canon at the fifth below, in a characteristic manner combining two principles. The third movement presents a canon at the seventh with a free part, and the chorale in the treble; the fourth movement has a canon by augmentation and a free part for the hands, and the chorale on the pedals. The last movement is a singular *tour de force.* It begins with a canon by inversion at the sixth on the tune of the chorale, which is given entire in that abstruse canonic form with a free bass, and the music, without staying its course, immediately presents the chorale in canon by inversion at the third, and going on in the same fashion, as soon as one canon is finished presenting another by inversion at the second, then at the ninth, and ending in five parts, including pedal, with a profusion of little canons in diminution, which seem to be tumbling over one another in their eagerness to get into the scheme before the inexorable limits of formal proportion shut the door with the final cadence.

The musical effect in these variations is subordinated to the display of skill. The third and fourth variations contain some beautiful music: otherwise the work illustrates the type referred to above in which the tribute to the chorale is rather of the head than of the heart. Bach had so constantly used his highest skill for the purposes of devotional expression that he seems to have arrived at the frame of mind which, through association, felt the skill itself to be something sacred and devotional. Such a situation is not unfamiliar with other composers besides Bach, when diminution of spontaneously inventive powers impels them to lay stress on their technical attainments. But on the other hand Bach may have been impelled to produce a sample of his amazing mastery, such as no other man living or indeed any man of any other time could emulate, in order to gratify the members of the Leipzig Musical Society, who prided themselves on their excessive valuation of theory, and were more likely to appreciate his feats of skill than the most deeply felt music he could set before them.

It is said that the manuscript of this work betrays in several places the signs of failing sight. Bach had subjected his eyes to a truly immense strain from the first. Very few men have ever transferred such a prodigious mass of original work to paper; and besides his own compositions he had copied a vast quantity of other people's, and he often wrote out the parts of his own works for performances. Besides all this huge quantity of writing, his daily work must have been in great part done by reading from manuscript, which is much more trying to the eyes than print. So the wonder is rather that his eyes lasted so long than that they showed ominous signs of collapse about the time that he was sixty years old. In the later years of the fifth decade of the eighteenth century the state of affairs was so serious that he was induced to submit to two operations, which were worse than unsuccessful, as they left him blind. This appears to have been at the beginning of 1750. In July, however, his sight was for a time partially restored; but his health was quite broken and his family and friends foresaw the inevitable end. So it came about that his last work, in the form that he loved so dearly, was finished on his death-bed.

It is said that some time before he had begun a chorale prelude on the tune *Wenn wir in höchsten Nöthen sein* ("When we are in deepest need"). He now completed it—tradition says by dictating the music to his pupil and son-in-law Altnikol—and with touching sincerity of devotion he altered the title from the piteous expression of deepest need to the words *Vor deinen Thron tret' ich* ("I come before Thy throne!"). Death had always had a strange fascination for him, and many of his most beautiful compositions had been inspired by the thoughts which it suggested. And now he met it, not with repinings or fear of the unknown, but with the expression of exquisite peace and trust. Music had been his life. Music had been his one means of expressing himself, and in the musical form which had been most congenial to him he bids his farewell; and only in the last bar of all for a moment a touch of sadness is felt, where he seems to look round upon those dear to him and to cast upon them the tender gaze of sorrowing love.

And with that last phrase his earthly labours ended, on July 28, 1750.

CHAPTER XVII

POSTSCRIPT

For over a hundred and fifty years since Bach's death composers have been constantly endeavouring to enhance their artistic resources; and yet with all their devoted and unsparing efforts they do not appear to have got much beyond the standard of his achievements. In some respects, indeed, they seem like people who have turned aside from a path which appeared rather too arduous and have gone a long way round, only to find themselves after a long climb at much the same place as they started from.

No doubt the aspect of art has enormously changed. The whole story of the development of the classical sonata, and the orchestral symphony, and the music drama, and chamber music, and the modern song and romantic and pyrotechnical pianoforte music has intervened; and, as Bach dealt in none of these things, it may be admitted that his range of art was limited, inasmuch as it is devoid of many of the features which they represent. The effect is most noticeable in his use of his orchestral forces, and the gaps induced by his acceptance of that unfortunate makeshift, the figured bass; and it is also noticeable in the lack of stress laid on formal distribution of contrasting keys in his work. As has frequently been said, Bach's ways of using his instrumental forces can hardly be described as orchestration in the modern sense. With occasional exceptions, he writes for all his instruments, whether wind or strings, on free contrapuntal principles and on equal terms, just as he would write for voices; and when such usage is eked out by a figured bass to fill up gaps in the harmony, it must be admitted that the problems of orchestration have not been completely solved.

In such matters as the effective use of tone quality and all that appertains to genuine orchestral effect, modern music has made gigantic strides. And it has made some also in the understanding of harmonic and tonal relations. Very nearly the whole function of the long story of the classical sonata was to teach men to regard relations of keys as the basis of artistic organisation. And since that important period was completed, the efforts of composers have been applied to turn the recognition of key relationships to account for the purposes of expression. Bach had little concern with relationships of keys in the formal sense, though he made some interesting experiments in such directions which have been discussed. His chief business was with polyphonic work; and the early phases of the new kind of harmonic music of the sonata order, though they were due to lead to great results, were too poor and invertebrate in his time to beget any impulse to follow them seriously or strenuously. In fact, considering the infantile standard of harmonic music of his time, it would have been almost impossible to be strenuous in it at all. The familiar fact referred to at the beginning of the chapter was confirmed most amply, as at the beginning of the seventeenth century. When men think they have found a new path in art they do not start from the point at which the old path has arrived, but a very long way back. And they have to toil a long way up the old ascent once more, before they can pick up again the level they had left. And then they go forward by combining the new forms of artistic activity with the old. So true is it that there is no break of continuity in the story of the development of art.

Bach's sphere was the final exposition of the possibilities of polyphonic art, and when the composers after his time had developed the principles of harmonic music far enough to feel assurance and freedom in the use of them, they combined their kind of art with Bach's polyphonic methods, and made them most effective in the very department of art in which Bach was most deficient—namely, orchestration. The difference being that the various instruments representing different tone qualities are employed in modern orchestration in the enunciation of the musical passages which are most apt to their individualities, and not merely items in a contrapuntal network; and that the polyphonic treatment of the various instruments ministers to that extravagant delight in subtleties of colour or tone quality which threatens the possible disintegration of modern art.

Apart from these matters of orchestration and harmonic form, Bach does not lose much from not having the classical sonata behind him. The principle of contrast of key was in the air in his time and he caught it sufficiently to anticipate a great deal that was going to happen. In the use of modulations for the purposes of expression he often forestalled the most surprising effects of the most adventurous modern composers, both in vocal music (as in recitatives and ariosos) and in such instrumental works as the Chromatische Fantasie and the great Fantasia in G minor for the organ. His enrichment of harmony by polyphonic methods in choral music, organ music, and clavier music makes the effect as complete and rich as that of the most advanced modern achievements. Even the composers who appear to aim at being several generations ahead of their time are glad to take a hint from him now and again, and do not always surpass him in the issue.

It appears, therefore, that the sum total is unequal. On the one hand, certain large groups of works can be taken absolutely without reserve as being as fully and perennially mature and complete in every artistic requirement as works written nearly two hundred years later. In other branches, wherever, for instance, the figured bass comes in, the work has to be accepted with mental adjustments. But even where the effect, from the more exacting modern point of view, is inadequate, it can hardly ever be made good. The only torsos which can be completed are those which are not worth completing. The inadequate and incomplete work, which is characteristic of the time, is still John Sebastian's, and it is too characteristic of him to be meddled with. In its very inadequacies it often gives gleams of his unique individuality which would be marred in the mending. Even if it be admitted that there are a few points which might be modified,—as for instance the stupefying *da capo* at the end of the first chorus in

Mit Fried' und Freud', and the similar misfortune in *Es erhub sich ein Streit,* and the galling oboes in many places where they have no business nowadays, whatever may have been inevitable in St. Thomas's Church on Sundays and festivals,—it is only by knowing Bach's work intimately that such apparent sacrilege may be compatible with the most reverent respect.

There certainly is no composer whose work more fully repays intimate knowledge. But then there arises the awkward question, how such acquaintance can possibly be attained. Bach's life's output is so enormous that even the rare enthusiasts who chance to combine sincere intentions with an exceptional allowance of leisure may well be driven to despair of ever mastering a subject so vast. Moreover the old type-story of the treasure that is fenced about with an infinity of obstacles seems here to be revived. The knowledge of John Sebastian is not attained without much searching of spirit, and an expenditure of energy which requires an ample supply of faith and conviction to maintain. Like all art which is full to the brim, his work has proved difficult for average human beings to understand; and those who have not the natural aptitude for understanding run some risk of finding none to help them thereto. All great music is difficult to realise because it requires correspondence of spirit in the interpreter with the greatness of utterance, and a capacity to rise to its height; and there is not any music which calls for more interpretation than Bach's.

But a great deal of Bach's work is rendered difficult of access by other circumstances besides the difficulty of interpretation. The church cantatas, which form by far the largest part of his works (for in spite of losses there are still over a hundred and ninety of them) were composed for and under conditions so unique that comparatively few of them are fit to be performed with any hope of producing the effect intended. The stress under which they were composed limited precariously the consideration due to the human weaknesses of the solo singers; it caused the composer to omit many directions which would have helped his admirers (whom he did not anticipate) in later times. It caused him to put in many features which it gratified him to execute, which were quite admissible for the special performance which he had in mind when writing, but are stumbling-blocks in other conditions. The very limitations of the resources of performance which were available to him caused him to idealise the actual and physical possibilities of orchestra, chorus, and soli. As he could not have a competent collection of performers, he wrote as for the ideal performers he called up in imagination—the only thing he could do under the circumstances and in view of the nature of his artistic impulses. And owing to the changing circumstances, the ideal performers are as little likely to present themselves in later days as the ideal conditions of performance. The melancholy conclusion seems inevitable that the greater part of this vast region of art is inaccessible except to those who can read it in imagination, and divine the wonderful revelations of the personality of the composer without the aid of their ears.

But even if the majority of the church cantatas can be admitted to be knowable to average mortals only by a limited process of selection, the array of other works seems almost paralysing in its extent:—the great motets, which can be performed only by the largest choirs of exceptional efficiency; the great sacred works such as the Magnificat, the Passions, the B Minor Mass, which require all the machinery of orchestra, chorus, soli, and a conductor who understands what Bach wants—at least twenty suites of over five movements apiece which can be played only by performers gifted with highly developed intelligence and technique; concertos by the score, overtures, hundreds of preludes and fugues, variations, toccatas, fantasias for clavier and organ, and several hundreds of movements based on chorales—all deserve the fullest attention. There is hardly an item in the whole list whose performance would not require assiduous work and devotion. It is not merely a question of technique, but of getting into touch with the intentions. There are hundreds of pianists, who can play the most brilliant and difficult concert pieces by the most ingenious virtuosos, to one who can realise such exquisitely poetical inspirations as the chorale preludes and chorale-fantasias and arrangements of chorales for the organ. However great the demands upon the technique in Bach's work, the demands on the musical intelligence are greater. The technique is called upon to present the letter and the intelligence the spirit that is embodied in the letter, and the constant and concentrated work which Bach had devoted to mastering all the mysteries of art gave him such readiness in things that appertain to the letter that nothing stood in the way of prompt utterance of the things that represent the spirit. Given the type of method to be followed, it mattered little what was the difficulty of the procedure, the prompt mind supplied at once the adequate artistic expression.

Yet it cannot be pretended that he was easily satisfied. When the first drafts of compositions can be found, they show wholesale erasures, even impatient smudgings out of passages which he felt to be inadequate, and copious corrections of detail. Different versions of the same works, with amplifications and reconstructions, abound. The two versions of the Magnificat, of which the first is almost illegible from the haste in which it was written, show how carefully he reconsidered his works, and even in the case of the "Matthäus-Passion," trustworthy records tell of comprehensive revisions. Like Beethoven, he tried and tested the schemes and the details of his works from different points of view and in different attitudes of mind; and since he did not begin to engrave his works till late in life, he could always change as much as he pleased without having to withdraw a superseded edition. While Beethoven's revisions have to be looked for in the sketch books, Bach's are mainly found in the various versions of complete works. Their attitude of mind was almost identical. Both were men of great temperament, seeking the expression of their personalities on grand lines; and both had to face the necessity of exploring regions unknown and untried; and both, in doing so, set their feet securely on the known before they ventured into the unknown. Bach's transformation of the form of the fugue was exactly analogous to Beethoven's transformation of the classical sonata. In both of them the impulse was to infuse new life into a well-established, even hackneyed, form. The technicalities of the form in both cases served them as a basis on which to build; but the technicalities were soon made subordinate to the higher purpose of musical expression in the widest sense; and in both cases, the principles laid down as essential to the requirements of design were set aside when a more spacious view of the possibilities of music made clear to them the necessity for a wider interpretation of principles of form. It was the abandonment of mere traditions and regulations which made so much experiment and re-experiment inevitable. In the search for the satisfactory solution of new problems, instinct had to supply the place of tradition, and experiment to verify the results.

Bach not only took infinite pains to develop his musical insight, as has been shown, by the close scrutiny to which he subjected the works of other composers; the spirit of adventure was strong in him and impelled him constantly to speculative courses. This is shown in every phase of his work. When the mood was on him, his part-writing is sometimes positively reckless, and the voice parts occasionally almost unsingable. But yet it is not the clumsiness of the composer who does not know how to write otherwise, but the conviction of one who chooses the more stirring course because that expresses most decisively what is in his mind. His experimental ventures were serviceable in other ways; for, while the mere procedure of contrapuntal art had been thoroughly explored and tested before his time, the various structural types were far otherwise, and he was bent on finding as many different schemes as possible wherein to cast the musical impulses which welled up in him. It was for this end that he not only speculated in all kinds of forms such as concertos, suites, variations, sonatas, overtures, sinfonias, chorale-preludes, chorale-fantasias, but tried how one could be combined with another, and how they could be transferred from the sphere for which they had been devised into new conditions. It was with the view of widening his resources of design that he imported the form of the French and the Italian overtures and concertos into the choral movements of his cantatas; that he expanded the form of the chorale preludes and fantasias into immense choruses, adapted the orchestral concerto to a solo instrument, and adorned his instrumental fugues with unfugal episodes annexed from other types of art.

All such novel experiments were tested by his own musical instinct and not by reference to schemes propounded by theorists. He anticipated the fact that form is another word for organisation, and that organisation varies in its relation to the quality of the matter or ideas dealt with and the style adopted. His methods of organisation cover the field from one extreme to another. Such rhapsodical forms as some of the Toccatas, the great Fantasia in G minor, and the Chromatische Fantasie, with its bravura passages and its recitatives, represent the utmost of elasticity; while the systematic plans that he adopted in some of his cantata choruses are so decisive and clear as to verge, in extreme cases, on the mechanical.

It is worth observing that the forms of the rhapsodical movements appear in the end to be even more convincing than the forms which are easy to analyse on mechanical principles; and it may be added that he is almost invariably at his best in movements which have a rhapsodical character, because the type is most congenial to the Teutonic mind. The classical ideal was essentially Italian in the emphasis laid on mechanical symmetry of design; the romantic ideal lays stress on the demands of the spiritual, and claims the right to subordinate mechanical symmetry to poetic thought. In the end the symmetry is of equal force in the romantic forms, but it is based on deeper principles. In showing how congenial rhapsodical and original forms were to him, Bach showed his kinship with all the greatest German composers of a hundred years and more after his death. He was seeking for a psychological basis of form, as a type that was more deeply rooted than form which was entirely compassed by musical terms and formulas; and in arriving at the personal solution of such problems he was a good deal aided by the nature of the fugal form. For in the fugue more stress is laid upon the distribution of the thematic material than upon tonal form, and it is therefore more elastic in its general plan; and of this elasticity he took the fullest advantage. For, as has been shown, he was often driven by his impulses to abandon the accepted principles of fugal structure, even in the distribution of the thematic material, and to use his subjects rather as bonds of cohesion and as providing for the necessary intellectual side of art, while in the laying out of the movements he followed his instinct and rejoiced in appeals to the sensibilities.

These features are most in evidence in his organ works, which, however wonderful in texture, make their appeal to mankind in general by the supreme insight they display into the intrinsic power of the organ for stirring the susceptibilities of human creatures. The intellectualist is driven to confess that the composer affords him the amplest satisfaction by the superb manipulation of the thematic material, and the ordinary hearer who cares very little about thematic material finds ample provision made for him also in the appeals to his senses. This shows, among other things, that Bach's personality combined the primitive human qualities in large measure with the amplest outfit of the intellectual qualities.

His humanity manifested itself in many and various ways. He delighted in frank rhythm. No composer ever attained to anything approaching the spontaneity, freshness, and winsomeness of his dances, such as the gavottes, bourrées, passepieds, and gigues in the suites; while many of his great choruses and his instrumental fugues are inspired with a force of rhythmic movement which thrills the hearer with a feeling of being swept into space out of the range of common things. But his ample humanity is equally shown in his love of melody. He is wonderful enough in the more conventional and regular forms of tune, but far more so in the deeply expressive rhapsodical melody, the outpouring of copious and genuine feeling, such as is displayed in his ariosos, the slow movements for solo violin, and the slow movement of the Italian concerto. Here again he anticipates the trend of true Teutonic melody, free, unconstrained, welling out untrammelled by convention, the direct emanation of spiritual exaltation.

Bach's way of giving such rhapsodical melodies coherence emphasises the dependence of melody on harmony, and the degree to which harmony influences the meaning of melody; and in harmony is found Bach's sublimest attribute, the factor which completes his artistic outfit in the most decisive fashion. Men before him had tried to find the true sphere of harmony in the scheme of expression, such as Monteverde, Schütz, even Purcell; but he not only found and, perhaps unconsciously, realised its sphere, but attained almost at once to the command of the entire gamut of its possibilities. The frankest expression of the sheer might of his harmony is in the overwhelming successions of suspensions which are met with in his organ works, such as the Toccatas in C major (see p. 508) and D minor (see p. 64). His motive in some cases is the delight of interweaving great masses of sound to contrast with passages of elaborate figuration, but in others it is the delight in the supreme power of harmony as a means of expression. The endless variety of expression of the harmonies in the chorales which come at the end of most of his cantatas, the sublime expression of the last few bars of the Crucifixus, the central portion of the Confiteor, the conclusion of the Chorale-prelude *O Mensch, bewein' dein' Sünde gross*, show how fully he realised the highest capacities of harmony.

The influence of the classical sonata after his time set back the range of harmony as a factor in expression and tended to limit it to the functions of form, and it was not till Beethoven's latest works that anything like an equal recognition of its powers was shown again. Even then it was hampered by the newly developed harmonic conceptions. Bach's great opportunity lay in the polyphonic aspect of his art—the fruit of the habit of looking upon harmony as the result of combined parts, which facilitated the production of infinite varieties of combinations of sound as the result of independent concurrent melodies, when ornaments and passing notes clashed with one another without stint and made the possibilities of harmonic variety almost unlimited. And it was through this attitude of mind that his harmony attains such an extraordinary degree of vitality. He realised quite early in his career that mere bald harmony without inner motion is too often dead weight, and that the movement of its components, either by counterpoint or figuration, is necessary to give it full artistic life. And in this sphere the supreme mastery of technical resource which his ceaseless labours produced served him in the greatest stead. His readiness and the absolute ease with which he manipulated large numbers of parts produced texture of a richness which seems almost unapproachable. The choruses in which all the voices have their independent melodies, accompanied by instrumental parts which also go their own way independently of the voices, are phenomena of complex means to single ends which are entirely unique. But on the other hand the effects which are produced by an intentionally limited number of parts are as wonderful. For Bach was by no means of the order of composers who produce their effects only by multiplying the factors, and overwhelm with mere volume of sound. He knew as well as any composer how to overwhelm with sound, but he could also overwhelm by the subtlety with which he could manipulate two or three parts. Even a single part was made at times to represent harmony and to supply the suggestion of melody, combined with it, as may be seen in his sonatas for solo violin; and this method of quasi-multiplication is sometimes made use of even when many parts are employed, so that it may be said that some of his works in many parts imply and suggest even more parts than are actually engaged in the operations.

Such powers must have afforded him pleasure in the exercise, and there is not the least doubt that the results afforded him pleasure also. He could not have achieved the great effects of his organ works unless he himself enjoyed them; and the same must have been the case with the motets, however inadequate the performances may have been. Even when his works were not performed, the power of a musician to hear every detail of a complicated work in imagination supplied an approximate alternative; and, as a rule, the imaginative hearing is more critical than the actual, as the faculties are less likely to be swamped by the excitement of the senses. So the fact that he never heard some of his greatest works performed with even the most distant approach to adequacy, would not interfere with the pleasure such an artistic nature must have felt in contemplating them.

But in all this there is a deeper truth. Bach's ways of making one part serve for many, of combining an infinite variety of parts, of associating the richest harmony with expressively ornate melody in terms of the most spacious rhythms, all point to the copious variety of his vital energies. The powers of many successful composers have been limited to one department alone of the elements of art. Some are quite incapable of anything but tune, some are incapable of anything but harmony, and some limit their aspirations to counterpoint, some have only rhythmic sense and some only sense of colour; but to Bach it was indispensable that he should have equal command of every side of art, in order to make it match and adequately represent the spiritual wealth and complexity of his nature. With sundry intelligible exceptions, it may be taken as a rule that composers who only use one or two of the resources of art are men of small, narrow, or undeveloped minds. The limited range of language is adequate to reveal the limited soul. The great temperament wrestles and strives, concentrates the whole panoply of vital forces under the stress of the utmost craving to find adequate presentment of its subjective states. The complexity of Bach's work certainly gave him pleasure, but it was not because the contemplation of it flattered him, but because the use of the vast variety of resources represented an expression of his inmost and most sacred feelings with sufficient adequacy to reawaken and revive rare states of spiritual exaltation. There surely is nothing ignoble or debasing in a man's renewing in himself the finest moments of his spiritual life, by contemplating the record as manifested in his own art. When a man considers his work from the point of view which he supposes to be that of the public, he prunes off what he thinks they will not care about; but contemplation from the point of view of his own feelings begets self-criticism and the continuous expansion of scope.

As has been said elsewhere, the scope of a work of art lies in the range and variety of sentiment and resource which it displays; Bach's scope was so comprehensive and concentrated that he frequently cumulates several traits of thought and emotion simultaneously. One of his favourite devices is to throw in an independent comment on the sentiment expressed by the parts which are associated with the words, by characteristic figures in the accompaniment, by counter-subjects, even by references to extraneous chorale tunes. The idea may actually have come to him first in connection with counter-subjects of fugues, which often have a commentatory character. But he does not confine himself to combining sentiments in different parts. It is by no means uncommon to find a single part representing several different concepts, or different aspects of the same idea. The figure of two notes given to the pedals in the Chorale prelude *Durch Adams Fall* (see p. 184) is interpreted by one commentator to be the expression of profound sorrow at the awesome idea of the Fall and its consequences; by another it is held to be one of Bach's quaintly symbolic touches of realistic suggestion. The latter is obviously right, and so, perhaps, is the former; and if it were added that Bach wrote the figure because it was convenient to the pedals, and also because it introduced a characteristic rhythmic element into the movement, and also because the broken character of the passage was of æsthetic value in relation to the continuity of the passages given to the hands, he would not have half exhausted the multitudinous motives which impelled the composer. The justification of the practice of transferring movements originally written to secular words, to works which were to serve for sacred purposes, lies in such many-sided implications; for where a single passage or movement represents various combined intentions, different meanings may be specially emphasised.

Bach verified the fact, that has been overlooked by many well-meaning advocates of programme music, that music's relation to the external aspects of things is a very small part of its functions; but that it combines an unlimited number of sentiments and associations with a central idea, and includes such a vast variety of connotations of any particular concept that words cannot either cope with or summarise its richest manifestations. Its sphere is different from that of words; and those who maintain that technical analysis covers the ground of what artistic souls may admire, are as much at fault as the idealists and impressionists who appear to think that great masters have provided the resources of art to enable moderns to represent the concrete facts of human life and the external aspects of cosmic cataclysms. The really imaginative poet-musician feels the almost infinite suggestions which radiate even from a domestic incident, which to the ordinary complacent person is purely a commonplace fact; and can move mankind by telling them what he feels about it in real music far more than the unimaginative maker of effects could do by a realistic representation of the eruptions of Krakatoa and Mont Pélée and the earthquakes in Valparaiso and San Francisco all rolled into one. It is the range of the field of imagination excited by the initiatory thought which shows the scope of the temperament. Music does not require cataclysms to evoke its power; the slightest incident which has any touching, beautiful, elevating, or otherwise emotional associations is sufficient, if, as in Bach's case, the range of command of artistic resources is proportionate to the imaginative activity.

This inevitably leads to the threshold of the important question whether great art should admit the expression of the baser qualities of human nature or only select the nobler. There, obviously, the question of opera comes in. For the adequate presentation of a dramatic subject it is indispensable that music should accept frankly the mission of expressing the vicious, the spiteful, even the mean and crafty and base. The responsibility of the composer is shifted. The music ceases to be representative of his own personality, and only suggests his imaginative self-transference into some other personality — the extent to which the practice of performing operatic excerpts in concert rooms has modified the conception of unoperatic music cannot be gainsaid. It is obvious, in any case, that the sense of personal responsibility for music which is not intended for the stage has been weakened. But in Bach's time such a situation was not even foreshadowed on the most distant horizon. Mild as was the operatic standard of his time, he had next to nothing to do with it. He studied the operatic airs of his forerunners and contemporaries, and, pressure of time and urgent labour constraining him, accepted the mere form of the operatic aria for the majority of his solo movements in the cantatas. It may further be admitted in a passing parenthesis that the arias are for the most part the least personal and the least successful manifestations of his powers. But apart from them it is the quality of the personality in Bach's works which is of such supreme importance and interest. Even if men on the advice of their chosen prophets abandon the old theory of the sincerity and nobility of art, human nature at least will pay tribute to the greatness of spirit, nobility of disposition, sincerity and singleness of heart which are so amply displayed. The foundation of Bach's musical personality is devotionalism. But it was a devotionalism so spacious and comprehensive that a large portion of its manifestations were emotions applicable to human life at large in its noblest phases. All the purely ornamental part of ritual is conspicuously absent from his religious works; and even if Lutheran theology influenced the product, it did not cause the drying up of the sources of independent inspiration.

As has been shown, the line of demarcation between his sacred and secular works is not at all decisive. The moods which manifested themselves in the latter are, for the most part, not at all out of place in sacred surroundings, and the loftiness of the standard of style makes all the phases akin. The conditions of his life ministered constantly to this emphasis on personality, for the persistent labour in which it must have been passed in order to develop his powers and produce the enormous mass of his works, inevitably enhanced the predisposition to meditation:—to his paying more attention to the art as it affected himself than as it affected other people. As has been said, he was never much of a public man, though his organ works show an ample measure of the characteristics of a public performer. But even as a public performer he was an idealist, and thought more of those who might be on a level with himself in perception than of the hosts of those who can be imposed upon by vain show. His instinct of responsibility to his art had grown to such a strength by the time he attained to a more public position at Leipzig that he still went on writing as if it were mainly for himself. His supreme interest was to explore all the possibilities of art, and to go on from strength to strength until the end.

But it is well not to lose sight of the fact that the

conditions of his life were not without their drawbacks. The stress under which his work was often done made him reiterate any scheme which had proved efficacious to the extent of nearly arriving at monotony. This has been pointed out in connection with the plan of his later cantatas, it must certainly be admitted in connection with his *da capo* arias, and also with certain features of his instrumentation. It made him adopt a certain procedure at relatively the same points in many movements; such as the sequences which so frequently manifest themselves after the presentation of his subjects. It also betrayed him into allowing his wonderful susceptibility to respond too hastily. He was susceptible to everything; a salient word, or an analogy, or an association of sentiment all quickly generated the musical response, and sometimes the salient word was not the one which gave the true meaning of the sentence. Moreover the salient word too often invited the realistic suggestion, of which many examples have been given, such as the laughter in *Unser Mund sei voll Lachens* and the *Erschrecke* passage in the tenor aria in *Herr Deine Augen sehen nach dem Glauben* (p. 444).

Such realistic suggestions, which were doubtless symbolic to him, caused him, in the stress of work, not to apply the full measure of his judgment. Yet they are, after all, but one feature out of many in the complex presentation of his inner nature, and they are generally amply counterbalanced by simultaneous musical traits of higher efficacy. Their existence is probably due to lack of time for reconsideration, and they occur for the most part only in works which had to be finished by a given time.

When trying to estimate the reasons for the lack of general appreciation of Bach's work in his own time it is obvious that whereas he concentrated so much of his powers on the infinite possibilities of polyphony, by an odd fatality, those were just the artistic phenomena which the world in general was ceasing to care about. Bach's career just coincides with the first stages of the era of the classical sonata and the Italian opera. The two things went together because they both represented a simplified form of art in which clearness and orderliness of design were the main requirements, and these properties made music much easier to listen to. The effect was to make the fashionable people who patronised art disinclined for concentration of mind and for the attitude of energetic receptivity which is indispensable to the appreciation of art's highest manifestations. The musical pabulum of the majority of the prosperous and fashionable folk was innocent and polite babble carefully administered in unvarying conventional quantities. Later on, more strenuous lovers of instrumental music were led step by step back to a higher standard of the new kind of art, by Philipp Emanuel Bach, Mozart, Haydn, and Beethoven; but the impetus of the downward tendency of the opera continued for a century, till it arrived at the unspeakable humiliations of the Italian opera of the first half of the nineteenth century.

Over and above these influences, the world was just beginning to turn its back on true devotional music. Bach said the last word in that line for nearly a century; while other composers were engaged in supplying smart Sunday congregations with colourless samples of the same sort of music they had been listening to at the opera in the week, leaving the insignificant few whose religion was a reality to look for their music in humble corners. In fact, the section of the world which had any connection with music was like a mob that suddenly turns its back on an orator to look at mountebanks, whose amiable antics amuse without calling for any exercise of energetic attention. Bach went on his way and expended the full powers of his well endowed nature in developing every available side of his art, so that it might minister ever more and more to the full expression of every phase of sentiment, association, æsthetic interest, and emotional utterance; and the more he achieved, the farther he got away from the trend of the art of his time. Indolence is always ready to accept any subtle hint which excuses the relaxation of attention. It was sufficient for the little petty weaknesses of human nature that it should be rumoured abroad that one John Sebastian Bach was a queer old sedentary organist, who devoted the greater part of his life to the contriving of extraordinary musical puzzles, and that such dry mechanical futilities were quite old-fashioned and out of the pale of any intelligent connoisseur's attention. Not only were the ears deaf, but what filtered through them found the mental machinery out of gear. The attitude of the world to Bach was so absolutely indifferent that as soon as he was dead it almost seemed as if a humble and obscure story was ended.

A certain fame he had as an organ player, as one who could do sundry things which other people could not, as a strong and independent personality. When his funeral took place on July 31, 1750, it was emphasised mainly as that of an official of St. Thomas's School, and was attended by the school. The indefatigable Philipp Spitta found a note written on a quarto sheet, in the library of the Historical Society at Leipzig, which records that the preacher at St. Thomas's Church on that date made the bare announcement that "the worthy and venerable Herr Johann Sebastian Bach, Hofcomponist to His Kingly Majesty of Poland and Cantor to the School of St. Thomas in this town, having fallen calmly and blessedly asleep in God, his body has this day, according to Christian usage, been consigned to the earth in St. John's Churchyard."

Of so little importance did the matter appear that Spitta, whose devoted efforts to discover every detail of interest in connection with his hero were quite inexhaustible, can only report vaguely that the grave was near the church; and that when, in the following century, rearrangement of public thoroughfares necessitated the removal of the ancient graveyard to make way for a road, the traces of its position were completely swept away, and the place of it was known no more. The reference which was made to Bach's death at a meeting of the Town Council shortly after was businesslike, unfriendly, and couched in terms which could not possibly have been used if anyone had had the very faintest glimmering of Bach's greatness as a composer. It spoke of him as "a great musician, but not a schoolmaster," and generally observed that "the school required a Cantor and not a Kapellmeister."

Even more piteous was what followed. Anna Magdalena, for whom, remembering her beautiful connection with her husband, it is difficult not to feel a personal affection, whose life had been intertwined with his so long by the tenderest strands, whose handwriting appears so often mingled with his, whose musical nature had been nurtured so tenderly by him, fell into the direst poverty, for a time was in receipt of charity, and died as an almswoman in 1760, and all traces of the place of her burial have disappeared.

As has been said, very few of Bach's compositions were printed in his lifetime, and most of his manuscripts were divided between his sons Friedemann and Philipp Emanuel after his death. To the carefulness and discreetness of the latter the world owes the greater part of what has remained accessible in later days. What Friedemann took was, owing to his dissipated habits, lost or sold piecemeal when destitution came upon him. Some works fell into the hands of men who appreciated their value, and have been recovered; some were hopelessly lost. Yet there must have been some continuity between the closing of his life's work and the reawakening of the world to his message some half a century and more later; and this was mainly supplied by the tradition which he handed down to his various pupils, and the permanent influence he established upon their artistic convictions.

Sufficient has been said of his discomforts in connection with the choir of St. Thomas's Church, and of his relations with the authorities of the school, to justify the inference that he lacked the disposition for managing boys or inspiring them with any regard for his authority. But it must certainly have been otherwise with young men of sense and ability who had the privilege of becoming his pupils, for he left behind a remarkable group of distinguished musicians who were sufficiently imbued with the influence of his spirit to keep the memory of his work alive. Several of such pupils were of his own stock, such as his unfortunate eldest son Friedemann, by whose gifts he set such store, and Philipp Emanuel, who at least had the advantage of living in such a glorious musical atmosphere and imbibing ennobling influences, even if his disposition and the conditions of the time led him into the cultivation of a different field of art from his father's. The youngest of the sons, Johann Christian, must assuredly also have learnt from his father, for he was fifteen when he died. But the line he took in art was strangely different from his father's, as he became a popular composer of Italian operas, and exerted much influence on Mozart. Besides these there was his nephew Samuel Anton, son of Johann Ludwig Bach of Meiningen, who lived in the house with his uncle's family for some time; and also a son of Bernhard Bach of Eisenach, who joined the ranks of the pupils. In one case Bach had the pleasure of having two generations as pupils; for Johann Tobias Krebs, who had been a pupil in the Weimar time, sent his three sons to the Leipzig University, and one, at least, became a favourite pupil of John Sebastian's, who is said to have called him "der einzige Krebs in meinem Bache." This same Johann Ludwig Krebs was held to be one of the greatest organists of the time after Bach's death, and lived till 1780. Another pupil, Johann Schneider, who had been with Bach at Cöthen, came to him again in Leipzig, and ultimately became organist of the Church of St. Nicholas. Among the most distinguished of all the pupils was Johann Friederich Agricola, who was at the University of Leipzig and studied with Bach from about the year 1738. He went to Berlin in 1741 and gained the reputation of being the finest organist in the city, and in 1759 also became court composer. He was loyal to the memory of his master, and is said to have helped Philipp Emanuel to draw up records of his life and ways. Another well-known pupil was Johann Philip Kirnberger, who was with Bach from 1739 to 1741. The name of J. T. Goldberg has been mentioned for his fortunate connection with one of Bach's greatest works; and J. C. Altnikol has also been mentioned for his pathetic connection with his master's last hours, and for his having become a member of the family by marrying Bach's daughter in 1749. He did not survive many years, but died in 1759. To these may be added L. C. Mizler, who was one of the first to put on record some of the facts of his master's life; and J. F. Doles, who was at St. Thomas's School when Mozart came to Leipzig many years after, and roused his enthusiasm by showing him some of the Choral Motets. Of the few pupils who survived till the eve of the reawakening, J. C. Kittel seems to have been the longest lived. He is said to have been thoroughly loyal to his master's teaching, and to have passed it on to his pupils. He lived till 1809; and in that same year died the last of Bach's actual family, the youngest daughter, Regina Johanna, who, like her mother, was mainly dependent upon charity in the latter part of her life.

In the minds of pupils, and of a few who were capable of realising dimly what Bach was, the traditions lingered on. After more than half a century of almost complete oblivion, men began to look with astonishment at the few works which were still available to the world, and began to guess what a dire oversight had been made. It began to dawn upon them that these were no products of mere pedantry and mechanical skill, but the utterances of such a splendid and poetic personality as had rarely appeared in the world.[1] The "Wohltemperirtes Clavier" and the organ works began to inspire men with enthusiasm; Mendelssohn in 1829 performed the "Matthäus-Passion" in Leipzig a hundred years after the first performance. Impetus was generated. The greatest performers found things worthy of their steel; the greatest interpreters found things of such moment and such depth of meaning as invited the happiest exercise of all their highest qualities. A perfect army of workers joined in the labour of searching for and disinterring works that had lain in the dust of decades, in collating, editing, suggesting readings of things incomplete, in developing the technique and even the attitude of mind most apt to understand, and in expounding and disseminating the knowledge of such an inexhaustible mine of wealth. At last the very waifs and strays of great cities come to hear his message, and children find a ready delight in things which seem to have been made especially for their innocent pleasure.

The unremitting labour of a long lifetime seems to have brought little reward to the labourer himself but

[1] Among those to whom the heartiest recognition is due for the service he did in attracting attention to Bach's works, was Samuel Wesley, the father of Samuel Sebastian Wesley who, as early as 1808, was writing and working with the utmost enthusiasm to awaken men's minds, and soon after that time brought out with Horn the first edition of the "Forty-eight" in England.

the content of having achieved, the satisfaction of the need of the artistic impulse which would not be gainsaid. For such a nature the joy of doing and accomplishing was reward enough Had it been otherwise, the world would not have the opportunity of rejoicing in the revelation of a personality so noble and so inspiring as that of John Sebastian Bach.

INDEX

I

J

K

L

M

N

O

P

T

U

ADDITIONS TO INDEX